THE INTERNATIONAL LAW ON THE RIGHT OF THE CHILD TO SURVIVAL AND DEVELOPMENT

THE INTERNATIONAL LAW ON THE RIGHT OF THE CHILD TO SURVIVAL AND DEVELOPMENT

Khadeija Elsheikh Mahgoub

intersentia
Cambridge – Antwerp – Portland

Intersentia Ltd
Sheraton House | Castle Park
Cambridge | CB3 0AX | United Kingdom
Tel.: +44 1223 370 170 | Fax: +44 1223 370 169
Email: mail@intersentia.co.uk
www.intersentia.com | www.intersentia.co.uk

Distribution for the UK and Ireland:
NBN International
Airport Business Centre, 10 Thornbury Road
Plymouth, PL6 7 PP
United Kingdom
Tel.: +44 1752 202 301 | Fax: +44 1752 202 331
Email: orders@nbninternational.com

Distribution for Europe and all other countries:
Intersentia Publishing nv
Groenstraat 31
2640 Mortsel
Belgium
Tel.: +32 3 680 15 50 | Fax: +32 3 658 71 21
Email: mail@intersentia.be

Distribution for the USA and Canada:
International Specialized Book Services
920 NE 58th Ave. Suite 300
Portland, OR 97213
USA
Tel.: +1 800 944 6190 (toll free) | Fax: +1 503 280 8832
Email: info@isbs.com

The International Law on the Right of the Child to Survival and Development

ISBN 978-1-78068-233-4
D/2016/7849/9
NUR 828

GPRC
Guaranteed Peer Reviewed Content

British Library Cataloguing in Publication Data. A catalogue record for this book is available from the British Library.

ACKNOWLEDGEMENTS

My thanks first and foremost go to Allah the Almighty. Only because of his blessings could I write this book.

The image of a 'miserable' child has always broken my heart. On a very hot summer afternoon in 2001, I was walking in a crowded street in central Khartoum. The area was full of beggar children. Some of them looked very malnourished. Others were walking in bare feet and wore shabby and ragged clothes. Some of them were of school age and others were babies carried by their mothers, or perhaps by a woman who had paid their parents so that she could walk around with them and beg. The heat was extreme; most of the people around the area looked dehydrated. But the beggar children who walked in bare feet were suffering more, because the ground was also very hot. Suddenly, the loud noise of police cars could be heard. The convoy of an important State official drove past at high speed. Everybody on the street had to jump to the side of the road or they could easily have been hit by the cars. The beggar children jumped away for their safety as well. The State official was in his air-conditioned car. He did not look at any of the children or the people on the street; he looked very busy admiring himself and the 'glamour of his position'. And yet the Sudanese government has claimed that Sudan is a poor country and cannot afford to guarantee to every child his or her right to survival and development!

I am indebted to Professor Mashood Baderin and Professor Karin Arts for their encouragement and endorsement of this book. I also thank Professor Karin Arts for her critique of the early draft of the book.

I would like to thank Intersentia for their cooperation. In particular, I wish to express my sincere appreciation to Tom Scheirs for his patience and professionalism. I also thank my PhD supervisor, Professor William Schabas.

On a private level, I would like to thank my parents, Inaam and Elsheikh, for all the encouragement, love and help they have given me. I also appreciate that they instilled in me the importance of always defending justice and not to feel fear. My gratefulness and love also go to my children Rawan, Muhammad and Rawah. My hope is that they develop and survive in a better world, together with all the other children on earth. My thanks also go to my husband. Last but not least, I would also like to thank all my friends and relatives who encouraged me along the way.

CONTENTS

INTRODUCTION

One of the big achievements of the 1989 United Nations Convention on the Rights of the Child (CRC) is a provision designated for the survival and development of the child. Article 6(2) of this Convention reads: 'State parties shall ensure to the maximum extent possible the survival and development of the child.' This article is unique, for two reasons: firstly, because it guarantees for the child a rights-based approach for his or her survival and development. This means that the survival and development of the child is no longer merely charity that is given to the child by individuals, society and more significantly the State, who have jurisdiction over the child.[1] Secondly, it is unique because it allows for terms such as 'survival' to be included in the body of a legally binding document. This has not been an easy thing to achieve, as will be explained later in the book.

The exceptional existence of article 6(2) requires a comprehensive interpretation that fulfils the spirit and aims of this provision. This is also important when considering the significant position of the Convention on the Rights of the Child as a whole. Suffice to say, in this respect, that with the exception of the United States, Somalia and South Sudan, the Convention on the Rights of the Child has achieved universal ratification.[2]

The wide ratification of the Convention also makes it necessary to have an updated understanding of its provisions, particularly article 6(2). This kind of knowledge should be useful for the fulfilment and implementation of the right of the child to survival and development in almost every country around the globe.

In addition, human-rights instruments in general, and the Convention on the Rights of the Child in particular, are meant to be living documents. This requires the interpretation of the Convention to be constantly reviewed and renewed. The legal interpretation presented in this book is one step in this direction. Obviously, there is always going to be a need for a deeper and updated understanding of the right of the child to survival and development.

Chapter 1 of the book discusses the rather difficult process that led to the adoption of article 6(2). The historical analysis in this chapter sheds light on the discussions, concerns, and elucidations that were made during the drafting

---

1 See article 2(1) of the Convention on the Rights of the Child.

2 There are some reports that Somalia ratified the CRC. See United Nations (UN News Centre): <www.un.org/apps/news/story.asp?NewsID=49845#.VNivTWb6hMS> accessed 23 April 2015. However, according to the United Nations Office of the High Commissioners for Human Rights, Somalia did not ratify the CRC. See <http://tbinternet.ohchr.org/_layouts/TreatyBodyExternal/Treaty.aspx?CountryID=161&Lang=EN> accessed 23 April 2015.

process of article 6(2). The chapter also speculates on the possible factors that could have played a role in the successful adoption of the article. In particular, the chapter highlights the possible role of the 1986 United Nations Declaration on the Right to Development; and the role played by the United Nations Children's Fund (UNICEF) in the adoption of article 6(2).

The historical analysis in Chapter 1 paves the way for the understanding of the survival and development of the child during the interpretative stage of the entire Convention, which is an ongoing process. In the wider context of the dynamic interpretation of the Convention on the Rights of the Child, Chapters 2 and 3 examine the recommendations of the Committee on the Rights of the Child with regard to the right of the child to survival and development. The main incentive behind this is to highlight the literature of the main body that monitors the degree of State Party compliance with, and implementation of, article 6(2). This role is guaranteed for the Committee on the basis of article 43(1) of the Convention, which reads: 'For the purpose of examining the progress made by States Parties in achieving the realization of the obligations undertaken in the present Convention, there shall be established a Committee on the Rights of the Child, which shall carry out the functions hereinafter provided.'

The Committee on the Rights of the Child classifies article 6(2) as a right of its own and as a general principle of the Convention.[3] Chapter 2 of this book focuses on the survival and development of the child as a right, while Chapter 3 focuses on survival and development as a general principle. It also argues for other classifications. The main literature that is examined is that of the Committee on the Rights of the Child. Both chapters identify various aspects of thinking and criteria that could prove to be helpful in the understanding and later the implementation and realisation of article 6(2). Arguably, an effective approach for achieving this is the conviction that article 6(2) has a larger scope. Therefore, this offers a good opportunity to open new windows on the understanding of the child's right to survival and development. For instance, in its 2010 State of the World's Children report, UNICEF identifies a number of survival and development rights which demonstrate the wide scope of the two concepts.[4] Accordingly, survival and development include, for example, parental rights in accordance with the evolving capacities of the child, right to identity and right not to be separated from parents, such as articles 5, 8 and 9 of the CRC. In addition, survival and development include rights on birth registration, name and access to information.[5] The discussion in this book supports the belief that article 6(2) has a very broad range. The discussion focuses on the understanding that there is still more to the interpretation, classification and implementation of article 6(2).

---

3 UN Doc. CRC/C/5 (30 October 1991), paras. 19 and 13.

4 UNICEF, *The State of the World's Children 2010* (UNICEF, November 2009), p. 16.

5 *Ibid.*

The right of the child to be registered and to have a name and identity is important for the survival and development of the child in exactly the same way as the right to health services, the right to leisure and play and the right to education. In this respect, one advantage of the Convention on the Rights of the Child is that it includes within one document different kinds of rights. The classic, traditional division of 'generations' or 'kinds' of rights does not exist within the CRC. As Cohen and Kilbourne pointed out, 'Only the Convention on the Rights of the Child ... has followed the Universal Declaration's Comprehensive model by establishing a full panoply of rights for children which includes civil-political rights, economic-social-cultural rights and humanitarian rights.'[6]

This is a good chance for article 6(2) to be classified in a way that conforms to the comprehensiveness of the Convention on the Rights of the Child. In this context there is, however, some tendency to link article 6(2) to the category of economic, social and cultural rights. It is true that the Committee on the Rights of the Child has emphasised the importance of the holistic approach of the Convention and this is helpful for the implementation and realisation of article 6(2). But it is also important to emphasise that it is not only the holistic approach that guarantees the implementation on the basis of different kinds of rights. Arguably, article 6(2), as a right on survival and development, holds this power within itself. In fact, the subject matter of article 6(2) as an article that guarantees for the child his or her survival and development supports both the economic, social and cultural aspect of article 6(2) and the other aspects as well. For example, article 7(1) provides for the right of the child to a name and to be registered: 'The child shall be registered immediately after birth and shall have the right from birth to a name, the right to acquire a nationality and, as far as possible, the right to know and be cared for by his or her parents.' This is a very important aspect of the right of the child to survival and development, as our world today is the world of papers and identities; therefore, the child needs to be named and registered in order to survive and develop. Lack of registration can seriously interfere with the child's survival and development.

Another point that Chapter 2 discusses, and which is in the background of the implementation of article 6(2) by any party who is involved with it in general, and the Committee on the Rights of the Child in particular, relates to the implementation of the article in practice and not only in theory. This requires a deep understanding that the survival and development of the child is somehow contextual. What realises the child's survival and development in one context might not in another. In this regard, the survival and development of the child is similar to the principle of the best interest of the child. The near-universal ratification of the Convention means that the Convention covers a

6 C. Cohen and S. Kilbourne, 'Jurisprudence of the Committee on the Rights of the Child: A Guide for Research and Analysis' (1998) 19 *Michigan Journal of International Law* 633, 635.

huge number and variety of backgrounds, legal systems, cultures and societies. This requires a deep understanding from the Committee and a willingness to keep away from abstracts. As Adam Lopatka has pointed out, 'The subject matter of the Convention is extremely sensitive. Its provisions had to reconcile various approaches rooted in different traditions, cultures, religions, stages of economic development, legal systems, and indeed politics.'[7] This does not mean that the Committee has to lower the standards that were adopted by the Convention, or the standards that evolved out of the interpretation stage of the CRC. The point is that some domestic standards are more conducive to the survival and development of the child than the Convention. This is the general rule according to article 41: 'Nothing in the present Convention shall affect any provisions which are more conducive to the realization of the rights of the child and which may be contained in: (a) The law of a State party; or (b) International law in force for that State.'

The main argument in Chapter 3 is related to the capacity of article 6(2) to be classified in a number of contexts within the entire CRC. Accordingly, the right of the child to survival and development is a general principle of the Convention, a right in itself, an aim of the Convention, and a quality-control factor.

Arguably, the Committee's classification of article 6(2) as a general principle of the Convention is not always reflected in the recommendations of the Committee. There are some incidences that need elucidation, for instance the Committee's concluding observations on the initial report of Cyprus, where the Committee spoke about the general principles but did not mention article 6(2):

> The Committee also expresses its concern that the State party has not yet fully taken into account in its legislation and policy-making the general principles of the Convention … article 2 (principle of non-discrimination), article 3 (principle of the best interest of the child) and article 12 (respect for the views of the child).[8]

Arguably, the multi-identification and multi-classification of article 6(2) is closer to the implementation and fulfilment of the spirit of the survival of the child and his or her development. In addition, this understanding is also a step towards the realisation of the child's human dignity. In this context, Chapter 4 focuses on the interrelationship between the right of the child to survival and development and the human dignity of the child.

The Convention is about the child as a right holder and the fact that it is the duty of the State to protect and realise the survival and development of the child. Chapter 5 of the book argues for the multi-identities of article 6(2) to be visible when creating the measures and conditions for the implementation

---

7 A. Lopatka, 'Importance of the Convention on the Rights of the Child' (1992) 91/2 *Bulletin of Human Rights* 56–65, 58.

8 Committee on the Rights of the Child, 'Concluding Observations on Cyprus's Initial Report', UN Doc. CRC/C/15/Add.59 (7 June 1996), para. 11.

and realisation of the right of the child to survival and development. This is approached by attempting to understand the nature of the obligation to 'ensure' the survival and development of the child, and the standard of 'to the maximum extent possible'. Ensuring or guaranteeing the survival and development of the child includes the famous tripartite obligations of respect, protect and fulfil. The chapter discusses, briefly, the way States could formulate their policies, legislations and other types of measures. For instance, the obligation to raise awareness of the survival and development of the child means that children should be able to have informed knowledge about the Convention and factors that interfere with their right to survival and development. In achieving this, the State Party needs to adopt measures that support survival and development as both a means and an aim.

In guaranteeing the survival and development of the child, the State Party needs to identify the factors that impede the implementation of the Convention. This should be helpful in providing answers or justifying why, despite the Convention on the Rights of the Child being in force for twenty-five years, children are still suffering. Why, despite the near-universal ratification of the Convention on the Rights of the Child, are images of suffering still visible almost everywhere around the globe? Why can sand-eaters and street-beggars and miserable children be seen on the streets of many cities around the word?[9] Could all of this be solved simply by the existence and effectiveness of 'the principle of "equality of opportunity"... with powerful legal and public policy implications'?[10] There is no doubt that these are important factors in realising the child's development, as Himes, for example, pointed out: 'It is especially important in terms of the basic health, nutritional and educational opportunities essential for child development.'[11] However, there is definitely more to be done. In this context, Chapter 5 of this book argues for the adoption of some 'effective', 'understanding', and 'realistic' measures and approaches that could support the implementation and realisation of the right of the child to survival and development.

The book also includes four case studies. The first one is on the interaction between the right of the child to survival and development, human dignity and corporal punishment. The second one is on the relationship between the right of the child to survival and development, juvenile justice and human dignity. The third one is on the complex relationship of climate change and the right of the child to survival and development. The fourth one is on the interaction between the right of the child to survival and development and breastfeeding. The first two case studies are included in Chapter 4. In children's rights literature,

---

9 Author's personal observations.

10 J.R. Himes, 'Children's rights: Moralists, lawyers and the right to development' (1993) 1 *International Journal of Children's Rights* 81, 85.

11 *Ibid.*

frequent links are made between juvenile justice, corporal punishment and human dignity. The discussion in Chapter 4 brings into the debate, in some detail, the survival and development aspect of the matter. As for the other two case studies, they are included in Chapter 6. The variety of the four topics represents the fact that article 6(2) has a very comprehensive and wide spectrum.

Overall, the book joins the ongoing debate on article 6(2) of the Convention on the Rights of the Child by attempting to understand what the article is really about and, later, what can be achieved from this particular concept. In this regard, the reflections included in this book represent an effort towards having a comprehensive study of article 6(2) on the survival and development of the child.

CHAPTER 1
HISTORICAL BACKGROUND

'Its language had been left more broadly stated than some would have liked.'

James Grant, Former Executive Director of UNICEF

1. INTRODUCTION

On 20 November 1989 the United Nations (UN) General Assembly (GA) adopted Resolution A/RES/44/25, to which the Convention on the Rights of the Child (CRC) is annexed. Article 6(2) of this Convention is concerned with the right of the child to survival and development and reads as follows: 'States Parties shall ensure to the maximum extent possible the survival and development of the child.' This article speaks about two rights: the right of the child to survival and the right of the child to development.

This chapter analyses the drafting history of article 6(2). The discussion starts with an analysis of the relationship between the concept of development, including human development, and the Convention on the Rights of the Child. This is important in order to put article 6(2) of the CRC in its original context as a right to development. The chapter then includes a descriptive analysis of the international instruments on the protection of the rights of the child in general and his or her right to development in particular prior to the adoption of the CRC. Following that, a detailed analysis of the drafting history of article 6(2) is included. Lastly, in an attempt to have a comprehensive historical analysis of article 6(2), the chapter discusses what can be called the 'unofficial' historical background of article 6(2), examining, in this regard, the role of United Nations Children's Fund (UNICEF) in the drafting of the article and the possible reflection of the adoption of the 1986 Declaration on the Right to Development.

This historical analysis is crucial in relation to the comprehensive interpretation, classification and implementation of article 6(2). It is also very important to point out that this analysis is not approached philosophically. Moreover, it is not about debating the nature or the historical evolution of the concept of children's rights or the arguments concerned with whether to grant children any rights or not.[1]

2. THE CONCEPT OF DEVELOPMENT AND THE UNITED NATIONS CONVENTION ON THE RIGHTS OF THE CHILD

2.1. BASIC FACTS

Logically, the aims of the Convention on the Rights of the Child should be seen within those of the United Nations, as it was issued under its umbrella. In this regard, the Convention is basically a further step towards the achievement of the United Nations' goals, priorities and concerns.

Initially, the UN was established to promote, among other aims, the development of human beings. This is stated in article 55 of the United Nations Charter: 'The United Nations shall promote: a. higher standards of living, full employment, and conditions of economic and social progress and development'.

The achievement of development and its strong relationship with human rights is also an important aspect of the United Nations' work. As Kofi Anan, the former UN Secretary General, stated: 'Development – furthering the well-being of people – is central to all that we undertake at the United Nations.'[2] In this context, protection of human rights is part of the overall well-being of people. He also added in his statement to the General Assembly on his report 'In Larger Freedom': 'I am profoundly convinced that the threats which face us are of equal concern to all. I have called the report "In Larger Freedom", because I believe those words from our Charter convey the idea that development, security and human rights go hand in hand.'[3] Under the UN, respect for human rights is an important factor in the attainment of development. Hence, the adoption of the United Nations Convention on the Rights of the Child should be seen as a step towards the attainment of this goal. 'Development cannot be attained in the absence of peace and security or in the absence of respect for all human rights and fundamental freedoms.'[4]

Practice also proved that stagnation of development could seriously affect the right of the child to survival and development. The following words of Miss

1 G. Van Bueren, *The International Law on the Rights of the Child* (Martinus Nijhoff Publishers, The Hague, 1998), p. 6.

2 United Nations Agenda for Development, Part 489 (United Nations Department of Public Information, 1997), foreword by Kofi Annan.

3 Former United Nations Secretary-General Kofi Annan, 'Secretary-General's statement to the General Assembly on his report "In Larger Freedom", New York, 21 March 2005. Available at <http://www.un.org/sg/STATEMENTS/index.asp?nid=1355> accessed 08.04.2015.

4 United Nations General Assembly, 'Agenda for Development'; UN Doc. A/RES/51/240, Annex (15 October 1997), para. 4.

Dieguez, which were addressed to the UN General Assembly in 1989 during the Discussion in the Third Committee of the General Assembly on 8–10 and 13–16 November 1989 with regard to the adoption of the CRC, highlight the interrelationship between development and human rights:

> [T]he draft convention was the international community's greatest achievement on the subject to date. Its adoption would be a most important step, because it would mean recognizing adult society's responsibility for the survival, development and protection of children. They were the first to suffer in crisis situation; as UNICEF had revealed, the debt problem and recession of the 1980s had hit children particularly hard, and half a million of them had died in the past years as a result of the stagnation of development.[5]

In this respect, article 6(2) on the right of the child to survival and development, as a part of the CRC, and, due to its comprehensive meaning (as will be discussed later in the book), should be seen as a step towards the achievement of the human development of people (children). This is clear as 'in order to promote development, equal attention and urgent consideration should be given to the implementation, promotion and protection of civil, political, economic, social and cultural rights',[6] in addition to other kinds of rights.

2.2. THE INTERNATIONAL YEAR OF THE CHILD AND DEVELOPMENT

Additionally, this special link with development is historically evident, as will be discussed later, since the CRC came as a result of a proposal from Poland, in 1978, to mark the International Year of the Child (IYC). The IYC in its turn had a strong developmental background. An important reason for the proclamation on the International Year of the Child was to highlight one of the major responsibilities of States towards their child populations, i.e., '[t]o promote recognition of the fact that programmes for children should be an integral part of economic and social development plans'.[7] In other words, one of the concerns of the IYC was the importance of the overall economic and social-progress programmes benefiting children, as child-focused programmes were seen as a step towards the achievement of these goals. This relationship has been clearly stated on the UN General Assembly Resolution on the IYC 'Recognizing the fundamental importance in all countries, developing and industrialized, of

---

5 UN Doc. A/C.3/44/SR.40 (27 November 1989), para. 56 (Miss Dieguez), available in Office of the United Nations High Commissioner for Human Rights, *Legislative History of the Convention on the Rights of the Child*, Volume I (United Nations, New York, 2007), p. 257.

6 United Nations General Assembly, 'Right to Development', UN Doc. A/RES/53/155 (25 February 1999), preambular para. 5.

7 United Nations General Assembly, 'International Year of the Child', UN Doc. A/RES/31/169 (21 December 1976), para. 2(b).

programmes benefiting children not only for the well-being of the children but also as part of broader efforts to accelerate economic and social progress'.[8]

Another reason for this proclamation was to recall the 1975 New International Economic Order on Development and International Economic Co-operation (NIEO):

> Recalling in this connexion ... resolutions 2626 (XXV) of 24 October 1970 containing the International Development strategy for the second United Nations Development Decade, ... of 1 May 1974 containing the Declaration and the Programme of Action on the Establishment of a New International Economic Order ... of 16 September 1975 on development and international economic co-operation ...
>
> ...
>
> Proclaims the year 1979 International Year of the Child...[9]

Maggie Black, who has written extensively about the history of UNICEF, has argued against the idea that the background of the International Year of the Child was of a developmental nature. She concludes that, for this reason, UNICEF was reluctant to show support for the IYC as this might have resulted in a loss of focus on development. She argues:

> The initiative for a children's 'Year' came not from Unicef but from international children's NGOs. Their starting point was not 'the child in development' but simply 'the child', whose cause – they felt – was being drowned out by the clamour surrounding more fashionable debates. Unicef was hesitant about a 'Year of the Child', disliking the language of rights and fearing a loss of focus on development.[10]

Based on Black's conclusions, it is possible to argue that UNICEF's reluctance could probably be attributed to progress in the formulation of the concept of the rights-based approach to development or the right to development. This is because the concept of the right to development was not fully developed yet.[11] In fact, what made UNICEF accept the International Year of the Child, with some reluctance, was that it feared a shallow focus on a 'celebratory and possibly superficial affair'.[12] A rights-based approach to development, which the current article 6(2) of the CRC is strongly connected to, was not

---

8 *Ibid*, preambular para. 2.

9 *Ibid*, preambular paragraph 3 and article 1. For the relationship between the NIEO and the right to development, generally, also see, K. Iqbal, *The Right to Development in International Law: The Case of Pakistan* (Routledge, London, 2012), pp. 132–141.

10 M. Black, *Children First: The Story of UNICEF, Past and Present* (Oxford University Press, Oxford, 1996), p. 13.

11 A. Sengupta, 'On the Theory and Practice of the Right to Development' [2002] HRQ Vol. 24, 837, 839.

12 UNICEF, 'The State of the World's Children 1996: Fifty years for children' (1996), online version <www.unicef.org/sowc96/1970s.htm> accessed 13 August 2015.

fully developed. This kind of understanding prevailed to the extent that some important UN organisations, such as UNICEF, were not active from the outset in the drafting process of the CRC because they did not see, at that time, any strong link between child survival and development and the concept of children's rights. The words of Newman-Williams explain this argument:

> Like other development agencies of the United Nations system UNICEF's traditional concern with the survival and basic needs of children seemed at odds with concerns for human rights. Many in the organization were convinced that human rights and development were not a good mix. The normative process of treaty bodies and the stark divisions created by the cold war between civil and political rights, and economic, social and cultural rights had convinced UNICEF that its programmes of cooperation should be best kept separate from the polarized world of human rights.[13]

In general, the gradual evolution of the concept of a rights-based approach to development reached a high level with the adoption of the CRC in general and article 6(2) in particular. The adoption of the CRC meant that the child has a 'right', i.e., that the child would enjoy all the consequences of having a right, and that the child's right to survival and development is a right and not a question of charity from any party.

> [T]he draft convention on the rights of the child was an important international instrument that would provide a framework for the coordination of national efforts to promote child survival, protection and development. Its ratification would not only lead to achieving national, regional and global child welfare objectives but would also make the world community realize that the rights of children were not a matter of charity but an integral component of human rights.[14]

3. MODERN INTERNATIONAL LAW AND RECOGNITION OF THE RIGHT OF THE CHILD TO SURVIVAL AND DEVELOPMENT PRIOR TO THE ADOPTION OF THE CRC

Within modern international law, in which the State and International Governmental Organisations (IGOs) are the main subjects, the international legal recognition of children's rights prior to 1989 can be found in two types of

---

13 M. Newman-William, 'How Things Changed', in *UN Chronicle*, Volume 36, Issue 2, 1999. p. 38.

14 UN Doc. A/C.3/44/SR.38 (20 November 1989), para. 48 (Mrs Joshi), available in Office of the United Nations High Commissioner for Human Rights, *Legislative History of the Convention on the Rights of the Child*, Volume I (United Nations, New York, 2007), p. 250.

documents: documents that are solely concerned with the rights of the child, and documents that include only some provisions on children's rights.

3.1. DOCUMENTS THAT ARE SOLELY CONCERNED WITH THE RIGHTS OF THE CHILD

3.1.1. *Declaration of Geneva (1924)*

The first example of a document solely concerned with the rights of the child is the 1924 Declaration of Geneva on the Rights of the Child.[15] It was adopted by the Fifth Assembly of the League of Nations. Some NGOs, such as Save the Children International Union, played an important role in its adoption.[16] This declaration contains five principles. Responsibility towards children is placed on mankind as a whole, which owes to the child the best that it can give. Principle 3 of the Declaration states that: 'The child must be first to receive relief in times of distress'. The significance of this principle, which speaks about children in times of war, comes from the fact that the Declaration was adopted following World War I. It is noticeable that the 1924 Declaration approaches the rights of the child from a welfare perspective only. For instance, the Declaration speaks about the child's development, in principle 1, in terms of the way the child should be given the means needed for his or her normal development, both materially and spiritually. The Declaration does not speak about how the child can contribute to achieving his or her physical and spiritual development.

The word 'right', which conveys the legal strength of the principles set out in the Declaration, was used only once, namely in the title of the Declaration. The Declaration suggests that material and spiritual development are part of the overall development of the child, but does not elaborate on the other aspects of the child's development. However, this aspect of the Declaration could represent the basis for the holistic approach to the child's right to development, under modern international law. Van Bueren, for instance, argues that the 1924 Declaration represents 'the first attempt at a holistic approach to children's rights'.[17] In this context, the Declaration constitutes an important step by the

---

15 Adopted by the Fifth Assembly of the League of Nations, Declaration on the Rights of the Child, 1924 (Declaration of Geneva). See also records of the Fifth Assembly, League of Nations Official Journal, Spec. Supp. No. 23, p. 179, available in Office of the United Nations High Commissioner for Human Rights, *Legislative History of the Convention on the Rights of the Child*, Volume I (United Nations, New York, 2007), p. 3.

16 G. Van Bueren, *The International Law on the Rights of the Child* (Martinus Nijhoff Publishers, The Hague, 1998), p. 8.

17 G. Van Bueren, 'International Children's Rights-A Stop-go History', in E. Verhellen (ed.), *Understanding Children's Rights* (Ghent Papers on Children's Rights, Children's Rights Centre, University of Ghent, Ghent, 1996), p. 313.

international community towards the recognition of children as a category in society that needs special care and protection.

3.1.2. 1959 United Nations Declaration of the Rights of the Child

The second main document predating the 1989 Convention on the Rights of the Child is the 1959 United Nations Declaration of the Rights of the Child.[18] It was adopted by the United Nations General Assembly on 20 November 1959, i.e., thirty years before the adoption of the CRC.[19] During the discussion in the General Assembly on 20 November 1959 it was pointed out that having a happy childhood is about something deeper than just pampering the child. The importance of having the right conditions for the development of the child was also highlighted:

> That sound foundation can only be provided by a happy childhood; not happy in the empty sense of mere pampering, or of building a wall to protect the child from the realities of life, but happy in the sense that the child is given every opportunity to develop the powers with which he has been endowed and to grow into a complete human being so that he will be able to contribute to the progress of mankind. One way in which he can do that – and undoubtedly the most important and effective way – will be by making the world a united and peaceful whole.[20]

Contrary to the five principles contained in the 1924 Geneva Declaration, the 1959 UN Declaration of the Rights of the Child covers a broader spectrum of children's rights in its ten principles. For instance, the 1959 Declaration speaks about the child and his or her right to enjoy the rights and freedoms mentioned in the Declaration, as this is for the benefit of the child and society as a whole. The 1959 Declaration is also, understandably, more strongly-worded and focused, as it came after the adoption in 1948 of the Universal Declaration on Human Rights.[21] This is relevant, since both of the documents were adopted by the UN's General Assembly. The 1948 Declaration is concerned with children, among others. As will be discussed later, article 25(2) guarantees the right of the child to special care and assistance: 'Motherhood and childhood are entitled to special care and assistance. All children, whether born in or out of wedlock, shall

---

18 United Nations General Assembly, Declaration of the Rights of the Child, UN Doc A/RES/1386 (XIV) of 20 November 1959.

19 For further reading see G. Van Bueren, *The International Law on the Rights of the Child* (Martinus Nijhoff Publishers, The Hague, 1998), pp. 9–12; also see Office of the United Nations High Commissioner for Human Rights, *Legislative History of the Convention on the Rights of the Child* Volume 1 (United Nations, New York, 2007), pp. 5–25.

20 UN Doc. A/4249 and Corr.2, para. 45, available in Office of the United Nations High Commissioner for Human Rights, *Legislative History of the Convention on the Rights of the Child*, Volume I (United Nations, New York, 2007), p. 23.

21 United Nations General Assembly, Universal Declaration of Human Rights, UN Doc. A/RES/3/217(III)A (10 December 1948).

enjoy the same social protection.' Using weaker language in the 1959 Declaration than that of the 1948 Declaration would have been considered to be a setback. It is worth mentioning, however, that the 1959 Declaration explicitly refers to the 1948 Universal Declaration on Human Rights in paragraph two of its preamble. This reflects the complementary nature of the international human-rights documents of the United Nations.

The 1959 Declaration of the Rights of the Child speaks about the child's development in five places. Firstly, in principle 2:

> The child shall enjoy special protection, and shall be given opportunities and facilities, by law and by other means, to enable him to develop physically, mentally, morally, spiritually and socially in a healthy and normal manner and in conditions of freedom and dignity. In the enactment of laws for this purpose, the best interests of the child shall be the paramount consideration.

This principle resembles article 6(2) of the CRC in terms of the comprehensive aspects of development that it covers and the requirement for the development of the child to be implemented under conditions of freedom and dignity.[22] Secondly, the Declaration refers to the child's development in principle 4:

> The child shall enjoy the benefits of social security. He shall be entitled to grow and develop in health; to this end, special care and protection shall be provided both to him and to his mother, including adequate pre-natal and post-natal care. The child shall have the right to adequate nutrition, housing, recreation and medical services.

The child's development under this principle is directed to the child's physical development and growth by focusing on the overall welfare of the child and his or her mother. Thirdly, the 1959 Declaration refers to the child's development in principle 6:

> The child, for the full and harmonious development of his personality, needs love and understanding. He shall, wherever possible, grow up in the care and under the responsibility of his parents, and, in any case, in an atmosphere of affection and of moral and material security; a child of tender years shall not, save in exceptional circumstances, be separated from his mother. Society and the public authorities shall have the duty to extend particular care to children without a family and to those without adequate means of support. Payment of State and other assistance towards the maintenance of children of large families is desirable.

---

22 The UN Committee on the Rights of the Child, when interpreting the CRC, asked States to 'describe specific measures taken to guarantee the child's right to life and to create an environment conducive to ensuring to the maximum extent possible the survival and development of the child, including physical, mental, spiritual, moral, psychological and social development, in a manner compatible with human dignity', in UN Doc. CRC/C/58 (Basic Reference Document), (20 November 1996), para. 40.

This principle focuses on the importance of having the appropriate environment in order for the child to reach his or her full and harmonious development. The article considers the parents as the first party responsible for the provision of this environment. Fourthly, the development of the child is mentioned in principle 7 of the Declaration:

> The child is entitled to receive education, which shall be free and compulsory, at least in the elementary stages. He shall be given an education which will promote his general culture and enable him, on a basis of equal opportunity, to develop his abilities, his individual judgement, and his sense of moral and social responsibility, and to become a useful member of society.

This principle focuses on the child as a social being and on the importance of education for his or her social development. Finally, principle 9 focuses on the protection of the child from exploitation, particularly economic exploitation, and from any form of child trafficking:

> The child shall be protected against all forms of neglect, cruelty and exploitation. He shall not be the subject of traffic, in any form.
>
> The child shall not be admitted to employment before an appropriate minimum age; he shall in no case be caused or permitted to engage in any occupation or employment which would prejudice his health or education, or interfere with his physical, mental or moral development.

All of these principles are reflected in the Convention on the Rights of the Child. This demonstrates that the 1959 Declaration, somehow, provided a holistic approach to the child's development before the CRC. The Declaration observed the conditions of dignity which are necessary for the child's development and the importance of the family as the most suitable environment for achieving the harmonious development of the child. The Declaration also provided for some aspects of the child's development, as it focused on the child's spiritual, material, physical, mental and moral development. It is worth mentioning that paragraph eight of the preamble of the Convention on the Rights of the Child cites both the 1924 and the 1959 Declarations, it reads:

> Bearing in mind that the need to extend particular care to the child has been stated in the Geneva Declaration of the Rights of the Child of 1924 and in the Declaration of the Rights of the Child adopted by the General Assembly on 20 November 1959 and recognized in the Universal Declaration of Human Rights, in the International Covenant on Civil and Political Rights (in particular in articles 23 and 24), in the International Covenant on Economic, Social and Cultural Rights (in particular in article 10) and in the statutes and relevant instruments of specialized agencies and international organizations concerned with the welfare of children…

Basically, both the 1924 and 1959 Declarations speak about the 'development' of the child, but the 1959 Declaration, in particular, elaborates on the meaning of the concept of 'development'. The 1959 Declaration also uses the expression 'to develop', which conveys an on-going process, as will be discussed later, with respect to article 6(2) of the Convention on the Rights of the Child. The main difference from the two previous declarations is that article 6(2) added the word 'survival' to the word 'development'. Another difference is that the word 'development' was used without any elaborations on its meaning or any reference to a particular aspect of development. More importantly, article 6(2) represents an obligatory designated article for the child's right to development.

3.2. DOCUMENTS THAT ARE NOT SOLELY CONCERNED WITH THE RIGHTS OF THE CHILD

The other types of documents that provided international protection of children's rights prior to 1989 are the ones that included some provisions on children's rights. These documents are concerned with a broader spectrum of human rights, in addition to those of children. Reference to children is made either directly or indirectly as part of the rights of the overall categories included. As regards their legal effect, these types of documents include both binding and non-binding instruments.

3.2.1. Non-Binding Document

In terms of the non-binding documents, the 1948 Universal Declaration on Human Rights (UDHR) indirectly acknowledges the child in many instances. Some articles of the Declaration make reference to the term 'everybody' which could be interpreted so as to include the child. The Declaration probably guaranteed the child some rights which are not explicitly assured in the Convention on the Rights of the Child. A typical example of this is article 17 of the Declaration, which guarantees the right to own property. The right belongs to children as well as to adults. However, the fact that children's rights were considered to be covered by the UDHR and other international human-rights documents was one of the arguments claimed by some parties against the adoption of a new specific convention on children's rights back in 1978.

The Universal Declaration provides protection to the child as a part of the term 'everyone' in article 22, which speaks about the dignity and the free development of the child's personality:

> Everyone, as a member of society, has the right to social security and is entitled to realization, through national effort and international co-operation and in accordance with the organization and resources of each State, of the economic, social and cultural rights indispensable for his dignity and the free development of his personality.

Article 26(2) of the UDHR also refers to the importance of directing education towards the full development of the human personality:

> Education shall be directed to the full development of the human personality and to the strengthening of respect for human rights and fundamental freedoms. It shall promote understanding, tolerance and friendship among all nations, racial or religious groups, and shall further the activities of the United Nations for the maintenance of peace.

In addition, article 29 states that the full development of the human being could be achieved if the individual performs his or her duties towards the community: 'Everyone has duties to the community in which alone the free and full development of his personality is possible.'[23] Of importance here is the reference to community duties.

Article 25(2) of the Declaration, explicitly, refers to children. It speaks about the special needs of motherhood and childhood:

> Motherhood and childhood are entitled to special care and assistance. All children, whether born in or out of wedlock, shall enjoy the same social protection.

It is worth noting here that the preamble of the CRC refers to the UDHR in paragraph 3 in relation to non-discrimination. Reference to the UDHR in the preamble of the CRC is also made in paragraphs 4 and 8.

3.2.2. Binding Documents

The Universal Declaration of Human Rights was intended as a declaratory instrument, but it was to be complemented by one or more international treaties that could impose binding obligations on States. Two major substantive treaties resulted in 1966: the International Covenant on Civil and Political Rights (ICCPR) and the International Covenant on Economic, Social and Cultural Rights (ICESCR). Article 23 of the ICCPR is of particular relevance to the child as it speaks about the importance of family. It also provides for the necessary protection of children in cases of dissolution of marriage in article 23(4):

> States Parties to the present Covenant shall take appropriate steps to ensure equality of rights and responsibilities of spouses as to marriage, during marriage and at its dissolution. In the case of dissolution, provision shall be made for the necessary protection of any children.

---

23 It is worth noting that the African Charter on the Right and Welfare of the Child adopted this approach of imposing responsibilities on the child. For example article 31 is titled 'Responsibility of the Child'. African Charter on the Rights and Welfare of the Child, OAU Doc. CAB/LEG/24.9/49 (1990), entered into force 29 November 1999.

Moreover, article 24 of the ICCPR is specifically concerned with the civil rights of the child and explicitly refers to the child:

> 1. Every child shall have, without any discrimination as to race, colour, sex, language, religion, national or social origin, property or birth, the right to such measures of protection as are required by his status as a minor, on the part of his family, society and the State.
> 2. Every child shall be registered immediately after birth and shall have a name.
> 3. Every child has the right to acquire a nationality.

Article 24 of the ICCPR was a further step towards more international recognition of the civil rights of children, which later became the subject of two separate articles in the CRC, namely articles 2 and 7. This reflects the importance of the Convention on the Rights of the Child as the main convention designated for children's rights, which gives the chance for the inclusion of detailed elaborations as regards the recognition and protection of children's rights. This is relevant when considering that many States Parties to the ICCPR used to underestimate their obligations under article 24 of the Covenant: in this context, the Human Rights Committee had to point out that the 'reports submitted by States parties often seem to underestimate this obligation and supply inadequate information on the way in which children are afforded enjoyment of their right to a special protection.'[24] The importance of article 24 of the ICCPR was emphasised by the Human Rights Committee: 'Article 24 of the International Covenant on Civil and Political Rights recognizes the right of every child, without any discrimination, to receive from his family, society and the State the protection required by his status as a minor.'[25] Rights of children (juveniles) are also explicitly referred to in article 14(4) of the ICCPR. In addition, there is a prohibition on execution for crimes committed under the age of 18 in article 6(5) of the ICCPR.

Similar to the Universal Declaration on Human Rights, it is possible to consider that the ICCPR refers to the child as well when it uses generalised terms such as '[e]very human being'. Article 9(1) of the ICCPR, for instance, which reads: '[e]veryone has the right to liberty and security of person'. It could be argued, however, that some rights in the Covenant are granted to mentally competent adults only, such as the right to vote as guaranteed by article 25(b) of the Covenant. The Human Rights Committee also makes the following comment with regard to voting age:

> Any conditions which apply to the exercise of the rights protected by article 25 should be based on objective and reasonable criteria. For example, it may be reasonable to require a higher age for election or appointment to particular offices than for exercising

24 Available in 'Compilation of the General Comments and General Recommendations Adopted by Human Rights Treaty Bodies', UN Doc. HRI/GEN/1/Rev.7 (12 May 2004), p. 144.

25 *Ibid.*

> the right to vote, which should be available to every adult citizen. The exercise of these rights by citizens may not be suspended or excluded except on grounds which are established by law and which are objective and reasonable.[26]

Nevertheless, in some States children younger than eighteen years old are given the right to vote. For example, in Austria and Brazil voting age starts at sixteen.

The Human Rights Committee interpreted the generalised term 'everyone' in its views adopted on 3 April 1995 regarding a communication against Argentina. The Human Rights Committee considered the falsification of the birth certificate of Ximena Vicario, who was a minor, and her adoption as violations of Ximena's privacy and family life according to article 17 of the Covenant, which speaks about the right of 'everyone', as it states 'no one' and not specifically the child.

> As to Ximena Vicario's and her grandmother's right to privacy, it is evident that the abduction of Ximena Vicario, the falsification of her birth certificate and her adoption by S.S. entailed numerous acts of arbitrary and unlawful interference with their privacy and family life, in violation of article 17 of the Covenant.[27]

Under the ICCPR the specific articles on children's rights provide extra protection to those rights already existing under the other generalised articles of the Covenant that use the term 'everyone':

> In the specific circumstances of this case, the Committee finds that the protection of children stipulated in article 24 of the Covenant required the State party to take affirmative action to grant Ms. Vicario prompt and effective relief from her predicament. In this context, the Committee recalls its General Comment on article 24, in which it stressed that every child has a right to special measures of protection because of his/her status as a minor; those special measures are additional to the measures that States are required to take under article 2 to ensure that everyone enjoys the rights provided for in the Covenant.[28]

The International Covenant on Economic, Social and Cultural Rights (ICESCR) also refers to children's rights in article 10:

> The States Parties to the present Covenant recognize that:
>
> 1. The widest possible protection and assistance should be accorded to the family, which is the natural and fundamental group unit of society, particularly for its establishment and while it is responsible for the care and education of dependent children. Marriage must be entered into with the free consent of the intending spouses.

---

26 See General Comment No. 25 on the right to participate in public affairs, voting rights and the right of equal access to public service (Art. 25), UN Doc. CCPR/C/21/Rev.1/Add.7 (12 July 1996), para. 4.

27 *Mónaco v. Argentina*, UN Doc. CCPR/C/53/D/400/1990, Annex, para. 10.4.

28 *Ibid.*, para. 10.5 (footnotes omitted).

2. Special protection should be accorded to mothers during a reasonable period before and after childbirth. During such period working mothers should be accorded paid leave or leave with adequate social security benefits.

Importantly as well, article 10(3) is concerned with the repercussions of discrimination; and economic and social exploitation of children on the child's normal development:

> Special measures of protection and assistance should be taken on behalf of all children and young persons without any discrimination for reasons of parentage or other conditions. Children and young persons should be protected from economic and social exploitation. Their employment in work harmful to their morals or health or dangerous to life or likely to hamper their normal development should be punishable by law. States should also set age limits below which the paid employment of child labour should be prohibited and punishable by law.

The Covenant also refers to the child's right to healthy development in article 12(2)(a) on the right to the highest attainable standard of health. It reads, 'The steps to be taken by the States Parties to the present Covenant to achieve the full realization of this right shall include those necessary for: (a) The provision for the reduction of the stillbirth-rate and of infant mortality and for the healthy development of the child'.

Other rights of the child are also referred to in article 13(3) of the ICESCR on the rights of the child to receive moral and religious education in conformity with the convictions of his/her parents:

> The States Parties to the present Covenant undertake to have respect for the liberty of parents and, when applicable, legal guardians to choose for their children schools, other than those established by the public authorities, which conform to such minimum educational standards as may be laid down or approved by the State and to ensure the religious and moral education of their children in conformity with their own convictions.

The Covenant also speaks about the importance of the right to education as part of everyone's full development, including the child, in article 13(1). Education shall enable children to participate effectively in a free society, which is an important principle of the right to development:

> The States Parties to the present Covenant recognize the right of everyone to education. They agree that education shall be directed to the full development of the human personality and the sense of its dignity, and shall strengthen the respect for human rights and fundamental freedoms. They further agree that education shall enable all persons to participate effectively in a free society, promote understanding, tolerance and friendship among all nations and all racial, ethnic or religious groups, and further the activities of the United Nations for the maintenance of peace.

3.3. OTHER INTERNATIONAL AND REGIONAL DOCUMENTS

Apart from the main United Nations instruments, various other international and regional documents relate to children's rights, such as the International Labour Organization (ILO) conventions. The 1950 European Convention on Human Rights also provides further protection for children's rights. Article 5(1)(d), for instance, regulates the detention of minors:

> 1. Everyone has the right to liberty and security of person. No one shall be deprived of his liberty save in the following cases and in accordance with a procedure prescribed by law;
>
> (d) the detention of a minor by lawful order for the purpose of educational supervision or his lawful detention for the purpose of bringing him before the competent legal authority; …

The examples illustrate that, prior to the adoption of the CRC, the recognition of children's rights by the international community and within the framework of international law (including regional conventions) was somehow limited and lacked comprehensiveness. Each of the previously mentioned documents addresses some issues concerned with children's rights but, obviously, none of them constitutes a comprehensive and an inclusive international document on children's rights. As for the right of the child to development, these instruments provide a certain degree of protection. It could be argued, however, that the 1959 Declaration of the Rights of the Child provided some level of comprehensive protection. This is correct to a limited degree, especially when considering that the 1959 Declaration is not a legally binding document. Basically, prior to the adoption of the CRC, there was a need for a more focused, inclusive and binding internationally recognised document guaranteeing children their rights, including the right of the child to survival and development.

4. THE DEVELOPMENT OF THE CONVENTION ON THE RIGHTS OF THE CHILD

In December 1976 the United Nations General Assembly adopted a resolution in which it proclaimed the year 1979 to be the 'International Year of the Child'. This Declaration came as a response to initiatives made by the international child-related non-governmental organisations.[29] The IYC is considered to be a

[29] M. Black, *Children First: The Story of UNICEF, Past and Present* (Oxford University Press, Oxford, 1996), p. 13.

significant event in the history of the adoption of the Convention on the Rights of the Child. In fact, Poland initially proposed the adoption of a convention on the rights of the child in order to mark the International Year of the Child.[30] The following comments by Cynthia Cohen describe the importance of the IYC as one of the milestones in the drafting history of the CRC:

> There might well be no Convention on the Rights of the Child had it not been for the 1979 International Year of the Child (IYC). It was in response to IYC's commemoration of the 1959 Declaration of the Rights of the Child that the Polish government proposed the drafting of a treaty that would put the ideals enumerated in the Declaration into legally binding form.[31]

With concerns about children's conditions being the basis of the 1979 International Year of the Child, the government of Poland, in 1978, submitted the first proposal of the Convention on the Rights of the Child to the thirty-fourth session of the UN Commission on Human Rights.[32] The aim was that the IYC should be marked by the adoption of a Convention on the Rights of the Child.[33] An additional concern was also the special need to assist children in the developing world.[34]

Accordingly, the Commission on Human Rights requested the Secretary-General to forward the draft Convention to Member States, competent specialised agencies, regional intergovernmental organisations, and regional non-governmental organisations, inviting them to communicate to him their views, observations and suggestions regarding such a convention.[35] The Economic and Social Council (ECOSOC), in its turn, being aware of the special need to assist children in developing countries in a manner consistent with the goals of the New International Economic Order (NIEO), took note of

---

30 See UN Doc. E/CN.4/1284 (18 January 1978), available in Office of the United Nations High Commissioner for Human Rights, *Legislative History of the Convention on the Rights of the Child*, Volume I (United Nations, New York, 2007), p. 31.

31 C. Cohen, 'Drafting of the United Nations Convention on the Rights of the Child: Challenges and Achievements', in E. Verhellen (ed.), *Understanding Children's Rights* (Ghent Papers on Children's Rights, Children's Rights Centre, University of Ghent, Ghent, 1996) p. 324.

32 UN Doc. E/CN.4/L.1366/ (7 February 1978), available in Office of the United Nations High Commissioner for Human Rights, *Legislative History of the Convention on the Rights of the Child*, Volume I (United Nations, New York, 2007), pp. 32–35.

33 UN Doc. E/CN.4/1284 (18 January 1978), available in Office of the United Nations High Commissioner for Human Rights, *Legislative History of the Convention on the Rights of the Child*, Volume I (United Nations, New York, 2007), p. 31.

34 Available in Office of the United Nations High Commissioner for Human Rights, *Legislative History of the Convention on the Rights of the Child*, Volume I (United Nations, New York, 2007), p. 32.

35 Commission on Human Rights resolution 20 (XXXIV) on the 'Question of a convention on the rights of the child' adopted on 8 March 1978, available in Office of the United Nations High Commissioner for Human Rights, *Legislative History of the Convention on the Rights of the Child*, Volume I (United Nations, New York, 2007), pp. 43–44.

the possibility of the General Assembly adopting the Convention during the International Year of the Child.[36]

In response to the Commission's request, the report of the Secretary-General was submitted during the thirty-fifth session of the Commission on Human Rights.[37] The responses reflected the general atmosphere and reactions towards children's rights that prevailed at that time. Initially, there was an environment that was in favour of the idea of the Convention. Nevertheless, there were some reservations with regard to various matters. Firstly, reservations were made with regard to the wording of the draft Convention. The wording of the initial draft of the Convention was very similar, and in some parts identical to that of the 1959 Declaration of the Rights of the Child, which was adopted by the General Assembly on 20 November 1959. The Swedish government, for instance, considered it logical enough to seek inspiration from the 1959 Declaration; nevertheless, it argued, among other things, that the wording of an international convention should not be identical to that of a declaration, as the two documents have different legal impacts.[38] The wording of a declaration is generally flexible and contains mainly principles, but the wording of a convention should be more precise and consistent with the legally binding nature of such a document. The Swedish government commented that: 'The 1959 Declaration contains general statements which do not have their proper place in the operative part of a convention which, being an agreement between States, should lay down concrete, mutual obligations.'[39] The less precise wording of the initial Polish draft was seen as a negative point that might leave the articles of the Convention open to different interpretations. 'The present text of the draft convention … is in many respects vague and open to widely differing interpretations. If there is to be a convention, there will be a need to elaborate a more precise text than the present one'.[40] Based on this kind of argument, it was considered more appropriate to review the wording of the draft Convention before adopting the final version in 1979, the International Year of the Child. This kind of reservation with regard to wording is relevant for the drafting history of article 6(2), as there was a focus on the issue of 'precise wording'. A lot of the debates during the drafting of article 6(2), as will be discussed later, related to the fact that the suggested concept of 'survival' does not have a precise meaning; therefore it is not suitable

---

36 United Nations Commission on Human Rights Economic and Soical Council resolution 1978/18 on the 'Question of a convention on the rights of the child' adopted on 5 May 1978, available in Office of the United Nations High Commissioner for Human Rights, *Legislative History of the Convention on the Rights of the Child*, Volume I (United Nations, New York, 2007), p. 47.

37 See UN Doc. E/CN.4/L.1366/Rev.2 (1 March 1978), available in Office of the United Nations High Commissioner for Human Rights, *Legislative History of the Convention on the Rights of the Child*, Volume I (United Nations, New York, 2007), p. 37.

38 See Office of the High Commissioner for Human Rights, *Legislative History of the Convention on the Rights of the Child*, Volume I (United Nations, New York, 2007), p. 62.

39 *Ibid.*

40 *Ibid.*, p 63.

to be put in a legally binding document. 'During the course of the debate, several governmental representatives commented that the concept of survival was not legally defined'.[41]

Secondly, there were some reservations regarding the timing of the adoption of the draft Convention. Certainly, twenty years after the adoption of the Declaration, it was seen that the proposed Convention should be a more up-to-date document. The government of the Netherlands, for instance, argued that the proposed Convention should take into consideration all the changes and developments that had occurred since 1959. 'In elaborating this idea, however, it is not considered sufficient to merely try and copy the Declaration of the Rights of the Child which dates back as early as 1959 and does not reflect the social, economic and cultural developments and changes since then.'[42] Changes at the international level were to be considered as well. A convention is an international agreement; therefore, all newly independent States should participate in the drafting of the proposed Convention, as stated by the Swedish government: 'It may also be recalled that since 1959 a large number of States have been admitted as members of the United Nations. These States – which did not participate in the drafting of the 1959 Declaration – ought to be given an opportunity to influence the drafting of the new convention.'[43]

Consideration of developmental and progress changes in the international situation also seemed to be useful for the adoption of article 6(2), as will be discussed later in this chapter, since it was adopted against a background of slowing down or reversal of progress in the developing world. As Van Bueren pointed out:

> Each day 40,000 children die from malnutrition and disease. Also, according to UNICEF, 'at least half a million young children have died in the last twelve months as a result of the slowing down or the reversal of progress in the developing world.' This is the background against which India, working closely with UNICEF, proposed article 6 of the Convention on the Rights of the Child.[44]

Coupled with this kind of reservation were those regarding the contents and exhaustiveness of the draft Convention. Some concerns were raised about the

---

41 UN Doc. E/CN.4/1988/28, available in Office of the United Nations High Commissioner for Human Rights, *Legislative History of the Convention on the Rights of the Child*, Volume I (United Nations, New York, 2007), para. 15, p. 364.

42 UN Doc. E/CN.4/1324 (27 December 1978), available in Office of the United Nations High Commissioner for Human Rights, *Legislative History of the Convention on the Rights of the Child*, Volume I (United Nations, New York, 2007), p. 60.

43 *Ibid.*, available in Office of the United Nations High Commissioner for Human Rights, *Legislative History of the Convention on the Rights of the Child*, Volume I (United Nations, New York, 2007), p. 62.

44 G. Van Bueren, *The International Law on the Rights of the Child* (Martinus Nijhoff Publishers, The Hague, 1998), p. 293. Citing UNICEF, 'The State of the World's Children 1989' (footnotes omitted).

comprehensiveness of the draft Convention and the factors that could influence it, as pointed out by the World Health Organization (WHO): 'In order to be comprehensive we would like such a convention to place the child in his various contexts, such as the family, the society, the legal context, the new international economic order.'[45]

5. THE OPEN-ENDED WORKING GROUP

With different kinds of reservations being expressed, the Commission on Human Rights decided to establish an open-ended Working Group to consider the proposal for the adoption of the Convention on the Rights of the Child, or what was called, at that time, agenda item 13 'Question of a convention on the rights of the child'. Professor Adam Lopatka of Poland was appointed as the Chairman Rapporteur of the Working Group. He continued to chair the drafting sessions till the adoption of the Convention in 1989.

The 'open-ended' nature of the Working Group was related to the membership of the group. The words of LeBlanc explain this: 'To say that the group was open-ended means that participation in it was open to states and nonstate actors such as IGOs and NGOs.'[46] However, there was another unintentional aspect of the group's work that came to match its 'open-ended' title. The time-frame within which the Working Group completed its mission matches its title of the 'open-ended Working Group'. It was not intended at the beginning that the drafting of the Convention would take ten years. The United Nations General Assembly, for instance, kept frequently calling on the bodies concerned to speed-up the drafting process so that the Convention could be adopted the following year.

The Working Group convened its meetings publicly. Notably, the set-up of the Working Group reflected all the elements that could influence the contents and, subsequently, the implementation of the Convention. All States represented at the Commission on Human Rights had the right to participate in the work of the Working Group. Other Member States of the UN and States that were not yet members of the UN but maintained observer status, such as Switzerland, were also allowed to participate as non-voting observers. Certainly, the issue of participation in the Working Group's work was a voluntary matter.[47] Intergovernmental organisations were able to send observers with the right to take the floor. United Nations Specialised Agencies were among the members of

---

45 UN Doc. E/CN.4/1324 (27 December 1978), available in Office of the United Nations High Commissioner for Human Rights, *Legislative History of the Convention on the Rights of the Child*, Volume I (United Nations, New York, 2007), p. 65.

46 L.J. LeBlanc, *The Convention on the Rights of the Child: United Nations Lawmaking on Human Rights* (University of Nebraska Press, 1995), p. 25.

47 *Ibid.*, p. 27.

the Working Group. Non-governmental organisations which had a consultative status with the Economic and Social Council were also represented during the sessions, but they did not have an absolute right to speak. However, in practice they were always given the chance to do so.[48] Many parties influenced the adoption of articles that were of close relevance to their work. This fact is particularly relevant in the case of article 6(2) on the right of the child to survival and development, because the article came as a result of the direct influence of India and UNICEF, which had an interest in articles related to the child's survival and development.[49]

Nevertheless, the mere presence of one of the above-mentioned organisations, particularly the UN organisations and specialised agencies, in the meetings of the Working Group did not necessarily imply an influential or active role in all of these sessions. This is very evident, for instance, in the case of UNICEF. It was present in most of the drafting sessions but became an active participant only late in the drafting process of the Convention, when it became one of the major influential participants. The late influential participation of UNICEF in the drafting process of the CRC is reflected in the method of adoption of article 6(2). This, however, does not mean that UNICEF was the only body that was interested in the child's survival and development. In fact there were other States as well, such as India, who brought the initial proposal for the article before the Working Group.[50] But UNICEF was going through major changes in its policies and understandings. These changes in its policies led UNICEF to focus on the child's survival and development. Accordingly, when later UNICEF became more interested in the adoption of a convention on the rights of the child, it was more interested in the articles that were related to its policies.[51]

As for the open-ended Working Group, it held annual sessions that lasted for one week before the annual sessions of the Commission on Human Rights. A number of factors affected the nature of the drafting group's work and its length. For instance, when the Working Group started its work back in 1978, the world was politically divided into blocs – the Western Bloc, the Eastern Bloc and, in

48 N. Cantwell, 'The Origins, Development and Significance of the United Nations Convention on the Rights of the Child', in S. Detrick (ed.), *The United Nations Convention on the Rights of the Child: A Guide to the Travaux Préparatoires* (Martinus Nijhoff Publishers, Dordrecht, 1992) p. 22.

49 UNICEF was interested in the articles that focused on the child's development. See UNICEF, 'The State of the World's Children 1996'.

50 UN Doc. E/CN.4/1988/28, available in Office of the United Nations High Commissioner for Human Rights, *Legislative History of the Convention on the Rights of the Child*, Volume I (United Nations, New York, 2007), para. 14, p. 364.

51 UNICEF was not interested at the beginning of the drafting of the CRC. See also M. Newman-William, 'How Things Changed', *UN Chronicle*, Volume 36, Issue 2, 1999. p. 38. See also M. Black, *Children First: The Story of UNICEF, Past and Present* (Oxford University Press, Oxford, 1996), p. 22.

between, the rest of the world – which negatively impacted on the duration of the drafting process, As Cohen described:

> Interest on the Convention on the Rights of the Child did not develop quickly. Some Western nations, the United States in particular, viewed the convention as an Eastern Bloc project focusing mostly on economic, social and cultural rights; rights which are considered by many governments as not being rights at all but merely 'good social policy'. However, beginning in 1983 these prejudices were modified to a large extent, primarily because the original Polish model convention was slowly being expanded by the Working Group to incorporate more and more civil and political rights.[52]

By 1985 there were changes in the international political climate, which cleared the way for the Convention to be adopted in 1989. As Cantwell describes it:

> Another major factor which affected the functioning of the Working Group, more especially in its early years, was the political climate. The change in the atmosphere of the meetings as of 1985, when East–West relations began to thaw in earnest, was remarkable. It contributed greatly to the Working Group being able gradually to move into top gear from then on, since it reduced to a minimum the purely political statements and negotiation that had previously been a hallmark of the discussions.[53]

However, this lengthy drafting process was, in some ways, useful for article 6(2) because India proposed the draft provision only in 1988, i.e., nine years after the establishment of the open-ended Working Group.

6. THE DRAFTING HISTORY OF ARTICLE 6(2) ON THE RIGHT OF THE CHILD TO SURVIVAL AND DEVELOPMENT

6.1. FIRST STEPS

The proposal to include article 6(2) on the right of the child to survival and development was made in 1988, at the very late stages of the CRC's drafting process. It was proposed as a result of the high number of children in developing countries who die every year as a result of diseases that can easily be cured.[54]

---

52 C. Cohen, 'United Nations Convention on the Rights of the Child: Introductory Note' (1989) 28 *International Legal Materials* 1448.

53 N. Cantwell, 'The Origins Development and Significance of the United Nations Convention on the Rights of the Child', in S. Detrick (ed.), *The United Nations Convention on the Rights of the Child: A Guide to the Travaux Préparatoires* (Martinus Nijhoff Publishers, Dordrecht, 1992), p. 22.

54 G. Van Bueren, *The International Law on the Rights of the Child* (Martinus Nijhoff Publishers, The Hague, 1998), p. 293.

Initially, the Indian delegation to the Working Group on the Convention on the Rights of the Child submitted a proposal for the adoption of an article that could, basically, remind States of their obligations: 'the States Parties to the present Convention undertake to create an environment, within their capacities and constitutional processes, which ensures, to the maximum extent possible, the survival and healthy development of the child.'[55] The focus on States to 'create an environment' emphasises the importance of the State as the duty holder to create the conditions necessary for the right of the child to survival and development. This has been later known to be the responsibility of the State under article 6(2) and the reason for its adoption.

Nevertheless, it is possible to argue that there was already some basis for the idea of focusing on the right of the child to development, as it had appeared in article II and probably article IV as well, since it focuses on some aspects of the child's development, of the initial Polish proposal for a Convention on the Rights of the Child in 1978.[56] Article II of the initial Polish proposal reads: 'The child shall enjoy special protection, and shall be given opportunities and facilities, by law and by other means, to enable him to develop physically, mentally, morally, spiritually and socially in a healthy and normal manner and in conditions of freedom and dignity. In the enactment of laws for this purpose, the best interests of the child shall be the paramount consideration.' Article IV reads: 'The child shall enjoy the benefits of social security. He shall be entitled to grow and develop in health; to this end, special care and protection shall be provided both to him and to his mother, including adequate prenatal and post-natal care. The child shall have the right to adequate nutrition, housing, recreation and medical services.' But for India, which initiated the idea of article 6(2) in 1988, the huge number of children who died every year as a result of malnutrition was actually the background of this important step.

6.2. REACTIONS AND DRAFTING PROCESS

In reaction, several governmental representatives, who participated in the drafting process, were worried about the inclusion of the word 'survival' because it lacked a legally defined meaning. 'During the course of the debate, several governmental representatives commented that the concept of survival was not legally defined and one representative expressed the belief that it could even prove harmful to the concept of the right to development, as her delegation

55 UN Doc. E/CN.4/1988/28, available in Office of the United Nations High Commissioner for Human Rights, *Legislative History of the Convention on the Rights of the Child*, Volume I (United Nations, New York, 2007), para. 14, p. 364.

56 UN Doc. E/CN.4/L.1366 (7 February 1978), available in Office of the United Nations High Commissioner for Human Rights, *Legislative History of the Convention on the Rights of the Child*, Volume I (United Nations, New York, 2007), p. 33.

understood it.'[57] Le Blanc, for instance, describes the reactions of the drafters to the Indian proposal as follows:

> Some delegates opposed the adoption of the Indian proposal on the ground that the right to survival did not have a widely accepted legal definition and would, therefore, prove difficult to implement. However, it was widely recognized that one of the advantages of the proposal was that it took a positive approach to the right to life by taking into account economic and social conditions that affect the survival of children.[58]

The 1959 Declaration, which addressed the issue of the rights of the child, had included concepts similar to those of article 6(2). As would often be seen within the legislative process of international law, the principles or concepts of a particular article would be based on an already existing article or principle from a previous international declaration.[59] Accordingly, it is possible to argue that article 6(2) was founded on the model of principle II of the 1959 Declaration of the Rights of the Child.

There were some attempts to change the wording of the Indian proposal, and alternatives were proposed. For instance: 'The States Parties to the present Convention shall respect the right of the child to survival. The State Parties shall, within their capacities and constitutional processes, take all necessary measures to ensure, to the maximum extent possible, the survival and healthy development of the child.'[60] Unfortunately, the UN Document does not state the party who proposed it; however, it is notable that this kind of suggestion emphasised the right of the child to survival twice: firstly by asking States to respect it, and then by asking States to ensure its implementation, although the respect for the right is part of its implementation. The suggestion also differs from the present article 6(2) as it specifies that States should ensure the 'healthy development' of the child. The present article 6(2) uses simple language and asks States Parties to ensure the development of the child, leaving the door open for further elaborative interpretations.

There were another two suggestions made by the drafters of article 6(2) in relation to specifying an aspect of the child's development. The first suggestion focused on the child's 'full' development: 'The States Parties to the present

---

57 UN Doc. E/CN.4/1988/28, available in Office of the United Nations High Commissioner for Human Rights, *Legislative History of the Convention on the Rights of the Child*, Volume I (United Nations, New York, 2007), para. 15, p. 364.

58 L.J. LeBlanc, *The Convention on the Rights of the Child: United Nations Lawmaking on Human Rights* (University of Nebraska Press, Lincoln, 1995), p. 77.

59 C. Cohen, 'The Developing Jurisprudence of the Rights of the Child' [1993–1994] 6 *St. Thomas Law Review* 1, 1–96.

60 UN Doc. E/CN.4/1988/28, available in Office of the United Nations High Commissioner for Human Rights, *Legislative History of the Convention on the Rights of the Child*, Volume I (United Nations, New York, 2007), para. 15, p. 365.

Convention undertake to create within the available resources the psychological conditions which will guarantee, to the maximum extent possible, the life and the full development of the child.'[61] The second suggestion focused on the child's healthy development: 'States Parties to the present Convention undertake to promote conditions which guarantee the life and healthy development of the child.'[62] However, there was another suggestion that resembled, to some extent, the present article 6(2), although it omitted a major part of it, i.e., the right to development. 'The States parties to the present Convention undertake to promote conditions which ensure, to the maximum extent possible, the survival of the child.'[63] However, it is possible to argue that the changes that were proposed in relation to the term 'development' were not focused on its precise legal definition because the concept of development had already existed in previous declarations, whereas the proposal to include the word 'survival' in the CRC was not preceded by similar inclusions.

Subsequently, both India, the main initiator of article 6(2), and UNICEF were given the chance to explain what they meant by the 'controversial' word 'survival'; the Chairman asked the observer of UNICEF to explain what his organisation understood by survival.[64] This step indicates the importance of UNICEF's views about survival and development for the drafting of article 6(2). The representative of India 'was of the view that the right to survival should be stressed, bearing in mind, as indicated by UNICEF, that many children died from preventable causes and that children could also survive in very poor conditions, the right to survival should be supplemented by the notion of healthy development.'[65]

Following that, the discussion in the Working Group continued and focused mainly on 'the definition of the concepts of survival, right to survival, right to development and the child's development.'[66] Some participants even expressed the importance of survival to the child's life, indicating that both life and survival are complementary and not mutually exclusive and that survival could even mean the reduction of infant mortality or could be the result of a reduction in infant mortality.[67] The discussion then continued to focus on the difference between the right to life and the right to survival.[68] Despite the great attention and clarification that the right to survival received, it was still difficult for some drafting parties to accept its inclusion in the Convention: 'Two speakers stated that, despite the explanations that had been given on the word "survival", they

61 *Ibid.*
62 *Ibid.*
63 *Ibid.*
64 *Ibid.*, para. 16.
65 *Ibid.*, para. 17.
66 *Ibid.*, para. 18.
67 *Ibid.*
68 *Ibid.*, para. 19.

continued to have serious doubts about the inclusion of this concept in the convention.'[69] A proposal that omitted any reference to survival or development was made: 'The States Parties to the present Convention undertake to promote conditions which protect, to the maximum extent possible, the life of the child.'[70] There was also a suggestion that focused on the textual differences between the different authentic languages of the Convention, particularly the English, French and Spanish texts: 'The States Parties to the present Convention undertake to promote conditions which ensure, to the maximum extent possible, the survival and healthy development of the child (The word "survival" in English to be put in brackets in the French and Spanish texts.)'[71] There was also another suggestion that grouped the components of the present article 6 – the right to life, survival and development – into one article: 'States Parties shall protect the right to life of children and ensure the survival and healthy development of children.'[72] As mentioned before, the UN documents do not indicate from whom these proposals came, but the number of suggestions and comments made conveys the environment in which article 6(2) was being drafted, i.e., the controversy about words and their specific legal meanings. This controversy was a reminder of the reservations about the wording that were raised back in 1978 when the initial Polish proposal was made.

During the drafting of the CRC, articles were not adopted on the basis of votes. The chairman of the group decided that the articles would be drafted by obtaining a consensus. Unlike the word 'unanimity', a consensus does not mean the unanimity of all the opinions; in fact, it means that there was some sort of an agreement or a compromise. Cynthia Cohen describes the consensus as 'agreeing not to disagree'.[73] Obviously, not all parties might necessarily be agreeable to an article and, therefore, in order for it to be adopted, some form of compromise would be inevitable. During the drafting of the Convention on the Rights of the Child, this kind of compromise was reached through 'sub-working groups' that emerged from the original drafting group on the article under consideration. 'Usually, they were successful in hammering out a compromise text and it would be quickly adopted by the Working Group.'[74] As might be expected, based on the controversy that the words 'survival' and 'development' caused, article 6(2) was the result of a compromise.

The sub-group would include 'delegations that had made comments about the proposed texts, plus an appropriate representative from a United Nations body

69 *Ibid.*

70 *Ibid.*

71 *Ibid.*, para. 20.

72 *Ibid.*

73 C. Cohen, 'Drafting of the United Nations Convention on the Rights of the Child: Challenges and Achievements', in E. Verhellen (ed.), *Understanding Children's Rights* (Ghent Papers on Children's Rights, Children's Rights Centre, University of Ghent, Ghent, 1996), p. 341.

74 *Ibid.*, p. 344.

and one or two NGOs'.[75] Unsurprisingly; among the members of the sub-group on article 6(2) were the initiator, India, and UNICEF. When the Chairman-Rapporteur was summing up the debate, he proposed that a small drafting group should work out a compromise text. This small drafting group was formed of Argentina, Bulgaria, India, Italy, Norway, UNICEF and the United Kingdom.[76] Following the submission of the compromise text the representative of India clarified a very important point that would prove to be essential, indeed, for any interpretation and implementation of article 6(2): namely, the reason for drafting article 6(2) in this way.

> The representative of India stated that the text had been drafted in order to cover the following main concerns: (a) the inherent right to life of the child, and (b) the focus on obligations for States parties to promote measures and conditions for the survival and development of the child.[77]

This sounds like common sense, since the aim of having a convention on the rights of the child is to obligate States to promote and protect children's rights. Nevertheless, it had to be emphasised. Unlike the declarations, the Convention is meant to adopt a rights-based approach, rather than a charity-based one, to children's rights.[78] It is, therefore, justifiable enough to exert more focus on duty bearers. The 1959 Declaration of the Rights of the Child, for instance, provides principles only and does not stress the State-obligation aspect.[79] The Indian explanation, in fact, indicates a deeper and more specific form of State Party obligation.

However, despite this compromise, there was an extensive discussion and the representative of Venezuela pointed out that she regretted the inclusion of paragraph 2 (presently article 6(2)), 'since, in her view, it will diminish the concept of the right to life conferred on all human beings in existing international instruments; she requested that some thought should be given to that, and that her position should be reflected in the report to be submitted to the Commission on Human Rights.'[80] There was no agreement for her demand and the Working Group accepted the text submitted by the small drafting group.

---

75 *Ibid.*, p. 355.

76 UN Doc. E/CN.4/1988/28, available in Office of the United Nations High Commissioner for Human Rights, *Legislative History of the Convention on the Rights of the Child*, Volume I (United Nations, New York, 2007), para. 21, pp. 365–366.

77 *Ibid.*, para. 23, p. 366.

78 N. Cantwell, 'Veni, Vidi... et Vici? A review of the history and impact of the CRC', in A. Weyts (ed.), *Understanding Children's Rights* (Ghent Papers on Children's Rights, Children's Rights Centre, University of Ghent, Ghent, 2004), pp. 289–290.

79 See UN Doc. A/4249 and Corr.2, para. 33, available in Office of the United Nations High Commissioner for Human Rights, *Legislative History of the Convention on the Rights of the Child*, Volume I (United Nations, New York, 2007), p. 21.

80 UN Doc. E/CN.4/1988/28 (6 April 1988), para. 24, available in Office of the United Nations High Commissioner for Human Rights, *Legislative History of the Convention on the Rights of the Child*, Volume I (United Nations, New York, 2007), p. 366.

The compromise was made; the word 'survival' was put into the body of a legally binding document and no specification or aspect of development was attached to the right of the child to development. As Schabas suggests, 'Treaties are the fruit of diplomatic compromise'.[81] Any specifications were for the future interpreters of the Convention to clarify. The compromise text included three rights of the child: the right to life, the right to survival and the right to development. It reads:

1. The States Parties to the present Convention recognize that every child has the inherent right to life.
2. States Parties shall ensure, to the maximum extent possible, the survival and development of the child

In January 1988 the Working Group of the Commission on Human Rights 'decided that a technical review of the text of the draft convention should be carried out in accordance with United Nations technical standards and practices regarding that kind of international instrument.'[82] During this review there were no comments on article 6(2) and its wording.[83]

6.3. FINAL DRAFTING PROCESS

In 1988 the Commission on Human Rights also decided to continue its work on the elaboration of the draft Convention on the Rights of the Child as a matter of the highest priority. It asked the Economic and Social Council to authorise the convening of an open-ended Working Group for a period of up to two weeks, with a view to completing the second reading of the draft Convention.[84] During this second reading some States submitted new proposals on the present article 6(2) for the Working Group to consider. The observer of Kuwait submitted a proposal that omitted any reference to the child's survival and development: 'The State Parties to the present Convention shall respect the child's right to life and, to this end, shall take all constitutional and legal measures needed

81 W. Schabas, 'The Right of the Child, Law of Armed Conflict and Customary International Law: A Tale of Two Cases', in K. Arts and V. Popovski (eds.), *International Criminal Accountability and the Rights of Children* (Hague Academic Press, The Hague, 2006), p. 34.

82 UN Doc. E/CN/.4/1989/WG.1/CRP.1 (15 October 1988), available in Office of the United Nations High Commissioner for Human Rights, *Legislative History of the Convention on the Rights of the Child*, Volume I (United Nations, New York, 2007), p. 187.

83 *Ibid.*; also see UN Doc. E/CN.4/1988/WG.1/WP.1/Rev.1, available in Office of the High Commissioner for Human Rights, *Legislative History of the Convention on the Rights of the Child,* Volume 1 (United Nations, New York, 2007), p. 366.

84 UN Doc. E/CN.4/1989/48 (2 March 1989) (I. Introduction), para. 1, available in Office of the United Nations High Commissioner for Human Rights, *Legislative History of the Convention on the Rights of the Child*, Volume I (United Nations, New York, 2007), p. 196.

to guarantee the right.'[85] The representative of Venezuela, who was previously one of the opponents of the inclusion of the word 'survival', also submitted the following proposal:

> 1. For the purposes of the present Convention, 'child' means every human being up to the age of 18 years unless, under the law of his state, he has attained the age of majority earlier,
> 2. The States parties to the present Convention recognize that every child has the inherent right to life
> 3. States Parties shall ensure to the maximum extent possible the healthy growth and development of the child...[86]

Venezuela maintained its opposing position until the last minute. Then the representative of the World Health Organization (WHO) stated reservations with regard to the replacement of the word 'survival'. He also made a very significant explanation, which was in reference to a proposal submitted by Venezuela, in which the word 'survival' was replaced by the word 'growth':

> The observer for the World Health Organization expressed reservation with regard to the replacement of the word 'survival' and explained that the term 'survival' had a special meaning within the United Nations context, especially for his organization and UNICEF. 'Survival' included growth monitoring, oral rehydration and disease control, breast feeding, immunization, child spacing, food and female literacy; the term 'growth' represented only a part of the concept of 'survival' and the change would be a step backwards from standards already accepted.[87]

This statement by the observer for the WHO emphasised the importance of the particular meaning of the words that were to be used as components of the term 'survival'. This clarification by the WHO was an example of the great determination to maintain the terminologies as they were and demonstrated recognition of the fact that any attempt to change them might result in adverse change to the standards already recognised. It is noticeable that most of the meanings of the word survival which the WHO representative referred to are centred on the issue of early childhood development.

There were also other reactions from delegates of States who participated in the drafting sub-working group on article 6(2), including Norway, Italy and India, the

85 UN Doc. E/CN.4/1989/WG.1/WP.18, available in Office of the United Nations High Commissioner for Human Rights, *Legislative History of the Convention on the Rights of the Child*, Volume I (United Nations, New York, 2007), pp. 366–367.

86 UN Doc. E/CN.4/1989/48, para. 87; see also UN Doc. E/CN.4/1989/WG.1/WP.10, available in Office of the United Nations High Commissioner for Human Rights, *Legislative History of the Convention on the Rights of the Child*, Volume I (United Nations, New York, 2007), p. 367.

87 UN Doc. E/CN.4/1989/48, para. 88, available in Office of the United Nations High Commissioner for Human Rights, *Legislative History of the Convention on the Rights of the Child*, Volume I (United Nations, New York, 2007), p. 367.

State that had initially proposed the provision. There were also reactions from some States who were part of the main drafting group, such as Australia and Sweden. All of these parties stated their preference for the word 'survival', 'reminding the Working Group of the Spirit of Collaboration under which this particular article was drafted 10 months ago.'[88] The representative of Italy explained the strong relationship between the two terms, i.e., 'survival' and 'development':

> The representative of Italy indicated that in the language of international organizations the two words 'survival' and 'development' had come to acquire the special meaning of ensuring the child's survival in order to realize the full development of his or her personality, both from the material and spiritual points of view.[89]

In relation to adopting new articles during the Convention's second reading, Cynthia Cohen refers to the 'Target 89' slogan. She explains that after spending a long time on the drafting of the CRC many NGOs were beginning to worry that the Convention's drafting might continue indefinitely. It was at this time that 'Target 89' was adopted. The aim was to finish the drafting of the Convention by 1989, which was the thirtieth anniversary of the 1959 Declaration of the Rights of the Child.[90] It led to a rush in finishing the drafting stage of the Convention in order to meet this target.[91] This, however, was not intended to be a reason for adopting articles that might weaken the existing recognised children's rights. Accordingly, the Working Group suggested to the Secretary-General that a technical review of the first reading should be undertaken.[92] Arguably, it is probably because of the 'Target 89' campaign that there was no interest in reopening the discussion on the wording of article 6(2).

However, following the strong statements that were made, the representative of Venezuela withdrew the amendment but stated that the problem would be an issue of interpretation by local authorities.[93] This was an indication that the representative of Venezuela was not convinced by the explanations of the matter that had already been made. Following that, the present article 6(2) of the Convention on the Rights of the Child was adopted in the Working Group's second reading of the CRC.[94]

---

88 *Ibid.*, para. 89.

89 *Ibid.*

90 C. Cohen, 'Drafting of the United Nations Convention on the Rights of the Child: Challenges and Achievements', in E. Verhellen (ed.), *Understanding Children's Rights* (Ghent Papers on Children's Rights, Children's Rights Centre, University of Ghent, Ghent, 1996), p. 327.

91 *Ibid.*, p. 328.

92 *Ibid.*

93 UN Doc. E/CN.4/1989/48 (2 March 1989), para. 90, available in Office of the United Nations High Commissioner for Human Rights, *Legislative History of the Convention on the Rights of the Child*, Volume I (United Nations, New York, 2007), p. 367.

94 *Ibid.*, para. 91, available in Office of the United Nations High Commissioner for Human Rights, *Legislative History of the Convention on the Rights of the Child*, Volume I (United Nations, New York, 2007), p. 368.

7. THE ROLE OF THE UNITED NATIONS CHILDREN'S FUND (UNICEF) IN THE DRAFTING OF ARTICLE 6(2)

7.1. PARTICIPATION OF UNICEF AT THE DRAFTING SESSIONS

It is important to emphasise that the official UN documents on the drafting of article 6(2) do not emphasise the role of UNICEF in the drafting of article 6(2).[95] However, there is one reference to, for example, UNICEF's role in the 1988 report of the Working Group, when it states that: 'At the request of the Chairman, the observer of the United Nations Children's Fund explained what the Fund understood by survival.'[96]

Nevertheless, there are many signs that convey the fact that UNICEF played an active role in the drafting of article 6(2). Firstly, in its 1996 State of the World's Children report, UNICEF explains how it worked hard to get article 6(2) included in the Convention, i.e., how it pushed for the inclusion of UNICEF's own vision on child survival and development:

> In the early 1980s, the group of rights that UNICEF was most anxious to promote – and upon whose inclusion in the Convention it had insisted – were child rights to survival and development. The Convention asserts on behalf of children that their basic rights to health and education should ultimately be guaranteed by the State. When UNICEF could see those rights converging with the campaign for child survival and development, it gave the Convention energetic support both in the final drafting stages and also after adoption by the General Assembly.[97]

In 1996 UNICEF celebrated its fiftieth anniversary. The success in getting article 6(2), i.e. the right to survival and development, included in the Convention was regarded by UNICEF as one of its major accomplishments within those fifty years.[98] Secondly, in an interview in December 2004, Nigel Cantwell, who participated in the drafting of the Convention as the Director of

95 UN Doc. E/CN.4/1988/28, paras. 14–26, available in Office of the United Nations High Commissioner for Human Rights, *Legislative History of the Convention on the Rights of the Child*, Volume I (United Nations, New York, 2007), pp. 364–366 and UN Doc. E/CN.4/1989/48, paras. 86–91 available in Office of the United Nations High Commissioner for Human Rights, *Legislative History of the Convention on the Rights of the Child*, Volume I (United Nations, New York, 2007), pp. 367–368.

96 UN Doc. E/CN.4/1988/28, para. 16, available in Office of the United Nations High Commissioner for Human Rights, *Legislative History of the Convention on the Rights of the Child*, Volume I (United Nations, New York, 2007), p. 365.

97 UNICEF, 'The State of the World's Children 1996' (online version) <www.unicef.org/sowc96/1990s.htm> accessed 19 April 2015.

98 UNICEF, 'The State of the World's Children 1996' (online version) <www.unicef.org/sowc96/> accessed 12 April 2015.

Defence for Children International, confirmed that, despite the fact that India had formally proposed the article, it was in fact UNICEF that pushed for its inclusion in the Convention.[99] Thirdly, the inclusion of article 6(2) was proposed to the Working Group shortly after UNICEF started taking the Convention more seriously in 1987 as will be discussed in the following paragraphs. All of these signs, significantly, represent an unwritten and unofficial history of article 6(2).

Initially, UNICEF was not interested in the Convention on the Rights of the Child. There is much speculation about the reasons for a lack of interest on UNICEF's part. For instance, some explain it on the basis that UNICEF did not want any confrontation with the governments as UNICEF, for some reason, assumed that a Convention on the Rights of the Child would be a reason for conflict. Black, for instance, refers to the negative attitude of UNICEF towards the concept of children's rights, which manifested itself even before the drafting of the CRC:

> In this movement Unicef played little part, or was at best passive. It did not wish to embroil itself in the controversial field of human rights in such a way as to antagonize its governmental partners and jeopardize what has become its main activity since the development era: cooperation in child-centred development programmes.
>
> Accordingly, when the NGO children's lobby pressed the UN to declare 1979 an 'International Year of the Child', the proposal evoked a sense of unease at Unicef. It feared a diversion of energy and resources away from 'development via basic services' – as yet making only limited headway...[100]

Cohen, who was also involved with the drafting of the CRC, also argues that UNICEF was reluctant to use the language of rights and describes the lack of interest from UNICEF during the drafting of the CRC:

> At that time, the Convention was not popular among governments and UNICEF viewed the idea of 'rights' for children as being so controversial that it might interfere with its ability to deliver services at the national level. This situation began to change after UNICEF's fortieth anniversary in 1986. From then on, UNICEF began to take a more active role in the Convention's drafting process and a UNICEF delegate was present at most of the Working Group sessions.[101]

---

99 Interview with Nigel Cantwell, a drafter of the Convention on the Rights of the Child, as the Director of Defence for Children International (Ghent, Belgium, December 2004).

100 M. Black, *Children First: The Story of UNICEF, Past and Present* (Oxford University Press, Oxford, 1996), p. 22.

101 C. Cohen, 'Drafting of the United Nations Convention on the Rights of the Child: Challenges and Achievements', in E. Verhellen (ed.), *Understanding Children's Rights* (Ghent Papers on Children's Rights, Children's Rights Centre, University of Ghent, Ghent, 1996), p. 327.

Another argument is made by LeBlanc. He argues that the Convention was meant to be a standard-setting document and that UNICEF is an operational rather than a standard-setting organisation. As for UNICEF, he argues:

> It is also not clear how much more could have been expected of specialized agencies like UNICEF. Although it may rightly be considered the premier international agency concerned with the status and welfare of children, UNICEF is primarily an operating agency and is only secondarily, if at all, a standard-setting agency. In fact, although it may possess substantial expertise that, in an ideal setting, should be shared with states and other actors involved in the elaboration of international norms, it faces realities that limit its potential value and effectiveness in such a process. It was created by governments and, for the most part, remains a creature of governments. Governments prescribe its mandate, establish much of its agenda, and provide most of its budget – all of which can serve to limit its independence or autonomy. Like other agencies or organizations of this type, it may be susceptible to political pressures and therefore may find an advantage to being prudent in its relations with states, allowing them to be primarily responsible for standard-setting and focusing its own energies on operational concerns.[102]

One can observe that UNICEF, in contrast to some other IGOs, was present in almost all of the drafting sessions that took place between 1979 and 1989. This in fact is a credit to be given to UNICEF. However, this presence did not always reflect a positive participatory role and was, at times, just for the sake of attendance, with no positive contribution made to the discussions. As LeBlanc explains:

> UNICEF, of course, was credited for its financial contributions … but it was widely criticized for not having taken a broader interest in the convention, particularly in the normative provisions. Overall, the NGOs were dissatisfied with what they considered low levels of attendance by the IGOs and specialized agencies at the sessions of the working group and claimed that the IGOs and agencies had been timid in bringing their expertise to bear in substantive issues.[103]

Moreover, it is necessary to distinguish between poor participation and effective participation as regards the role of UNICEF during the drafting of the CRC. During the early years of the drafting, the participation of UNICEF did not exceed the level of attendance at the sessions. Van Bueren criticises UNICEF's failure, at that time, to advocate for children's rights: 'Rather than a lion roaring on behalf of children as it is now, UNICEF was more a mouse squeaking at the foot of the secretary general.'[104]

---

102 L.J. LeBlanc, *The Convention on the Rights of the Child: United Nations Lawmaking on Human Rights* (University of Nebraska Press, 1995), p. 40.

103 *Ibid.*, pp. 38–39.

104 G. Van Bueren, 'International Childrens Rights – A Stop-Go History', in E. Verhellen (ed.), *Understanding Children's Rights* (Ghent Papers on Children's Rights. Children's Rights

7.2. CHILD SURVIVAL AND DEVELOPMENT REVOLUTION

In the period between the early eighties and the mid-nineties, UNICEF's policies and actions were guided by what was called at that time 'the Child Survival and Development Revolution'. UNICEF did not adopt a rights-based approach to it. However, in 1987, UNICEF and its director started to recognise the importance of the children's rights approach in strengthening the child survival and development revolution. Black describes this era of UNICEF's history and how UNICEF was determined to include its vision of the child survival and development revolution in the body of the Convention:

> By 1987, Unicef had begun to recognize the potential convergence of the world wide campaign for child survival with the thrust for children's rights. Grant, previously sceptical that governments would accept that children had independent rights of their own, came fully behind the Convention with the proviso that the rights to survival and development be given their due weight within the text. A timetable was set for completing the draft Convention and orchestrating its tour through the necessary international committees and machinery of the UN approval system. Although the Commission on Human Rights was administratively and technically responsible for this process, Unicef's role in mobilizing support for the Convention's adoption was extremely important.[105]

For UNICEF, the concept of survival started earlier than 1982. It emerged in the post-colonial era, when there was a huge amount of poverty and underdevelopment in the 'third world'.[106] Later, in 1978, the important health conference of the Health Ministers of the developing countries took place in Alma Ata (now called Almaty) in the former USSR. They agreed to restructure the health systems in their countries based on the so-called 'Primary Health Care' (PHC), for all citizens. The concept included, among others, growth monitoring, oral rehydration, breastfeeding and immunisation. When UNICEF started the survival revolution in 1982 it focused, mainly, on the reduction of under-five mortalities. Based on that, UNICEF concentrated on four aspects from the Primary Health Care package, as they were vital in reducing under-five mortalities. In other words, these four concepts were vital for the survival of the child.

> UNICEF now proposed to vanquish common infections of early childhood using simple medical technologies. From the primary health care package, it singled out four techniques, which collectively were referred to as 'GOBI': 'G' for growth

Centre, University of Ghent, Ghent, 1996), p. 316.

105 M. Black, *Children First: The Story of UNICEF, Past and Present* (Oxford University Press, Oxford, 1996), pp. 24–25.

106 *Ibid.*, p. 5.

> monitoring to keep a regular check on child well-being; 'O' for oral rehydration therapy to treat bouts of child diarrhoea; 'B' for breastfeeding as the perfect nutritional start in life; 'I' for immunization against the six vaccine-preventable childhood killers: tuberculosis, diphtheria, whooping cough, tetanus, polio and measles. One of the strengths of this prescription was that all the techniques were low cost.[107]

The comments of the representative of the WHO in 1988 during the Convention's second reading about the specific meaning of the term 'survival' are a reminder of the agreement in Alma Ata. Jim Grant directed UNICEF during the ten years that witnessed the drafting of the Convention on the Rights of the Child. He believed that human progress is essential in the development process and that investment in health and education should have developmental implications. Thus he focused on the general concept of development and on worldwide development. His idea was to cooperate with governments in 'child-centred development programmes'.[108]

> By the end of the decade the child survival and development revolution was estimated to have saved the lives of 12 million children. However, it was never aimed exclusively at saving children's lives and preventing childhood disease and disability. The wider purpose of the revolution was to revitalize the flagging cause of human-centred development and to place children at the leading edge.[109]

The comments made by Jim Grant reflect the significance of survival as an indicator of and instrument for development. Child-mortality levels were used as indicators to measure the overall development of the State: 'Rates of infant and young child mortality had previously been seen as measurements of a country's development. Now UNICEF suggested a direct attack on infant and child mortality as an instrument of development.'[110]

The environment that prevails during the drafting of a convention can have a significant effect on its contents. This environment might either positively or negatively influence the inclusion of a particular article or concept in the body of the convention. The active participation and engagement of UNICEF in the drafting of the Convention in 1987 resulted in the creation of a welcoming environment. This welcoming environment probably facilitated the inclusion of UNICEF's interest in child survival and development, i.e., article 6(2) and other related articles, in the substantive part of the CRC, specifically if we take into

107 UNICEF, 'The State of the World's Children 1996' (online version) <www.unicef.org/sowc96/1980s.htm> accessed 12 April 2015.

108 M. Black, *Children First: The Story of UNICEF, Past and Present* (Oxford University Press, Oxford, 1996), p. 22.

109 UNICEF, 'The State of the World's Children 1996' (online version) <www.unicef.org/sowc96/1980s.htm> accessed 12 April 2015.

110 *Ibid.*

account that focus on the survival and development of the child was, in itself, convincing enough. In this respect, it might be argued that the proposal for the inclusion of article 6(2) was not welcomed by all States and that, in fact, it confronted considerable objections. This fact, however, does not contradict the above argument as regards the welcoming environment which eventually resulted in the adoption of article 6(2) with a compromise. Cynthia Cohen, who participated in the drafting of the Convention, describes some other aspects of the environment that prevailed at the time of the drafting of the Convention, as follows:

> participants came to the Working Group armed only with old fashioned notions of children as being in need of 'care and protection' and the text of a Polish model Convention. They did not have a 'great plan', and, contrary to the myths that have grown up since the Convention has gone into force, there was no idea that children's rights should embody the 'three P's' of protection, provision and participation. Instead a mixed group of delegates, from differing cultures and varying backgrounds met to hammer out a international human rights instrument that would be appropriate for children. In doing this, the different actors behaved in a variety of ways which ultimately resulted in the completion of a treaty protecting the rights of the child.[111]

It could also be argued that the fact that UNICEF has a particular interpretation of survival and development does not necessarily mean that this interpretation was shared by those who adopted the Convention. It could also be said that it is not good law to conclude that article 6(2) should be interpreted as UNICEF intended simply because UNICEF was important in its adoption. Articles 45(a) and 45(b) of the CRC answer back to both of these arguments:

> In order to foster the effective implementation of the Convention and to encourage international co-operation in the field covered by the Convention:
> (a) The specialized agencies, the United Nations Children's Fund, and other United Nations organs shall be entitled to be represented at the consideration of the implementation of such provisions of the present Convention as fall within the scope of their mandate. The Committee may invite the specialized agencies, the United Nations Children's Fund and other competent bodies as it may consider appropriate to provide expert advice on the implementation of the Convention in areas falling within the scope of their respective mandates. The Committee may invite the specialized agencies, the United Nations Children's Fund, and other United Nations organs to submit reports on the implementation of the Convention in areas falling within the scope of their activities;
> (b) The Committee shall transmit, as it may consider appropriate, to the specialized agencies, the United Nations Children's Fund and other competent bodies, any

111 C. Cohen, 'Drafting of the United Nations Convention on the Rights of the Child: Challenges and Achievements', in E. Verhellen (ed.), *Understanding Children's Rights* (Ghent Papers on Children's Rights, Children's Rights Centre, University of Ghent, Ghent, 1996), p. 340.

> reports from States Parties that contain a request, or indicate a need, for technical advice or assistance, along with the Committee's observations and suggestions, if any, on these requests or indications; ...

Accordingly, UNICEF's special relationship with article 6(2) on the survival and development of the child did not end with its adoption into the CRC. UNICEF is expected to play an important role in the implementation of the entire CRC, including article 6(2). In achieving this, UNICEF would be guided by its inner policies on the survival and development of the child.

8. THE 1986 UNITED NATIONS DECLARATION ON THE RIGHT TO DEVELOPMENT AND THE DRAFTING OF ARTICLE 6(2) ON THE RIGHT OF THE CHILD TO SURVIVAL AND DEVELOPMENT

8.1. BASIC FACTS ABOUT THE DECLARATION ON THE RIGHT TO DEVELOPMENT

The United Nations General Assembly adopted the Declaration on the Right to Development (DRD) in 1986, only two years prior to the proposal on article 6(2) of the CRC.[112]

> The right to development is an inalienable human right by virtue of which every human person and all peoples are entitled to participate in, contribute to, and enjoy economic, social, cultural and political development, in which all human rights and fundamental freedoms can be fully realized.[113]

Based on this article, Arjun Sengupta, the former UN Independent Expert on the Right to Development, points out that there is an inalienable human right that is called the right to development. It includes issues such as full sovereignty over natural resources, self-determination, popular participation in development and equality of opportunity.[114] It also includes responsibility for the creation of favourable conditions for the enjoyment of other civil, political, economic, social and cultural rights. It is beyond the discussion on this chapter whether this inalienable human right to development is an individual or collective right,

---

112 See UN Doc. E/CN.4/1988/28, para. 14, available in Office of the United Nations High Commissioner for Human Rights, *Legislative History of the Convention on the Rights of the Child*, Volume I (United Nations, New York, 2007), p. 364.

113 United Nations General Assembly, 'Declaration on the Right to Development', UN Doc. A/RES/41/128 (4 December 1986), article 1.

114 More information is available at: <www.ohchr.org/EN/Issues/Development/Pages/Backgroundrtd.aspx> accessed 24 April 2015.

however, it is probably better to mention that some academics argue against the individual's right to development for the benefits of a people's right to development.[115]

For the DRD, there is a particular process of economic, social, cultural and political development, in which all human rights and fundamental freedoms can be fully realised. There is a right to development process as explained by the former Independent Expert on the Right to Development.[116] Finally, 'the right to development is a human right by virtue of which every human person and all peoples are entitled to participate in, contribute to and enjoy that particular process of development'.[117] Sengupta also adds that: 'The right to development builds upon the notion of human development and can be described as the right to human development, defined as a development process that expands substantive freedoms and thereby realizes all human rights.'[118]

In this context, the question that arises is about the link between the right of the child to survival and development and the right to development as stated by the DRD? There is no doubt that the adoption of article 6(2) was a major step towards saving the lives of millions of children from death and crippling diseases. The human development aspect of article 6(2) is definite. The link with 'development' is also very clear as article 6(2) was proposed against the background of the slowing down of progress in developing countries.[119] This emphasises the importance of the separate right of the child to development, in the form guaranteed by the 1986 Declaration on the Right to Development, in relation to article 6(2).

8.2. DRD AND THE DRAFTING OF ARTICLE 6(2)

The question here is: was there any influence from the adoption of the DRD in 1986 on the drafting and adoption of article 6(2)? Arguably, the adoption of the United Nations Declaration on the Right to Development could have been among some of the changes at the international level that led to the proposal of an article on the right of the child to development, i.e., article 6(2). The role that the adoption of this Declaration played in the adoption of article 6(2) is, possibly, part of the 'unofficial' history of the CRC, especially when focusing on Sengupta's explanation of the meaning of article 1 of the Declaration on the Right to

115 See K. Iqbal, *The Right to Development in International Law. The Case of Pakistan* (Routledge, London, 2012), pp. 54–58.

116 For further reading also see K. Iqbal, *The Right to Development in International Law. The Case of Pakistan* (Routledge, London, 2012).

117 A. Sengupta, 'On the Theory and Practice of the Right to Development' (2002) 24 *Human Rights Quarterly* 837, 847.

118 *Ibid.*, p. 851.

119 G. Van Bueren, *The International Law on the Rights of the Child* (Martinus Nijhoff Publishers, The Hague, 1998), p. 293.

Development. His explanation proves the importance of the State obligation of creating conditions and measures for the benefit of the right to development, in particular human development. The concept of the State as the duty-holder in both the national and international level is also reflected in articles 3(1) and 8 of the DRD.[120] Responsibility at the national level is also mentioned in article 2(3). State creation of conditions was part of the basis for the way in which article 6(2) was drafted. The fact that the right to development is about human development also indicates this close link, since article 6(2) is about the right of the child to 'survival' and 'human development'.

Van Bueren also suggests a link between the right of the child to development as it appears in article 6(2) and the international right to development:

> The right to development is also a dynamic concept. The right to development is the right of individuals, groups and arguably peoples to participate in, contribute to and enjoy continuous economic, social, political and cultural development in an environment in which all human rights can be realised. Within the context of the Declaration on the Right to Development the right includes concepts of equality of opportunity and distributive justice for all including children. When presenting the draft which became article 6 India argued strenuously that the concept of development was necessary to reinforce the notion of survival.[121]

Van Bueren, also, stresses that the right to development, as guaranteed by the Declaration on the Right to Development, has a special interrelated facet:

> Specifically, in relation to children, the right to development has a second interrelated facet. The right to development also refers to the health and the development of the individual child to a level which enables the child to benefit from the exercise of all the other rights of the child.[122]

Arguably, this indicates or conveys the important link or relationship between the right to development and other individual children's rights such as the right to health and the right to education. However, it also emphasises that the right to development and survival is separate from other children rights. Moreover, it brings to the focus the value added of a separate formulation of a right of children to development; over many more specific provisions on children's rights.

---

120 For a discussion on the difficulties facing the concept of the State as the duty-holder see K. Iqbal, *The Right to Development in International Law. The Case of Pakistan* (Routledge, London, 2012), pp. 53–54.

121 G. Van Bueren, *The International Law on the Rights of the Child* (Martinus Nijhoff Publishers, The Hague, 1998), p. 293 (footnotes omitted).

122 *Ibid.*

Also with consideration of the principle of the best interests of the child, the link between the right to development and the right of the child to survival and development as guaranteed by article 6(2) is significant. Any future interpretation of article 6(2) is to benefit from this possible link.

9. CONCLUSION

Prior to the adoption of the Convention on the Rights of the Child (CRC), the protection of the right of the child to development was scattered among different international human-rights instruments. Some of these instruments had a weak legal status, such as the 1959 Declaration of the Rights of the Child. Others had a stronger legal status but were not designated only to the child and his or her rights.

For many, the CRC is a unique human-rights instrument.[123] This opinion is based on the fact that the CRC is a document that is solely designated to recognise, protect and realise the rights of the child. In addition, the CRC is part of the overall United Nations' focus on the comprehensive development of human beings and human rights, article 6(2) of the CRC on the right of the child to survival and development, in particular, represents an emphasis on human development.

The drafting of the CRC was not an easy and smooth process. In fact, it took the drafters ten years, from 1979 to 1989, to agree on the final version of the text. In 1988 the Working Group had before it a proposal from India: 'States Parties to the present Convention undertake to create an environment, within their capacities and constitutional processes, which ensures, to the maximum extent possible, the survival and healthy development of the child.'[124] Some Parties in the drafting group opposed the inclusion of the term 'survival' on the basis that it lacked a precise legal definition. The term 'development' was also subject to some proposals that tried to attach an aspect of the child's development, such as 'healthy development'. Following that, the Chairman appointed a sub-working group in order to produce a 'compromised' text, i.e., a text that would bring together all the conflicting opinions about the inclusion of the proposed article in the CRC. The 'compromised' text read as follows: '1. States Parties recognize that every child has the inherent right to life. 2. States Parties shall ensure to the maximum extent possible the survival and development of the child.'

The representative of India, which was part of the sub-working group that drafted article 6(2), pointed out a very important matter for the future

123 C. Cohen, 'United Nations Convention on the Rights of the Child: Introductory Note' (1989) 28 *International Legal Materials* 1448.

124 UN Doc. E/CN.4/1988/28, para. 14, available in Office of the United Nations High Commissioner for Human Rights, *Legislative History of the Convention on the Rights of the Child*, Volume I (United Nations, New York, 2007), p. 364.

implementation of the article, namely the reason for drafting the text in this way. The representative emphasised that the article was drafted in order to focus on the obligations of States Parties to create measures and conditions for the survival of the child.

During the drafting process, a definition of the word 'survival' was also put forward by the World Health Organization (WHO) representative. He made this clarification on behalf of his organisation and the United Nations Children's Fund (UNICEF). His comments were – and still are – vital for the future interpretation and implementation of article 6(2).

The role that UNICEF played in the drafting of article 6(2) cannot be denied. Before working hard for the inclusion of article 6(2) in the Convention on the Rights of the Child, UNICEF was going through major changes in its policies and its vision of the child's survival and development. These changes developed and reached their peak in the 1980s, when UNICEF had its child survival and development revolution, and when article 6(2) was drafted and adopted in the CRC. The historical development of UNICEF's child survival and development revolution and its role in the adoption of article 6(2) represent an 'unofficial' history of article 6(2) of the CRC.

However, UNICEF's survival and development revolution is not the only example of the 'unofficial' history of article 6(2). Changes within the United Nations in general, and the adoption of important international documents such as the 1986 United Nations Declaration on the Right to Development, can also serve as examples of the unofficial history. The DRD has a strong focus on the right of the individual to human development, which is the same focus of article 6(2). Moreover, the DRD promotes the principles of participation, which is essential for the realisation of the right to development. The DRD meets with article 6(2) also in the fact that both require States to focus on the creation of condition for the realisation of human rights, i.e. the right to development.

The 'unofficial' history of article 6(2) is important for the future comprehensive interpretation and implementation of article 6(2), as any such act should prove to be beneficial for elaborations on the concept of the child's right to survival and development. The adoption of article 6(2) on the survival and development of the child is an important step towards the realisation of the international right of the child to human development as stated in the 1986 UN Declaration on the Right to Development.

CHAPTER 2

CURRENT AND POSSIBLE INTERPRETATIONS OF ARTICLE 6(2)

Analytical Perspectives to the Work of the Committee on the Rights of the Child

1. INTRODUCTION

Most of the major international United Nations human rights conventions provide for a body responsible for supervising and monitoring the convention concerned. In this context, article 43(1) of the Convention on the Rights of the Child (CRC) establishes the Committee on the Rights of the Child: 'For the purpose of examining the progress made by States Parties in achieving the realization of the obligations undertaken in the present Convention, there shall be established a Committee on the Rights of the Child, which shall carry out the functions hereinafter provided.' The first members of the Committee were elected in 1991. They are elected 'for a term of four years by States parties in accordance with article 43 of the CRC. Members serve in their personal capacity and may be re-elected if nominated.'[1] More details of the Committee, its members and its work are mentioned later in this chapter.

This chapter focuses mainly on the Committee's interpretation and understanding of article 6(2) of the CRC on the right of the child to survival and development. It is important to emphasise that most of the discussion in this chapter is generated from the Committee's handling of article 6(2). The Committee's role in monitoring the implementation of article 6(2) by States' Parties is evident. In this respect, it is important to study the Committee's literature in relation to article 6(2).

Furthermore, the chapter discusses the possible reasons that led the Committee to choose its opinions for the interpretation of article 6(2). It is probably worth mentioning that this is not an easy task. Earlier Cohen and Kilbourne observed in their analysis of the 'jurisprudence' of the Committee on the Rights of the Child back in 1998: 'Unfortunately, establishing the

---

1 More information is available at: <www2.ohchr.org/english/bodies/crc/members.htm>.

jurisprudence of the Committee on the Rights of the Child is largely a matter of guesswork. Scholars and researchers cannot state with any certainty exactly how the Committee interprets a given article of the Convention. That task is probably difficult even for members of the Committee themselves.'[2] More than twenty years have passed since the establishment of the Committee; this gives a chance, at least, to study its methodology in interpreting the articles of the Convention. This will be discussed later in the chapter. However, it is probably possible to argue that the Committee's interpretations are influenced, among other things, by the overall views and perceptions of the United Nations. This is based on the fact that the CRC is a UN Convention. In addition, one can also point out that the Committee's interpretations are influenced by the cooperation that takes place between the Committee on the Rights of the Child and other human rights bodies.[3] Human rights monitoring bodies coordinate their activities in number of ways.[4] Furthermore, it is probably possible to add that as the Committee progresses with its interpretations of the articles of the Convention, it does not quickly break the established links and understandings that took place during the drafting of the CRC.[5]

As a basic current interpretative body of article 6(2), this chapter attempts to answer the following questions. Why did the Committee decide to put article 6(2) under the heading 'basic health and welfare rights', and to which 'type' of rights do the basic health and welfare rights of the child belong? From a rights-based approach, what are the results of classifying article 6(2) under the heading 'basic health and welfare rights'? Finally, is there a possibility of classifying article 6(2) under other 'types' of rights?

The chapter begins with a general overview of the Committee on the Rights of the Child. This includes an understanding of its interpretative capacity. Following that, the chapter identifies the 'Recommendations' of the Committee on the Rights of the Child in relation to article 6(2). The discussion then proceeds to analyse the Committee's recommendations on article 6(2). The chapter also includes a discussion on the reasons for the interpretation so as to include the link that the Committee made between article 6(2) and a number of specific developmental domains. There is a discussion of the results of this interpretation in order to understand the outcome of associating article 6(2) with

---

2 C. Cohen, and S. Kilbourne, 'Jurisprudence of the Committee on the Rights of the Child: A Guide for Research and Analysis' (1998) 19 *Michigan Journal of International Law* 633, 636.

3 For more information see the Committee's website at: <www2.ohchr.org/english/bodies/crc/workingmethods.htm#a7> accessed 12 April 2015.

4 More information is available at: <www2.ohchr.org/english/bodies/icm-mc/index.htm> accessed 15 April 2015.

5 For example, the Committee keeps the historical link between article 33 on the protection of children from the use of illicit drugs and article 24 on the right to health. For further reading see K. Mahgoub, 'Article 33 of the Convention on the Rights of the Child: The Journey from Drafting History to the Concluding Observations of the Committee on the Rights of the Child' (2012) 2(1) *Human Rights and Drugs* 45–63.

certain economic, social and cultural rights. The chapter also includes a detailed discussion of the basic health and welfare rights that the Committee associated with article 6(2). Finally, the chapter looks at the possibility of identifying article 6(2) with other types of rights.

2. THE COMMITTEE ON THE RIGHTS OF THE CHILD

2.1. MAIN FEATURES OF THE COMMITTEE'S INTERPRETATIVE WORK

The Committee's interpretations and recommendations can be found in two types of documents. The first one is the documents that the Committee specifically issues for explanation and interpretation reasons, i.e. the 'General Comments', and the 'Report and Recommendations' that are based on the Days of General Discussion.[6] As Harris put it in relation to the International Covenant on Civil and Political Rights (ICCPR) 'General Comments are being increasingly supplemented as interpretations of the ICCPR by Committee'.[7] Schabas also provides a description to the general comments of the Human Rights Committee, that could also apply to the general comments of the Committee on the Rights of the Child as becoming 'very close to being a form of official or authentic commentary on the Covenant.'[8] The second type of the Committee's interpretative documents are the documents that include the concluding comments and responses that the Committee makes with regard to each individual State Party report. Presently, these are the main sources for finding the Committee's recommendation. However, the UN General Assembly adopted on 19 December 2011 the Optional Protocol to the CRC on a complaints mechanism for violations of children's rights. The optional protocol opened to signature on 28 February 2012 and came into force on 14 April 2014. Over time, the activation of the protocol should provide more sources for finding the Committee's interpretations.

The State Party reports are themselves relevant legal information and they represent the interpretation of the State Party. However, the discussion on

6 D. Weissbrodt, J.C. Hansen and N.H. Nesbitt, 'The Role of the Committee on the Rights of the Child in Interpreting and Developing International Humanitarian Law' (2011) 24 *Harvard Human Rights Journal* 115, 147.

7 D.J. Harris, *Cases and Materials on International Law*, 7th edition (Sweet and Maxwell, London, 2010), p. 562.

8 W.A. Schabas, *The Abolition of the Death Penalty in International Law*, 3rd edition (Cambridge University Press, Cambridge, 2002), p. 94.

this chapter is limited only to the understanding and interpretations of the Committee on the Rights of the Child.[9]

Article 44(1) of the CRC obligates the States Parties to report to the Committee on the progress and the implementation of the Convention within each individual State Party: 'States Parties undertake to submit to the Committee, through the Secretary-General of the United Nations, reports on the measures they have adopted which give effect to the rights recognized herein and on the progress made on the enjoyment of those rights.' First implementation reports were to be submitted within two years of the entry into force of the CRC for the State Party concerned and after that every five years. The first initial reports were due in September 1992, and more than 70 State reports had reached the Committee by December 1995.[10]

> At its first session, in October 1991, the Committee adopted guidelines to help States parties writing and structuring their initial reports. Governments are recommended to prepare their reports according to these guidelines, which stress that the report should indicate 'factors and difficulties' encountered by the State in the implementation of the Convention – in other words, that it should be problem-oriented and self-critical.[11]

States are also asked to 'specify "implementation priorities"' and 'specific goals for the future'.[12] Relevant legal texts and statistical data are to be submitted with the report.[13] More details about the reporting process are discussed later in the chapter.

2.2. MAIN FRAMEWORK OF THE COMMITTEE'S INTERPRETATION OF ARTICLE 6(2)

This will be discussed in detail later in the chapter. However, a brief discussion is included here for the purposes of this section. During the drafting of the Convention on the Rights of the Child, the inclusion of the word 'survival' in article 6(2) was not an easy or smooth task. For opposing parties, the word lacked precise and legal definitions; hence, some parties argued that it could not be included into the body of a legally binding document such as the CRC. Towards the end of the drafting sessions a recognised definition for the term 'survival' was made, but the same could not be said about the term 'development'. This

9 United Nations General Assembly, 'Optional Protocol to the Convention on the Rights of the Child on a Communications Procedure', UN Doc. A/RES/66/138, Annex (27 January 2012).

10 Human Rights Committee, 'The Rights of the Child' Fact Sheet No. 10 (Rev.1).

11 Human Rights Committee, 'The Rights of the Child' Fact Sheet No. 10 (Rev.1) (footnote omitted).

12 Human Rights Committee, 'The Rights of the Child' Fact Sheet No. 10 (Rev.1).

13 Human Rights Committee, 'The Rights of the Child' Fact Sheet No. 10 (Rev.1).

was the situation with regard to the terms 'survival' and 'development' as they appear in article 6(2) when the Committee initiated its interpretation.[14]

Basically, the Committee's framework of article 6(2) can be summarised as follows. As regards the definition of the word 'development', the Committee in its general comment on the measures of implementation in 2003 stated and confirmed the following definition for the word development: 'The Committee expects States to interpret "development" in its broadest sense as a holistic concept, embracing the child's physical, mental, spiritual, moral, psychological and social development. Implementation measures should be aimed at achieving the optimal development for all children.'[15] More recently, the Committee has confirmed this in it general comment on violence against children, where it stated that:

> the obligation of the State party includes comprehensive protection from violence and exploitation which would jeopardize a child's right to life, survival and development. The Committee expects States to interpret 'development' in its broadest sense as a holistic concept, embracing the child's physical, mental, spiritual, moral, psychological and social development. Implementation measures should be aimed at achieving the optimal development for all children.[16]

Here the Committee made reference to the entire article 6, i.e., right to life, survival and development. As for the right to development the Committee identified a framework for the possible interpretation of the word 'development'. This framework only specifies some aspects or domains of the term 'development', so as to include physical, mental, spiritual, moral, psychological and social development. This framework is helpful for the Committee as regards the areas and aspects of the child's development that need to be targeted. However, it does not elaborate on the meaning of the word 'development' itself. In addition it excludes other aspects of the child's development such as economic or cultural development, for instance.[17]

---

14 This was all addressed in details in Chapter 1. For more details see Office of the High Commissioner for Human Rights, *Legislative History of the Convention on the Rights of the Child: Part I* (United Nations, New York, 2007), pp. 364–369.

15 Committee on the Rights of the Child, 'General Comment No. 5: General measures of implementation for the Convention on the Rights of the Child (arts. 4, 42 and 44, para. 6)', UN Doc. CRC/GC/2003/5 (27 November 2003), para. 12.

16 Committee on the Rights of the Child, 'General Comment No. 13: The Right of the Child to Freedom from All Forms of Violence', UN Doc. CRC/GC/13 (18 April 2011), para. 62. See also Committee on the Rights of the Child, 'General Comment No. 16: State obligations regarding the impact of the business sector on children's rights', UN Doc. CRC/C/GC/16 (17 April 2013), Section III, para. 18.

17 For more information on aspects of the right to development see:
صفاء الدين محمد عبد الحكيم الصافي, حق الانسان في التنمية الاقتصادية و حمايته دوليا (الطبعة الاولى), منشورات العربي الحقوقية, بيروت, 2005, ص 109- 340.

2.3. DIRECT CONSEQUENCES OF THE COMMITTEE'S FRAMEWORK FOR ARTICLE 6(2)

Importantly, the Committee's orientation of article 6, including 6(1) and 6(2), included an identification of the legal status of the article within the CRC. Thus, article 6(2) has two legal statuses. Firstly, it is to be considered as one of the 'general principles' of the Convention on the Rights of the Child. Secondly, the Committee classified article 6(2) as a 'basic health and welfare right'. As a result the article became closely associated with the economic and social rights of the child that are enshrined in the CRC. Worth noting, however, is that article 6(1) on the right to life has not been classified as a 'basic health and welfare right'. A more detailed discussion follows later in the chapter.

3. THE NATURE OF THE COMMITTEE ON THE RIGHTS OF THE CHILD'S WORK

3.1. INTERPRETATIVE CAPACITY OF THE COMMITTEE ON THE RIGHTS OF THE CHILD

As previously mentioned, the Committee on the Rights of the Child was established to monitor the implementation of the Convention and, later, its two Optional Protocols; one on the involvement of children in armed conflict, and the other on the sale of children, child prostitution and child pornography. The Committee will also provide for the Third Optional Protocol on a communications procedure, which came into force on 14 April 2014.[18] The Committee is among a group of treaty bodies established by human rights treaties within the United Nations system. However, for practical reasons, in addition to the monitoring responsibilities, the treaty bodies also provide interpretation of the convention concerned. The need to understand and examine the degree of State Party implementation of each individual article of the Convention requires the Committee to make its own interpretations of the Convention.

In the case of the Committee on the Rights of the Child, article 43 does not speak expressly about the Committee's interpretative capacity; it speaks only about its monitoring capacity. Article 17(1) of the Convention on the Elimination of All Forms of Discrimination Against Women (CEDAW), for instance, also states that the CEDAW Committee was established '[f]or the purpose of considering

[18] According to article 19(1) which reads: 'The present Protocol shall enter into force three months after the deposit of the tenth instrument of ratification or accession'. For more information see <https://treaties.un.org/pages/viewdetails.aspx?src=treaty&mtdsg_no=iv-11-d&chapter=4&lang=en> accessed 23 April 2015.

the progress made in the implementation of the present Convention'.[19] Harris, for example, explains that the Committee interprets the provisions of the convention concerned so that it could perform its functions. He was referring to the Committee on Elimination of Racial Discrimination, but, arguably, the same could be said about the Committee on the Rights of the Child: 'While the Committee has not been given general competence to interpret the Convention, as a treaty organ, the Committee may be competent to interpret the Convention insofar as is required for the performance of the Committee's functions'.[20]

Harris also observes that the recommendations of the treaty monitoring bodies (TMBs) are not legally binding upon States. As for the general comments of the TMBs, he comments, 'Outside of the reporting system, all TMBs adopt general comments or recommendations in which they state their interpretation of particular articles or address other matters.'[21] However, he could see that their general comments, despite not being legally binding upon States Parties they are of considerable importance in practice.[22] He also adds, 'Nonetheless all such supervisory bodies contribute in their functioning to the meaning of the rights their treaties guarantee '.[23] Cohen, for instance, gives a standard, according to which it is probably possible to argue for the interpretative capacity of the Committee or not. She suggests that all laws, whether national or international, require interpretation by an authoritative body before they are applied,

> Ultimately, no law, whether it is local, national or international, can be understood until it has been interpreted and applied to a given set of circumstances by some 'authoritative source.' The authoritative source could be an arbitration panel, an administrative hearing or other similar body, as long as it is recognized as having the authority to interpret the text of the legal material it is writing.[24]

Cohen calls a source an authority on the basis that it is recognised as having the authority to interpret. Arguably, when applying this standard, according to article 43 of the CRC, it does not express any reference to the interpretive authority of the Committee. However, it is probably possible to argue that the Committee

---

19 Convention on the Elimination of All Forms of Discrimination against Women, 18 December 1979, 1249 U.N.T.S. 13.

20 D.J. Harris, *Cases and Materials on International Law,* 4th edition (Sweet and Maxwell, London, 1991), p. 677.

21 D.J. Harris, *Cases and Materials on International Law,* 7th edition (Sweet and Maxwell, London, 2010), p. 547.

22 *Ibid.*, p. 547.

23 D.J. Harris, *Cases and Materials on International Law,* 4th edition (Sweet and Maxwell, London, 1991), p. 602.

24 C. Cohen, 'A Guide to Linguistic Interpretation of the Convention on the Rights of the Child Articles 1, 4, 41 and 45', in C. Cohen and H.A. Davidson (eds.), *Children's Rights in America: U.N. Convention on the Rights of the Child Compared with United States Law* (American Bar Association Center for Children in the Law and Defense for Children International, Washington D.C., 1990), p. 33 (footnote omitted).

interprets the articles of the Convention for practical reasons. These reasons are related to its work on examining the State Party implementation of the Convention.

Moreover, it is also possible to argue that some States could view the Committee as a source of valuable guidance in the interpretation of the Convention, but they could quarrel with the suggestion that the Committee is authoritative, and that its interpretations are 'binding'. States could insist that they can ignore interpretations by the Committee, where they find that such interpretations are unjustified. Usually, in these cases, the Committee would insist on its interpretation and it will keep reminding the State Party in its Concluding Observations to follow the Committee's interpretation, for instance by calling on the State Party to review its position on a particular area of concern to the Committee. The Committee will probably follow an approach similar to that of the Human Rights Committee, which has called on States Parties to reconsider its interpretation because this undermines the recognition of the competence of the Committee to consider communications.[25] For example the United States argues with regard to the interpretative role or nature of responsibility of the Human Rights Committee:

> The last sentence of paragraph 11 states that "a reservation that rejects the Committee's competence to interpret the requirements of any provisions of the Covenant would also be contrary to the object and purpose of that treaty". This statement can be read to present the rather surprising assertion that it is contrary to the object and purpose of the Covenant not to accept the Committee's views on the interpretation of the Covenant. This would be a rather significant departure from the Covenant scheme, which does not impose on States Parties an obligation to give effect to the Committee's interpretations or confer on the Committee the power to render definitive or binding interpretations of the Covenant.[26]

Such disagreements between human rights monitoring bodies and States Parties are common. Since both parties might have a different interpretation for a particular provision in the human rights document concerned. The most reasonable approach would be is to bring the two sides into one common ground. With reference to the right to privacy under article 17 of the ICCPR, for instance, Mashood Baderin argues for the application of the doctrine of margin of appreciation 'because of its utility for resolving cases involving public sensibility and moral issues confronted by States Parties to the Covenant.'[27] Baderin counts on the cultural background and orientation of the Human Rights Committee members at the point in time to have an influential role in this regard.[28]

---

25 Human Rights Committee, 'Concluding Observations: Australia', UN Doc. A/55/40(SUPP) (24 July 2000), para. 520.

26 United Nations General Assembly, 'Fiftieth Session Report of the Human Rights Committee', UN Doc. A/50/40, Annex VI (3 October 1995), para. 1.

27 M.A. Baderin, *International Human Rights and Islamic Law* (Oxford University Press, Oxford, 2003), pp. 117–118.

28 *Ibid.*, p. 118.

The Committee on the Rights of the Child started exercising its interpretative capacity in 1991 when it issued its first guidelines for the State Party reports.[29] The guidelines included the Committee's clarifications on individual provisions of the State Party reports and established a framework for them. It continues to build on these interpretations whenever it issues more guidelines or one of its recommendations, for example during its Days of General Discussions, its General Comments, or its series of Concluding Observations, which are the Committee's replies to State Party reports. Since its establishment in 1991, the Committee has issued a total of eighteen General Comments. As for the guidelines, the Committee adopted the first general guidelines regarding the form and content of initial reports to be submitted by States parties under article 44(1)(a), of the Convention at its twenty-second meeting (first session) on 15 October 1991. In 1996 the Committee adopted, general guidelines regarding the form and contents of periodic reports to be submitted by States Parties under article 44(1)(b), of the Convention, at its 343rd meeting (thirteenth session). Later, in 2005, the Committee adopted 'General guidelines regarding the form and content of periodic reports to be submitted by States Parties under article 44(1)(b), of the Convention. Finally, in 2010 the Committee replaced the 2005 guidelines with Treaty-specific guidelines regarding the form and content of periodic reports to be submitted by States Parties under article 44(1)(b), of the Convention.[30]

The success of the Convention in obtaining almost universal acceptance was reflected in the amount of work and the composition of the Committee. Initially, article 43(2) of the Convention stated that the Committee should consist of ten members of high moral standing and recognised competence in the field of human rights and children's rights, which is the field covered by the Convention. However, in order to ease the blockage of accumulated State Party reports, changes regarding the increasing of the number of the Committee members from ten to eighteen were inevitable.[31]

---

29 The Committee adopted its first guidelines in 1991 see Committee on the Rights of the Child, 'General guidelines regarding the form and content of initial reports to be submitted by States parties under article 44, paragraph 1 (a), of the Convention', UN Doc. CRC/C/5 (30 October 1991).

30 See *ibid.* Committee on the Rights of the Child, 'General guidelines regarding the form and contents of periodic reports to be submitted by States Parties under article 44, paragraph 1 (b), of the Convention', UN Doc. CRC/58 (20 November 1996); Committee on the Rights of the Child, 'General guidelines regarding the form and content of periodic reports', UN Doc. CRC/C/58/Rev.1 (29 November 2005); and Committee on the Rights of the Child, 'Treaty-specific guidelines regarding the form and content of periodic reports to be submitted by States parties under article 44, paragraph 1 (b), of the Convention on the Rights of the Child', UN Doc. CRC/58/Rev.2 (25 November 2010).

31 The United Nations General Assembly, in resolution 50/155 of 21 December 1995, approved the amendment to article 43(2), of the Convention on the Rights of the Child; the word 'ten' was replaced with the word 'eighteen'. This amendment entered into force on 18 November 2002 when it had been accepted by a two-thirds majority of the States Parties (128 out of 191). See <http://www.ohchr.org/en/professionalinterest/pages/crc.aspx> accessed 27 April 2015.

3.2. OTHER DUTIES OF THE COMMITTEE

As previously mentioned, article 43(1) explicitly states that the Committee was fundamentally established in order to examine the progress of States Parties in implementing the Convention on the Rights of the Child. Despite that, the Committee lacks an enforcement capacity, and it has no authority to impose the Convention directly. However, as previously stated, in 2011 the UN General Assembly adopted the Third Optional Protocol to the CRC on a complaints mechanism.[32] This important step will surely have its influence in the Committee's recommendations.[33] According to article 10(5) of the Optional Protocol on individual complaints the Committee is expected 'After examining a communication … without delay, transmit its *views* on the communication, together with its *recommendations*, if any, to the parties concerned.'[34] Article 10(5) speaks about the views of the Committee. However, Schabas, for instance, argues with regard to the Human Rights Committee's similar views, that in reality they are a judgment.[35] As a follow-up the State Party to the Protocol is expected, according to article 11(1):

> The State party shall give due consideration to the views of the Committee, together with its recommendations, if any, and shall submit to the Committee a written response, including information on any action taken and envisaged in the light of the views and recommendations of the Committee. The State party shall submit its response as soon as possible and within six months.[36]

The Committee is not a court and this justifies its limited powers. The Optional Protocol on individual communications, will not make the committee's views legally binding.[37] Nevertheless, the Human Rights Committee argues in favour of its own views in cases of individual communications:

> While the function of the Human rights Committee in considering individual communications is not, as such, that of a judicial body, the views issued by the

32 United Nations General Assembly, 'Optional Protocol to the Convention on the Rights of the Child on a communications procedure', UN Doc. A/RES/66/138 (27 January 2012).

33 For a similar comment on the Optional Protocol to the International Covenant on Civil and Political Rights see D.J. Harris, *Cases and Materials on International Law,* 7th edition (Sweet and Maxwell, London, 2010), p. 562 and the following pages.

34 United Nations General Assembly, 'Optional Protocol to the Convention on the Rights of the Child on a communications procedure', UN. Doc. A/RES/66/138 (27 January 2012), article 10(5) (emphasis added).

35 W.A. Schabas, *The Abolition of the Death Penalty in International Law,* 3rd edition (Cambridge University Press, Cambridge, 2002), p. 94.

36 United Nations General Assembly, 'Optional Protocol to the Convention on the Rights of the Child on a communications procedure', UN Doc. A/RES/66/138 (27 January 2012).

37 D.J. Harris, *Cases and Materials on International Law,* 7th edition (Sweet and Maxwell, London, 2010), p. 565.

Committee under the Optional Protocol exhibit some important characteristics of a judicial decision. They are arrived at in a judicial spirit, including the impartiality and independence of Committee members, the considered interpretation of the language of the Covenant, and the determinative character of the decisions.'[38]

3.3. BASES OF INTERPRETATION

When the Committee interprets the Convention a number of factors are put into consideration. Before detailing them, it is probably worth emphasising that from an international law point of view the Convention is a treaty. Thus, its interpretation could be guided by the Vienna Convention on the Law of Treaties.[39] Article 31 of this instrument regulates the general principles that bind the Committee on the Rights of the Child when interpreting article 6(2): '1. A treaty shall be interpreted in good faith in accordance with the ordinary meaning to be given to the terms of the treaty in their context and in the light of its object and purpose.'

Furthermore, the Vienna Convention lists different bases of interpretation in article 31, such as:

2. The context for the purpose of the interpretation of a treaty shall comprise, in addition to the text, including its preamble and annexes:
   (a) any agreement relating to the treaty which was made between all the parties in connection with the conclusion of the treaty;
   (b) any instrument which was made by one or more parties in connection with the conclusion of the treaty and accepted by the other parties as an instrument related to the treaty.
3. There shall be taken into account, together with the context:
   ...
   (b) any subsequent practice in the application of the treaty which establishes the agreement of the parties regarding its interpretation;
   (c) any relevant rules of international law applicable in the relations between the parties.
4. A special meaning shall be given to a term if it is established that the parties so intended.

In addition, the Committee, when faced with vague words, such as the term 'development' in article 6(2), can use some supplementary resources to

38 Human Rights Committee, 'General Comment No. 33: The Obligations of States Parties under the Optional Protocol to the International Covenant on Civil and Political Rights', UN Doc. CCPR/C/GC/33 (5 November 2008), para. 11.

39 W.A. Schabas, *The Abolition of the Death Penalty in International Law,* 3rd edition (Cambridge University Press, Cambridge, 2002), p. 93.

those stated on article 31 of the Vienna Convention. Article 32 of the Vienna Convention explains these supplementary means:

> Recourse may be had to supplementary means of interpretation, including the preparatory work of the treaty and the circumstances of its conclusion, in order to confirm the meaning resulting from the application of article 31, or to determine the meaning when the interpretation according to article 31:
> (a) leaves the meaning ambiguous or obscure; or
> (b) leads to a result which is manifestly absurd or unreasonable.

In the case of the interpretation of article 6(2) of the Convention, the Committee on the Rights of the Child is also bound by some concomitant factors. Firstly, the CRC is a United Nations (UN) Convention. It was made by the organisation of the UN; therefore, its interpretations are expected to be consistent with those aims and purposes that are stated in article 1 of the United Nations Charter, i.e., to maintain international peace and to develop friendly relations among nations based on respect for the principle of equal rights and self-determination of peoples. In addition, achieving 'international co-operation in solving international problems of an economic, social, cultural, or humanitarian character, and promoting and encouraging respect for human rights and for fundamental freedoms for all without distinction as to race, sex, language, or religion'.[40]

Secondly, the Committee, in its interpretation, is guided by the principles of the Convention on the Rights of the Child itself because they are meant to help with this task. For instance, the principle of the best interests of the child should be present when interpreting each article of the Convention.[41] Any possible interpretation that could jeopardise this principle should itself be disregarded.

Furthermore, the Committee on the Rights of the Child is also influenced by the dynamic interpretation of the Convention. This is a basis for interpretation that aims mainly at expanding the scope of the interpretation and the rights included. The Committee on the Rights of the Child made reference to dynamic interpretation, for instance, in 1998 it raised the issue in relation to inheritance rights of children born out of wedlock in Japan. The Committee considered dynamic interpretation to be part of the holistic interpretation of the Convention.

> Although article 2 of the Convention was not clear on the matter, a holistic interpretation of the Convention that included not only discrimination but also the best interests of the child could not but reach the conclusion that member States should adopt a dynamic interpretation of the Convention with regard to the inheritance rights of children born out of wedlock.[42]

---

40 The preamble of the Convention makes a number of references to the United Nations and its charter, such as the reference on the first paragraph to the principles of the Charter.

41 Vienna Declaration and Programme of Action, A/CONF.157/24 (12 July 1993), para. 21, p. 26.

42 Committee on the Rights of the Child, 'Summary record of the 464th meeting: Japan', UN Doc. CRC/C/SR.464 (2 June 1998), para. 35.

Dynamic interpretation is a well-established method in the interpretation of human-rights treaties. For example, the European Court of Human Rights considered it in a number of cases. Soering v. UK is a leading case in this regard.[43] The Court also adopted it in Marckx v. Belgium, in relation to the rights of children born out of wedlock.[44] Generally speaking dynamic interpretation intends to take societal changes in to consideration. The Court has done this in earlier cases as well.[45]

Arguably, dynamic interpretation also guarantees the human dignity of the child since updated interpretations of the Convention are expected to provide consideration and respect to the dignity of the child. Cassese refers to the relationship between human dignity and dynamic interpretation. He observes that the UN has succeeded in moving from a static concept of human rights conceived as a means of realising international peace to a dynamic doctrine which goes so far as to promote conflict and the disruption of the status quo for the sake of introducing social justice and respect for human dignity.[46] Furthermore, dynamic interpretation of treaties is not only confined to human rights treaties. The International Court of Justice (ICJ), for example, referred to it in the Aegean Sea Continental Shelf Case:

> Having regard to the foregoing considerations, the Court is of the opinion that the expression in reservation (b) ... must be interpreted in accordance with the rules of international law as they exist today, and not as they existed in 1931. It follows that in interpreting and applying reservation (b) with respect to the present dispute the Court has to take account of the evolution which has occurred in the rules of international law concerning a coastal State's rights of exploration and exploitation over the continental shelf.[47]

Nevertheless, while the concept of dynamic interpretation could prove to be important in keeping the Convention alive and up to date, it is wiser to emphasise that it should be made on the bases of the aims and principles of the Convention. The Convention is a standard-setting document, but this should not interfere with the fact that it covers almost all the countries in the world. It is a fact now that all the countries around the world, with the exception of the United States, Somalia and South Sudan, are parties to the CRC.[48] This means

---

43 *Soering v. United Kingdom* (Series A, vol. 161, II E.H.R.R.) (1989) 439.

44 *Marckx v. Belgium*, 13 June 1979, Series A no. 31.

45 See A. Cassese, *International Law* (Oxford University Press, Oxford, 2001), p. 373.

46 A. Cassese, *International Law* (Oxford University Press, Oxford, 2001), p. 373.

47 *Aegean Sea Continental Shelf (Greece v. Turkey)* (Judgment) [1978] ICJ Rep 33–34.

48 There are some reports that Somalia ratified the CRC. See United Nations (UN News Centre) <www.un.org/apps/news/story.asp?NewsID=49845#.VNivTWb6hMS> accessed 23 April 2015. However, according to the United Nations Office of the High Commissioners for Human Rights, Somalia did not ratify the CRC. See <http://tbinternet.ohchr.org/_layouts/TreatyBodyExternal/Treaty.aspx?CountryID=161&Lang=EN> accessed 23 April 2015.

that the Convention is faced with a variety of cultures and societies. For example, it is very important to point out that what constitutes the best interests of a child might vary from one State to another. In fact, even within one society or even one family, the best interests of the child is subjective and contextual. The same applies to the survival and development of the child: what guarantees the survival and development of the child might vary from one society or one family to another. This demands deep understanding from the Committee and anyone who attempts to interpret the CRC. This kind of deep understanding is ensured by article 43(2) of the CRC, which guarantees diversity among the members of the Committee. It states that: 'The Committee shall consist of eighteen experts of high moral standing and recognized competence ... consideration being given to equitable geographical distribution, as well as to the principal legal systems.' As pointed out earlier, in his call for the Human Rights Committee to adopt the margin of appreciation doctrine, Baderin counts on the cultural background and orientation of the Human Rights Committee members at the point in time to have an influential role in this regard.[49] Additionally, in his argument for the empowerment of local societies in relation to the child-survival policies, Kent explains the way in which local standards could prove to be better than international standards in the case of the child's survival:

> Many of the most important questions relating to child survival work are related to cultural relativism and cultural sensitivity. Why do child survival programs typically treat people as objects? Why aren't people's views taken more fully into account? Why aren't people more fully engaged in the formulation and the implementation of child survival programs?
>
> ...
>
> Also, *we* who provide programs tend to assume that they who receive programs – the targets of our campaigns – understand malnutrition, diseases, and children's mortality in much the same ways *we* do. Where differences in understanding are noted, the reflexive response is to assume they are wrong, and perhaps foolish or superstitious. Very regularly, the prescribed remedy is that they should be administered some education, which means getting *them* to see things as we see them. The idea that we might benefit from some education regarding their way of understanding is rarely entertained.[50]

However, it might be argued that consideration for the individuality of the State opposes the concept of the universality of human rights. The Vienna Declaration

---

Also see <http://treaties.un.org/Pages/ViewDetails.aspx?src=TREATY&mtdsg_no=IV-II&Chapter=4&lang=en> accessed 23 April 2015.

49 M.A. Baderin, *International Human Rights and Islamic Law* (Oxford University Press, Oxford, 2003), p. 118.

50 G. Kent, *The Politics of Children's Survival* (Praeger Publishers, New York, 1991), pp. 53–54 (footnotes omitted).

and Programme of Action, in fact, replies to such arguments and recognises the individuality of the State and the regional differences in paragraph 5:

> All human rights are universal, indivisible and interdependent and interrelated. The international community must treat human rights globally in a fair and equal manner, on the same footing, and with the same emphasis. While the significance of national and regional particularities and various historical, cultural and religious backgrounds must be borne in mind, it is the duty of States, regardless of their political, economic and cultural systems, to promote and protect all human rights and fundamental freedoms.[51]

Furthermore, the Convention on the Rights of the Child itself recognises that in some cases local measures could support the right of the child to development more than the international ones. Accordingly, it confirms in article 41 that the State Party does not have to stick only to the CRC. If there are other measures that provide for stronger obligations, the State can follow them. Article 41 of the CRC guarantees this attitude, as it was intentionally put in the Convention in order to prevent the CRC from weakening existing standards of law applicable to the child:[52]

> Nothing in the present Convention shall affect any provisions which are more conducive to the realization of the rights of the child and which may be contained in:
> (a) The law of a State party; or
> (b) International law in force for that State.

The Committee on the Rights of the Child has referred to article 41, and has stated that other international human rights apply to all persons under the age of 18:

> The Committee encourages all States parties to enact and implement within their jurisdiction legal provisions that are more conducive to the realization of the rights of the child than those contained in the Convention, in the light of article 41. The Committee emphasizes that the other international human rights instruments apply to all persons under the age of 18 years.[53]

---

51 Vienna Declaration and Programme of Action, A/CONF. 157/24 (12 July 1993), para. 5, p. 23. See also M. Nowak, *Introduction to the International Human Rights Regime* (Martinus Nijhoff Publishers, Leiden, 2003), pp. 26–27.

52 C. Cohen, 'A Guide to Linguistic Interpretation of the Convention on the Rights of the Child Articles 1, 4, 41 and 45', in C. Cohen and H.A. Davidson (eds.), *Children's Rights in America: U.N. Convention on the Rights of the Child Compared with United States Law* (American Bar Association Center for Children in the Law and Defense for Children International, Washington D.C., 1990), pp. 45–46. See also UN Doc. E/CN.4/1989/48, paras. 623–636, available in Office of the High Commissioner for Human Rights, *Legislative History of the Convention on the Rights of the Child*, Volume II (United Nations, New York, 2007), pp. 809–812.

53 Committee on the Rights of the Child, 'General Comment No. 5: General measures of implementation for the Convention on the Rights of the Child (arts. 4, 42 and 44, para. 6)', UN Doc. CRC/GC/2003/5 (27 November 2003), para. 23.

In its General Comment No. 17, which is concerned with the rights of the child, the Human Rights Committee also stated that the State Party can make consideration to social and cultural conditions when speaking about the attainment of majority.

> The right to special measures of protection belongs to every child because of his status as a minor. Nevertheless, the Covenant does not indicate the age at which he attains his majority. This is to be determined by each State party in the light of the relevant social and cultural conditions. In this respect, States should indicate in their reports the age at which the child attains his majority in civil matters and assumes criminal responsibility. States should also indicate the age at which a child is legally entitled to work and the age at which he is treated as an adult under labour law. States should further indicate the age at which a child is considered adult for the purposes of article 10, paragraphs 2 and 3.[54]

Dynamic interpretation can also make use of the survival and development of the child as a gauge in addition to other measures, such as the best interest of the child. Dynamic interpretation aims at keeping human rights conventions valid. However, it should be carefully realised so that it will not jeopardise the aims and purposes of the Convention.

For the purpose of interpreting the Convention the Committee gives consideration to the overall recognised understandings and meanings that are shared by the other human rights bodies as well. It can, however, also expand on them. United Nations Human Rights Bodies meet together and sometime they echo each other's work. Barrett and Veerman, for instance, highlight a case where

> In 2010, for example, the Human Rights Committee raised concerns about the use of the military in fighting organised crime in Mexico ... this was mirrored not long after by the Committee on the Rights of the Child, reviewing Mexico under the Optional Protocol to the CRC on the involvement of children in armed conflict. This, in turn, highlighted the relevance of the OPAC to the drug trade. The Committee criticised the use of children in fighting against the drug cartels.[55]

3.4. FACTORS THAT INFLUENCE THE COMMITTEE'S INTERPRETATIONS

There is an important factor that needs to be mentioned in relation to the Committee's interpretation, not only with regard to article 6(2), but also in

---

54 Available in Economic and Social Council, 'Compilation of the General Comments and General Recommendations Adopted by Human Rights Treaty Bodies', UN Doc. HRI/GEN/1/Rev.7 (12 May 200), p. 145. However, in some cases, the Human Rights Committee disagrees with some States as regards the low age of children that is adopted by the State concerned.

55 D. Barrett and P.E. Veerman, *Article 33 Protection of Children from Narcotic Drugs and Psychotropic Substances* (Martinus Nijhoff Publishers, Leiden, 2012), para. 26 (footnotes omitted).

relation to the entire Convention. This is related to the right of the Committee to listen to other sources. It is a right that is guaranteed by article 45(a), which reads:

> In order to foster the effective implementation of the Convention and to encourage international co-operation in the field covered by the Convention:
>
> (a) The specialized agencies, the United Nations Children's Fund, and other United Nations organs shall be entitled to be represented at the consideration of the implementation of such provisions of the present Convention as fall within the scope of their mandate. *The Committee may invite the specialized agencies, the United Nations Children's Fund and other competent bodies as it may consider appropriate to provide expert advice on the implementation of the Convention in areas falling within the scope of their respective mandates. The Committee may invite the specialized agencies, the United Nations Children's Fund, and other United Nations organs to submit reports on the implementation of the Convention in areas falling within the scope of their activities;*
>
> ...
>
> (d) The Committee may make suggestions and general recommendations based on information received pursuant to articles 44 and 45. (emphasis added)

Back in 1998 Cohen and Kilbourne referred to the significant influence of the information that the Committee receives from the specialised agencies on the Committee's interpretations: 'Perhaps the most significant outside influence is the input the Committee receives under article 45 of the Convention. This article gives the Committee the power to obtain information from various United Nations bodies, such as the International Labour Organisation, the World Health Organization and UNICEF.'[56] There are some treaty bodies that do not take information from the specialised agencies. The Human Rights Committee, for instance, has decided that specialised agencies should not be invited to comment on State reports but may submit information to individual members of the Committee, who are free to use it as they think fit.[57]

Before explaining the way this factor interferes with the interpretation of the Committee to article 6(2), it is useful to emphasise that the United Nations Children's Fund (UNICEF) played an important role in the drafting of article 6(2).[58] In the context of the Committee's considerations to the opinion of the UN bodies in general and UNICEF in particular, it should be acceptable to say that UNICEF's understanding and interpretation of the concept of the child's survival and development influenced the interpretations of the Committee. This

56 C. Cohen, and S. Kilbourne, 'Jurisprudence of the Committee on the Rights of the Child: A Guide for Research and Analysis' (1998) 19 *Michigan Journal of International Law* 633, 639.

57 D.J. Harris, *Cases and Materials on International Law*, 4th edition (Sweet and Maxwell, London, 1991), p. 622.

58 This has been explained in detail in Chapter 1.

does not mean that the Committee's opinion and interpretation is based only on UNICEF's understandings, but they are a significant factor.

4. THE REPORTING MECHANISM

Similar to the concept of a monitoring body, the reporting mechanism is a feature that is common to the main human rights treaties. Both concepts are complementary. Article 44 of the CRC regulates the reporting process and explains its aims as follows:

> 1. States Parties undertake to submit to the Committee ... reports on the measures they have adopted which give effect to the rights recognized herein and on the progress made on the enjoyment of those rights ...
> 2. Reports ... shall indicate factors and difficulties, if any, affecting the degree of fulfilment of the obligations under the present Convention. Reports shall also contain sufficient information to provide the Committee with a comprehensive understanding of the implementation of the Convention in the country concerned...

The reporting process aims at giving a clear understanding and follow-up to the situation of children's rights in the State Party. The Committee on the Rights of the Child has confirmed these aims of the reporting mechanism on different occasions. For instance, in its concluding observations on the report of Nigeria, the Committee stated the aim of the reporting process as to 'indicate not only the measures adopted but also the progress made since the entry into force of the Convention and priorities identified for action, as well as the difficulties encountered in guaranteeing the rights provided for in the Convention.'[59]

The State Party reports also represent the understanding of each individual State Party on a particular aspect of the Convention. The fact that the Committee can interpret the articles of the Convention does not suggest that the States Parties are not eligible to interpret the Convention as well. For practical reasons, the State Party needs to interpret the article before implementing it. The interpretative capacity of the State has been recognised in the Convention. For instance, according to article 1 of the CRC, 'For the purposes of the present Convention, a child means every human being below the age of eighteen years unless under the law applicable to the child, majority is attained earlier.' This article was intentionally worded in a manner that would give each individual State the chance to interpret the article, with regards to the age of majority, as it deemed fit. The article does not specify the age of the child. It states only

59 Committee on the Rights of the Child, 'Concluding Observations: Nigeria', UN Doc. CRC/C/15/Add.61 (30 October 1996), para. 2.

that the child is any person under the age of 18 unless, under the law applicable to the child, majority is attained earlier. This loose wording was intended to attract more ratifications of the Convention because it would give the States Parties more freedom in determining the age of childhood and the duties of the States Parties that would result from this age specification.[60] States Parties' interpretations are more associated with the practice and not the theory. This emphasises the importance of the State Party interpretations. The Convention is meant to be a 'standard-setting document', which is associated with the theory, but each State Party report should reflect and represent the practice and the difficulties associated with it.

The Committee has issued guidelines for States Parties on the contents and forms of their reports.[61] It has been very strict in requiring the States Parties to follow the guidelines. For instance, after the submission of its initial report, the Committee asked the Republic of Tanzania to resubmit a comprehensive revised initial report following the guidelines for the submission of State Party reports. The process took five years to resubmit the revised initial report.[62]

Article 44 does not name the parties who should participate in the preparation of the State reports. A participatory approach has been encouraged by the Committee. In this regard, the participation of different sectors in society, such as community and political leaders, civil society and the general public, is always welcomed.[63] Over time, the identities of the participants were extended so as to include children themselves, as in the 'What do you think?' programme, which involves children in the preparation of the children's rights report.[64] In Belgium, for instance, the programme is a method for the implementation

---

60 N. Cantwell, 'The Origins, Development and Significance of the United Nations Convention on the Rights of the Child', in S. Detrick (ed.), *The United Nations Convention on the Rights of the Child: A Guide to the Travaux Préparatoires* (Martinus Nijhoff Publishers, Dordrecht, 1992), pp. 26–27.

61 The Committee adopted its first guidelines in 1991 see Committee on the Rights of the Child, 'General guidelines regarding the form and content of initial reports to be submitted by States parties under article 44, paragraph 1 (a), of the Convention', UN Doc. CRC/C/5 (30 October 1991). Committee on the Rights of the Child, 'General guidelines regarding the form and contents of periodic reports to be submitted by States Parties under article 44, paragraph 1 (b), of the Convention', UN Doc. CRC/58/ (20 November 1996); Committee on the Rights of the Child, 'General guidelines regarding the form and content of periodic reports', UN Doc. CRC/C/58/Rev.1 (29 November 2005); and Committee on the Rights of the Child, 'Treaty-specific guidelines regarding the form and content of periodic reports to be submitted by States parties under article 44, paragraph 1 (b), of the Convention on the Rights of the Child', UN Doc. CRC/58/Rev.2 (23 November 2010).

62 Committee on the Rights of the Child, 'Concluding Observations: Tanzania's Initial Report', UN Doc. CRC/C/15/Add.156 (9 July 2001), para. 1.

63 Committee on the Rights of the Child, 'Concluding Observations: Palau's Initial Report', UN Doc. CRC/C/15/Add.149 (21 February 2001), para. 3.

64 Committee on the Rights of the Child, 'Consideration of Reports Submitted by States Parties Under Article 44 of the Convention, Second periodic reports of States Parties due in 1999 Addendum Belgium', UN Doc. CRC/C/83/Add.2 (25 October 2000), para. 66.

of the participation rights of the child because they prepare a report for the Committee on the Rights of the Child. The Committee praised the idea that it was with the support of the State Party that children can make their views known. This support includes conferences, courses on children's rights, councils in schools and communities. However, in some possibly relevant instances, the Committee also raised concerns that children are not adequately informed on how they can have input into policies that affect them, or how their views will be taken into consideration once they have been solicited. Furthermore, the Committee expressed concern that sufficient attention has not been accorded to the participation of primary and secondary students in school governance. This including areas such as school regulations and management of discipline.

5. THE RECOMMENDATIONS OF THE COMMITTEE ON ARTICLE 6(2)

5.1. THE REPORTING PROCESS

In the context of this chapter, the term 'recommendations' means the interpretations, opinion and philosophy of the Committee as regards a particular issue. The recommendations of the Committee on the Rights of the Child started to take shape when the Committee issued its uniform interpretations of the provisions of the Convention. This uniform interpretation is expected to assist the States Parties in implementing the Convention and later reporting to the Committee on this matter.[65] As pointed out earlier, the Committee's interpretations and recommendations can be found in two types of documents.[66] Firstly, there are the documents that the Committee specifically issues for explanation and interpretation reasons. For example, the 'General Comments' of the Committee or 'Report and Recommendations' that are based on the days of general discussion. Secondly, there are the documents that include the comments and observations that the Committee adopts in response to each individual State Party report.[67] It might be possible to argue against the qualification of the days of general discussion as an interpretation and recommendation of the Committee. The Committee, in fact, refers to their purpose as 'to foster a deeper understanding of the contents and implications of

65 N.H. Kaufman, and M.L. Blanco, 'Drafting and Interpreting Article 27', in A.B. Andrews and N.H. Kaufman (eds.), *Implementing the U.N. Convention on the Rights of the Child: A Standard of Living Adequate for Development* (Praeger Publishers, Westport, 1999), p. 23.

66 See also United Nations General Assembly, 'Optional Protocol to the Convention on the Rights of the Child on a communications procedure', UN Doc. A/RES/66/138 (27 January 2012).

67 D. Weissbrodt, J.C. Hansen and N.H. Nesbitt, 'The Role of the Committee on the Rights of the Child in Interpreting and Developing International Humanitarian Law' (2011) 24 *Harvard Human Rights Journal* 115, 118, 126–127.

the Convention as they relate to specific articles or topics.'[68] After the discussion the Committee adopts its recommendations, taking into account the issues raised.[69] Some authors also argue, in favour, that '[t]he Committee occasionally cites these Recommendations for support in Concluding Observations, so at a minimum they act as persuasive interpretations of Convention obligations.'[70] The Committee did not issue a general comment or a general day of discussion on article 6. However, it has referred to the right of the child to survival and development in several general comments.[71]

In an ongoing process, the Committee's response to the State Party's report takes different stages and ends with the Concluding Observations. Under article 44(1)(b) of the CRC, States Parties are obliged to submit to the Committee, in addition to the initial report, a periodic report every five years. This process is continuous. Together, the State Party reports and the Committee's response can be considered as a dialogue, which is constructive in nature.[72] The Committee itself considers the reporting process as an essential vehicle for the establishment of a meaningful dialogue between the States Parties and the Committee.[73] This process of 'reporting and responding' has led to the development of the Committee's recommendations on the CRC. It has resulted in a focused analysis of each article of the CRC. This ongoing process has helped to narrow the gaps between the theory that is represented in the CRC and the actual practice, which is represented by the implementation of the Convention by the States Parties. The continuous nature of the dialogue brings an evolutionary factor to the interpretation of the articles of the Convention that should help in expanding, strengthening and laying the basis for a particular understanding.

---

68 See <http://www.ohchr.org/EN/HRBodies/CRC/Pages/Discussion2014.aspx> accessed 13 April 2015.

69 See <http://www.escr-net.org/docs/i/521548> accessed 13 April 2015.

70 D. Weissbrodt, J.C. Hansen and N.H. Nesbitt, 'The Role of the Committee on the Rights of the Child in Interpreting and Developing International Humanitarian Law' (2011) *Harvard Human Rights Journal* 115, 147 (footnotes omitted).

71 For example, in its General Comment on adolescent health, the Committee stated: 'The Committee understands the concepts of "health and development" more broadly than being strictly limited to the provisions defined in articles 6 (right to life, survival and development) and 24 (right to health) of the Convention.' See Committee on the Rights of the Child, 'General Comment No. 4: Adolescent health and development in the context of the Convention on the Rights of the Child', UN Doc. CRC/GC/2003/4 (1 July 2003), para. 4. See also Committee on the Rights of the Child, 'General Comment No. 3: HIV/AIDS and the rights of the child', UN Doc. CRC/ GC/2003/3 (17 March 2003), para. 5.

72 P. David, 'Fifteen Years of Work of the UN Committee on the Rights of the Child Monitoring Child Rights: Achievements and Limits of a Crucial Process', in A. Weyts (ed.), *Understanding Children's Rights* (Ghent University, Ghent, 2004), p. 303.

73 Committee on the Rights of the Child, 'General guidelines regarding the form and content of initial reports to be submitted by States parties under article 44, paragraph 1(a), of the Convention' (30 October 1991) UN Doc. CRC/C/5, para. 4.

5.2. THE COMMITTEE'S EVOLVING RECOMMENDATIONS WITH REGARD TO ARTICLE 6(2)

The question that arises in this context is: what are the Committee's recommendations as regards article 6(2) of the CRC? Initially, the language used in article 6(2) is solitary. In this regard, one of the main tasks and challenges for the Committee, after it started its work back in 1991, was to interpret and transfer the wording of article 6(2) into a legal language; i.e. the language of rights, including all so-called 'types of rights'.

One of the main characteristics and successes of the Convention on the Rights of the Child is that it includes within one document different types of rights. Initially, this gave the Committee the chance to choose a classification of article 6(2) from a wide variety of types of rights. In this context, the Committee was faced with the task of categorising the 'right to survival' and the 'right to development' of the child. To decide on this, the Committee had to choose between all types of rights. It probably had to answer questions such as: to which type of rights' does the word 'development' belong? This task remained following the drafting sessions of the Convention.[74]

As detailed earlier, in Chapter 1, the United Nations Children's Fund (UNICEF) played an important role in the drafting and adoption of article 6(2) in the CRC. Originally, together with India, it initiated it and managed successfully to bring it, with the support of India and others, into the body of a legally binding document such as the Convention on the Rights of the Child.[75] UNICEF wanted the adoption of article 6(2) on survival and development because it complemented UNICEF's policy at the time. The concept of the child's development existed in international documents before the adoption of the CRC, such as principle 2 of the 1959 Universal Declaration on Children's Rights:

> The child shall enjoy special protection, and shall be given opportunities and facilities, by law and by other means, to enable him to develop physically, mentally, morally, spiritually and socially in a healthy and normal manner and in conditions of freedom and dignity. In the enactment of laws for this purpose, the best interests of the child shall be the paramount consideration.[76]

---

74 During the drafting of the Convention the representative of Venezuela did not agree with the inclusion of paragraph 6(2) because in her view it would diminish the right to life. See UN Doc. E/CN.4/1988/28, para. 24. The representative later stated that the issue of the interpretation of the article would be a matter for local authorities (see UN Doc. E/CN/1989/48, para. 90). Both documents are available in Office of the High Commissioner for Human Rights, *Legislative History of the Convention on the Rights of the Child* (Volume I, United Nations, New York, 2007, pp. 366 and 367.

75 See Office of the High Commissioner for Human Rights, *Legislative History of the Convention on the Rights of the Child* (Volume I, United Nations, New York, 2007), pp. 364–367.

76 United Nations General Assembly, 'Declaration of the Rights of the Child', UN Doc. A/RES/1386 (XIV) (20 November 1959), Principle 2.

However, most of these documents did not adopt a rights-based approach. In fact, they were more policy-based, community-based, and needs-based approaches.[77] For instance, UNICEF was convinced that the State's expenditure on armaments, an aspect of the right of the child to survival and development, should decrease and that it should be increased on education and health, but there was no rights-based approach for that. This was seen from a policy-based perspective and not a rights-based one. According to these pre-CRC understandings of survival and development, the challenge for the Committee on the Rights of the Child was how to change such lack of a rights-based approach and interpret and formulate such an approach for the right of the child to survival and development.

The recommendations of the Committee on the Rights of the Child on article 6(2) started to emerge in 1991, when the Committee issued its general guidelines regarding the form and content of initial reports to be submitted by States Parties under article 44(1)(a). In these guidelines the Committee divided the articles of the Convention, which are included in the substantive part of the Convention, into eight clusters. The clusters were made according to the overall general spectrum of the Convention, in a logical order and according to content.[78] The clusters were not made to differentiate between the various child's rights; nor to state any preferences. In fact, the clusters aim at achieving a number of tasks, such as making the work of the Committee more organised.[79] To facilitate a more structured discussion, the clustering of the articles also aims at confirming the fact that the articles of the Convention should be dealt with using a holistic approach:

> The ... guidelines group the articles of the Convention in clusters with a view to assisting States parties in the preparation of their reports. This approach reflects the holistic perspective on children's rights taken by the Convention: i.e. that they are indivisible and interrelated, and that equal importance should be attached to each and every right recognized therein.[80]

The Committee, in its Guidelines for Periodic Reporting,[81] also mentioned that the clusters were made in order to guide the States Parties in terms of the contents and

77 See UNICEF, 'The State of the World's Children 1996' <http://www.unicef.org/sowc96/1980s.htm> accessed 23 April 2015.

78 See Committee on the Rights of the Child, 'General guidelines regarding the form and content of initial reports to be submitted by States parties under article 44, paragraph 1(a), of the Convention', UN Doc. CRC/C/5 (30 October 1991). See also Committee on the Rights of the Child, 'Overview of the Reporting Procedures' (24 October 1994) UN Doc. CRC/C/33, para. 5.

79 P. David, 'Fifteen Years of Work of the UN Committee on the Rights of the Child Monitoring Child Rights: Achievements and Limits of a Crucial Process', in A. Weyts (ed), *Understanding Children's Rights* (Ghent University, Ghent, 2004), p.304.

80 Committee on the Rights of the Child, 'General guidelines regarding the form and content of periodic reports' (29 November 2005) UN Doc. CRC/C/58/Rev.1, para. 3.

81 As mentioned earlier, the Committee issued a number of guidelines.

form of their reports.[82] However, in both of these documents, article 6(2) appeared, mainly, under two headings: 'General Principles' and 'Basic Health and Welfare'. This applies to its 2010 guidelines as well, with the addition of the Annex.[83]

5.3. THE LEGAL STATUS OF ARTICLE 6(2) ACCORDING TO THE INTERPRETATION OF THE COMMITTEE ON THE RIGHTS OF THE CHILD

Following its previous guidelines, in 2010 the Committee identified four articles of the Convention and declared that they are to be treated as the general principles that will guide the implementation of the entire Convention. The articles in question are: article 2 on non-discrimination; article 3 on the best interests of the child; article 6 on the right to life, survival and development; and article 12 on the right of the child to have his or her views listened to and respected.

> General principles
> Relevant information, including the principal legislative, judicial, administrative or other measures in force or foreseen, factors and difficulties encountered and progress achieved in implementing the provisions of the Convention, and implementation priorities and specific goals for the future should be provided in respect of:
> ...
> (c) The right to life, survival and development (art. 6);

The other heading under which article 6(2) appears in its 2005 guidelines is 'Basic Health and Welfare':

> Under this section States parties are requested to provide relevant information, including the principal legislative, judicial, administrative or other measures in force; the institutional infrastructure for implementing policy in this area, particularly monitoring strategies and mechanisms; and factor in difficulties encountered and progress achieved in implementin the relevant provisions of the Convention, in respect of: Survival and Development (art. 6, para. 2) ... Under this cluster, States parties are requested to follow the provisions in paragraphs 5 and 6, and general comment No. 3 (2003) on HIV/AIDS and the rights of the child and general comment No. 4 (2003) on adolescent health and development in the context of the Convention on the Rights of the Child.

---

82 Committee on the Rights of the Child, 'General guidelines regarding the form and content of periodic reports', UN Doc. CRC/C/58/Rev.1 (29 November 2005), para. 3.

83 See Committee on the Rights of the Child, 'Treaty-specific guidelines regarding the form and content of periodic reports to be submitted by States parties under article 44, paragraph 1 (b), of the Convention on the Rights of the Child', UN Doc. CRC/58/Rev.2 (23 November 2010), pp. 82 and Section C, para. 1(6).

31. States parties should provide relevant information in respect of:
(a) Survival and development (art. 6, para. 2)[84]

The Committee reconfirmed this clustering of article 6(2) in its 2010 guidelines. In this document article 6(2) appears under the heading 'Disability, basic health and welfare (arts. 6, 18 (para. 3), 23, 24, 26, 27 (paras. 1–3) and 33)'. The Committee states in paragraph 34: 'Under this same cluster, States parties should provide relevant and updated information in respect of: (a) Survival and development (art. 6, para. 2)'.[85]

This heading includes article 6(2); article 18(3) on the right of children of parents who are both working to benefit from child-care services and facilities; article 23 on the rights of disabled children; and article 24 on the child's right to health and health services. In addition it includes article 26 on the child's right to benefit from social security; and article 27(1)–(3) on the right of the child to an adequate standard of living. It also includes the first part of article 33 that deals with the protection of children from the use of illicit drugs and psychotropic substances. Significantly, under this heading, article 6(2) is a basic health and welfare right. This is how the Committee, generally, classifies article 6(2). Worth mentioning, in this context, that no special relationship with the neighbouring article 6(1) on the right to life was emphasised by the Committee.

The discussion on this chapter will focus mainly on article 6(2) in its second classification, i.e., as a basic health and welfare right. As regards the classification as a general principle, this will be dealt with in detail in Chapter 3.

It is worth noting, however, that the guidelines include other cases of double classification as well. For instance, article 39 appears under the heading 'Family Environment and Alternative Care' and the heading 'Special Protection Measures'.[86] Theoretically, this double classification aims at giving article 6(2) the ultimate chance to be fully and effectively realised. According to this classification, every aspect of the article that will lead to its full realisation is expected to be covered. However, the practice might, arguably, show some confusion that might result from this double classification. This confusion, in the case of article 6(2), is basically caused by the fact that the general principles of the Convention enjoy a stronger presence within the Convention than that enjoyed by the basic health and welfare rights of the child. The implementation of the general principles is expected to be reflected in relation to all the rights

84 Committee on the Rights of the Child, 'General guidelines regarding the form and content of periodic reports', UN Doc. CRC/C/58/Rev.1 (29 November 2005), paras. 30–31.

85 Committee on the Rights of the Child, 'Treaty-specific guidelines regarding the form and content of periodic reports to be submitted by States parties under article 44, paragraph 1 (b), of the Convention on the Rights of the Child', UN Doc. CRC/58/Rev.2 (23 November 2010), para. 34.

86 Committee on the Rights of the Child, 'General guidelines regarding the form and content of periodic reports', UN Doc. CRC/C/58/Rev.1 (29 November 2005), paras. 16 and 23.

in the Convention and not only the basic health and welfare ones. The question remains, however, as to whether these differences are contradictory or not.

At this stage in the discussion, the question that probably needs to be asked is: to which type of rights do the basic health and welfare rights of the child belong?

6. SPECIAL LINK WITH THE ECONOMIC AND SOCIAL RIGHTS OF THE CHILD

Basically, the inclusion of several types of rights in one document, such as the CRC, denotes that all of these rights are legally equal and cannot be divided. Furthermore, it can be considered as a step towards the strengthening of the notion of the indivisibility and interdependence of all types of human rights. The Committee recognises the equal importance of the economic and social rights and the civil and political rights, by stating that both types of rights are justiciable.[87] The equal legal strength of economic and social rights will be discussed later in the chapter.

The Committee's rights-based interpretation explicitly makes article 6(2) an economic and social right of the child (ESR). The link with this type of rights was later reconfirmed by the Committee in various places. For instance, the Committee recommended in its Concluding Observations on Kyrgyzstan's second periodic report that, with regard to street children, the State had to ensure that they are provided with adequate nutrition, clothing, housing, health-care and educational opportunities, including vocational and life-skills training, for the sake of supporting their full development.[88]

6.1. BASES FOR IDENTIFYING ECONOMIC SOCIAL AND CULTURAL RIGHTS

An important question however is: how can one identify an economic and social right of the child? Philip Alston, for instance, has provided a criterion to identify the ESR of the child. He argues that one aspect of economic and social rights is that they are always limited by the use of a 'resource qualifier'. He states:

> [T]here are two indicators that may be used. The first is the presence of phrases which constitute 'resource qualifiers' in the body of various articles. Thus, for example, phrases such as 'subject to available resources' … and 'free of charge, whenever

87 Committee on the Rights of the Child, 'General Comment No. 5: General measures of implementation for the Convention on the Rights of the Child (arts. 4, 42 and 44, para. 6)', UN Doc. CRC/GC/2003/5 (27 November 2003), para. 25.

88 Committee on the Rights of the Child, 'Concluding Observation: Kyrgyzstan's Second Periodic Report', UN Doc. CRC/C/15/Add.244 (3 November 2004), para. 64(a).

> possible' ..., are a good indication that the right has an 'economic and social' component. The second indicator is a significant similarity between the formulation used in the Convention and a right recognized in the International Covenant on Economic, Social and Cultural Rights.[89]

According to Alston's criteria, one can argue that the CRC includes not less than a total of nine economic, social rights, including article 6(2). Article 6(2) reads, 'States Parties shall ensure to the maximum extent possible the survival and development of the child.' The 'resource qualifier', according to Alston, is referred to in the term 'to the maximum extent possible'.[90]

Nevertheless, the word 'ensure', which is considered as a relatively strong word in human rights documents language when compared to others, is used in the first part of the article.[91] The Human Rights Committee, in its General Comment No. 31, argues in favour of the strong and prompt nature of the obligation to ensure:

> The article 2, paragraph 1, obligation to respect and ensure the rights recognized by the Covenant has immediate effect for all States parties. Article 2, paragraph 2, provides the overarching framework within which the rights specified in the Covenant are to be promoted and protected. The Committee has as a consequence previously indicated in its General Comment 24 that reservations to article 2 would be incompatible with the Covenant when considered in the light of its objects and purposes.[92]

This unique compilation of a 'resource qualifier' and the strong level of obligation, represented by the obligation to 'ensure' makes it clear that article 6(2) is special and unique. It is definitely more than an economic, social and cultural right of the child.

6.2. LEGAL STATUS OF ECONOMIC, SOCIAL AND CULTURAL RIGHTS WITHIN THE CRC

Is the word 'ensure' that has been stated in article 6(2) stronger than the words 'respect' or 'protect'? The word 'respect' obliges the State to immediately refrain

---

89 P. Alston, 'The legal framework of the Convention on the Rights of the Child' (1992) 91/2 *Bulletin of Human Rights* 1, 11.

90 The broad scope of the standard 'to the maximum extent possible' will be discussed in Chapter 5.

91 C. Cohen, 'A Guide to Linguistic Interpretation of the Convention on the Rights of the Child Articles 1, 4, 41 and 45', in C. Cohen and H.A. Davidson (eds.) *Children's Rights in America: U.N. Convention on the Rights of the Child Compared with United States Law* (American Bar Association Center for Children in the Law and Defense for Children International, Washington D.C., 1990), pp. 34–38. See also N. Cantwell, 'Veni, Vidi... et Vici? A review of the history and impact of the CRC', in A. Weyts (ed.), *Understanding Children's Rights* (Ghent University, Ghent, 2004), p. 296.

92 Human Rights Committee, 'General Comment No. 31 [80]: Nature of the General Legal Obligation Imposed on States Parties to the Covenant', UN Doc. CCPR/C/21/Rev.1/Add.13 (26 May 2004), para. 5.

from a particular act that will negatively influence the child's right. The word 'protect' obliges the States Parties to immediately take steps that will directly aim at the elimination of factors that will negatively influence the right, such as third-party violations.[93] In this regard, the word 'ensure' involves a more positive approach, since it requires a guarantee for actions to be taken and for results. The State Party will be obliged to immediately guarantee the implementation of the right.[94] It is possible also to argue that there is no significant difference between the obligation to ensure to the maximum extent possible under article 6(2) and the obligation to ensure respect under article 1 that is common to the Four Geneva Conventions.[95] But the obligation to ensure, however, means to guarantee, or due diligence and it has an immediate effect. In addition, it has a positive and negative nature, i.e., the State needs to refrain from some acts and persist with others.[96]

As regards the 'resource qualifier', based on Alston's indicators, can one argue that the term 'ensure', in article 6(2), is later weakened in the second part of the article by the use of the phrase 'to the maximum extent possible'? This is because it puts a limitation on the level of States Parties' responsibilities. According to Philip Alston's second indicator, the resource qualifier for identifying the economic, social and cultural rights is represented by the term 'to the maximum extent possible'. But article 6(2) uses the comprehensive statement 'to the maximum extent possible' and not 'to the maximum extent of its available resources', which, arguably, speaks mainly about financial and other materialistic resources.

More details on the nature of State Party obligations are available in Chapter 5. However, to summarise, under the CRC there is no variation in the legal positions of the economic and social rights and the civil and political rights. The Committee has classified article 6(2) as a basic health and welfare right of the child, i.e., an economic, social right of the child. However, in the light of the basis of the understanding of the obligation to 'ensure' and the standard of 'to the maximum extent possible' it is possible to argue that article 6(2), on the survival and development of the child contains, the elements that allow it to be classified as more than an economic and social right. Aspects of the obligation to ensure

---

93 Committee on Economic, Social and Cultural Rights, 'General Comment No. 16: Substantive Issues Arising in the Implementation of the International Covenant on Economic, Social and Cultural Rights. The equal right of men and women to the enjoyment of all economic, social and cultural rights (art. 3 of the International Covenant on Economic, Social and Cultural Rights)', UN Doc. E/C.12/2005/4 (11 August 2005), paras. 18–31.

94 UN Doc. E/CN.4/1984/71, para. 87, available in Office of the High Commissioner for Human Rights, *Legislative History of the Convention on the Rights of the Child,* Volume II (United Nations, New York, 2007), p. 613.

95 'The High Contracting Parties undertake to respect and to ensure respect for the present Convention in all circumstances'.

96 Human Rights Committee, 'General Comment No. 31 [80]: Nature of the General Legal Obligation Imposed on States Parties to the Covenant', UN Doc. CCPR/C/21/Rev.1/Add.13 (26 May 2004), paras. 5–6.

provide for other classifications of article 6(2). This should be considered as a further step towards the conceptual strengthening of the article.[97]

6.3. SPECIAL LINK BETWEEN ARTICLE 6(2) AND SOME SPECIFIC ECONOMIC, SOCIAL AND CULTURAL RIGHTS

6.3.1. *Special Link between Article 6(2) and Article 24 on the Right of the Child to Health*

The Committee's recommendations on article 6(2) make article 24 on the right to health the main article that is directly and explicitly linked and associated with article 6(2). The Committee has explicitly stated that it 'understands the concepts of "health and development" more broadly than being strictly limited to the provisions defined in articles 6 (right to life, survival and development) and 24 (right to health) of the Convention.[98] Article 24 (1) reads as follows:

> States Parties recognize the right of the child to the enjoyment of the highest attainable standard of health and to facilities for the treatment of illness and rehabilitation of health. States Parties shall strive to ensure that no child is deprived of his or her right of access to such health care services.

The obligation of the State Party in this article is not to ensure that every child is healthy but to ensure the right of the child to the highest attainable standards of health. In the context of this article, the quality of services and their provision should be ensured by the State Party. It is not enough for the State Party to provide the health services. States have to endeavour to ensure the provision of quality health services as well. For instance, the State has to provide qualified medical staff, quality equipment and quality follow-ups, or adopt policies that support the primary health-care programmes over those policies that support providing curative health care. In this regard, the Committee requires that there should be access to quality health services, especially when considering child mortality rates.[99] Placing the obligation on the State Party does not, however, prevent the State from using supplementary resources such as 'resources made

---

97 For further reading on the concept of the obligation to ensure, see L.B. de Chazournes and L. Condorelli, 'Common Article 1 of the Geneva Conventions revisited: Protecting collective interests' (31/03/2000) 837 *International Review of the Red Cross* 67–87 <https://www.icrc.org/eng/resources/documents/misc/57jqcp.htm> accessed 19 April 2015.

98 See Committee on the Rights of the Child, 'General Comment No. 4: Adolescent health and development in the context of the Convention on the Rights of the Child', UN Doc. CRC/GC/2003/4 (1 July 2003), para. 4.

99 Committee on the Rights of the Child, 'Concluding Observations: Tanzania's Initial Report', UN Doc. CRC/C/15/Add.156 (9 July 2001), para. 47.

available by other sources, including non-governmental organizations, the international community and the private sector.'[100] The State, however, will remain under an obligation to protect the child.

Article 24(2) continues:

> States Parties shall pursue full implementation of this right and, in particular, shall take appropriate measures:
> (a) To diminish infant and child mortality;
> (b) To ensure the provision of necessary medical assistance and health care to all children with emphasis on the development of primary health care;
> (c) To combat disease and malnutrition, including within the framework of primary health care, through, inter alia, the application of readily available technology and through the provision of adequate nutritious foods and clean drinking-water, taking into consideration the dangers and risks of environmental pollution...

The Committee recognises that, the two extremes, of malnutrition and obesity do not conform to the concept of healthy physical development. For instance, in its Concluding Observations on the periodic report of China, the Committee recognises both of these issues as problems, bearing in mind that obesity might occur within children who have varying financial capabilities: 'It further urges the States Party to develop policies and programmes to adequately address the problems of malnutrition and obesity in children'.[101] In turn, this represents a clear indication that the healthy development of a child can be impaired within all levels of a society, whether rich or poor. Article 24 continues:

> (d) To ensure appropriate pre-natal and post-natal health care for mothers;
> (e) To ensure that all segments of society, in particular parents and children, are informed, have access to education and are supported in the use of basic knowledge of child health and nutrition, the advantages of breastfeeding, hygiene and environmental sanitation and the prevention of accidents...

Significantly, article 24(c) refers to environmental pollution. This is important because it highlights external aspects that affect the right of the child to development. In this regard, the Committee raises the issue of environmental health conditions in many terms, such as solid waste management.[102]

As far as breastfeeding is concerned, problems of low levels of breastfeeding mothers are sometimes linked to financial resources. For instance, in poor

---

100 Committee on the Rights of the Child, 'General Comment No. 15: The Right of the Child to the Enjoyment of the Highest Attainable Standard of Health (Art. 24)', UN Doc. CRC/C/GC/15 (17 April 2013), para. 23.

101 Committee on the Rights of the Child, 'Concluding Observations: China's (including Hong Kong and Macau Special Administrative Regions)', UN Doc. CRC/C/CHN/CO/2 (24 November 2005), para. 63.

102 Committee on the Rights of the Child, 'Concluding Observations: Palau's Initial Report', UN Doc. CRC/C/15/Add.149 (21 February 2001), para. 47.

countries, mothers depend on breastfeeding because it is cheaper. Nevertheless, in the past, false concept about breastfeeding, have negatively affected its provision, for example considering it less fashionable. Moreover, the deterioration of the health of mothers who do not have access to nutritious food also negatively affected breastfeeding. In this context, the State is obliged to raise the awareness of breastfeeding and to provide improvements in mothers' health. According to article 24(f): 'To develop preventive health care, guidance for parents and family planning education and services.' States are encouraged to place more emphasis on pre-natal and post-natal services, with special attention paid to deprived communities, and to develop training programmes in parenting skills, stressing the positive effects of breastfeeding, nutritious diet for mother and child, as well as proper hygiene, on early childhood development and survival.'[103]

It is also useful to add here the relationship with HIV/AIDS and how it can negatively affect the right of the child to development. Especially when considering that in some cases orphaned children who are victims of HIV/AIDS are heads of households, and this can affect their development, particularly their psychological development.

The Committee provides a comprehensive understanding to article 24 on the right to health as an ESR. This inclusive understanding reveals the length the Committee went in to in making this direct and explicit link between article 6(2) and article 24. However, the distinction of article 6(2) as an article that guarantees two separate rights of the child – i.e., the right to survival and the right to development – should be emphasised.

The link between article 6(2) and article 24 was first made during the drafting of the Convention in 1988. When considering the original reasons for the inclusion of article 6(2) in the Convention, one can possibly argue that it is not surprising to see this merging of the two articles. In fact, during the drafting of article 24(c), in particular, while an agreed version of article 12 *bis* was thought to have been obtained in 1985, India proposed some amendments to the sub article in 1988. India made this proposal during the same session, in which, it proposed article 6(2). The representative of India justified the reasons for the revision of the earliest article by inserting a new subparagraph (c) before the already adopted subparagraph (c) of article 12 *bis*, as follows:

> [I]t was aimed at covering situations which existed, in particular, in developing countries, where almost all of the 14 million cases of premature death as a consequence of disease occurred. In countries where an important part of the population ran the risk of serious disease, due to economic and social problems, children were specially vulnerable and needed special protection. Such protection could be assured through

[103] Committee on the Rights of the Child, 'Concluding Observations: Romania's Third and Fourth Periodic Report', UN Doc. CRC/C/ROM/CO/4 (30 June 2009), paras. 30–31.

> the application of readily available technologies and low-cost measures such as oral rehydration therapy and immunization against the common childhood diseases.[104]

It was then stated clearly that the proposal was aimed at protecting the life of the child and was 'related to article 1 *bis*' (the number of article 6 before the final renumbering in 1989).[105] It is worth noting here that the second part of article 6(2), i.e., the right to 'development', was put in mainly to serve the first part of the article, i.e., the right to survival. Development was thus seen as a step towards the achievement of the child's survival. In this context, it is therefore possible to argue that when the Committee started its work back in 1991, it was not in favour of breaking the originally well-established link or relationship between the two articles, which was clearly established during the drafting sessions. This argument is supported by the fact that most of Committee's recommendations on the article are similar to the drafting notes. Article 24(c) is intrinsically linked to the concept of survival.[106]

However, there was a further step that the Committee was ready to take in relation to the *travaux préparatoires*, and it was a positive one. In that it did not limit article 6(2) to article 24(c). In fact, it merged article 6(2) and all of article 24, which is a very broad article and covers a number of aspects of the right to health. This merging is evident in the Committee's reporting guidelines, where both articles were associated together and listed under the heading 'Basic Health and Welfare'. It is also clear in other documents as well. For instance, in its day of general discussion on the rights of the child in early childhood, the Committee restated the holistic approach to the Convention while emphasising articles 24, 28 and 29.[107]

> The Committee reminds States parties (and others concerned) that the right to survival and development can only be implemented in a holistic manner, through the enforcement of all the other provisions of the Convention, including rights to health, adequate nutrition, social security, an adequate standard of living, a healthy and safe environment, education and play (articles 24, 27, 28, 29 and 31), as well as through respect for the responsibilities of parents and the provision of assistance and quality services (articles 5 and 18). From an early age, children should themselves be included in activities promoting good nutrition and a healthy and disease-preventing lifestyle.[108]

---

104 UN Doc. E/CN.4/1988/28 (6 April 1988), para. 60, available in Office of the High Commissioner for Human Rights, *Legislative History of the Convention on the Rights of the Child*, Volume II (United Nations, New York, 2007), p. 595.

105 *Ibid.*

106 See, for instance, M. Nowak, 'Article 6. The Right to Life, Survival and Development', in: A. Alen, J. Vande Lanotte, E. Verhellen, F. Ang, E. Berghmans and M. Verheyde (eds.), *A Commentary on the United Nations Convention on the Rights of the Child* (Martinus Nijhoff Publishers, Leiden, 2005), p. 14.

107 Committee of the Rights of the Child, 'Day of Discussion: Implementing Child Rights in Early Childhood' (17 September 2004), para. 8, Palais Wilson.

108 Committee on the Rights of the Child, 'General Comment No. 7: Implementing child rights in early childhood', UN Doc. CRC/C/GC/7/Rev.1 (20 September 2006), para. 10.

It is also possible to argue that the Committee made this link because the right to health has a special link with the child's physical, mental and psychological development.[109] According to the Committee's interpretation of article 6(2), these are some aspects of the child's development.

Before the adoption of the CRC, international law gave children the minimum protection in terms of the right to health. Article 12(1)–(2)(a) of the International Covenant on Economic, Social and Cultural Rights, for instance, is too vague in its wording as regards the right of the child to health. It reads:

> 1. The States Parties to the present Covenant recognize the right of everyone to the enjoyment of the highest attainable standard of physical and mental health.
> 2. The steps to be taken by the States Parties to the present Covenant to achieve the full realization of this right shall include those necessary for: The provision for the reduction of the stillbirth-rate and of infant mortality and for the healthy development of the child.

In comparison, one can clearly recognise the enhancement that article 24 of the Convention on the Rights of the Child provides. It is a very long article. It provides detailed and broad information regarding protection for different aspects of the right of the child to health. For instance, it provides for education, information and services in family planning, and education and awareness-raising on hygiene issues and the importance of breastfeeding. In addition it provides for decreasing the high number of under-five mortalities, which is very high, especially in developing countries, and the abolition of many traditional practices that are harmful to children.[110] The comprehensiveness of article 24 brings it more into line with the definition of the term 'health' that is included in the Constitution of the World Health Organization and that provides a comprehensive understanding of health: 'Health is a state of complete physical, mental and social well-being and not merely the absence of disease or infirmity.'[111] This is significant because it explains why the decision of the Committee to broaden the scope of the right of the child to development under article 6(2) by directly linking it to the right to health should be seen, in itself, as a positive step. In terms of its quality and comprehensiveness, article 24 includes varied and diverse access to the right of the child to health. This will widen the direct scope and effect of the concept of the right of the child to

---

109 A.B. Andrews, 'Securing Adequate Living Conditions for Each Child's Development' and N.H. Kaufman and M.L. Blanco, 'Drafting and Interpreting Article 27', in A.B. Andrews, and N.H. Kaufman (eds.), *Implementing the U.N. Convention on the Rights of the Child: A Standard of Living Adequate for Development* (Praeger Publishers, Westport, 1999), p. 6.

110 Unfortunately a proposal by the NGO ad hoc group for the inclusion of a sub article on the medical experimentation on children was not successful. See United Nations Commission on Human Rights, UN Doc. E/CN.4/1988/WG.1/WP.2, p. 11. Available in Office of the High Commissioner for Human Rights, *Legislative History of the Convention on the Rights of the Child*, Volume II (United Nations, New York, 2007), pp. 594–595.

111 Constitution of the World Health Organization, (1946) 14 UNTS 185.

development, represented by having a clear understanding of the concept of the right of the child to development. Nevertheless, it is important that this association should not affect the individuality of article 6(2) as a separate right.

Article 24 is not the only article that the Committee links to article 6(2). In fact, the Committee went further towards the realisation of the holistic approach in dealing with article 6(2) when it associated the article with other basic health and welfare rights as well, namely articles 23, 26, 27 and 33. This association is a positive step in itself, because it broadens the conceptual understanding of article 6(2). Nevertheless, it links it again with the economic and social rights of the child and conveys that article 6(2) belongs to this category of rights only.

6.3.2. Special Link between Article 6(2) and Article 23 on the Rights of the Disabled Child

Article 23 regulates State Party responsibility towards physically or mentally disabled children. It is the second article among the group of rights that the Committee associates with article 6(2). An important aspect of article 23 is that it deals with disabled children not as a group of vulnerable children but as a recognised and specific category or group of children who have the right to receive special attention and treatment.[112] On these bases it is relevant that, while the article does not include the term 'discrimination' at all, it is initiated from the perspective of protecting this specific group of children from discrimination. Accordingly, the aim of the entire article is to protect this group of children from the point of view of empowering them; by promoting their chances to be self-reliant and active participants in the community. Most of the Committee's recommendations on article 23 focus on the issue of discrimination: 'Prevent and prohibit all forms of discrimination against children with disabilities and ensure equal opportunities for their full participation in all spheres of life by implementing the domestic laws and by including disability aspects in all relevant policy-making and national planning'.[113] For example:

> (b) Ensure that equal access to services is provided to children with disabilities, taking into consideration the Standard Rules on the Equalization of Opportunities for Persons with Disabilities … and
> (c) Provide equal educational opportunities for children with disabilities, including by providing the necessary support and ensuring that teachers are trained to educate children with disabilities within the regular schools.[114]

---

112 UN Doc. E/CN.4/1983/62, para. 58, available in Office of the High Commissioner for Human Rights, *Legislative History of the Convention on the Rights of the Child*, Volume II (United Nations,, New York, 2007), pp. 570–571.

113 Committee on the Rights of the Child, 'Concluding Observations: Uganda' (Unedited Version), UN Doc. CRC/C/15/Add.270 (30 September 2005), para. 47(a).

114 Committee on the Rights of the Child, 'Concluding Observations: Denmark', UN Doc. CRC/C/DNK/CO/3 (23 November 2005), paras. 39 (b) and (c).

Article 23 places the primary responsibility to care for the disabled child on his or her parents, but the primary responsibility to provide the services and required equipment to the disabled child is placed on the State. Article 23(3) explicitly speaks about the concept of the 'individual development' of the child, with special emphasis on cultural and spiritual development. As mentioned above, the Committee refers in its guidelines to spiritual development as an aspect of the child's development under article 6(2), but does not refer to cultural development. It is worth noting, however, that the final version of this paragraph was also made by UNICEF during the drafting of the CRC.[115] This conveys that, during the drafting, UNICEF was especially interested in the concept of development and worked for the inclusion of some articles that target the development of the child in the CRC, including article 6(2).

States Parties are obliged under article 23(3) to provide 'education, training, health care services, rehabilitation services, preparation for employment and recreation opportunities in a manner conducive to the child's achieving the fullest possible integration and individual development, including his or her cultural and spiritual development.' This paragraph was inserted as an alternative to a proposal to include a clause that would create provisions for the disabled child to receive religious education.[116] This in fact should be regarded as an expansion on the concept of development; nevertheless, article 23(2) limits this. Limitation is caused by links to the provision of particular services, such as education and health-care services. Accordingly, the wording of article 23(2) does not allow for an unlimited definition of the term 'development' and links it with a number of economic and social rights that do not suggest a high level of responsibility on the State Party. In addition, the wording of the text of article 23(3) is very soft as regards the level of State Party obligation. Based on that, States are obliged to provide the services 'free of charge, whenever possible, taking into account the financial resources of the parents or others caring for the child'. It is very important, however, that while the article aims at the empowerment and prevention of discrimination of the disabled child, it is completely paralysed by the use of a number of weak clauses. These weak clauses convey that the State Party's level of responsibility in terms of realization and fulfilment is not very high. In many cases the level of the State's responsibility does not go beyond mere recognition, which does not convey more than just the acceptance of the one particular aspect of the overall rights of the disabled. States Parties are obliged to provide the services or facilities required only when their facilities and the available resources permit.

115 UN Doc. E/CN.4/1989/WG.1/CRP.1, p. 28, available in Office of the High Commissioner for Human Rights, *Legislative History of the Convention on the Rights of the Child*, Volume II (United Nations, 2007), pp. 576–571.

116 UN Doc. E/CN.4/1983/62, para. 61, available in Office of the High Commissioner for Human Rights, *Legislative History of the Convention on the Rights of the Child*, Volume II (United Nations, New York, 2007), p. 571.

In addition to article 4 of the CRC, which explicitly puts a 'verbal' limitation on the implementation of the economic and social rights of the child, most of the individual articles on this type of right reconfirm this important point. The wording restates within the article itself that the implementation will be dependent on the available resources, such as article 23(2), or on the basis of international co-operation, such as article 24(4).

Nevertheless, while the link that the Committee has made between article 6(2) and article 23 does not enhance the legal position of article 6(2), it links article 6(2) with the overall concept of development and issues of international development. Article 23 does not provide any definition of the reasons for mental or physical disablement. However, it might be possible to argue that by focusing on some of the reasons for disablement, the Committee has created an indirect link between the right of the child to development, under article 6(2), and the overall concepts of development and international development.[117] To illustrate, there is no doubt that armed conflicts, for example, can cause major disabilities to children through the use of land mines. This in turn is highly relevant to the concept of international peace. In this context, the right of the child to development, when linked with the rights of the disabled, has its implied links with the right to development and the right to peace. However, this indirect link does not have a recognised positive effect in terms of the legal status of both articles, i.e. article 6(2) and article 23.

6.3.3. *Special Link between Article 6(2) and Article 26 on the Right of the Child to Benefit from Social Security*

The wording of article 26 is in no way stronger than that of articles 23 and 24. In fact, during the drafting sessions, there was one proposal that had a stronger wording, because it used the word 'ensure' instead of the word 'recognise'; it read: 'The States Parties to the present Convention shall, in a manner appropriate to national conditions, ensure to every child the right to benefit from social security'.[118] The representative of the United States proposed the use of the word 'recognise' in lieu of the word 'ensure' in order to prevent any suggestion that the right should be implemented immediately, 'because that would imply that the right to benefit from social security was recognized as a goal or objective whose realization would be sought progressively rather than a legal right requiring immediate implementation'.[119]

117 UNICEF, *Implementation Handbook for the Convention on the Rights of the Child* (New York, UNICEF, 2007), p. 334.

118 UN Doc. E/CN.4/1984/71, para. 84, available in Office of the High Commissioner for Human Rights, *Legislative History of the Convention on the Rights of the Child,* Volume II (United Nations, New York, 2007), p. 612.

119 UN Doc. E/CN.4/1984/71, para. 87, available in Office of the High Commissioner for Human Rights, *Legislative History of the Convention on the Rights of the Child,* Volume II (United

> Article 26 concerns financial support for children provided by the State. Children are usually economically dependent upon adults. However, when the adults with responsibility for children are unable to provide for them, either because they are unable to find gainful employment or because their circumstances ... prevent them from working, then the State has an obligation to ensure that the child has some form of financial support, either paid directly to the child or via a responsible adult ... Article 26 is subject to the proviso of article 4: '... With regard to economic, social and cultural rights, States Parties shall undertake such measures to the maximum extent of their available resources and, where needed, within the framework of international cooperation.' During the drafting of article 26, proposals were made to make the right to social security explicitly dependent on the availability of national resources, but this was perceived to be unnecessary in view of article 4 ... the child has a right to 'benefit from' social security rather than a right 'to' social security. This reflects the fact that children's economic security is generally bound up with that of their adult caregivers. This dependence also led to the drafting of the second paragraph of article 26, making social security contingent on the caregiver lacking resources...[120]

Article 26 raises the issue of entitlement. Who is entitled to receive social security? Article 26(1) recognises the main principle that every child has the right to benefit from social security. This conveys that all children, no matter what their financial status is, have the right to social security. Later, this generalisation was limited by the wording of article 26(2): 'The benefits should, where appropriate, be granted, taking into account the resources and the circumstances of the child and persons having responsibility for the maintenance of the child, as well as any other consideration relevant to an application for benefits made by or on behalf of the child.' Hodgkin and Newell, point out that the drafters did agree to make it clear that children could apply for benefits directly.[121]

> The Convention underlines the financial as well as caring responsibilities of parents and others with child-rearing responsibilities ...
>
> In addition, means-testing of child social security is generally regarded as desirable, given the need to target limited resources effectively. It should, however, be noted that some degree of financial support for all children, regardless of their parents' circumstances, is neither unreasonable nor unviable ... families with children can be encouraged and supported by tax rebates or direct benefits.
>
> Universal benefits to all children have the added advantage of ensuring full take-up rates with very low administrative costs, since no means-testing is involved.[122]

Nations, New York, 2007), p. 613.

120 R. Hodgkin and P. Newell, *Implementation Handbook for the Convention on the Rights of the Child* (UNICEF, Geneva, 2007), p. 385.

121 *Ibid.*, p. 385.

122 *Ibid.*, p. 389.

When joined together, article 6(2) grants the child the right to survival and development. Article 26 grants the child the right to benefit from social security, although it allows for this to happen through the persons who care for the child. Arguably, the careful scrutiny of article 26 allows the possible interpretation that it is concerned with the financial empowerment of the child. Nevertheless, this is to be considered on the basis of whether the child or his or her parents owns the money.[123] If it is the child, then this could probably be considered as a financial and economic development of the child. According to the Committee's statement on the aspects of the 'development' under article 6(2), financial development is not an aspect of the child's development in article 6(2).

Article 26 is extremely significant in terms of the obligations of the States Parties to ensure to the maximum extent possible the survival and development of the child. This is momentous, considering that there were huge concerns about the inclusion of articles that would bring within them a large burden of financial obligations. This was pointed out on different occasions during the drafting of the Convention. For instance, the representative of Bangladesh submitted a statement in which he emphasised the position of developing countries with regard to such cases:

> Articles sponsored by the NGO, Defence for Children International, are broadly acceptable. However, articles such as 'health' 'standards of living' "compulsory free education" should be made subject to a clause on the economic feasibility in particular countries. For example, it is estimated that to accommodate the school-going population in Bangladesh it would cost an amount of 200 million dollars per annum over the next few years before we can attain the objective of free compulsory primary education. Some recognition of the economic problems faced by developing countries is essential if the draft is to enjoy the support of the vast majority of developing countries including the least developed countries.[124]

The statement was made during the drafting of article 27, but it is probably an argument by developing and least-developed States in relation to all the articles that impose a financial responsibility on the State Party. This includes the financial obligations under article 6(2), which obliges the State to create measures and conditions for the survival and full development of the child.

---

123 For further reading on the entitlement of the child to apply for the social benefit and applications to be made on behalf of the child see R. Hodgkin and P. Newell, *Implementation Handbook for the Convention on the Rights of the Child* (UNICEF, Geneva, 2007), pp. 389–390.

124 UN Doc. E/CN.4/1986/39, Annex IV, available in Office of the High Commissioner for Human Rights, *Legislative History of the Convention on the Rights of the Child,* Volume II (United Nations, New York, 2007), p. 625.

6.3.4. *Special Link between Article 6(2) and Article 27 on the Right of the Child to an Adequate Standard of Living*

Similar to article 6(2), article 27 appears under the heading 'Basic Health and Welfare' in the Committee's guidelines. Article 27 enshrines the right of every child to a standard of living adequate for the child's physical, mental, spiritual, moral and social development. It is a lengthy provision, and consists of four paragraphs. The second and third paragraphs set out the responsibility of the parents or those responsible for the child and the responsibility of the State Party as regards the provision of adequate standards of living for the development of the child. Paragraph four is concerned with the recovery of maintenance, which includes cases in which the parent and the child do not live in the same State.

During the drafting of article 27, the Algerian government proposed to the Working Group an article that represented a comprehensive understanding of the concept of the right of the child to development and of the conditions and requirements involved with its implementation. The proposal recognised the shared international responsibility for the creation of an adequate standard of living for the child. 'Children have the right to an adequate standard of living. To this end, the State Parties shall cooperate in the economic, social, cultural, scientific and technical field to promote economic and social progress throughout the world and particularly in the developing countries.'[125] This proposal focused on international cooperation. According to article 4 of the CRC, international cooperation is an integral part of the realisation of these kinds of rights, including article 6(2) (on the basis of the Committee's clustering). 'With regard to economic, social and cultural rights, States Parties shall undertake such measures to the maximum extent of their available resources and, where needed, within the framework of international co-operation.'

Article 27(1) explicitly identifies some aspects of the child's development and requires the States Parties to recognise them. 'States parties recognize the right of every child to a standard of living adequate for the child's physical, mental, spiritual, moral and social development.' Highlighting the Committee's interpretation of the word development in article 6(2), it is very similar to that of article 27(1).[126] The only difference is that the Committee's interpretation adds psychological development. In this sense it is possible to argue that the link that the Committee made between article 6(2) and article 27 expands on the definition of the word development, and that this is a positive step.

---

125 UN Doc. E/CN.4/1983/WG.1/WP.27, available in UN Doc. E/CN.4/1988/28 (6 April 1988), para. 60. Cited in Office of the High Commissioner for Human Rights, *Legislative History of the Convention on the Rights of the Child,* Volume II (United Nations, New York, 2007), p. 621.

126 On the link between article 6(2) and article 27(1) see R. Hodgkin and P. Newell, *Implementation Handbook for the Convention on the Rights of the Child* (UNICEF, Geneva, 2007), p. 393.

Importantly, article 27 raises the issue of the level of State Party responsibility. Article 27 (2) reads as follows: 'The parent(s) or others responsible for the child have the primary responsibility to secure, within their abilities and financial capacities, the conditions of living necessary for the child's development.' This paragraph raises the issue of private responsibility versus State responsibility. Arguably, since the adoption of the Universal Declaration of Human Rights in 1948, the core principle of the entire concept of human rights has been viewed as being to guarantee the rights of the individual vis-à-vis the State to which the individual falls under its jurisdiction.[127] However, there are some instances where this main aspect of human rights is not clear. For example, article 29(1) of the Universal Declaration of Human Rights states that everyone has duties to community. The African Charter on the Rights and Welfare of the Child also speaks about the responsibility of the child. In fact all of article 31 of the African Charter focuses on the responsibility and the duties of the child. Article 31, however, does not interfere with the realisation of article 1 of the African Charter, which is concerned with the obligation of the State party.

Arguably the core principle of State responsibility has not been clearly embedded into the wording of article 27. The article adopts the concept of primary parental financial responsibility. When compared to its counterpart article in the International Covenant on Economic, Social and Cultural Rights, namely article 11 (ICESCR), it is possible to point out the difference. According to article 11, the State holds the primary responsibility for ensuring an adequate standard of living for individuals. Whereas in article 27(2) the State steps in only when the parents are unable to fulfil their financial duty of securing the standard of living necessary for their child's development. 'Parents have primary responsibility for securing this right; States must if necessary assist parents in doing so and in cases of need must provide material supports to the child, such as food, clothing and housing.'[128] Hodgkin and Newell explain the financial responsibility of the State and comment on some reported cases where the State has passed up its duties to the parents:

> The primary responsibility of parents and other carers to meet the child's needs reflects the principles stated in article 3(2), article 5 and article 18. Where provision

---

127 For the responsibility of the child see Organization of African Unity, 'The African Charter on the Rights and Welfare of the Child', OAU Doc. CAB/LEG/24.9/49 (1990) (11 July 1990), article 31. See also United Nations General Assembly, 'The UN Declaration on the Right and Responsibility of Individuals, Groups and Organs of Society to Promote and Protect Universally Recognized Human Rights and Fundamental Freedoms', UN Doc. A/RES/53/144 (8 March 1999), Annex, where according to article I of this Delcaration: 'Everyone has the right, individually and in association with others, to promote and to strive for the protection and realization of human rights and fundamental freedoms at the national and international levels.'

128 R. Hodgkin and P. Newell, *Implementation Handbook for the Convention on the Rights of the Child* (UNICEF, Geneva, 2007), p. 393 (emphasis added); see also p. 397.

for the child's development is concerned under article 27, parental responsibility is expressly qualified by the proviso 'within their abilities and financial capacities'.

This is an important reminder that, where parents lack the requisite skills or resources, the State must assist the parents in meeting their responsibilities, including the provision of material assistance such as food, clothing and housing. The Committee commented to the Democratic Republic of the Congo that:

'The Committee agrees with the State Party in expressing deep concern that the State seems increasingly to be shifting its duties and responsibilities onto parents and persons effectively or legally responsible for a child's upbringing...' ... legislation can be very precise about what is expected from parents by defining 'parental responsibility' in law in terms of meeting the child's material, emotional, developmental and intellectual needs. That such legislation might be hard to enforce is not the point; the law has an important educational function as well.[129]

Article 27(3) confirms the responsibility of the State: 'State parties, in accordance with national conditions and within their means, shall take appropriate measures to assist parents or others responsible for the child to implement this right and shall in case of need provide material assistance and support programmes, particularly with regard to nutrition, clothing and housing.' When compared to article 11 of the ICESCR, article 27 is expected to provide stronger protection. This is due to the CRC being a specialised convention on children's rights. Furthermore, the CRC was adopted at a later stage than the ICESCR; therefore, it would make no sense for the CRC article to provide less protection than the one that already existed.[130]

It is very important, in the context of article 27, to distinguish between the responsibility of the individuals and the responsibility of the State. What is the level of the State Party's obligation under article 27? Is it possible to argue that article 27, when read together with article 4 of the Convention, introduces two levels or two types of State Party responsibility, namely what can be called 'the primary responsibility' of the State and 'the secondary responsibility' of the State? Van Bueren has made a comparison between the level of State responsibility under article 6(2) and that under article 27(2) and concluded that the CRC is not clear in this matter with relation to the right to development. She has pointed out that the State Party responsibility in article 27 is secondary to that of the parents:

Article 6(2) places the duty clearly on the state whereas article 27(2) places the primary responsibility on parents to secure within their abilities and financial

129 R. Hodgkin and P. Newell, *Implementation Handbook for the Convention on the Rights of the Child*, (UNICEF, Geneva, 2007), p. 395.

130 See UN Doc. E/CN.4/1989/WG.1/CRP.1, p. 32, available in UN Doc. E/CN.4/1988/28 (6 April 1988), para. 60. Cited in Office of the High Commissioner for Human Rights, *Legislative History of the Convention on the Rights of the Child*, Volume II (United Nations, New York, 2007), p. 629.

> capacities the conditions of living which are necessary for the child's development. The duty on States Parties is a secondary one to take appropriate measures 'within their means' to assist parents and others responsible for the child in implementing the child's right to an adequate standard of living.[131]

The level of the primary responsibility is guaranteed by article 4 of the CRC: 'States Parties shall undertake all appropriate legislative, administrative and other measures for the implementation of the rights recognized in the present Convention.' Article 4 is a major article of the CRC because it is concerned with the general rules regarding the State Party's responsibility towards the implementation of all the rights guaranteed in the Convention. It clearly promotes the primary responsibility of the State with regard to the implementation of all the articles in the CRC. Article 27(2) places the primary *financial* responsibility for securing the adequate standard of living on the parents. However, this does not exempt the State from securing, for instance, the legislations necessary for supporting the parents in fulfilling their obligations. The existence of such appropriate legislation is a primary responsibility of the State. The State also holds the primary responsibility for respecting and protecting the right of the child to a standard of living adequate for the child's development.

The secondary responsibility of the State is related to the failure of the parents to fulfil their primary responsibility. State responsibility is considered secondary because it starts only when the parents fail to fulfil their primary responsibility in securing the adequate standard of living. This level of responsibility is guaranteed in article 27(3), where the responsibility takes the form of providing material and financial assistance, within the means of the State, after the parents fail to provide it. Sharon Detrick comments on the responsibility of individuals as 'horizontal effects'. She uses the term as regards the effects that human rights have in relations between private parties as opposed to the relation with the State. She stresses that the term is not to be confused with the misconception that human rights treaties can impose responsibilities on any party other than the State. 'The term "horizontal effects" is used here in the sense that the right in question corresponds to a positive obligation of States parties to adopt domestic measures concerning the acts (or omissions) of private parties.'[132] Initially, the relationship between parent and child is crucial in the CRC. The nature of childhood requires responsibility to be imposed on the parents because children need someone to take care of them. Responsibility of parents towards their children is guaranteed by articles 5 and 18 of the CRC. The terms 'primary responsibility' and 'secondary responsibility' do not convey that the State will be exempted from issuing laws, for instance for the realisation of the child's right to an adequate standard of living.

131 G. Van Bueren, *The International Law on the Rights of the Child* (Martinus Nijhoff Publishers, The Hague, 1998), pp. 317–318.

132 S. Detrick, *A Commentary on the United Nations Convention on the Rights of the Child* (Martinus Nijhoff, The Hague, 1999), p. 31.

The terms convey that with regard to financial support, State Party responsibility is recognised through two steps: firstly, the legislation or any other relevant step that guarantees State intervention in the case of failure of parents; and, secondly, the actual intervention by providing the financial support.

However, Hodgkin and Newell argue that:

> Article 27's emphasis on the State assisting parents in the exercise of their primary responsibility to secure children's living conditions, rather than directly assisting the child, is both self-protective and principled: self-protective, because the drafting nations were anxious not to be placed under duties to support the children of rich parents, or to allow parents generally to offload their responsibilities onto the State; principled, because – as the Convention stresses – children have a right wherever possible to be cared for by their parents and kept within a family environment. Article 27 reaffirms the principle established in article 18 that while both parents have primary responsibility for their children, the State also has obligations to support parents in the role of protecting and promoting the well-being of their children. The Committee has expressed concern that States might not recognize that some parents were unable to undertake their responsibilities and needed support: … steps should be taken to strengthen the system of assistance to both parents in the performance of their childrearing responsibilities, in particular in the light of articles 18 and 27 of the Convention.[133]

It is worth noting in this context that the level of individual responsibility is in fact higher than that of the State Party because the parents are obliged to 'secure' the adequate standard of living for the child, but the State's responsibility does not go beyond taking the 'appropriate measures' to assist the individual(s) responsible for the child. In comparing article 27 to the other articles in the Convention, particularly those of an economic and financial nature, it is possible to argue that this division of responsibilities does not exist. For instance, according to article 24 on the right to health standards, the State is primarily responsible for providing the required health services as well as being primarily responsible for passing the required legislation.

Considering that article 6(2) was included in the Convention in order to oblige the State to focus on the promotion and creation of measures for the survival and development of the child, one has to ask the following question: what credit will article 6(2) gain when being associated with article 27?

The Committee has followed the tradition of reminding the State Party of its obligations under this article. For instance, the concluding observations on the initial report of Tanzania reads as follows:

> [T]he Committee recommends that the State party reinforces its efforts to provide support and material assistance to economically disadvantaged families to guarantee

---

133 R. Hodgkin and P. Newell, *Implementation Handbook for the Convention on the Rights of the Child* (UNICEF, Geneva, 2007), p. 397.

> the right of children to an adequate standard of living. In this connection, the Committee recommends that the State party pay particular attention to the rights and needs of children in the implementation of the Poverty Reduction Strategy Programme and all other programmes intended to improve the standard of living in the country … the State party establish mechanisms to ensure that children living and/or working on the streets are provided with nutrition, clothing and housing. Moreover, the state party should ensure that these children are provided adequate access to health care; rehabilitation services for physical, sexual and substance abuse; services for reconciliation with their families; and education, including vocational and life-skills training … that the States Party cooperate and coordinate its efforts with civil society and local communities.[134]

6.3.5. *Special Link between Article 6(2) and Article 33 on the Right of the Child to be Protected from the Use of Illicit Drugs*

The association between article 6(2) and the part of article 33 that protects children from the use of illegal drugs came in only in 2010. The article reads 'States Parties shall take all appropriate measures, including legislative, administrative, social and educational measures, to protect children from the illicit use of narcotic drugs and psychotropic substances as defined in the relevant international treaties'. In its 2010 guidelines the Committee put this part of article 33 under the subheading 'Disability, basic health and welfare'.[135]

One major aspect of the Committee's interpretation of article 33 focuses on the obligation of the State Party to protect children from the illicit use of narcotic drugs and psychotropic substances as an obligation to provide related health and social services.[136] For instance the Committee has required States Parties to provide 'specialized and youth-friendly drug dependence treatment and harm-reduction services for children and young people'. The Committee has also supported some educational measures to protect children, noting that 'it is further recommended that programmes be introduced within the school environment to educate children about the harmful effects of narcotic drugs and psychotropic substances.' The Committee also speaks about 'Providing children with accurate and objective information about the harmful consequences of substance abuse', and 'Considering children and adolescents affected by the use of drugs and harmful substances, as victims, including

---

134 Committee on the Rights of the Child, 'Concluding Observations: Tanzania's Initial Report', UN Doc. CRC/C/15/Add.156 (9 July 2001), para. 55.

135 Committee on the Rights of the Child, 'Treaty-specific guidelines regarding the form and content of periodic reports to be submitted by States parties under article 44, paragraph 1 (b), of the Convention on the Rights of the Child', UN Doc. CRC/58/Rev.2 (23 November 2010), section F.

136 K. Mahgoub, 'Article 33 of the Convention on the Rights of the Child: The Journey from Drafting History to the Concluding Observations of the Committee on the Rights of the Child' (2012) 2(1) *Human Rights and Drugs* 45, 54.

by providing them with easily accessible drug abuse treatment and social reintegration'.[137]

Basically, the Committee's interpretation of article 33 reveals a strong link with the right to health.[138] In this context, it is possible to argue that this association between article 6(2) and article 33 provides limited expansion on the concept of the child's survival and development.

6.4. CONSEQUENCES OF ASSOCIATING ARTICLE 6(2) WITH ECONOMIC, SOCIAL AND CULTURAL RIGHTS

The association that the Committee made between article 6(2) and the basic health and welfare rights of the child, which are mainly economic and social rights, gave article 6(2) some benefits, although limited ones. The major credit that article 6(2) gained is the expansion on the definition of the concept of the right to development.

Despite grouping article 6(2) with basic health and welfare rights, the Committee did not stop on linking article 6(2) with the aforementioned rights only. This is probably because it considers article 6(2) as a general principle of the CRC. This, however, is also due to the holistic approach to the implementation of the Convention. The holistic approach to the implementation of the CRC gave the Committee the chance to link article 6(2) with the other economic and social rights of the child as well, covering issues such as child labour, poverty, dropping out of school, and development of the child. For instance, the Committee recommended in its Concluding Observations on Kyrgyzstan's second periodic report that the State had to ensure that street children were provided with 'adequate nutrition, clothing, housing, health care and educational opportunities, including vocational and life-skills training, in order to support their full development'.[139]

7. ASPECTS OF THE CHILD'S DEVELOPMENT

The second main question that this chapter poses is concerned with the reasons that led the Committee to formulate its present interpretation of article 6(2) of the CRC: why did the Committee decide to put article 6(2) under the heading 'Basic Health and Welfare Rights'? This question could also be asked in a different way: why did the Committee make this specific link between

137 *Ibid.*, p. 54.
138 *Ibid.*, p. 62.
139 Committee on the Rights of the Child, 'Concluding observation: Kyrgyzstan's Second Periodic Report', UN Doc. CRC/C/15/Add.244 (3 November 2004), para. 64(a).

article 6(2) and the economic and social rights of the child? Arguably, the answer could be found within the definition that the Committee gave to the word 'development'. The Committee stated in its General Comment No. 5 that it expects States to interpret development in its broadest sense as a holistic concept, embracing the child's physical, mental, spiritual, moral, psychological and social development. In addition, implementation measures for article 6(2) should be aimed at achieving the optimal development for all children.[140] In other words, the Committee adopts the view that the right of the child to development, under article 6(2), represents the right of the child to 'human development'. Accordingly, the Committee named specific developmental domains that represent some aspects of human development.

Earlier, Cohen and Kilbourne have, momentously, highlighted the importance of child-development theories in the Committee's interpretation of the Convention. 'The developing jurisprudence of the Committee on the Rights of the Child is influenced by many factors. While the most significant of these factors is probably the nature of the information made available to the Committee, other factors include ... changes in child development theory'.[141]

7.1. SPECIFIC DEVELOPMENTAL DOMAINS

The child's physical development is probably the most obvious aspect of his or her development. It is highly related to problems of malnutrition and poverty. Other developmental domains are also related. UNICEF referred to this fact in its 2009 State of the World's Children report:

> Given the current global financial crisis, which has put the prosperity of future generations at risk, it is more relevant than ever to put children at the forefront of our partner relationships. History shows that children are especially vulnerable to recessions, as they are often removed from school to work or suffer malnutrition as food becomes scarce.
>
> This can have a permanent impact on children's development, with important future implications for society as a whole.[142]

140 Committee on the Rights of the Child, 'General Comment No. 5: General measures of implementation for the Convention on the Rights of the Child (arts. 4, 42 and 44, para. 6)', UN Doc. CRC/GC/2003/5 (27 November 2003), para. 12.

141 Obviously there are other issues that affect the Committee's interpretations and understandings. See, for instance, C.P. Cohen, and S. Kilbourne, 'Jurisprudence of the Committee on the Rights of the Child: A Guide for Research and Analysis' (1998) 19 *Michigan Journal of International Law* 633, 639–640.

142 L. Michel, 'The Ideal Gift', in UNICEF, 20 Years, The Convention on the Rights of the Child, p. 56 <www.unicef.org/rightsite/364_587.htm> accessed 13 April 2015.

Many children around the world still die from malnutrition. Back in 1990 the World Declaration on the Survival, Protection and Development of Children stated the huge number of children who die every day from malnutrition: 'Each day, 40,000 children die from malnutrition and disease, including acquired immunodeficiency syndrome (AIDS), from the lack of clean water and inadequate sanitation and from the effects of the drug problem.'[143] The Food and Agriculture Organization of the United Nations (FAO) states that: 'Countries in protracted crisis are characterized by high or very high levels of undernutrition and recurrent high levels of acute malnutrition (wasting, or low weight-for height). These limit the development of individuals and societies: undernutrition kills (contributing to a third of the 8.8 million annual child deaths worldwide'.[144] Children's development is also related to issues of housing and poverty.[145]

Furthermore, the right of the child to physical development has strong links with the right of the child to health. For young children, particularly those under eight years, physical development is highly dependent on the family and 'is best provided for within a small number of consistent, caring relationships. Typically, these relationships are with the combination of mother, father, siblings, grandparents and other members of the extended family, along with professional caregivers specialized in childcare and education.'[146]

Changes in the climate, as will be discussed in Chapter 6, also affect the child's physical development such as desertification and famine. Other affecting factors also include:

> access to clean drinking water, adequate sanitation, appropriate immunization, good nutrition and medical services, which are essential for young children's health, as is a stress-free environment. Malnutrition and disease have long-term impacts on children's physical health and development. They affect children's mental state, inhibiting learning and social participation and reducing prospects for realizing their potential. The same applies to obesity and unhealthy lifestyles...[147]

Physical development of the child is probably the most common domain of human development, although all of them are interrelated. Mental development, for instance, is 'the development of such abilities as perceiving, remembering, planning, evaluating others, and exchanging information'.[148] It varies from one

143 United Nations, 'World Declaration on the Survival, Protection and Development of the Child' (30 September 1990), para. 6.

144 Food and Agriculture Organization of the United Nations, 'The State of Food Insecurity in the World: Addressing food insecurity in protracted crises' (Rome, 2010), p. 33.

145 R. Hodgkin and P. Newell, *Implementation Handbook for the Convention on the Rights of the Child* (UNICEF, Geneva, 2007), pp. 398–401. See also UN General Assembly, 'United Nations Millennium Declaration', UN Doc. A/RES/55/2 (18 September 2000), para. 11.

146 Committee on the Rights of the Child, 'General Comment No. 7: Implementing Child Rights in Early Childhood', UN Doc. CRC/C/GC/7/Rev.1 (20 September 2006), para. 19.

147 *Ibid.*, para. 27(a).

148 P.Y. Hashima and S.P. Limber, 'An Adequate Standard of Living Necessary for Children's Cognitive (Mental) Development', in A.B. Andrews, and N.H. Kaufman (eds.), *Implementing*

child to another, depending on many things, including cultural experiences. Accordingly, it 'must be understood within the social context in which the child is embedded'.[149] This probably supports the argument for the importance of having proper understanding and consideration for the individuality of the State and the community concerned. This understanding should be made on bases that avoid stereotyping and judgemental approaches.

In its turn, mental development is important in achieving spiritual development. The ability to look, observe and think represents a very important aspect in achieving spiritual relief. The spiritual development of the child will help him or her to find answers for questions such as 'who created the sky?' and 'who created the earth?' Spiritual development represents an important aspect of a child's development, and even of an adult's development. Spiritual development is a lifelong process when taking into consideration that there are two aspects to a human being: a spiritual aspect and a material aspect.

It is important to emphasise that many aspects of the child's development are influenced by:

> Events in early life … the development of the brain's circuitry, the dynamic gene–environment interactions and the programming of the body's immune, neurological and endocrine systems. This has implications for subsequent trajectories of human development. Both the architecture of skills (coping abilities and cognitive and noncognitive competences) and the process of skill formation are strongly influenced by neural circuits that develop as a result of dynamic interactions between genes and early-life environments and experiences. In other words, the environment can affect individuals differently depending on their genetic endowments, and the same genetic endowment produces different outcomes depending on the environment … Studies from New Zealand and the United States have linked childhood abuse and other adversities.[150]

The social development of the child is very closely related to his or her ability to interact with others. For instance, participation of children is important for building democracy and other participatory forms of governance. A democratic society is one of the conditions that the State needs to create in order to ensure the survival and development of the child.[151] Social development covers a wide range of issues, such as the fight against poverty

---

the U.N. Convention on the Rights of the Child: A Standard of Living Adequate for Development (Praeger Publishers, Westport, 1999), p. 69.

149 *Ibid.*, p. 69.

150 United Nations Development Programme (UNDP), Human Development Report 'Sustaining Human Progress: Reducing Vulnerabilities and Building Resilience' (New York, 2014), pp. 57–58.

151 M.G. Flekkøy and N.H. Kaufman, 'The Social Development of the Child', in A.B. Andrews and N.H. Kaufman (eds.), *Implementing the U.N. Convention on the Rights of the Child: A Standard of Living Adequate for Development* (Praeger Publishers, Westport, 1999), p. 117.

and children's education. Children have the right to enjoy social development and to contribute to it. Arguably, social development can be achieved in two main ways. The first is by focusing on children themselves and the way they interact and participate in the society through a number of participation rights that the Convention on the Rights of the Child includes. In this context, children have to learn the rules, methods and norms of interaction. Some arguments in this regard are:

> Social development assumes that certainties within society are of special importance. Among these are the relationship values necessary for building democracy. Therefore, sustaining positive social development includes learning democracy. Since democracy requires participation from all members of society who exercise critical and creative thinking, the participation rights are highly significant...[152]

Article 8(2) of the 1986 Declaration on the Right to Development also emphasises the importance of participation for the realisation of children's rights: 'States should encourage popular participation in all spheres as an important factor in development and in the full realization of all human rights.'

The second way to achieve social development is by focusing on the identification and the creation, on the basis of what has been identified, of an environment and conditions that are suitable for its achievement. In this context, the achievement of social development requires article 6(2) to be placed under different headings and not only under the heading 'Basic Health and Welfare Rights'. Arguably, the right of the child to survival and development can sit very well under the heading 'Civil Rights and Freedoms', which is one of the clusters that the Committee made in its guidelines.[153] It is even possible to argue that in addition to the child's social development, other aspects of development require this as well. This will be discussed in more detail later in the chapter.

However, a pressing question that could be asked in this context is about the economic development of the child. Why didn't the Committee include the

---

152 *Ibid.*

153 The Committee adopted its first guidelines in 1991 see Committee on the Rights of the Child, 'General guidelines regarding the form and content of initial reports to be submitted by States parties under article 44, paragraph 1 (a), of the Convention', UN Doc. (CRC/C/5) (30 October 1991). Committee on the Rights of the Child, 'General guidelines regarding the form and contents of periodic reports to be submitted by States Parties under article 44, paragraph 1 (b), of the Convention', UN Doc. UN/CRC/58/ (20 November 1996); Committee on the Rights of the Child, 'General guidelines regarding the form and content of periodic reports', UN Doc. CRC/C/58/Rev.1 (29 November 2005); and Committee on the Rights of the Child, 'Treaty-specific guidelines regarding the form and content of periodic reports to be submitted by States parties under article 44, paragraph 1 (b), of the Convention on the Rights of the Child', UN Doc. CRC/58/Rev.2 (23 November 2010).

child's economic development as an aspect of development? The same could also be asked with regard to the child's cultural development.

7.2. INTERACTION BETWEEN ARTICLE 6(2) AND HUMAN DEVELOPMENT

The definition of human development is influenced by the context under consideration. In a political and economic setting, for example, human development is related to stability, security, prosperity, prevention of poverty, and allocation of budgetary resources. In a legal context, human development is involved with the prevention of juvenile delinquency and so on. The wording of article 6(2) does not indicate that the human development of the child should be viewed from the perspective of psychological development only, for instance. Human development is expected to be at the centre of the developmental process of any country.

In the Convention on the Rights of the Child, references to the child's development have been made more than once. The term 'development' has been explained by reference to particular aspects of the child's development. For instance, article 27(1) explicitly states that 'States Parties recognize the right of every child to a standard of living adequate for the child's physical, mental, spiritual and moral development.' Article 23(3) speaks about the 'individual development of the child'. But references to the child's development appear in four places in the CRC without any specifications or indications to any aspect of development, namely it appears once in article 6(2), twice in article 18(1), and once in article 27(2). Article 6(2) focuses mainly on the responsibility of States Parties to create measures and conditions necessary for the child's development. Contrary to the focus of article 6(2), both articles 18(1) and 27(2) speak explicitly about the responsibility of the parents or the guardians to provide for the development of the child. Obviously, the capability of the individuals, i.e. parents, is very limited when compared to that of the State. This suggests that the term 'development' in article 6(2) refers to the right of the child to human development in a broad sense and in various settings. These various settings should be consistent with the high abilities of the States. The term development in article 6(2) should be viewed in political, social, economic, administrative and environmental settings, etc. as this is the nature and spectrum of the State responsibility. State responsibility is varied because the State can offer different, varied and large-scale solutions. For instance, in a political setting, the right of the child to mental or social development requires the State to provide a stable, democratic, or other participatory form of governance, and a secure environment to protect the right of the child to this aspect of development.

7.3. DIFFERENCE BETWEEN THE RIGHT TO DEVELOPMENT UNDER ARTICLE 6(2) AND OTHER CRC PROVISIONS

However, as regards the question posed as to why the Committee decided to put the right of the child to survival and development under the heading 'Basic Health and Welfare Rights', it could be argued that, in addition to the child development theories, the vision of the Committee can be attributed mainly to the existence of the right to survival in the same article with the right to development. The right of the child to survival, basically, is strongly linked to the right of the child to growth monitoring, oral rehydration and disease control, breastfeeding, immunisation, child spacing, food and female literacy.[154] In fact, during the drafting of the Convention, India, which submitted the formal proposal for the inclusion of article 6(2) in the Convention strongly argued 'that the concept of development was necessary to reinforce the notion of survival.'[155] It is probable that when the Committee started its work back in 1991, its vision for the interpretation of article 6(2) was not far from that of the Indian delegation. Arguably, it did not want to break the originally established link between the two concepts and, therefore, classified article 6(2) on the basis of the meaning of the right to survival. This will probably justify the implicit interpretation that links the right of the child to development to the right to education; a possible reason for this could be female literacy, which is linked to the right to survival.[156] The Committee's broad definition of the term 'development' represents a basic reference in the matter, but this does not mean that the adoption of a broader, yet positive, definition is blocked. Still, human rights norms are subject to both dynamic interpretation and teleological interpretation.[157] In fact, even literal interpretation favours a broader reading of the provision, because the text of article 6(2) is broadly designed. As an example, the Committee's recommendations include a reference to the special needs of the particular categories of children. In its general comment on adolescents' health, the Committee stated that the reason for issuing the comment was that adolescents need special recognition and attention from the States. The Committee also indirectly reminded States Parties of their obligations in terms of the interpretation and the implementation of the right to development in its

---

154 UN Doc. E/CN.4/1989/48 (2 March 1989), para. 88, available in Office of the High Commissioner for Human Rights, *Legislative History of the Convention on the Rights of the Child*, Volume I (United Nations, New York, 2007), p. 367.

155 G. Van Bueren, *The International Law on the Rights of the Child* (Martinus Nijhoff Publishers, The Hague, 1998), p. 293.

156 The beginnings of the child survival and development revolution, which UNICEF initiated in the early 1980s, started with the notion of survival only – after that, the notion of development was added. See UNICEF, 'The State of the World's Children 1996' (online version), available at <www.unicef.org/sowc/1980s.htm> accessed 23 April 2015.

157 The interpretation of human rights norms under the international conventions is a broad topic and is subject to a number of factors.

broadest sense. The Committee's approach in this regard is motivated by the special needs of adolescents. To illustrate, the right to development in its broadest sense is not limited to adolescents: it is a right that the Convention guarantees to all children. The State Party therefore holds this obligation towards all children. The obligation of the States Parties to give particular attention to the needs of adolescents provides a broad definition to the concept of development. Another example of a dynamic and an evolving interpretation is when the Committee adds new standard factors to the term development, such as 'positive development'. The Committee has referred to the concept of positive development of girls in relation to the production of animated cartoon characters, such as Sara in Tanzania.[158] Although the Committee has provided no clarifications as to what it could possibly mean, it is probably generally related, in this context, to gender equalities. In this context, it is important to say that the Committee uses the method of the holistic approach for the implementation of the Convention and the classification of article 6(2) as a general principle in order to broaden the scope of the child's survival and development.

8. LEGAL AND CONCEPTUAL RESULTS OF CLUSTERING ARTICLE 6(2) AS AN ECONOMIC AND SOCIAL RIGHT OF THE CHILD

8.1. LEGAL RESULTS

The third question that the chapter poses is about the results of the recommendations that the Committee chose to adopt with regard to article 6(2). In a rights-based approach context, what are the results of classifying article 6(2) under the heading 'Basic Health and Welfare Rights'? This question focuses on the conceptual and implementation results of classifying article 6(2) as an economic and social right of the child. There are two main effects, one is related to the legal status of article 6(2) and the other is related to the concept of development.

Within the Convention on the Rights of the Child, the legal status of economic, social and cultural rights is governed by article 4 of the CRC, which reads:

> States Parties shall undertake all appropriate legislative, administrative, and other measures for the implementation of the rights recognized in the present Convention. With regard to economic, social and cultural rights, States Parties shall undertake such measures to the maximum extent of their available resources and, where needed, within the framework of international co-operation.

158 Committee on the Rights of the Child, 'Concluding Observations: Tanzania's Initial Report', UN Doc. CRC/C/15/Add.156 (9 July 2001), para. 20.

This provision represents a step towards the strengthening of the legal capacity and implementation of economic and social rights of the child under the CRC. The article explicitly recognises the possible financial incapability of some States Parties to fulfil the required standards to realise this type of rights; therefore, it requires the States Parties to implement the article to the maximum extent possible. Later, in its General Comment No. 5, the Committee confirmed the equal importance of economic and social rights and civil and political rights, by stating that both types of rights are justiciable: 'the Committee emphasizes that economic, social and cultural rights, as well as civil and political rights, must be regarded as justiciable. It is essential that domestic law sets out entitlements in sufficient detail to enable remedies for non-compliance to be effective.'[159] In addition, the Committee often stresses the holistic approach as regards the implementation of all the articles of the Convention. All of these efforts have their positive effects as regards the legal status of the economic, social and cultural rights in the CRC, including article 6(2) in its capacity as a health and welfare right.

However, the question remains as to what the effects of the Committee's association between ESR and article 6(2) are on the legal status of article 6(2). Is article 6(2) on the right of the child to survival and development justiciable? Is it justiciable on its own or is it dependant on another right such as the right to health for example? In relation to the level of State Party obligation, it is obvious that article 6(2) uses stronger language than article 24, which is classified by the Committee as a basic health and welfare right. Under the Convention of the Rights of the Child, and probably under the other international human rights documents, the wording of the text reflects the level of the State Party's obligation. It is true that once the State has ratified or acceded to the Convention, it is then under a legal obligation to fulfil the particular obligations of each individual article. In this context, the important point is that not all of the articles require the same level of responsibility. Arguably, the wording of some economic and social rights imposes a lesser degree or level of responsibility, with regard to the immediateness of the realisation. However, States Parties are obliged to take immediate steps to initiate their actions towards the full implementation of ESR; which are generally, implemented progressively.[160] Literally, when applying this understanding to article 6(2), on the basis of the Committee's classification, this suggests that the survival and development of the child should be progressively implemented. It is true that the Committee avoided this kind of reading by stating that the Convention should be implemented using a holistic approach and that article 6(2) is actually a general

159 Committee on the Rights of the Child, 'General Comment No. 5: General measures of implementation for the Convention on the Rights of the Child (arts. 4, 42 and 44, para. 6)', UN Doc. CRC/GC/2003/5 (27 November 2003), para. 25; see also para. 6.

160 The Committee on Economic, Social and Cultural Rights has pointed out that some aspects of the State obligations require immediate implementation.

principle of the Convention. This, however, does not stop the issues as regards, for example, how the State Party can progressively implement the right of the child to breastfeeding.

Furthermore, not all of the economic and social rights share the same level of State Party responsibility either. Article 6(2), assuming that it is an economic and social right, for instance uses a stronger language than that of articles 24 or 23. The State Party under article 6(2) is obliged to ensure while under article 24 it is obliged to recognise only. In this context, and from the legal status perspective, the Committee on the Rights of the Child's merging of article 6(2) and article 24 does not have a visible positive effect on the legal status of the article. As Ksentini explains, article 24 is not one of the stronger articles of the CRC:

> States do not recognize the right of the child to health, but the right of the child to the enjoyment of the highest attainable standard of health. They do not guarantee the child right of access to medical treatment and rehabilitation services, but undertake to 'strive to ensure' that no child is deprived of his or her right of access to health care services.[161]

Based on this, it is possible to argue that the theoretical interpretation of article 6(2) by the Committee, which links it to the ESR, does not clearly strengthen the legal position of the article. In essence, the wording of article 24(4) explicitly reconfirms that its realisation is highly dependent on international cooperation: 'States Parties undertake to promote and encourage international co-operation with a view to achieving progressively the full realization of the right recognized in the present article. In this regard, particular account shall be taken of the needs of developing countries.' Under the CRC, international cooperation is compulsory for both donor and recipient States. The first part of article 4, which is applied to all provisions in the Convention, uses a strong word as regards the level of the State Party's obligation. The word 'undertake' is stronger than the word 'recognize' because it requires positive action: 'The obligation to undertake the measure is of immediate application and cannot be deferred until a more propitious moment. Moreover, the obligation is not subject to the availability of resources'.[162] The pressing and immediate nature of the word undertake made the drafters of article 4 exempt the State Party from this prompt implementation of economic and social rights by adding the condition 'to the maximum extent of their available resources'. However, the obligation to implement the economic and

---

161 F.Z. Ksentini, 'The Convention on the Rights of the Child: norms for protection and an instrument of co-operation for the survival, development and well-being of the child' (1992) 91/2 *Bulletin of Human Rights* 43, 49.

162 P. Alston, 'The legal framework of the Convention on the Rights of the Child' (1992) 91/2 *Bulletin of Human Rights* 1, 10.

social rights through international cooperation is a prompt one but puts the realisation of the rights under the authority of international cooperation.

8.2. CONCEPTUAL RESULTS

The other result of the Committee's grouping of article 6(2) with the basic health and welfare right of the child is related to the scope and definition of the right to development. There is no doubt that the interpretation of article 6(2) by the Committee has broadened the concept of the right of the child to development. The direct link with some other rights has led to the expansion of the meaning of the word 'development': for example the general setting of the right to health as regards the overall concept of development. To elucidate, in 1979, the United Nations General Assembly adopted a resolution entitled 'Health as an Integral Part of Development'.[163] In this resolution, the General Assembly endorsed the concepts of primary health that were adopted in the 1978 Alma Ata Declaration. The important point is that the General Assembly confirmed in this resolution that health and the right to health should be seen as part of the overall concept of development, particularly social and economic development. The relationship between the right to health or the right to healthy development and the overall concept of development has been confirmed by members of the Committee on different occasions as well. For instance, in her statement at the World Summit for Population and Development as early as 1994, Hoda Badran, the former president of the Committee on the Rights of the Child, pointed out this relationship:

> In terms of the linkage between children's state of well being and development it is an indisputable healthy childhood leads to healthy productive adulthood which is a basic requirements for societal development.
>
> As well stated in a recent publication 'respect for and protection of children's rights is the starting point for the full development of the individual's potential in an atmosphere of freedom, dignity and justice'.[164]

In this context, it can be argued that article 6(2) does not just include a single individual right. In fact, article 6(2) has been elaborated so as to include other articles within it as well. In doing this, the Committee was guided by its own interpretations as regards the meaning of the word development.

---

163 United Nation General Assembly, 'Health as an integral part of development' (29 November 1979) UN Doc. A/RES/34/58.

164 Statement delivered by Hoda Badran, the former Chairperson of the Committee on the Rights of the Child at the International Conference on Population and Development (ICPD) in Cairo, Egypt (7 September 1994).

9. POSSIBILITY OF OTHER CLASSIFICATIONS OF ARTICLE 6(2)

9.1. RIGHT TO DEVELOPMENT

Although the Committee has classified article 6(2) as a basic health and welfare right, it has relied on the holistic approach to widen the scope of article 6(2). This is a technique that the Committee uses towards the implementation of all the articles of the Convention. However, the question arises as to whether article 6(2), separately, and without depending on the holistic approach, could be classified and associated with other kinds of rights? This depends on the understanding and interpretations that could be given to the concept of 'right-based approach to survival' and 'right-based approach to development'. Is there a possibility of classifying article 6(2) under other headings? The question aims at understanding if there is another dimension to article 6(2) in addition to the one that the Committee already gave.

Initially, it is worth mentioning that the Committee itself stated that article 6(2) includes aspects of civil and political rights:

> Article 4, while reflecting States parties' overall implementation obligation, suggests a distinction between civil and political rights and economic, social and cultural rights in its second sentence ... There is no simple or authoritative division of human rights in general or of Convention rights into the two categories. The Committee's reporting guidelines group articles 7, 8, 13–17 and 37 (a) under the heading 'Civil rights and freedoms', but indicate by the context that these are not the only civil and political rights in the Convention. *Indeed, it is clear that many other articles, including articles 2, 3, 6 and 12 of the Convention, contain elements which constitute civil/political rights,* thus reflecting the interdependence and indivisibility of all human rights. Enjoyment of economic, social and cultural rights is inextricably intertwined with enjoyment of civil and political rights.[165]

In her argument for extra-territorial obligations of the State, Skogly has explained the value added by having a rights-based approach to development:

> Thus, the value added by the right to development as a human right is twofold: first there is a right to a process that aims towards the complete and comprehensive fulfilment of all human rights as guaranteed through the International Bill of Rights;

---

165 Committee on the Rights of the Child, 'General Comment No. 5: General measures of implementation for the Convention on the Rights of the Child (arts. 4, 42 and 44, para. 6)', UN Doc. CRC/GC/2003/5 (27 November 2003), para. 6 (emphasis added). The Committee also made a link between article 6 and the right of the child to identity under the heading civil and political rights when speaking about 'baby boxes' in: Committee on the Rights of the Child, 'Concluding Observations on the Second Periodic Report of the Holy See', UN Doc. CRC/C/VAT/CO/2 (25 February 2014), para. 36.

and that the quality of 'development' is evaluated by focusing on the human rights effects of the development process.[166]

When applying Skogly's understanding to article 6(2) one can possibly say, firstly, that there is a right to a process that aims towards the complete and comprehensive fulfilment of all the rights of the child as guaranteed by the CRC. Is it possible, then, in this context, to say that the right of the child to development under article 6(2) means that the child has a right to the existence of conditions such as political freedoms, economic facilities, social opportunities, transparency guarantees and protective security?[167] In addition, it is important to emphasise that the child has such a right on the basis of article 6(2) only and not through the holistic approach.

Secondly, one can say that the quality of development is evaluated by focusing on the child rights effects of the development process. This means that there is a relationship between the concept of the overall development of the State and the concept of human development as guaranteed by article 6(2). For instance, as the Arab human development report points out in relation to the Arab countries, this means that the basic priority for policy is 'to create a virtuous cycle whereby economic growth promotes human development and human development in turn promotes economic growth.'[168] Human development is both a process and an outcome. It is concerned with the process through which choices are enlarged, but it also focuses on the outcomes of enhanced choices. Human development thus represents an equation, the left-hand side of which reflects human capabilities, and the right-hand side economic, political and social opportunities to use those capabilities.[169] 'In the ultimate analysis, human development is development of the people, development for the people, and development by the people.'[170] In this context, is it possible to formulate the same relationship between the concept of the child's human development in article 6(2) and the overall development of the State? And, if so, how can the State make use of the capabilities of children? Based on the Arab Human Development Report, development of the people involves building human capabilities through the development of human resources. Development for the people implies that the benefits of growth must be translated into the lives of people, and development by the people emphasises that people must be able

166 S. Skogly, *Beyond National Borders: States' Human Rights Obligations in International Cooperation* (Intersentia, Antwerp, 2006), p. 138 (footnote omitted).

167 These are conditions that are identified in the Arab Human Development Report, that are, for empirical purposes, expected to suit the nature of the Arab world and lead to the enhancement of the well-being of the population of the Arab world, United Nations Development Programme (UNDP), *Arab Human Development Report 2002: 'Creating Opportunities for Future Generations'* (UNDP, New York, 2002), p. 19.

168 *Ibid.*, p. 13.

169 *Ibid.*, p. 15.

170 *Ibid.*, p. 16.

to participate actively in influencing the processes that shape their lives.[171] But it could be argued that participation by children in shaping the processes that shape their lives is somehow limited. This is somehow true in relation to voting, for example (although some countries allow for children at the age of 16 and 17 to vote). Otherwise, the CRC opens the door for children to participate in processes that shape their lives. In his Statement to the UN Conference on Population and Development in 1994, James Grant confirmed that the concept of development includes participation of people in the development process: 'If it is to be sustainable today, development must not only produce economic growth, sustainable in the environmental sense. It also must be sustainable in a human sense – it must break the grip of poverty on the bottom half or third of society and slow population growth, while sustaining democracy, human rights, people's participation in the development process and peace.'[172] In addition, UNICEF, in its Mission Statement, explicitly confirms its commitment to a gendered-based approach to the participation of women and girls: 'UNICEF aims, through its country programmes, to promote the equal rights of women and girls and to support their full participation in the political, social, and economic development of their communities.'[173] Convictions about the importance of youth participation continue to grow. For development to have its effects on children's rights, and vice versa, youth participation is important. As concerned forums are now speaking about the post-2015 Development Agenda, youth participation in governance, for instance, is important:

> Youth concerns are critical for the post-2015 agenda: Given that young people are the leaders of the future and the primary beneficiaries and inheritors of ongoing inter-generational challenges, they must be involved in the design and ownership of a new development agenda. They need to be involved in policy shifts towards green technologies and environmentally-efficient modes of development, as well as in a growing focus on opportunities for employment, innovation and shared wealth-creation for the next and successive generations.[174]

The Arab Human Development Report also explains the importance of the human development approach to the development of the State:

> The human development concept is broader than other people-oriented approaches to development. Human-resource development emphasizes only human capital and treats human beings as an input in the development process, but not as its

171 *Ibid.*, p. 16.

172 James P. Grant, Statement of UNICEF at the International Conference on Population and Development, Cairo (6 September 1994), available at: <www.un.org/popin/icpd/conference/una/940907130633.html> accessed 13 April 2015.

173 'UNICEF's mission statement', available at: <www.unicef.org/about/who/index_mission.html> accessed 24 April 2015.

174 Available at: <https://www.worldwewant2015.org/node/361674> accessed 28 April 2015.

> beneficiaries. The basic-needs approach focuses on minimum requirements of human beings, but not on their choices. The human-welfare approach looks at people as recipients, but not as active participants in the processes that shape their lives. Human development, by encompassing all these aspects, represents a more holistic approach to development.[175]

The question remains as to whether the same formulation can be made with regard to article 6(2) separately, i.e., without depending on the holistic approach. In the author's view, article 6(2) on the right of the child to survival can provide for this separately, and without dependence on the holistic approach. This is in fact one of the values added for having a separate right on the right of the child to survival and development.

9.2. THE HOLISTIC APPROACH

The following is a brief explanation as to the way in which the Committee implements the holistic approach.

In its general comment on adolescents' health, for instance, the Committee on the Rights of the Child states that in order for the child to develop, he or she needs more than the right to health:

> The Committee understands the concepts of 'health and development' more broadly than being strictly limited to the provisions defined in articles 6 (right to life, survival and development) and 24 (right to health) ... One of the aims of this general comment is precisely to identify the main human rights that need to be promoted and protected in order to ensure that adolescents do enjoy the highest attainable standard of health, develop in a well-balanced manner, and are adequately prepared to enter adulthood and assume a constructive role in their communities and in society at large. This general comment should be read in conjunction with the Convention and its two Optional Protocols ... as well as other relevant international human rights norms and standards.[176]

The Committee has also confirmed the link with the right of the child to participation in order to achieve adolescents' health and development and participation as an integral part of the right of the child to development. Participation includes the right of the child to express his or her own views freely and have them duly taken into account; and the Committee considers it

---

175 United Nations Development Programme (UNDP), *Arab Human Development Report 2002: Creating Opportunities for Future Generations* (UNDP, New York, 2002), p. 17.

176 Committee on the Rights of the Child, 'General Comment No. 4: Adolescent health and development in the context of the Convention on the Rights of the Child', UN Doc. CRC/GC/2003/4 (1 July 2003), para. 4.

fundamental in realising adolescents' right to health and development. States Parties are obliged to ensure that adolescents are given a genuine chance to express their views freely on all matters affecting them, especially within the family, in school, and in their communities. States have to create the appropriate environment to allow for this, and to ensure that adolescents are able to safely and properly exercise this right. Furthermore, States Parties have to ensure that public authorities, parents and other adults working with children 'create an environment based on trust, information-sharing, the capacity to listen and sound guidance that is conducive to adolescents participating equally, including in decision-making processes.'[177]

The above examples show that the Committee considers the holistic approach to the implementation of the entire Convention is crucial in connecting the articles of the Convention together. All of the articles of the Convention are interrelated.[178] The holistic approach has made it possible for the Committee to link article 6 with other rights of the child, such as the civil and political rights of the child.

In its general guidelines regarding the form and contents of the periodic report, the Committee has identified the rights contained in articles 7, 8, 13–17 and 37(a) as being concerned with civil rights and freedoms. It has made links with article 24, on the right to health, and the civil and political rights of the child when it spoke about adolescents' health:

> The Convention defines the civil rights and freedoms of children and adolescents in its articles 13 to 17. These are fundamental in guaranteeing the right to health and development of adolescents. Article 17 states that the child has the right to 'access information and material from a diversity of national and international sources, especially those aimed at the promotion of his or her social, spiritual and moral well-being and physical and mental health'. 'The right of adolescents to access appropriate information is crucial if States parties are to promote cost-effective measures, including through laws, policies and programmes, with regard to numerous health related situations...'[179]

In order to promote the health and development of adolescents, the Committee also encourages States Parties to respect their right to privacy and confidentiality, including respect to advice and counselling on health matters (article 16). According to the Committee, health-care providers have an obligation to keep medical information concerning adolescents confidential, bearing in mind the basic principles of the Convention. Such information may only be disclosed with

177 *Ibid.*, para. 8.

178 See for instance D. Barrett and P.E. Veerman, *Article 33 Protection of Children from Narcotic Drugs and Psychotropic Substances* (Martinus Nijhoff Publishers, Leiden, 2012), para. 102.

179 Committee on the Rights of the Child, 'General Comment No. 4: Adolescent health and development in the context of the Convention on the Rights of the Child', UN Doc. CRC/GC/2003/4 (1 July 2003), para. 10.

the consent of the adolescent, or in the same situations applying to the violation of an adult's confidentiality. The Committee also states that: 'Adolescents deemed mature enough to receive counselling without the presence of a parent or other person are entitled to privacy and may request confidential services, including treatment.'[180]

Also, as a general principle, the Committee has linked article 6(2) to various other rights of the child. In its Concluding Observations on France's initial report, the Committee made a link between the general principles and articles 7, 9, 10 and 22. In this regard, the Committee was concerned about the new laws (at that time) on nationality and the entry and residence of foreigners, refugees and asylum-seekers, as well as family reunification. Of concern was how such legislation would affect the enjoyment of the rights of the child, particularly those in articles 7, 9, 10 and 22, taking into due account the general principles of the Convention.[181]

The Committee has also made an indirect reference to the right of the child to development, in its capacity as a general principle, with respect to juvenile justice. For instance, in its concluding observations on Kyrgyzstan's second periodic report, the Committee recommended that the State Party should ensure that the 'Akzakal Courts (Elders' Courts), when dealing with children in conflict with the law, fully apply the principles and provisions of the Convention'.[182] The principles of the Convention include the right of the child to survival and development because article 6(2) is one of the four general principles of the Convention and because the Committee adopts a holistic approach to the implementation of the Convention.

The Committee has also made references in some cases to the link between the articles on family environment and alternative care. In the Concluding Observations on Albania's report, it stated: 'The Committee is concerned that family reunification procedures may not always be dealt with in a manner consistent with the general principles (arts. 2, 3, 6 and 12)'.[183] The articles on family environment and alternative care are articles 5, 18 (paras. 1–2), 9–11, 19–21, 25, and 27 (paras. 4 and 39). However, these links were mainly made with article 6 in its capacity as a general principle.

In some cases, the Committee has created a relationship between article 6(2) and article 7, which is concerned with the registration of births. In its

180 Committee on the Rights of the Child, 'General Comment No. 4: Adolescent health and development in the context of the Convention on the Rights of the Child', UN Doc. CRC/GC/2003/4 (1 July 2003), para. 11.

181 Committee on the Rights of the Child, 'Concluding Observations: France's Initial Report', UN Doc. CRC/C/15/Add.20 (25 April 1994), para. 25.

182 Committee on the Rights of the Child, 'Concluding Observations: Kyrgyzstan's Second Periodic Report', UN Doc. CRC/C/15/Add.244 (3 November 2004), para. 67(f).

183 Committee on the Rights of the Child 'Concluding Observation on Albania's Initial Report', UN Doc. CRC/C/15/Add.249 (31 March 2005), para. 42.

Concluding Observations on Angola's initial report, the Committee pointed out this relationship when it mentioned that the registration of children at birth should be made by the government at the National Forum on Early Childhood Care and Development in June 2004. Children who are not registered at birth can be at risk due to inaccessibility to health services and education, and that can seriously affect their development.[184] In this context the Committee is taking into consideration the child's individual interest.

The holistic approach to article 6(2) and the context of the collective approach to the articles of the Convention require that all articles be dealt with together and not individually. However, this approach, while it strengthens the article and expands its context, may in some cases jeopardise its independence. This in fact might suggest that if the other articles, such as the right to health, are not properly or fully implemented, then the same will apply to the right of the child to development under article 6(2).

9.3. RIGHT TO DEVELOPMENT ASPECTS OF ARTICLE 6(2)

In a related context, questions may be raised on the relationship between the right of the child to development and the 'right to development'. One narrow aspect of the right to development is to deal with it through the framework of social and economic rights. Realisation of the right to development requires the implementation of the whole set of human rights. In this respect, the link that the Committee made with economic and social rights is one aspect of the right of the child to development. The 'right to development' requires the implementation of the civil and political rights of the child as well.[185] The Committee tried to compensate for this aspect of the right to development by stating that article 6(2) is a general principle of the Convention. In fact, as will be seen in Chapter 3, the wording of article 6(2) as a general principle, if misunderstood, may jeopardise the importance and independence of article 6(2). Tatjana Ansbach, when speaking about the interrelationship between the right to development and the other human rights, has argued that: 'The right to development is a human right itself; and it differs a lot from other human rights by virtue of its nature.'[186] The right to economic development is an aspect that has not been mentioned in the Committee's scope of the term development. Van Bueren, for instance, refers to the right to development and article 6(2) by stating that, with regard to article 6(2), the right to development is a dynamic

---

184 Committee on the Rights of the Child 'Concluding Observations: Angola's Initial Report', UN Doc. CRC/C/15/Add.246 (3 November 2004), paras. 26 and 27.

185 T. Ansbach, 'Peoples and Individuals As Subjects of the Right to Development', in S.R. Chowdhury, E.M.G. Denters, P.J.I.M. De Waart (eds.), *The Right to Development in International Law* (Law Research Institute, Calcutta, 1992), pp. 161–163.

186 *Ibid.*, p. 161.

concept.[187] Arguably, the reason for the adoption of article 6(2) in the CRC can largely be attributed to concerns about the influence of poverty on the general condition of children. Children in developing countries are considered the main victims of poverty. The State poverty of a big number of developing countries could be decreased by a number of factors, such as debt release, good governance and equal opportunities, and reducing spending on arming.[188] These concerns need to be visibly reflected in the definition of the word development under article 6(2).

In addition to being a quality-control factor, the right to development is also an empowering right for the less-privileged sectors of some societies, such as women and children. Article 3 of the Convention on the Elimination of All Forms of Discrimination against Women, for example, guarantees the right of women to development and empowers them:

> States parties shall take in all fields, in particular in the political, social, economic and cultural fields, all appropriate measures, including legislation, to ensure the full development and advancement of women, for the purpose of guaranteeing them the exercise and enjoyment of human rights and fundamental freedoms on a basis of equality with men.

The right to development empowers children. It is very significant that the right guaranteed under article 6(2) is not the right of the child to survival and growth, because the concept of growth is different from that of development. Development conveys quality, which leads to empowerment.[189]

In addition to being classified as a basic health and welfare right, it is also possible to argue that article 6(2) could be classified as a quality-control factor or right. During the drafting of article 6(2), the representative of India argued for the inclusion of the words 'survival' and 'development'. He believed that the right to survival and development would complement the right to life, which is guaranteed in article 6(1). LeBlanc summarises what is going on with article 6(2) in terms of practice, according to the Indian delegation who 'believed that if the convention affirmed that the right to life and the right to survival were "complementary and not mutually exclusive," many problems affecting children,

---

187 G. Van Bueren, *The International Law on the Rights of the Child* (Martinus Nijhoff Publishers, The Hague, 1998), p. 293.

188 These were, mainly, the factors of concern that led to the initiation of the child survival and development revolution that UNICEF was advocating when leading the lobbying and working for the inclusion of article 6(2) in the CRC. See UNICEF, 'The State of the World's Children 1996' (online version) <www.unicef.org/sowc96/> (accessed 10 December 2014). See also M. Black, *Children First: The Story of UNICEF, Past and Present* (Oxford University Press, Oxford, 1996), p. 13.

189 See UN Doc. E/CN.4/1988/28; and E/CN.4/1989/48, paras. 86–91, available in Office of the High Commissioner for Human Rights, *Legislative History of the Convention on the Rights of the Child*, Volume I (United Nations, New York, 2007), pp. 364–367.

such as infant mortality, could be attacked'.[190] The link between the right to life and the right to survival and development was highlighted during the drafting of the CRC. In other words, this means that the link was highlighted as far as the theoretical part of the CRC is concerned. This theoretical understanding suggests that, in cases of children's rights, the right to life needs a quality monitor, which is represented by the right to survival and development. In addition to staying alive, children need a quality factor to their lives. This quality factor is represented in terms of the survival rights in giving children immunisation, breastfeeding, growth monitoring and oral rehydration. In terms of the right to development, the Committee's definition and the direct link with economic and social rights made issues such as health, the rights of the disabled, social benefits and standard of living the factors that will determine whether the factor of quality has been added to the child's life. The question, in this context, should be: what are the other quality factors that can be added? Participation is essential; a child also needs a life where he or she can participate. This means that this link should be highlighted and reflected in practice as well. As LeBlanc asks, 'How is the survival and development of the child to be realized?'[191]

10. CONCLUSION

It is important to study the recommendations of the Committee on the Rights of the Child on article 6(2) as they stand as one of the current important interpretations of the article. The clustering that the Committee made to the substantive articles of the Convention on the Rights of the Child clearly classifies article 6(2) as a disability, basic health and welfare right of the child. The definition that the Committee on the Rights of the Child gives to the term 'development', which is mentioned in article 6(2) is significant. In this regard, the Committee mentioned a number of developmental aspects through which the term development can be defined. These developmental aspects are mainly concerned with the concept of human development. However, it is important to question why the Committee's development aspects do not refer to other aspects of human development such as the economic development of the child or the cultural development of the child.

The Committee states that all ESR and civil and political rights under the CRC are justiciable. The important question, however, that remains is whether article 6(2) is justiciable on its own or is it dependant on another right. The link that the Committee made with basic health and welfare rights, which are mainly economic and social rights, puts article 6(2) on the same level of legal status as

190 L.J. LeBlanc, *The Convention on the Rights of the Child: United Nations Law making on Human Rights* (University of Nebraska Press, Lincoln, 1995), p. 77.

191 *Ibid.*, p. 78.

these articles. Although article 4 of the CRC guarantees a high legal status for the economic and social rights of the child, this classification does not add much to the legal status of article 6(2). Nevertheless, the clustering expands on the definition of article 6(2).

Furthermore, the holistic approach to the articles of the Convention that the Committee has adopted also expands the definition of the word development. Accordingly, the Committee linked the right to development to some civil and political rights of the child, such as the right to registration at birth. The holistic approach, in addition to other factors, may strengthen the legal position of article 6(2). Neverheless, the holistic approach may affect the independence and the dynamic conceptual evolution of the right of the child to survival and development.

Generally speaking, the discussion in this chapter is based on the understanding that the way article 6(2) stands within the Convention on the Rights of the Child enables for a comprehensive interpretation of the article. This overall interpretation of article 6(2) would have its effects on the implementation and realisation of the right to survival and development. Associating the article with basic health and welfare rights should be done in a way that does not prevent the right to survival and development from being associated with other rights. The relaxed wording of article 6(2), in addition to the dynamic interpretation of the Convention on the Rights of the Child, allow for future expansions of the interpretations of article 6(2), such as using the article as a quality-measuring factor.

Article 6(2) is unique. The way it stands within the Convention on the Rights of the Child opens the door for having a very wide interpretation. This makes it legitimate enough to classify article 6(2) as the right of the child to 'everything'.[192] This includes the international right to development. Under article 6(2) of the CRC, States Parties shall ensure to the maximum extent possible the right of the child to 'everything'. This is discussed in further details in Chapters 5 and 6.

The chapter also highlights the important link between the right to development and other individual children's rights such as the right to health and the right to education. However, it emphasis also that the right to development and survival is separate and independent from other children rights. Moreover, it brings into focus the added value of a separate formulation of a right of children to development, over many more specific provisions on children's rights.

---

192 Description by Benyam Dawit Mezmur, the Vice-Chairperson of the Committee on the Rights of the Child, in a Lecture at the Children's Rights Summer School, Nottingham, United Kingdom, June 2013.

CHAPTER 3

THE NATURE OF ARTICLE 6(2) ON THE SURVIVAL AND DEVELOPMENT OF THE CHILD

1. INTRODUCTION

This chapter attempts to discuss the nature of article 6(2) on the survival and development of the child. Article 6(2) has been identified by many as a general principle of the Convention on the Rights of the Child (CRC). Other authors disagree and instead classify article 6(2) as an aim of the entire substantive article of the CRC. The main argument in this chapter is that the article is very complex and has multiple identities. Basically, article 6(2) is a right in itself, an aim of the Convention, a general principle and a quality-control factor.

In this regard, it is probably worth mentioning that having more than one categorisation of an article of the Convention is not new to the Convention on the Rights of the Child. For example, article 12 of the Convention includes the following on the participation of children:

> 1. States Parties shall assure to the child who is capable of forming his or her own views the right to express those views freely in all matters affecting the child, the views of the child being given due weight in accordance with the age and maturity of the child.
> 2. For this purpose, the child shall in particular be provided the opportunity to be heard in any judicial and administrative proceedings affecting the child, either directly, or through a representative or an appropriate body, in a manner consistent with the procedural rules of national law.

The Committee on the Rights of the Child has stated that this article is not only a general principle, but also a means for States to use: 'Listening to children should not be seen as an end in itself, but rather as a means by which States make their interactions with children and their actions on behalf of children ever more sensitive to the implementation of children's rights.'[1]

---

1 Committee on the Rights of the Child, 'General Comment No. 5: The general measures of implementation of the Convention on the Rights of the Child (arts. 4, 42 and 44, para. 6)', UN Doc. CRC/GC/2003/5 (27 November 2003), para. 12.

2. ARTICLE 6(2) AS A GENERAL PRINCIPLE: A DISPUTED IDENTITY

This identity of article 6(2) appeared very early on the children's rights literature that followed the adoption of the Convention on the Rights of the Child. Nevertheless this identity of article 6(2) has been disputed by many authors over the years. Those who argue against having article 6(2) as a general principle definitely have their justifications. For example, Doek, who is the former chairperson of the Committee, raises his concerns about article 6(2) and the entire article 6 as a general principle:

> But one can also raise questions: why would we call 'the inherent right to life' a general principle and what is the role and (or the added value) of this principle in the implementation of the (other) articles of the CRC?
>
> In the concluding observations the Committee sometimes raises concerns under article 6(1) regarding traffic accidents and suicide. But this 'principle' is almost never mentioned in relation to other articles of the CRC. The same applies to article 6(2). Or in other words: what could be the added value (e.g. the guiding force) of article 6(2) in the implementation of the other articles of the CRC next to the second part of article 4 CRC.
>
> In short: the role of article 6 as a general principle should be carefully considered and discussed.[2]

Doek speaks about the second part of article 4, which reads: 'With regard to economic, social and cultural rights, States Parties shall undertake such measures to the maximum extent of their available resources and, where needed, within the framework of international co-operation.' Arguably, Doek's comments are not far away from the understanding that limits article 6(2) to being just a health and welfare right. The logical question, in this context, would be: why should survival and development be limited only to welfare rights? Is there anything against connecting the survival and development of the child to civil rights and freedoms or, the right to development? Why not give article 6(2) a wider spectrum and consider it to be the right of the child to 'everything'?[3]

---

2 J.E. Doek, 'The CRC General Principles', in J. Connors et al. (eds), *The Convention on the Rights of the Child Reaches Majority* (Institut international des droits de l'enfant (IDE), Switzerland, 2007), pp. 36–37.

3 'Everything' is borrowed from the description by Benyam Dawit Mezmur's, the Vice-Chairperson of the Committee on the Rights of the Child, in a Lecture at the Children's Rights Summer School, Nottingham, United Kingdom, June 2013.

2.1. ARTICLE 6(2) AS A GENERAL PRINCIPLE IN THE JURISPRUDENCE OF THE COMMITTEE ON THE RIGHTS OF THE CHILD

Basically, the Committee on the Rights of the Child has identified and classified four articles of the Convention as being the general principles of the entire CRC:

> Relevant information, including the principal legislative, judicial, administrative or other measures in force or foreseen, factors and difficulties encountered and progress achieved in implementing the provisions of the Convention, and implementation priorities and specific goals for the future should be provided in respect of:
> (a) Non-discrimination (art. 2);
> (b) Best interests of the child (art. 3);
> (c) The right to life, survival and development (art. 6);
> (d) Respect for the views of the child (art. 12).[4]

The Committee has also stated that: 'States parties are encouraged to provide relevant information on the application of these principles in the implementation of articles listed elsewhere in these guidelines.'[5] This conveyed that the general principles are the guidelines for the implementation of the other articles of the Convention. The Committee has also highlighted the importance of the general principles, for instance in its concluding observations on the initial report of Honduras:

> The Convention must be seen as the framework for action to improve the condition of children. In this connection, the Committee wishes to emphasize the importance of the application of the general principles, as reflected in its articles 2, 3, 6 and 12, in guiding the action to be taken to implement the rights of the child.[6]

With reference to the important position of the general principles of the Convention, the following discussion aims at identifying, mainly from the Committee's recommendations, the nature of the general principles. The discussion also aims at understanding the way article 6(2) works as a general principle of the Convention. Lastly, the discussion identifies some areas of the Committee's recommendations that could, arguably, be confusing and need some clarification.

---

4 Committee on the Rights of the Child, UN Doc. CRC/C/5 (30 October 1991), para. 13.

5 *Ibid.*, para. 14.

6 Committee on the Rights of the Child, 'Concluding Observations on Honduras's Initial Report', UN Doc. CRC/C/15/Add.24 (24 October 1994), para. 20.

2.2. MAIN FEATURES OF THE GENERAL PRINCIPLES

It is very important to mention that the original text of the Convention on the Rights of the Child does not specify any article or articles as being the general principles. This means that the classification of the so-called general principles has been made at the interpretation stage of the Convention. This could explain the lack of consensus on the nature of article 6(2) and on which articles should constitute the general principles of the Convention. Authors such as Van Bueren, for instance, argue that the two main interpretation principles of the Convention are the best interest of the child and the evolving capacities: 'Underpinning the Convention on the Rights of the Child are two new principles of interpretation in international law: the best interests of the child, and the evolving capacities of the child.'[7]

It is relevant in this regard to identify the aspects that are shared between the four general principles, in order to decide whether the survival and development of the child can legitimately be considered a general principle of the Convention or not. Obviously, there are some aspects where the general principles do not meet and this is due to the differences in their individualities and the different core and nature of each individual principle.

A main feature in this regard is their position as general principles of the Convention and their legal status within it. To illustrate, in addition to being part of the substantive part of the CRC, the general principles enjoy the privilege of being 'general guidelines' of the Convention. This means that they should be implemented via two parallel methods. The first is direct implementation, which involves the implementation of just the individual general principle concerned – for example the implementation of article 6(2) as a substantive article and as a general principle. The second method is indirect implementation, which happens through the implementation of the other articles of the Convention, as in the implementation of article 6(2) through the implementation of article 24 of the CRC, for instance. This means that they should be applied and duly integrated into the implementation of each individual article of the Convention.[8] All articles of the Convention are expected to respect the factual principles of the best interests of the child, non-discrimination, life, survival and development of the child, and participation of the child. This attitude towards the general principles demonstrates the concept that the general principles represent the soul of each individual article of the Convention. As Thomas Hammarberg put it:

> An important aspect was that the new Convention defines some general principles which together form an approach to the rights of the child which guide national programmes of implementation…

---

7 G. Van Bueren, *The International Law on the Rights of the Child* (Martinus Nijhoff, The Hague, 1998), p.45.

8 Committee on the Rights of the Child, 'Concluding Observations on Myanmar's Initial Report', UN Doc. CRC/C/15/Add.69 (24 January 1997), para. 13.

> These Articles were put under a special heading in the guidelines before norms on civil rights, family aspects, health, education and other more substantive provisions. It was made clear that the Committee wanted governments to report on the application of these principles also in relation to the realization of the other Articles in the Convention. Thereby, the Convention became something more than a mere list of obligations, it got a 'soul'.[9]

For instance, in the case of articles 28 and 29 on the right to education and the aims of education, the full implementation and realisation of both articles requires the States Parties to ensure that school curricula are guided by the principles of the Convention.[10] In the case of article 6(2), this means that school curricula should be guided by the principle of the survival and development of the child. A similar example is the obligation of the States Parties to identify a plan of action for the implementation of the Convention. The general principles should guide this plan of action and they should be integrated into it.[11]

An important matter in terms of the legal status of a general principle is that the general principles should be related to the implementation of all the articles of the Convention, whether civil and political rights or economic, social and cultural rights. This means that the implementation of the general principle should not be impaired by whether the article under consideration is related to civil and political rights or to economic, social and cultural rights. This is due to the fact that the Convention on the Rights of the Child is considered to be promoting the concepts of indivisibility and interdependence of all human rights. All the rights of the child are considered equal and there should be no hierarchy as regards their implementation:

> The Committee expresses its deep concern at the insufficient attention paid to the implementation of the general principles of the Convention, namely its articles 2, 3, 6 and 12 and their relationship to the implementation of all the articles in the Convention, including those relating to the civil and political rights of children.[12]

---

9 T. Hammarberg, 'The Rights of the Child in Developing Countries: International Norms and Procedures for Real Change?', in P. Baehr, H. Hey, J. Smith and T. Swinehart (eds.), *Human Rights in Developing Countries*, Yearbook (Kluwer Law and Taxation Publishers, Deventer, 1994), pp 10–11.

10 Committee on the Rights of the Child, 'Concluding Observations on Bulgaria's Initial Report', UN Doc.CRC/C/15/Add.66 (24 January 1997), para. 17.

11 Committee on the Rights of the Child, 'Concluding Observations on Belarus's Initial Report', UN Doc. CRC/C/15/Add.17 (7 February 1994), para. 11.

12 Committee on the Rights of the Child, 'Concluding Observations on Sudan's Initial Report', UN Doc. CRC/C/15/Add.10 (18 October 1993), para. 12.

2.2.1. *General Principles should Guide the State Legislation and Administrative Decisions*

Another form of the domestic implementation of the general principles is that they should guide all domestic legislation, policies, decision-making, projects and programmes within the individual State Party.[13] These measurements are essential in order to make all the rights in the Convention a reality.[14] This is a requirement of article 4 of the CRC. For instance, the implementation of article 4 requires that the general principles should be integrated into every aspect of decision-making that has an effect on the enjoyment and fulfilment of children's rights, such as policies, laws, and actions and programmes affecting children at all levels, including on administrative and judicial levels.

According to article 4, for example, the State Party should consider the possibility of comprehensively and continuously reviewing its entire legislation to ensure that the principles of the Convention are incorporated into national laws and procedures.[15] In this regard, while consolidated children's rights statutes are highly welcomed, the Committee emphasises that in addition it is crucial that all relevant sectoral laws, e.g., educational and health laws, should reflect the principles and standards of the Convention consistently.[16] For example, in France, when a mother requested that her identity not be revealed during pregnancy, the Committee considered that related legislative measures did not reflect the general principles of the CRC:

> Regarding the right of the child to know his or her origins, including in cases of a mother requesting that her identity remain secret during the birth and declaration of the birth, adoption and medically-assisted procreation, the Committee is concerned that the legislative measures being taken by the State party might not fully reflect the provisions of the Convention, particularly its general principles.[17]

Maternity leave represents another example of the use of article 6(2) as a general principle, so as to guide the specialised legislation. Based on the interpretation and classification that the Committee has made to article 6(2), particular emphasis should be made so as to make some domestic and specialised laws

---

13 Committee on the Rights of the Child, 'Concluding Observations on Nigeria's Initial Report', UN Doc. CRC/C/15/Add.61 (30 October 1996), para. 32.

14 Committee on the Rights of the Child, 'Concluding Observations on Pakistan's Initial Report' UN Doc. CRC/C/15/Add.18 (25 April 1994), para. 15.

15 Committee on the Rights of the Child, 'Concluding Observations on Denmark's Initial Report', UN Doc. CRC/C/15/Add.33 (15 February 1995), para. 24.

16 Committee on the Rights of the Child, 'General Comment No. 5: The general measures of implementation of the Convention on the Rights of the Child (arts. 4, 42 and 44, para. 6)', UN Doc. CRC/GC/2003/5 (27 November 2003), para. 22.

17 Committee on the Rights of the Child, 'Concluding Observations on France's Initial Report', UN Doc. CRC/C/15/Add.20 (25 April 1994), para. 14.

– such as those on breastfeeding and maternity rights, and those that have, according to the Committee, a special relation with the classification of the article – compatible with article 6(2):

> The Committee is concerned about the apparent insufficiency of measures to encourage breast-feeding. The Committee notes that powdered milk for babies continues to be freely distributed in hospitals, contrary to international guidelines on this matter. Equally, the extent to which the statutory provisions relating to, *inter alia*, maternity leave and conditions of employment for nursing mothers are compatible with the principles and provisions of the Convention remains a matter of concern to the Committee.[18]

2.2.2. General Principles should Guide National Judicial Decisions

Judicial implementation of children's rights leads to their realisation. Once a State has ratified the CRC, its courts should abide by the soul of the Convention, i.e., the general principles. Judicial decisions should be formulated on the basis of the general principle. This aims to ensure that the general principles are fully and appropriately integrated into any judicial decision.[19] The Committee reconfirmed this opinion in many reports. For instance, in its concluding observations on the Azerbaijan initial report, it stated:

> The Committee wishes to express its general concern that the State party does not appear to have fully taken into account the provisions of the Convention, especially its general principles, as reflected in its articles 2 (non-discrimination), 3 (best interest of the child), 6 (right to life, survival and development) and 12 (respect for the views of the child), in its legislation, its administrative and its judicial decisions … relevant to children.[20]

The Committee sometimes uses the term 'harmonize' and sometimes the term 'integrate' in relation to the reflection of the general principles in the judicial decisions.[21] Both concepts imply a degree of conformity between the general principles and the judicial decisions within the State party.

---

18 Committee on the Rights of the Child, 'Concluding Observations: United Kingdom of Great Britain and Northern Ireland: Dependent Territories Hong Kong Initial Report', UN Doc. CRC/C/15/Add.63 (30 October 1996), para. 16.

19 See Committee on the Rights of the Child, 'Concluding Observations on Trindade and Tobago's Initial Report', UN Doc. CRC/C/15/Add.82 (10 October 1997), para. 29. Also Committee on the Rights of the Child, 'Concluding Observations on Ghana's Initial Report', UN Doc. CRC/C/15/Add.73 (18 June 1997), para. 33.

20 Committee on the Rights of the Child, 'Concluding Observations on Azerbaijan's Initial Report', UN Doc. CRC/C/15/Add.77 (17 June 1997), para. 15.

21 Committee on the Rights of the Child, 'Concluding Observations on Ghana's Initial Report', UN Doc. CRC/C/15/Add.73 (18 June 1997), para. 33.

2.2.3. *The Implementation of the General Principles should not be Dependent on Budgetary Resources*

Another main feature of the general principles is that their implementation should not be dependent on budgetary resources. For example, in its concluding observations on Bolivia's initial report, which was the first ever concluding observation, the Committee stated:

> The Committee emphasizes that the principle of non-discrimination, as provided for under article 2 of the Convention, must be vigorously applied, and that a more active approach should be taken to eliminate discrimination against certain groups of children, most notably girl children. In this connection, *the Committee notes that the application of this and the other general principles of the Convention cannot be dependent upon budgetary resources.*[22]

The Committee reconfirmed this statement later on, for instance, in its concluding observations on Indonesia's initial report:

> The Committee is concerned that insufficient attention is given to the implementation of the general principles of the Convention, particularly its articles 2, 3 and 12. The Committee wishes to emphasize that the implementation of these principles is not to be made dependent on budgetary resources.[23]

All the general principles are equal in relation to not being subject to budgetary allocations. Budgetary cooperation within different regions of the State Party should support this important feature of the general principles. A comprehensive approach to the implementation of the rights of the child that is consistent with the general principles of the Convention should therefore apply, irrespective of budgetary resources.[24]

2.2.4. *General Principles should be Realised at both* de jure *and* de facto *Levels*

De jure and *de facto* implementation of the General Principles should support their effective implementation. In addition to being reflected at the *de jure* level, the general principles should be reflected at the *de facto* one as well. The general principles are to be included in both practice and legislation.[25]

---

22 Committee on the Rights of the Child, 'Concluding Observations on Bolivia's Initial Report', UN Doc. CRC/C/15/Add.1 (18 February 1993), para. 14 (emphasis added).

23 Committee on the Rights of the Child, 'Concluding Observations on Indonesia's Initial Report', UN Doc. CRC/C/15/Add.7 (18 October 1993), para. 13.

24 Committee on the Rights of the Child, 'Concluding Observations on France's Initial Report', UN Doc. CRC/C/15/Add.20 (25 April 1994), para. 19.

25 Committee on the Rights of the Child, 'Concluding Observations on Guatemala's Initial Report', UN Doc. CRC/C/15/Add.58 (7 June 1996), para. 18.

In some instances the *de facto* implementation of the general principles has a considerable link to some negative social practices that may exist within society but have not yet found their way to the legislative level, especially when some of these social practices and attitudes are in conflict with the general principles of the Convention, for example gender-based stereotyping. This is not an easy task to achieve. It is the State Party's responsibility to undertake measures, such as raising awareness, to face the difficulties that have been caused by prejudices, intolerance and other social attitudes that are in contradiction with the general principles of the Convention.[26] Moreover, there are some problems with practicability. It is going to be a matter of definition when discussing which social practices are in conflict with the general principles and which ones are not. Many social practices need time to change because they are deeply rooted in the society. In some parts of Sudan, for example, the practice of *shulukh* (facial scars made for cosmetic reasons) was seen as a sign of beauty. Gradually, it started to diminish, partly because of a major shift in the way society viewed the practice and viewed beauty as well.

2.2.5. Implementation of the General Principles should Lead to the Effective Implementation of Children' Rights

Another extra feature of the general principles is related to the concept of prioritisation. The implementation of the general principles of the Convention requires that priority be given to children and their rights. For instance, the best interests of the child should be considered first. Governments have, in international forums, agreed to the principle of 'first call for children', included in the final document adopted by the World Conference on Human Rights.[27] Based on that, when a State Party formulates policy options and proposals, there should be an accompanying assessment of the possible impact on children. This would mean that the decision-makers are well advised and informed when formulating a policy as to its effect on the rights of the child.[28] In its concluding observations on the initial report of the United Kingdom, for example, the Committee recommended, with regard to the best interest principle, that 'children's rights be fully integrated into the discussions on issues concerning the transfer of sovereignty over Hong Kong and be accorded high priority in the dialogue on these and related matters in the Joint Liaison Group.'[29]

---

26 Committee on the Rights of the Child, 'Concluding Observations on Poland's Initial Report', UN Doc. CRC/C/15/Add.31 (15 January 1995), paras. 10 and 17.

27 'Report of the World Conference for Human Rights: Report of the Secretary General', UN Doc. A/CONF.157/24 (Part I) (13 October 1993), para. 45, p. 38.

28 Committee on the Rights of the Child, 'Concluding Observations on United Kingdom of Great Britain and Northern Ireland: Dependent Territories Hong Kong Initial Report', UN Doc. CRC/C/15/Add.63 (30 October 1996), para. 20.

29 *Ibid.*

3. EQUALITY OF THE 'GENERAL PRINCIPLES OF THE CRC'

The following paragraphs examine the Committee on the Rights of the Child's literature with regards to the equality of the four general principles. The question would be whether it is possible to argue that sometimes the Committee's comments do not clearly reflect that the four general principles, that it has identified, are equal? This is important as sometimes the Committee's recommendations do not reflect or convey the equality of the four general principles. In particular, they do not convey the equality of article 6 to the other general principles, as identified by the Committee. To illustrate, in the Committee's recommendations, there are several instances where it would be possible to argue that it had isolated article 6. Sometimes the Committee would be talking about all the general principles, but when it makes specifications it speaks only about articles 2, 3 and 12:

> In view of the fact that the Convention can only be referred to before the courts as a means of interpretation of national legislation, the Committee recommends that further steps be taken to ensure the effective implementation of the Convention at the national level. In this regard, the Committee also wishes to emphasise the importance of taking action to ensure that the general principles of the Convention, particularly those relating to non-discrimination, the best interest of the child and the respect for the views of the child as guaranteed under articles 2, 3, and 12 respectively, are reflected in domestic law.[30]

Another example can be found in the Committee's concluding observations on the initial report of Cyprus:

> The Committee also expresses its concern that the State party has not yet fully taken into account in its legislation and policy-making the general principles of the Convention ... article 2 (principle of non-discrimination), article 3 (principle of the best interest of the child) and article 12 (respect for the views of the child).[31]

Article 6 is also not mentioned in the concluding observations on the initial report of Yemen:

> The Committee is concerned about the unclear status of the Convention in the domestic legal framework and about the insufficient steps taken to bring existing legislation into full conformity with the Convention, including in the light of the general principles of the Convention, in particular the principles of non-discrimination (art. 2), the best interest of the child (art. 3) and respect for the views of the child (art. 12).[32]

---

30 Committee on the Rights of the Child, 'Concluding Observations on Canada's Initial Report', UN Doc. CRC/C/15/Add.37 (20 June 1995), para. 23.

31 Committee on the Rights of the Child, 'Concluding Observations on Cyprus's Initial Report', UN Doc. CRC/C/15/Add.59 (7 June 1997), para. 11.

32 Committee on the Rights of the Child, 'Concluding Observations on Yemen's Initial Report', UN Doc. CRC/C/15/Add.47 (13 February 1996), para. 6.

Another example can be found in the Committee's concluding observations on Antigua and Barbuda's initial report, where there is no mention whatsoever of article 6 under the heading 'General Principles'.[33] In fact, in some cases it would have been logical for the Committee to emphasise article 6(2) because it is also relevant, according to the Committee's classification of article 6(2), to the matter under discussion, but the Committee does not refer to the article, for instance, in the concluding observations on the initial report of Guatemala:

> In view of the historical disparities affecting indigenous children and children belonging to groups living below the poverty line, as well as girls, the Committee is concerned about the adequacy of measures to ensure the effective implementation of the economic, social and cultural rights of children at the national, regional and local levels, in the light of articles 2, 3 and 4 of the Convention.[34]

While all of the general principles of the Convention should be reflected in domestic legislations, the Committee did not speak about article 6, for example, in the concluding observations on Senegal's initial report:

> The Committee recommends that the State party ensure that national legislation conforms fully to the provisions and principles of the Convention, in the light of the concerns identified by the Committee and of the study on a comprehensive law reform conducted under the auspices of UNICEF. The principles of the Convention including those relating to the best interest of the child and the prohibition of discrimination and of participation of children in matters affecting them should be reflected in domestic law...[35]

While all children should enjoy their rights, those who belong to a particularly vulnerable group of children should receive special attention so as to guarantee that they are enjoying their rights. In this regard, the general principles should be fully implemented in order to guarantee the maximum enjoyment of the rights of these groups. Notably, the Committee did not refer to article 6(2) as a general principle in relation to the implementation of the rights of asylum-seeking children:

> The Committee remains concerned about the extent to which account is taken of the special needs and rights of children in asylum-seeking and refugee situations. ... In this respect the Committee notes that the guarantees provided for in the Convention, in particular in its articles 2, 3, 12, 22 and 37(d) do not appear to be complied with, while insufficient attention seems to have been ensured to the implementation of

33 Committee on the Rights of the Child, 'Concluding Observations on Antigua and Barbuda's Initial Report', UN Doc. CRC/C/15/Add.247 (3 November 2004), paras. 26–32.

34 Committee on the Rights of the Child, 'Concluding Observations on Guatemala's Initial Report', UN Doc. CRC/C/Add. 58 (7 June 1996), para. 16.

35 Committee on the Rights of the Child, 'Concluding Observations on Senegal's Initial Report', UN Doc. CRC/C/15/Add.44 (27 November 1995), para. 24.

> articles 9 and 10 of the Convention. The Committee also notes with concern that the provision of medical treatment and services to asylum-seeking children does not appear to be interpreted in the light of the principles and provisions of the Convention, in its articles 2 and 3.[36]

Another example is children born out of wedlock. The Committee required that they receive equal treatment, particularly at the legislative level. However, it rarely links this to article 6. It should be noted that the existence of legislation that regulates and guarantees the survival and development of this vulnerable group of children is extremely important:

> The State party should pursue its efforts with a view to fully reflecting in its legislation and practice the provisions and principles of the Convention, in particular the principles of non-discrimination, the best interest of the child and the right of the child to freely express his or her views. In this regard, the Committee recommends that existing legislation be modified to fully ensure equal treatment between children born in and out of wedlock.[37]

Also in its concluding observations on Ukraine's initial report:

> The Committee expresses its concern as to full compatibility of national legislation, measures and programmes with the provisions and principles of the Convention, particularly with regard to the principles of non-discrimination (art. 2), including in relation to the different age of marriage for girls and boys, the best interest of the child (art. 3) and the right of the child to express his/her opinion in all decisions affecting him/her (art. 12)...[38]

4. IS ARTICLE 6(2) A GENERAL PRINCIPLE OF A 'SPECIAL NATURE'?

Notably, sometimes the differentiation is against the entire article 6. When excluding article 6(2), the Committee does not differentiate between article 6(1) and 6(2). For instance, no reference was made to article 6 in the concluding observations on Finland's initial report:

> The Committee expresses its concern that the State party has not yet fully taken into account in its legislation and in its policies the general principles of the Convention,

36 Committee on the Rights of the Child, 'Concluding Observations on Germany's Initial Report', UN Doc. CRC/C/15/Add.43 (27 November 1995), para. 19.

37 Committee on the Rights of the Child, 'Concluding Observations on Italy's Initial Report', UN Doc. CRC/C/15/Add.41 (27 November 1995), para. 16.

38 Committee on the Rights of the Child, 'Concluding Observations on Ukraine's Initial Report', UN Doc. CRC/C/15/Add.42 (27 November 1995), para. 8.

> in particular non-discrimination (art. 2), the best interest of the child (art. 3) and respect for the views of the child (art. 12).[39]

Significantly, in some instances, the Committee did not mention article 6(2) even when speaking about the importance of the Convention as a whole. The Committee was referring to the CRC and the manner in which it is viewed as a document that guarantees the rights of children as children and not as future adults. For instance, no reference was made to article 6(2) in the concluding observations on the initial report of the Republic of Korea:

> The Committee is also concerned that the basic principles of the Convention, in particular the provisions of its articles 2, 3 and 12, have not been adequately reflected in legislation, policies and programmes. Insufficient measures have been adopted to create awareness of these basic values of the Convention with a view to changing the prevailing consideration and treatment of the child simply 'as a mini-adult or immature adult', as recognized in the report.[40]

As previously discussed in Chapter 2, in order to simplify the understanding and later the implementation of article 6(2), the Committee grouped it together with a number of rights in the CRC.[41] Nevertheless, the Committee sometimes failed to refer to article 6(2) even when speaking about the implementation of some of its associated articles:

> The Committee encourages the Government to pursue its efforts in order to ensure full compliance of its national legislation with the provisions and principles of the Convention, including non-discrimination (art. 2), the best interest of the child (art. 3) and respect for the views of the child (art. 12). The Committee particularly recommends that legislative measures be adopted with a view to ensuring ... the basic rights of all disabled children, in particular the right to education, in the light of article 23...[42]

Another example is in its comment about the national nutritional policy of Bangladesh. The Committee could have mentioned that the National Nutritional Policy of the State Party should be governed by the survival and development principle in its concluding observations on Bangladesh's initial report: 'Further steps should be taken in the area of health and welfare services. In

39 Committee on the Rights of the Child, 'Concluding Observations on Finland's Initial Report', UN Doc. CRC/C/15/Add.53 (13 February 1996), para. 13.

40 Committee on the Rights of the Child, 'Concluding Observations on the Republic of Korea's Initial Report', UN Doc.CRC/C/15/Add.51 (13 February 1996), para. 12.

41 As previously mentioned in Chapter 2, the Committee made a clustering of the articles of the Convention and article 6(2) was associated with the health and welfare rights of the child.

42 Committee on the Rights of the Child, 'Concluding Observations on the Republic of Korea's Initial Report', UN Doc.CRC/C/15/Add.51 (13 February 1996), para. 22.

particular, concerted efforts are needed to combat malnutrition and ensure the implementation of a National Nutritional Policy for children'.[43]

Also when speaking about malnutrition which is very much related to the child's survival and development, the Committee does not mention article 6(2): 'The Committee is worried about the insufficient measures taken to tackle the issues of child malnutrition, disability, mental health and early pregnancies, as well as cases of early marriage. It is also concerned about the problem of youth suicide.'[44]

In addition, in the concluding observations on Azerbaijan's initial report the Committee spoke about health and nutrition but made no specific reference to article 6(2):

> The Committee is gravely concerned about the general health situation of children, in particular with regard to the rise in the infant, child and maternal mortality rates, the decline of breastfeeding, the increase in the number of unwanted pregnancies, nutrition and iodine deficiencies, substance abuse, and the negative impact of environmental pollution.[45]

The Committee spoke about labour law and the general principles but did not mention article 6 at all, although labour law and family law are closely linked to survival and development. One example is in the concluding observations on Romania's initial report:

> Special efforts should be made to bring the existing legislation fully into line with the provisions of the Convention and thereby taking into account the principles of non-discrimination, the best interests of the child, and respect for the views of the child, as in the case of labour legislation. The Family Code of 1954 needs to be revised in the light of the Convention.[46]

In some occasions, the Committee also made connections with labour law and the best-interest principle but made no reference to the survival and development principle:

> In view of the significant risk of the exploitation of children through labour, particularly in the light of recent changes to national legislation, the Committee

---

[43] Committee on the Rights of the Child, 'Concluding Observations on Bangladesh's Initial Report', UN Doc. CRC/C/15/Add.74 (18 June 1997), para. 41.

[44] Committee on the Rights of the Child, 'Concluding Observations on Bulgaria's Initial Report', UN Doc. CRC/C/15/Add.66 (24 January 1997), para. 16.

[45] Committee on the Rights of the Child, 'Concluding Observations on Azerbaijan's Initial Report', UN Doc. CRC/C/15/Add.77 (17 June 1997), para. 24.

[46] Committee on the Rights of the Child, 'Concluding Observations on Romania's Initial Report', UN Doc. CRC/C/15/Add.16 (7 February 1994), para. 14. Later, Romania made some modifications to the family code see Committee on the Rights of the Child, 'Concluding Observations on Romania's third and fourth periodic report', UN Doc. CRC/C/ROM/CO/4, (30 June 2009), para. 3(d).

> suggests that this matter be urgently addressed and that the necessary action be taken in line with the Convention and in particular its article 3 as it relates to the best interests of the child.[47]

Finally, as previously explained, the Committee clearly states that the general principles should not be dependent on budgetary resources. However, it does not always refer to article 6(2) when speaking about this important aspect of all of the general principles. This lack of reference to article 6(2) provides the opportunity to ask the following theoretical question: does this convey that the Committee considers that article 6(2) to be dependent on budgetary resources? For instance, in the concluding observations on the initial report of Indonesia, the Committee stated:

> The Committee is concerned that proper attention has not yet been given to the implementation of the general principles of the Convention, particularly its articles 2, 3 and 12. The Committee reiterates that the implementation of these principles is not to be made dependent on budgetary constraints.[48]

In its concluding observations on France's initial report, the Committee explicitly mentioned the general principles that do not depend on budgetary resources and article 6(2) is not among them. The Committee was concerned about the cooperation between the central government and the local authorities, especially with regard to budgetary matters, in order to minimise the disparities that may arise between the regions as to the provision of services.[49]

Nevertheless, it is important to note the most of the above-mentioned positions of the Committee were made at the early years the followed the adoption of the CRC. In fact, in some rare cases, such as its concluding observations on Mongolia's initial report, the Committee speaks about article 6(2) when speaking about the other general principles and states that they should be incorporated into legislation.[50] In addition, its concluding observations to Jamaica's periodic report, the Committee mentioned article 6 specifically when talking about all four general principles of the Convention:

> With a view to strengthening its implementation of article 4 of the Convention and in the light of articles 2, 3 and 6, the Committee recommends that the State party

---

47 Committee on the Rights of the Child, 'Concluding Observations on Belarus's Initial Report' UN Doc. CRC/C/15/Add.17 (7 February1994), para. 16. See also 'Concluding Observations on Costa Rica's Initial Report', UN Doc. CRC/C/15/Add.11 (18 October 1993), para. 14.

48 Committee on the Rights of the Child, 'Concluding Observations on Indonesia's Initial Report', UN Doc. CRC/C/15/Add.25 (24 October 1994), para. 11.

49 Committee on the Rights of the Child, 'Concluding Observations on France's Initial Report', UN Doc. CRC/C/15/Add.20 (25 April 1995), para. 19.

50 Committee on the Rights of the Child, 'Concluding Observations on Mongolia's Initial Report', UN Doc. CRC/C/15/Add.48 (13 February 1996), para. 12.

prioritize budgetary allocations to ensure the implementation of the rights of children to the maximum extent of available resources and, where needed, within the framework of international cooperation.[51]

When talking about juvenile justice, the Committee spoke in detail about the relationship between the child's development and juvenile justice:

4c. The right to life, survival and development (art. 6).
This inherent right of every child should guide and inspire States Parties in the development of effective national policies and programmes for the prevention of juvenile delinquency, because it goes without saying that delinquency has a (very) negative impact on the child's development. Furthermore, this basic right should result in a policy of responding to juvenile delinquency in ways that support the child's development ... The use of deprivation of liberty has (very) negative consequences for the child's harmonious development and seriously hampers his or her reintegration in society. In this regard, article 37(b) CRC explicitly provides that deprivation of liberty, including arrest, detention and imprisonment, should be used only as a measure of last resort and for the shortest appropriate period of time, so that the child's right to development is fully respected and ensured...[52]

In addition, in its concluding observations to Ukraine's initial report the Committee stated in paragraph 17 of the same report:

The Committee encourages the Government of Ukraine to pursue the revision of the legislative framework in order to fully reflect the Convention and ensure the realization of children's rights ... and full compliance with the provisions and principles of the Convention on the Rights of the Child, especially the principles of non-discrimination (art. 2) and the best interest of the child (art. 3), the right to life, survival and development (art. 6) and the right of the child to express his/her opinion in all decisions affecting him/her (art. 12)...[53]

4.1. NO FORMAL DISTINCTION

In fact, the Committee does not make any formal distinction between, or create any hierarchy in relation to, the four general principles of the Convention, at least from a theoretical perspective. The Committee also has no doubts about the position of article 6(2) as a general principle. In this context the lack of reference, on many occasions, to article 6(2) when speaking collectively about the four

51 Committee on the Rights of the Child, 'Concluding Observations on Jamaica's Second Periodic Report', UN Doc. CRC/C/15/Add.210 (4 July 2003), para. 18.

52 Committee on the Rights of the Child, 'General Comment No. 10 on Children's rights in juvenile justice', UN Doc. CRC/C/GC/10 (25 April 2007), para. 11.

53 Committee on the Rights of the Child, 'Concluding Observations on Ukraine's Initial Report', UN Doc. CRC/C/15/Add.42 (27 November 1995), para. 17.

general principles of the CRC needs more elucidation. Could it be argued that this apparent contradiction is caused by a prevailing understanding by many who are involved in one way or another with the CRC (the Committee) that the survival and development of the child is linked only to a group of health and welfare rights? Accordingly, does this negatively reflect on the generalised nature of the principle? For example, Marta Santos Pais interprets the principle of survival and development as follows:

> The fourth general principle is the one of survival and development ... it means ensuring the right to an adequate standard of living in the full respect for the child's human dignity, the right to the highest attainable standard of health, to information and education in the basic knowledge of preventive health care, nutrition and environmental sanitation ... Areas which have been traditionally considered as measurable and where the goals of the World Summit for Children together with the national plans of action play a decisive role.
>
> And still gain another and deeper challenge of self-betterment of the child, ensuring the capacity of developing talents and abilities to their fullest potential, giving the child this essential feeling of belonging to a world made of solidarity where there will be no place for indifference towards mimetism inside extreme poverty...[54]

Thomas Hammarberg also clearly speaks about a direct relationship between economic, social and cultural rights and the survival and development principle, 'The principle most directly related to children's economic and social rights is formulated in the right-to-life Article. This Article goes further than just granting children the right not to be killed, it includes the right to survival and to development (Article 6(2)'.[55]

Moreover, in its general comment on business, the Committee gave the following as to how the general principles relate to business activities. Note that under the heading of right to life, survival and development, article 6(2) has been linked to a number of economic, social and cultural rights:

> The activities and operations of business enterprises can impact on the realization of article 6 in different ways. For example, environmental degradation and contamination arising from business activities can compromise children's rights to health, food security and access to safe drinking water and sanitation. Selling or leasing land to investors can deprive local populations of access to natural resources linked to their subsistence and cultural heritage; the rights of indigenous children may be particularly at risk in this context. The marketing to children of products such as cigarettes and alcohol as well

54 M.S. Pais, 'Monitoring Children's Rights A View from Within', in E. Verhellen (ed.), *Monitoring Children's Rights* (Martinus Nijhoff Publishers, The Hague, 1996), p. 138.

55 T. Hammarberg, 'The Rights of the Child in Developing Countries: International Norms and Procedures for Real Change?', in P. Baehr, H. Hey, J. Smith and T. Swinehart (eds.), *Human Rights in Developing Countries*, Yearbook (Kluwer Law and Taxation Publishers, Deventer, 1994), p. 12.

as foods and drinks high in saturated fats, trans-fatty acids, sugar, salt or additives can have a long-term impact on their health. When business employment practices require adults to work long hours, older children, particularly girls, may take on their parent's domestic and childcare obligations, which can negatively impact their right to education and to play; additionally, leaving children alone or in the care of older siblings can have implications for the quality of care and the health of younger children.[56]

5. ARTICLE 6(2) AS A RIGHT

Article 6(2) is basically composed of two rights: the right to survive and the right to develop. The State Party is obliged to respect, protect and fulfil these two rights, which means that the State needs to create conditions and provide measures for achieving this.

The Convention on the Rights of the Child includes civil, economic, social and cultural rights, in addition to civil and political rights, as Cynthia Cohen commented: 'In its final form, the Convention on the Rights of the Child is a comprehensive human rights treaty. Following the model of the Universal Declaration of Human Rights the Convention combines in one treaty both civil-political rights and economic-social-cultural rights'.[57] In this context, the logical question would be: to which kind of rights does article 6(2) belong? Is it a combination of both kinds of rights? Does it include the international right to development? This has been discussed in detail in Chapter 2; therefore, the discussion here will be somewhat brief.

Arguably, the nature of the wording of article 6(2) is relevant in this regard as it is possible to distinguish the nature of the right on the basis of its wording. The wording, for some, might be confusing, which means that as a right it is important to understand exactly what the article is referring to. Article 6(2), for instance, refers to development without specifying any aspect of it. Nevertheless, as was detailed in Chapter 2, the Committee's efforts produced a number of developmental aspects and domains.

Another point is whether article 6(2) is a provision right or a protection right or a participation right? The CRC is known for its three P's, i.e. provision, protection and participation. Cantwell explains that the terms are used in order to minimise any kind of distinction, 'which had been highlighted notably by the East–West divide on the conception of human rights.'[58] Within the context

56 Committee on the Rights of the Child, 'General Comment No. 16 on State obligations regarding the impact of the business sector on children's rights', UN Doc. CRC/C/GC/16 (17 April 2013), Section III, para. 19 (footnotes omitted).

57 C.P. Cohen, 'The Developing Jurisprudence of the Rights of the Child' (1993) 6 *St. Thomas L. Rev.* 18, 96 (footnotes omitted).

58 N. Cantwell, 'Veni, Vidi... et Vici? A review of the history and impact of the CRC', in A. Weyts (ed.), *Understanding Children's Rights* (Ghent University, Ghent, 2004), p. 295.

of these three P's, it is possible to argue that earlier classifications by the Committee classified article 6(2) as a provision and protection right of the Child: 'The Committee welcomes the fact that a national conference was organized in December 1991 for a discussion on priority areas of survival, protection and development of children.'[59] Eugeen Verhellen classifies the survival and development of the child as a provision right, which means that it is concerned with 'providing access to certain goods and services; the right to food and health care …, the right to education …, the right to enjoy social security…'[60] Being classified, earlier, by the Committee as a basic health and welfare right,[61] i.e., as an economic, social and cultural right, also puts article 6(2) in the category of provision rights. This means that, according to the Committee's understanding, it is possible to comprehend the scope of article 6(2) as a right from the articles that are associated with it according to the clustering that was made by the Committee for all the articles of the Convention.

Notably, many concluding observations of the Committee speak about the survival and development of the child only in the category of basic health and welfare rights. In some cases, all of article 6 – not just article 6(2) – became a second version of the right to health: 'Furthermore, in the light of article 6 of the Convention, the Committee expresses its concern at the health status of children of different socio-economic groups and those belonging to ethnic minorities.'[62] Based on the clustering that the Committee gave to the words survival and development, article 6(2), on many occasions, stood as a supporting article to article 24 on the right to health, as in the concluding observations on Belize's second periodic report:

> The Committee welcomes the revised and expanded Care and Growth Chart, which provides a detailed and personal health and development record for all children under 5 years of age. While noting with appreciation the State party's efforts to improve the primary health care, including the establishment of the National Health Insurance Scheme and the School Health and Physical Education Services (SHAPES) programme, the Committee is nevertheless concerned at the regional disparities in accessibility to health services, the high number of infant deaths and regional differences in this respect, and the situation of malnutrition among infants and children. The Committee is also concerned at the lack of access to safe drinking water and sanitation in the rural and most remote areas.

59 Committee on the Rights of the Child, 'Concluding Observations on Pakistan's Initial Report', UN Doc. CRC/C/15/Add.18 (25 April 1994), para. 5.

60 E. Verhellen, *Convention on the Rights of the Child: Background, motivation, strategies, main themes* (E. Verhellen and Garant Publishers, Leuven, 2000), p. 80.

61 Committee on the Rights of the Child, 'General guidelines regarding the form and content of initial reports to be submitted by States Parties under article 44, paragraph 1(a), of the Convention (Basic Reference Document)', UN Doc. CRC/C/5 (30 October 1991), para. 19.

62 Committee on the Rights of the Child, 'Concluding Observations on United Kingdom and Northern Ireland's Initial Report', UN Doc. CRC/C/15/Add.34 (15 February 1995), para. 13.

> Furthermore, the Committee reiterates its concern at the low prevalence of breastfeeding.[63]

The Committee has also made a link between malnutrition and survival, which conveys the meaning that the Committee gave to the word survival: 'Malnutrition continues to seriously hamper the survival and development of children in the State party, which has one of the highest rates of malnourished children in the world and where calorie intake has decreased over the past decades, resulting in a higher incidence of stunting and wasting.'[64]

The Committee made a reference to the child's development when it encouraged States Parties to assist families in their responsibilities in the upbringing and development of their children:

> The Committee encourages the State party to adopt further measures to ensure assistance for the family to ensure its responsibilities in the upbringing and development of the child, in particular in the light of articles 18 and 27 of the Convention. Special attention should be paid to the prevention of child abandonment, as well as to the prevention of, and appropriate assistance to, child-headed families.[65]

The development part of article 6(2), however, links it with participation rights as well. While the Committee spoke about specific types of development in its general comment no. 5, it also kept adding more types and qualities of development to the list in its concluding observations on the State Party reports. For instance, the Committee spoke about the concept of 'sound development' of children in its concluding observations on Croatia's initial report:

> The Committee is concerned that a number of unaccompanied children who have lost contact with their families are in institutions or in foster care. The Committee further notes with concern that some foster homes might accept responsibility for the care of children solely for the economic compensation provided to them. It stresses that the consequences for the children living under such conditions are not conducive to their sound development.[66]

---

63 Committee on the Rights of the Child, 'Concluding Observations on Belize's Second Periodic Report', UN Doc. CRC/C/15/Add.252 (31 March 2005), para. 52.

64 Committee on the Rights of the Child, 'Concluding Observations on Bangladesh's Initial Report', UN Doc. CRC/C/15/Add.74 (18 June 1997), para. 21.

65 Committee on the Rights of the Child, 'Concluding Observations on the Republic of Korea's Initial Report', UN Doc.CRC/C/15/Add.51 (13 February 1996), para. 27.

66 Committee on the Rights of the Child, 'Concluding Observations on Croatia's Initial Report', UN Doc. CRC/C/15/Add.52 (13 February 1996), para. 16.

The Committee also spoke about the concept of 'harmonious development':

> In view of the various concerns raised by the Committee with respect to the implementation of article 32 of the Convention, it wishes to highlight the importance of the State party ensuring that all children have access to health care, that education be made compulsory as a measure to prevent the economic exploitation of children and that further measures should be undertaken to combat exploitation, ... including legislative measures to ensure the effective protection of the child against the performance of any work that is likely to be hazardous or to ... or to be harmful to the child's health or full and harmonious development.[67]

The Committee had the following to say about placing children in institutions and harmonious development:

> The Committee also suggests that appropriate alternatives to institutional care be developed, with the best interests of the child as the primary consideration, as well as the promotion of his or her harmonious development and preparation for responsible participation in society.[68]

The Committee also spoke about 'cultural development': 'The Committee believes that opportunities for the cultural development of children are critical and recommends that measures be taken to give children access to child literature and media. The need for playgrounds and child-friendly parks should be considered in city planning.'[69] This was emphasised later by the Committee on its general comment no. 17 on article 31.[70] The Committee also made reference to 'social development:' 'The Committee notes with satisfaction the importance attached by the Government to education, considered as the "driving force of social and economic development".'[71]

But the scope of the child's development is also linked to the child's civil rights and freedoms. Participation of the child has been described by some as the 'breaking news' of the Convention on the Rights of the Child.[72] The principle is expected to achieve a number of benefits for the individual child and his or

---

67 Committee on the Rights of the Child, 'Concluding Observations on Nigeria's Initial Report', UN Doc. CRC/C/15/Add.61 (30 October 1996), para. 41.

68 Committee on the Rights of the Child, 'Concluding Observations on Bulgaria's Initial Report', UN Doc. CRC/C/15/Add.66 (24 January 1997), para. 27.

69 Committee on the Rights of the Child, 'Concluding Observations on Lebanon's Initial Report', UN Doc. CRC/C/15/Add.54 (7 June 1996), para. 36.

70 Committee on the Rights of the Child, 'General Comment No. 17 (2013) on the right of the child to rest, leisure, play, recreational activities, cultural life and the arts (art. 31)', UN Doc. CRC/C/GC/17 (17 April 2013), Section VIII.

71 Committee on the Rights of the Child, 'Concluding Observations on the Republic of Korea's Initial Report', UN Doc. CRC/C/15/Add.51 (13 February 1996), para. 5.

72 E. Verhellen, in a Presentation during an Interdisciplinary Course on Children's Rights in Ghent, Belgium, 2004.

her family, and for society.[73] With this in the background, participation is significantly of relevance to the child's development. This makes article 6(2) a participation right as well. In its General Comment No. 6, the Committee mentioned that information should be provided in a manner that is appropriate to the maturity of the child and his or her level of understanding:

> To allow for a well-informed expression of such views and wishes, it is imperative that such children are provided with all relevant information concerning, for example, their entitlements, services available including means of communication, the asylum process, family tracing and the situation in their country of origin ... In guardianship, care and accommodation arrangements, and legal representation, children's views should also be taken into account. Such information must be provided in a manner that is appropriate to the maturity and level of understanding of each child.[74]

Freedom of expression, assembly, association and movement, create an environment suitable for practising the right to participation. In addition, free and independent press media, peaceful demonstrations and meetings, and being able to criticise and to oppose are also important in creating the environment for the child to participate.[75] Security forces, for example, should apply the right of the child to survival and development during public demonstrations. For instance, the Committee asked Egypt to investigate cases of violations were children were affected by live and rubber bullets and tear gas during the mass public demonstrations in January 2011.[76] This is relevant to the understanding that participation of the child is a part of the overall concept of development. The participation of the child cannot be viewed separately from the overall concept of development that has been mentioned in article 6(2). Children may participate in the development of their countries. For example, when children are employed in a safe type of work (article 32), they are participating in the economic development process. When children work in good conditions or in accepted forms of work, this is a very good form of participation and it is even good for the child's development and his or her economic development. And when the child earns his or her money, this is a good thing for his or her dignity. Dignity is a main aim of the right to survival and development of the child as is discussed

---

73 Committee on the Rights of the Child, 'Concluding Observations on Syrian Arab Republic's Initial Report', UN Doc. CRC/C/15/Add.70 (24 January 1997), para. 12.

74 Committee on the Rights of the Child, 'General Comment No. 6 on the Treatment of Unaccompanied and Separated Children Outside their Country of Origin', UN Doc. CRC/GC/2005/6 (1 September 2005), para. 25.

75 Note: these factors have been mentioned at the Human Rights Committee's General Comment No. 25 on the right to vote, which is an adults' right. UN Doc. CCPR/C/21/Rev.1/Add.7, para. 25.

76 Committee on the Rights of the Child, 'Concluding Observations on the consolidated third and fourth periodic reports of Egypt', UN. Doc. CRC/C/EGY/CO/3-4 (15 July 2011), paras. 38-39.

in Chapter 4. In this context, it may be claimed that this is an argument for child labour. The term labour conveys a form of exploitation. The argument in this context is for the survival and development of the child as a right and an aim, which will be discussed later in the chapter. If any form of exploitation could be avoided, then it is possible to argue that child work as such could be in the interests of the child. Obviously, there are lots of detailed considerations that need to be taken into account before allowing any child to work.

Overall, in this context, it is important, however, to emphasise the comprehensiveness aspect of the survival and development of the child as a right: simply, as the right of the child to all kinds of rights, i.e. the right to 'everything'.[77]

6. THE SURVIVAL AND DEVELOPMENT OF THE CHILD AS AN AIM OF THE CONVENTION

Some argue that article 6(2) on the survival and development of the child is not a general principle of the Convention, but is rather the aim of the entire substantive part of the Convention.

Arts, for example, argues that she considers survival and development of a different order than the other general principles of the CRC. She considers that the other three general principles always have to be a primary consideration in order to achieve the survival and development of the child.

> The main substantive objective of the Convention is to ensure the survival and development of children. Following Unicef, many authors and organizations categorize the 'survival and development' of children as being also general principles of the CRC. In this author's view, 'survival and development' make up the overall substantive objective of the Convention and are thus of a different order than the three general CRC principles that (should) direct the form and orientation of all implementation measures (the best interest of the child, non-discrimination and participation).[78]

Arguably, it would probably be useful to understand the way article 6(2) works as an aim of the entire substantive part of the CRC. This should be helpful in understanding the difference between article 6(2) as a general principle, as a right, or as an aim of the Convention.

---

77 Words of Benyam Dawit Mezmur's, the Vice-Chairperson of the Committee on the Rights of the Child, in a Lecture at the Children's Rights Summer School, Nottingham, United Kingdom (June 2013).

78 K. Arts, 'General Introduction: A Child Rights-Based Approach to International Criminal Accountability', in K. Arts, and V. Popovski (eds.), *International Criminal Accountability and the Rights of Children* (Hague Academic Press, The Hague, 2006), p. 10.

The following words of Adam Lopatka explain the way article 6(2) works as an aim in relation to other articles of the CRC: 'Respect for the child's personality and care for his or her proper development demand that no child should be subjected to torture or other cruel, inhuman or degrading treatment or punishment.'[79] In other words, Adam Lopatka is saying that if the child gets subjected to torture or other cruel, inhumane or degrading treatment or punishment, then the child will not properly develop. Therefore, if we reverse Adam Lopatka's words, lack of survival and development could be attributed to the child being subjected to the act of torture or other cruel, inhuman or degrading treatment or punishment. This means that the State needs to ensure the survival and development of the child as an aim by not allowing any child to be subjected to torture or other cruel treatment.

In terms of the basis or techniques for determining what achieves the survival and development of the child and what does not, a subjective approach should be implemented. What might be suitable for one child might not be suitable for another one. This is just common sense, and supports efficient implementation. Arguably, survival and development, in this context, is similar to the best interests of the child. For example, the Committee mentions the following in its General Comment No. 6 in relation to the best interests principle:

> A determination of what is in the best interest of the child requires a clear and comprehensive assessment of the child's identity, including her or his nationality, upbringing, ethnic, cultural and linguistic background, particular vulnerabilities and protection needs.[80]

Another example can be found in the way the participation principle works as a method for the achievement of the child's social development. Social development is one aspect of the child's overall development under article 6(2).[81] For example, the concept of the responsibility of the child which is recognised by article 31 of the African Charter on the Rights and Welfare of the Child. When a child has responsibilities, this means that the child has to give. When the child gives, then the child is making an input. When the child makes an input, then the child is participating. And when the child is participating, then he or she is developing. Regardless of this, the participation of children on issues and policies that affect them is an individual human right that should lead to the full

79 A. Lopatka, 'The Rights of the Child are Universal: The Perspective of the UN Convention on the Rights of the Child', in M. Freeman and P. Veerman (eds.), *The Ideologies of Children's Rights* (Martinus Nijhoff Publishers, Dordrecht, 1992), p. 50.

80 Committee on the Rights of the Child, 'General Comment No. 6 on the Treatment of Unaccompanied and Separated Children Outside their Country of Origin', UN Doc. CRC/GC/2005/6 (1 September 2005), para. 20.

81 Committee on the Rights of the Child, 'General Guidelines for Periodic Reports (Basic Reference Document)', UN Doc. CRC/C/58 (20 November 1996), para. 40.

development of the child. This demonstrates a clear relationship between the development of the child as an aim and his or her participation.

Furthermore, article 6(2) as an aim can be achieved by the full implementation of article 4. This means that the full implementation of article 4 will also lead to the full implementation of the survival and development of the child.

6.1. SPECIFIC EXAMPLES ON ARTICLE 6(2) AS AN AIM

In some specific cases, such as the right of the child to enjoy the family environment, the Committee pointed out that some factors impede the best-interest principle. For example, in the concluding observations on Iceland's initial report, the Committee noted that the best interest of the child to spend time in his or her family environment may be infringed by the long working hours of parents and that sufficient measures had not been taken to prevent children from being alone at home during their parents' working hours. The concept of sufficient measures is infringed by the insufficient availability of places in nursery schools, which is of concern.[82] The same could be argued about the survival and development of the child. The safety of the child, which is central to his or her survival and development, could be affected if parents were not at home.

Any form of exploitation, particularly child labour, prostitution, drug-related activities and child trafficking and sale, could seriously interfere with the survival and development of the child as an aim. For example, in order to protect the right of the child to survival, the Committee asked the following of States:

> The Committee further recommends that firm measures be taken to ensure the right of survival of all children in Nepal, including those who live and/or work in the streets. Such measures should aim at the effective protection of children against any form of exploitation, particularly child labour, prostitution, drug-related activities and child trafficking and sale.[83]

Another example is the case of children in institutional care, who also need to reach their full development. In this regard the Committee made specifications in relation to the child's harmonious development:

> The Committee also suggests that appropriate alternatives to institutional care be developed, with the best interests of the child as the primary consideration, as well as

---

82 Committee on the Rights of the Child, 'Concluding Observations on Iceland's Initial Report', UN Doc. CRC/C/15/Add.50 (13 February 1996), para. 19.

83 Committee on the Rights of the Child, 'Concluding Observations on Nepal's Initial Report', UN Doc. CRC/C/15/Add.57 (7 June 1996), para. 35.

> the promotion of his or her harmonious development and preparation for responsible participation in society.[84]

Discrimination, as well, could interfere with the child's survival as an aim. For instance:

> With regard to the implementation of article 2 of the Convention, the Committee expresses its concern at the persistence of discriminatory attitudes and harmful practices affecting girls, as illustrated by serious disparities, sometimes starting at birth and affecting the enjoyment of the rights to survival, health, nutrition and education.[85]

The obligation of the State Party to identify the factors that impede the implementation of the Convention also helps in achieving the aim of survival and development of the child. Identifying the problem through the participation of the child supports the child's development, which leads to the overall development of his or her community. As Kent observed:

> It is not only goals but also the appreciation of obstacles and other considerations that must be shared. These common understandings arise out of continuing dialogue among the concerned individuals and organizations. That dialogue helps to build increasingly effective task orientation, and it also helps to build the sense of community.[86]

7. ARTICLE 6(2) AS A QUALITY-CONTROL FACTOR

As a quality-control factor article 6(2) can assist in determining whether the State Party has fulfilled its obligations for the implementation of the children's rights that are included in the Convention. Doek, for example, as previously pointed out, raises his concerns about article 6(2) as a general principle. In fact, he highlights another aspect of article 6(2), namely the qualifying factor. 'One could conclude that article 6 qualifies the measures a State Party has to undertake in implementing all other articles of the Convention, because they can all be considered as contributing to the survival and/or development of the child (ensure to the maximum extent possible).'[87]

As a quality-control factor, the survival and development principle is expected to play an important role in terms of the measures that the State Party will undertake in order to fulfil its obligations towards children and their

---

84 Committee on the Rights of the Child, 'Concluding Observations on Uruguay's Initial Report', UN Doc. CRC/C/15/Add.62 (30 October 1996), para. 23.

85 Committee on the Rights of the Child, 'Concluding Observations on Bangladesh's Initial Report', UN Doc. CRC/C/15/Add.74 (18 June 1997), para. 15.

86 G. Kent, *The Politics of Children's Survival* (Praeger Publishers, New York, 1991), p. 168.

87 J.E. Doek, 'The CRC General Principles', in J. Connors et al. (eds.), *18 Candles. The Convention on the Rights of the Child Reaches Majority* (Institut international des droits de l'enfant (IDE), Switzerland, 2007), pp. 36–37.

convention rights. For instance, in terms of the system for birth registrations, this may mean the adoption of measures that do not interfere with survival and development is significant. This could simply mean that, in some countries, where there is extremely hot weather, accompanied by poverty, or a lack of technology with which to register the child, the registration hour should be in the early hours of the day or late in the afternoon. This could help in protecting the survival of the babies, and probably older children, by stopping them from going out in the heat.[88]

As a qualifying factor to children's participation, the interaction between the participation principle and the survival and development principle is very clear, particularly where spiritual and cultural developments are concerned. For instance:

> Children with disabilities often require special services in health and education to allow them to achieve their fullest potential. However it should be noted that spiritual, emotional and cultural development and well-being of children with disabilities are very often overlooked. ... Furthermore, when their participation is invited, it is often limited to activities specifically designed for and targeted at children with disabilities. ... Programmes and activities designed for the child's cultural development and spiritual well-being should involve and cater to both children with and without disabilities in an integrated and participatory fashion.[89]

Earlier, Kent clarified the way in which article 6(2) may work as a qualifying factor:

> Participation is often interpreted in terms of involvement in decision making, implementation, supplying material and labor resources, or evaluation of programs. Here the focus is on participation in the *planning* of child survival programs. This means involvement in the formulation of the questions, the conceptual framework, the perspective, and the options, and not just having the opportunity to choose among options formulated by others. Full engagement in the planning of programs for child survival can be a potent means of empowerment for local people.[90]

He continues by stating that: 'Participation in the planning process in itself constitutes a means of development.'[91] This is relevant to article 6(2), because human development is a measure of overall development. The survival and development of the child as a qualifying factor also has a strong link with the child's participation. Empowerment requires participation and/or the opposite – participation leads to

---

88 Author's personal observations.

89 Committee on the Rights of the Child, 'General Comment No. 9 on the Rights of Children with Disabilities', UN Doc. CRC/C/GC/9 (27 February 2007), para. 33.

90 G. Kent, *The Politics of Children's Survival* (Praeger Publishers, New York, 1991), p. 167.

91 *Ibid.*, p. 168.

empowerment and empowerment is development: to be empowered is to increase capacity to define, analyse and act on one's own problem.[92]

8. CONCLUSION

Article 6(2) of the Convention on the Rights of the Child is unique. The way it stands within the Convention presents the opportunity to have the article identified and categorised in various settings. This is because the concepts of survival and development are both broad and varied in relation to their meaning. In addition, the two concepts are vital, and this gives the opportunity to have a dynamic and comprehensive categorisation of the survival and development of the child.

However, it is possible, for some, to argue against the concept of separate identification and categorisation of one article of the CRC; after all, the Convention should be implemented using a holistic approach. As Eugeen Verhellen pointed out:

> a subdivision of rights into different categories would be in breach of the spirit of the Convention, which makes no distinction between the different rights ... Indeed, the intention of bringing them all together in one *comprehensive instrument* was precisely to indicate that they were all equally important and even interdependent, none of these rights can stand alone ... The comprehensiveness of the Convention on the Rights of the Child is underlined especially by the fact that both first-generation and second generation human rights have been brought together here ... This emphasises the indivisibility and the non-hierarchy of these rights.[93]

While these arguments are undoubtedly legitimate, making such a categorisation could prove to be useful for having an in-depth understanding of the right of the child to survival and the right of the child to development. This kind of approach could prove to be helpful for the full, effective implementation and realisation of both rights. This supports the domestic implementation of the Convention that is compatible with the general principles and ensures the fulfilment of all the rights provided in the Convention, including the right to survive and develop.

Lack of consensus between authors and those who are involved with the Convention on the Rights of the Child in general, and article 6(2) in particular about the exact nature of article 6(2) is an illustration of the richness in meaning that the survival and development of the child have. This richness allows for quadrate categorisation of article 6(2). In particular, it allows for article 6(2) to be identified as a general principle of the Convention, a right of the Convention, an aim of the Convention, and a qualifying factor of the Convention.

---

92 *Ibid.*, p. 163.

93 E. Verhellen, *Convention on the Rights of the Child: Background, motivation, strategies, main themes* (E. Verhellen and Garant Publishers, Leuven, 2000), pp. 77–78.

CHAPTER 4

THE SURVIVAL AND DEVELOPMENT OF THE CHILD AND THE CHILD'S HUMAN DIGNITY

'Since when have you turned men into slaves, whereas they are born free of their mothers?'

Caliph Omar Ibn Alkhattab,
seventh century

1. INTRODUCTION

In its general guidelines for periodic reports, the Committee on the Rights of the Child states that article 6 of the Convention on the Rights of the Child (CRC) should be implemented in a manner that is compatible with the human dignity of the child. Precisely, the Committee on the Rights of the Child asks the States Parties to the Convention on the Rights of the Child to create a suitable environment in order to ensure to the maximum extent possible the survival and development of the child in a way that is compatible with the child's human dignity:

> Please describe specific measures taken to guarantee the child's right to life and to create an environment conducive to ensuring to the maximum extent possible the survival and development of the child, including physical, mental, spiritual, moral, psychological and social development, in a manner compatible with human dignity, and to prepare the child for an individual life in a free society.[1]

---

1 Committee on the Rights of the Child, 'General guidelines for periodic reports', UN Doc. CRC/C/58 (20 November 1996) (Basic Reference Document), para. 40. Please note that the Committee on the Rights of the Child replaced this document with 'General guidelines regarding the form and content of periodic reports to be submitted by States Parties under article 44, paragraph 1 (b), of the Convention', UN Doc. CRC/C/58/Rev.1 (29 November 2005). The new document does not make the same reference to the relationship between the survival and development of the child and his or her human dignity. In 2010 the Committee replaced the 2005 guidelines with 'Treaty-specific guidelines regarding the form and content of periodic reports to be submitted by States parties under article 44, paragraph 1 (b), of the Convention on the Rights of the Child', UN Doc. No. CRC/58/Rev.2 (23 November 2010).

This chapter studies the interrelationship between the human dignity of the child and article 6(2) of the CRC on the right of the child to survival and development. The chapter starts with an identification of the concept of human dignity in the context of article 6(2). Following this, the chapter highlights the universal importance of the concept of human dignity, by highlighting the importance of human dignity in various cultural and religious backgrounds. This is also achieved by focusing on some international and domestic legal documents and constitutions. The chapter highlights the importance of the concept as a base or foundation for human rights. Later there is more detailed discussion on the relationship between article 6(2) and the concept of human dignity. As pointed out in Chapter 3, under the Convention on the Rights of the Child, article 6(2) has various capacities, e.g., the general principle capacity, the aim capacity, the qualifying factor capacity and the right capacity. This chapter discusses the interaction between the human dignity of the child and article 6(2) under various capacities. In both cases, the chapter concludes that in relation to article 6(2) the human dignity of the child has two facets. It is both an end, i.e., an aim, and a criterion, i.e., a tool; or it is a method towards achieving the survival and development of the child.

Before proceeding with the discussion, it is important to highlight the significant relationship between the right of the child to survival and development and human dignity. In fact some might argue against the selection of dignity as an underlying concept to the entire article 6(2), especially considering that human dignity is not explicitly referred to in the text of the article. This legitimate argument could be based on the understanding that, as discussed in Chapter 3, article 6(2) has multi-identities. This already makes it of a complex nature. Therefore, the argument goes on that it might be confusing to choose the 'wide and vague' concept of dignity in helping with regard to the interpretation of the 'complex' right of the child to survival and development.

In this respect, it is important, from one side, to refer to the close relationship between international human rights norms and human dignity (this will be discussed later in detail). On the other side reference should be made to the wide spectrum of article 6(2) as a right to everything. The interaction with human dignity is just unbreakable with regard to all aspects of the right of the child to survival and development. This strong relationship is inevitable.

2. UNDERSTANDING HUMAN DIGNITY

2.1. IMPORTANCE OF THE UNIVERSAL CONCEPT OF HUMAN DIGNITY

The concept of human dignity, as such, is wide and vague. It is related to every aspect of human life, including legal, religious, philosophical, political, cultural and ethical features. The following few paragraphs aim at understanding the rationale behind such an importance of the concept of human dignity.

By looking at the human being in the centre of the world, one can point out a number of aspects in which the dignity of the human being is evident. For instance, humans are distinctive because they have minds. Minds are different from brains. Animals are like humans when it comes to brains, but the human being is more dignified than the animal because he or she has a mind. The mind leads to thinking, and thinking leads to inventing, and so on. Rabkin argues that the word 'dignity' requires some distinction:

> To start with, we might notice that the U.N. texts associated 'dignity' with equality. This is curious, since 'dignity' normally implies a point of distinction: what is dignified is in some way distinguished from the ordinary – or at least from the undignified.[2]

Does this argument suggest that the human being is the only living being that has dignity? Granting human beings dignity does not mean that other creatures should not be treated with dignity. Rabkin's argument about a 'point of distinction' should be valid only when humans are compared to other creatures, not when they are compared to each other as humans. This suggests that dignity for adults is the same as that for children.

Human beings, when compared to other creatures such as animals, are able to make use of and benefit from most of the available resources in the world. For example, human beings make use of the sun by generating solar energy from it. They also make use of water, seas and rivers by generating power from them or the simple act of travelling on them. Human beings make use of the other creatures that exist in this world, like animals, for instance, by using them for entertainment when riding on the back of a horse, or even by going to the circus and watching animals in shows that amuse human beings and enable them to enjoy themselves. If we try to imagine an opposite situation, where a human being is entertaining an animal, then this would be illogical and humiliating for the human being, which is contrary to his or her dignity.[3] Importantly as well, any positive or negative action that prejudices the mind is a violation of human dignity. In its turn, for a human, having a mind is accompanied by having a will, and being able to behave in accordance with one's will is also an aspect of human dignity.

All of this requires human beings to have dignity that is inherent in them by the mere fact that they are humans. This inherent dignity follows the human being even after his or her death. The respect for a dead body is a universal value.

---

2 J. Rabkin, 'What We Can Learn about Human Dignity from International Law' (2003) 27 *Harvard Journal of Law & Public Policy* 145, 145.

3 This is not to deny animals the right to be treated kindly and mercifully.

This is an observation of the human dignity. It is not acceptable to exhume bodies, except for exceptional reasonable reasons, such as investigations. In some societies, washing the body of a dead person after he or she dies and burying him or her in the ground is a sign of respect for his or her dignity. For these societies, this is seen as the most dignified way to treat the human body after death. Sometimes controversies and concerns with regard to respect for human dignity accompany exhibitions of Egyptian mummies and exhibitions that contain dead bodies, and that are claimed to be for educational reasons. This proves the importance of human dignity, which has always been a living concept in human life. The story of the son of Adam, who killed his brother and later saw a crow burying another crow, conveys that he violated his brother's dignity by killing him and then by leaving him exposed, rather than burying his dead body.

2.2. HUMAN DIGNITY AS A LIVING CONCEPT WITHIN VARIOUS RELIGIOUS, CULTURAL, IDEOLOGICAL, SOCIAL AND LEGAL BACKGROUNDS

Since the early existence of humanity, despite differences in human beings and human backgrounds, human dignity has been known and referred to. The story of the prophet Moses, who asked the Pharaoh to allow him to move with the Jews to another land, where they would not suffer the same maltreatment that they received from the Pharaoh and his people in Egypt, conveys this. The nobility and integrity of the Virgin Mary embodies the principle of human dignity. Human dignity is also embedded in the Islamic belief that God granted humans dignity and, therefore, provided other creatures for their use. In the Koran, human dignity is granted by God: 'Verily we have honoured the children of Adam. We carry them on the land and the sea, and have made provision of good things for them, and have preferred them above many of those whom we created with a marked preferment.'[4]

Human dignity also finds a place in legislation, such as those international conventions seeking to end slavery around the world, intellectual writings, and works of fiction. Human dignity was also not far away from the thinking and ideologies that were behind some revolutions and social movements, such as the French Revolution, the Mahdiyya Revolution in Sudan, the Bolshevik Revolution in Russia and the civil rights movements in America. These movements vary a lot in their ideologies but one may possibly argue that they all share a concern for human dignity in order to improve the quality of people's lives. While it might not have been clearly stated that the respect for human dignity and the prevention of humiliation were driving forces and aims that these movements hoped to achieve, one can perceive that human dignity and respect for it were present. This illustrates the living nature of human dignity. The respect for and

4 The Holy Koran, *Surah* 17, Verse 70.

protection of human dignity are rooted inside human beings. Obviously, this is not enough to prevent humans from violating respect for human dignity, but it is always there, at least, to help in stopping and preventing it.

2.3. SIGNIFICANCE OF HUMAN DIGNITY IN THE CONTEXT OF THIS CHAPTER

In the context of this chapter, the importance of having a definition or at least an understanding of the concept of human dignity in relation to article 6(2) comes from the fact that human dignity is an essential concept for all human beings and their rights, particularly article 6(2). All human beings have dignity and all of them should enjoy full respect for that dignity. Human beings should enjoy the respect of their dignity with regard to their lives, their minds, their bodies, their reputation and honour, and their properties, i.e., all the aspects of their lives. In this regard, children are no different from adults. Similar to human dignity, the right of the child to survival and development covers all the aspects of the child's life. In order to have a child who survives and develops with dignity, the child needs to enjoy recognition and protection of his or her quality of life.

2.4. DEFINITION OF HUMAN DIGNITY

Despite the importance and universality of the concept of human dignity, it is not easy to have a precise definition of it. It is probably easier to understand some of its features and its fields and domains but, arguably, the principle lacks a precise definition that will determine its meaning. However, from a linguistic point of view, 'dignity is the quality of being worthy of honour and respect'.[5]

Dominique Rousseau observes that discussing human dignity and attempting to offer an explanation of the principle of human dignity is not a straightforward process:

> While all European constitutions now include the right to respect for human dignity, none defines or spells it out. It emerges clearly … that human dignity is a vague concept capable of many interpretations. This seems to be due to the peculiarity of this right in comparison to other fundamental rights, be they civil, political, social, economic or cultural.[6]

5 A.S. Homby, *Oxford Advanced Learner's Dictionary of Current English,* 5th edition (Oxford University Press, 1995), p. 323.

6 D. Rousseau, 'Concluding Report. The principle of respect for human dignity', Montpellier, 2–6 July 1998, *Science and Techniques of Democracy*, No. 26 (Council of Europe Publishing, 1999), pp. 102–106, p. 104.

Arguably, the difficulties that arise in a discussion on human dignity can be summarised into two points. Firstly, the concept, i.e. the principle of human dignity, covers all the variable aspects of human life; therefore it is a very broad and wide principle. Walter, for instance, argues that this difficulty led the courts to deal with human dignity in connection with another basic right, for instance slavery and racial discrimination, where the violation of equality goes along with the violation of the human dignity clause.[7] Secondly, the issue of 'preciseness' is also of importance. Human dignity is a concept and a value, and, although strongly enduring, it is not tangible. This makes it more difficult to create a precise definition of the concept. In this context, it is probably more logical to focus on the features of the human dignity concept rather than attempt to give a precise definition.

2.5. FEATURES OF HUMAN DIGNITY

One important feature of human dignity is that it is universal and that it is for every human being around the globe, including children. Individuals have human dignity and the entire human race has dignity. The concept of human dignity is also absolute. Human beings should be treated in a dignified way. Human beings are living beings who have dignity; therefore, they should be treated with dignity, with regard to any aspect of their life. Based on this, human dignity is a principle that has the effect of determining how children, as human beings, are to be treated. Thus, it is indeed logical enough to expect a dignified treatment of a child when implementing the right of the child to health or the right of the child to education and so on.

Significantly, the universality and the absoluteness of the human dignity principle also have the effect of determining the rights and wrongs of human behaviour. For instance, if a child is harassing a dog, then it is not going to be possible to argue that the child should not be disciplined for the maltreatment of the dog just because the child has human dignity. In fact, the child's behaviour should reflect this dignity by showing and proving a dignified way of behaviour. This means that the principle of human dignity determines humans' behaviour towards others; therefore, it is a measuring tool, i.e., a criterion for quality. This understanding should regulate the understanding of the concept of human dignity.

However, while human dignity is absolute and inherent in humanity, and its protection and realisation should not be impaired in any way, there are some cases where the human dignity of the child might be 'jeopardised' if some caution is not taken, for instance in relation to the rights of parents to discipline

7 C. Walter, 'Human Dignity in German Constitutional Law. The principle of respect for human dignity', Montpellier, 2–6 July 1998, *Science and Techniques of Democracy*, No. 26 (Council of Europe Publishing, 1999), pp. 25–42, p. 41.

their children (more details on this are discussed later in the chapter). Parents have the right to discipline their children, but only under the umbrella of the human dignity of both the parent and the child. Human dignity regulates the parents' behaviour and the child as the person under parental authority. Rights of parents are guaranteed for in articles 5 and 18 of the CRC.

The Constitutional Court of South Africa, in a case about the religious right of parents in Christianity to discipline their children, referred to the debate on the human dignity of both sides as a 'complex factual and psychological setting':

> Then, the broad community has an interest in reducing violence wherever possible and protecting children from harm. The overlap and tension between the different clusters of rights reflect themselves in contradictory assessments of how the central constitutional value of dignity is implicated. On the one hand, the dignity of the parents may be negatively affected when the state tells them how to bring up and discipline their children and limits the manner in which they may express their religious beliefs. The child who has grown up in the particular faith may regard the punishment, although hurtful, as designed to strengthen his character. On the other hand, the child is being subjected to what an outsider might regard as the indignity of suffering a painful and humiliating hiding deliberately inflicted on him in an institutional setting. Indeed, it would be unusual if the child did not have ambivalent emotions. It is in this complex factual and psychological setting that the matter must be decided.[8]

This complex psychological setting is of great importance to the child's psychological and spiritual upbringing. The mere recognition of parental rights is not at all a violation of the human dignity of the child. It is actually the quality of the practice that might jeopardise the child's human dignity.

Christian Walter questions the absoluteness of human dignity from a different perspective. He raises this point with regard to the decision of a human being to end his own life, where he points out that as a basic principle, the only thing that human dignity can do is to establish general considerations. He argues that the details depend largely on the practical assessments, which vary from case to case.[9] Debates on human dignity and ending one's own life are of relevance. While practicability is an important factor, other factors need to be considered as well in order to determine the rules that would govern the concept of human dignity. Sources of human dignity are of relevance in this regard. A relevant debate, in this context, is whether human dignity is granted by divine

---

8 *Christian Education South Africa v. Minister of Education* (18 August 2000) (CCT4/00) [2000] ZACC 11 (Constitutional Court of South Africa), para. 15. For further analysis of the *Christian Education South Africa* case see C. Cornell et al. (eds.), *The Dignity Jurisprudence of the Constitutional Court of South Africa: Cases and Materials* (Fordham University Press, New York, 2013), pp. 390–405.

9 C. Walter, 'Human Dignity in German Constitutional Law. The principle of respect for human dignity', Montpellier, 2–6 July 1998, *Science and Techniques of Democracy*, No. 26 (Council of Europe Publishing, 1999), pp. 25–42, p. 37.

authority to human beings. When human dignity is a grant, this means that human dignity should be ruled by the divine rule of the granter.

All of these factors about the nature of human dignity and its features and issues of practice should be considered in regard to the discussion on the relationship between the human dignity of the child and article 6(2) on the survival and development of the child.

3. THE RESPONSIBILITY OF THE STATE TO PROTECT THE HUMAN DIGNITY OF THE CHILD

In the context of article 6(2) it is the responsibility of the State to respect the human dignity that is under consideration. This is whether it is the respect for human dignity that should occur between two individuals or the respect between the individual and the State. It is also the responsibility of the State to enhance parents', guardians' and carers' understanding of dignity. In its General Comment No. 7 the Committee on the Rights of the Child stated:

> In providing appropriate assistance to parents in the performance of their child-rearing responsibilities (art. 18.2), States parties should take all appropriate measures to enhance parents' understanding of their role in their children's early education, encourage child-rearing practices which are child-centred, encourage respect for the child's dignity and provide opportunities for developing understanding, self-esteem and self-confidence...[10]

But is the imposition of the responsibility on the State derived from the understanding that it should have an interest in the matter? The case of Christian Education South Africa v the Minister of Education, which involved corporal punishment according to Christian beliefs, discussed the issue on the basis that if the society believed in corporal punishment then the State had no interest:

> The second and more persuasive argument is to the effect that the state has an interest in protecting pupils from degradation and indignity. The respondent contended that the trend in Europe and neighbouring African countries was firmly in the direction of abolition of corporal punishment, and that the core value of human dignity in our Bill of Rights did not countenance the use of physical force to achieve scholarly correction. Accordingly, the respondent was under an obligation to prohibit such punishment, and to do so without exception and for the benefit of all children. The appellant replied that for believers, including the children involved, the indignity and degradation lay not in the punishment, but

10 Committee on the Rights of the Child, 'General Comment No. 7 on Implementing Child Rights in Early Childhood', UN Doc. CRC/C/GC/7/Rev.1 (20 September 2006), para. 29(a).

> in the defiance of the scriptures represented by leaving the misdeeds unpunished; subjectively, for those who shared the religious outlook of the community, no indignity at all was involved. It argued further that internationally there was widespread judicial support for the view that physical punishment only became degrading when it passed a certain degree of severity. Appellant would be bound by limits set by the common law, and these limits would establish the standards to be applied. It did not contend that corporal punishment should be permitted in all schools, but asserted that its use should be allowed within reasonable limits in independent schools where parents, out of their religious convictions, had authorised it. The state interest, accordingly, did not extend to protecting the children in the appellant's schools.[11]

In cases of conflict of interests between the State and the individual concerned, which one should prevail? Walter refers to the obligation of the State to protect human dignity and the fact that it may conflict with the interests of the individual whom the State wants to protect. He refers to 'dwarf throwing' cases and says that the human-dignity factor in them has been used as a basis for restraining freedom and not as a means for the protection of freedom.[12] He states that the Constitutional Court in Germany has qualified the basic rights, especially the human dignity clause, as an 'order of values'. He argues that value-oriented jurisprudence tends to reverse the basic function of the human dignity clause.[13] This kind of argument illustrates the lack of consensus, confusions and sometimes misconceptions about human dignity. For example, in the case of 'dwarf throwing' a contradictory argument could be established on the basis that human dignity is intended to protect the individual from any harm, even if he or she agrees to its infliction.

Arguably, conflict of interests could arise in many cases, such as child vaccinations. Some vaccines, such as the measles, mumps and rubella vaccine (MMR) for example, was falsely claimed to have a causal link with autism.[14] In this case, the State and the society from one side have an interest in stopping the illnesses, but the individual child also has an interest not to be subject to an act that will interfere with his or her right to survival, development and health. In this case, human dignity has a role to play.

However, in the context of article 6(2) of the CRC, the State is responsible for the protection of the human dignity of the child. The responsibility of the State in article 6(2) is derived from the fact that the CRC, initially, places the obligation

---

11 *Christian Education South Africa v. Minister of Education* (18 August 2000) (CCT4/00) [2000] ZACC 11[43] (Constitutional Court of South Africa) (footnotes omitted), para. 43.

12 For dwarf throwing also see *Manuel Wackenheim v. France*, UN Doc. CCPR/C/75/D/854/1999.

13 C. Walter, 'Human Dignity in German Constitutional Law. The principle of respect for human dignity', Montpellier, 2–6 July 1998, *Science and Techniques of Democracy*, No. 26 (Council of Europe Publishing, 1999), pp. 25–42, pp. 38–39.

14 M.A. Maglione et al., 'Safety of Vaccines Used for Routine Immunization of US Children: A Systamic Review' (2014) 134 *Paediatrics* 325, 331.

on the State Party. One question, however, is whether this can happen in a way that interferes with the child's beliefs and those of the concerned society? The Committee asks States Parties to create measures that are conducive to the human dignity of the child. This is a general statement. Later it will be debated whether it is up to the State to decide how to use the human dignity principle and whether it is acceptable to place any limits, under the theme of individual's interest, on it or not. The State will also decide whether to deal with the concept separately or in relation to other matters, by declaring them unconstitutional for instance.[15]

4. HUMAN DIGNITY IN INTERNATIONAL LAW AND NATIONAL CONSTITUTIONS

The concept or the principle of human dignity is not new in international law and its inclusion in a number of international and regional human rights conventions illustrates its importance. The Universal Declaration on Human Rights, for example, makes several references to human dignity in the preamble and the articles as well. Article 1, for instance, states that human beings are equal in their dignity, which means that no one or no race has more dignity than the others: 'All human beings are born free and equal in dignity and rights. They are endowed with reason and conscience and should act towards one another in a spirit of brotherhood.'[16] When drafting the Universal Declaration, human dignity was thought to be the principle that would bring various nations that have different cultural backgrounds together. The preamble of the International Covenant on Civil and Political Rights (ICCPR) also refers to human dignity as well: 'Recognizing that these rights derive from the inherent dignity of the human person…'[17] The wording of the International Covenant on Economic, Social and Cultural Rights (ICESCR) is exactly the same as that of the ICCPR.[18] Both of the Covenants consider that the principle of human dignity is actually the source of the rights. Human dignity is also a right under article 1 of the European Charter of Fundamental Rights: 'Human dignity is inviolable. It must be respected and protected.'[19] The principle also appears in the 1959 Declaration of the Rights of the Child:

---

15 J.M. Cardoso Da Costa, 'The Principle of Human Dignity in European Case Law. The principle of respect for human dignity', Montpellier, 2–6 July 1998, *Science and Techniques of Democracy*, No. 26 (Council of Europe Publishing, 1999), pp. 50–56, p. 54.

16 Universal Declaration of Human Rights (adopted 10 December 1948 UNGA Res 217 A (III) (UDHR).

17 International Covenant on Civil and Political Rights (adopted 16 December 1996, entered into force 23 March 1976) 999 UNTS 171 (ICCPR).

18 International Covenant on Economic Social and Cultural Rights (adopted 16 December 1966, entered into force 3 January 1976) 999 UNTS 171 (ICESCR).

19 European Union, Charter of Fundamental Rights of the European Union, 7 December 2000, Official Journal of the European Communities, 18 December 2000 (2000/C 364/01).

> Whereas the peoples of the United Nations have, in the Charter, reaffirmed their faith in fundamental human rights and in the dignity and worth of the human person, and have determined to promote social progress and better standards of life in larger freedom.[20]

The importance of the human dignity principle is also reflected in its adoption into a number of domestic legislations and constitutions. The principle is found in a number of constitutions around the world that have different ideological and cultural backgrounds. For instance, article 1 of the 1976 constitution of Portugal bases the sovereignty of the State on human dignity: 'Portugal is a sovereign Republic, based on the dignity of the human person and the will of the people, and committed to building a free and fair society that unites in solidarity.' The preamble to the 1937 constitution of the Republic of Ireland (Bunreacht na hÉireann) also refers to the dignity as an aim: 'And seeking to promote the common good, with due observance of Prudence, Justice and Charity, so that the dignity and freedom of the individual may be assured, true social order attained, the unity of our country restored, and concord established with other nations'. Article 23 of the Belgian Constitution also speaks about the right to lead a life with human dignity, such as the right to health, the right to decent housing, the right to the protection of a healthy environment, and the right to cultural and social fulfilment. The human dignity principle is also available in the Polish constitution in force since 17 October 1997. Article 30 explicitly states: 'The inherent and inalienable dignity of the person shall constitute a source of freedoms and rights of persons and citizens. It shall be inviolable. The respect and protection thereof shall be the obligation of public authorities.'

Most of these constitutions refer to human dignity in a manner that is relevant to the cultural experience and history of the particular State but without excluding the future. The South African constitution for example was passed with great consideration to the painful apartheid history and experience of South Africa.[21] The words of Langa DCJ in De Reuck v. Director of Public Prosecutions express this and explain the important position of the human dignity concept in the South African Constitution:

> The value of dignity in our Constitutional framework cannot therefore be doubted. The Constitution asserts dignity to contradict our past in which human dignity for black South Africans was routinely and cruelly denied. It asserts it too to inform the

20 United Nations General Assembly, 'Declaration of the Rights of the Child', UN Doc. A/RES/1386 (XIV) (20 November 1959).

21 See C. Cornell et al. (eds.), *The Dignity Jurisprudence of the Constitutional Court of South Africa: Cases and Materials* (Fordham University Press, New York, 2013), p. 67. G.E. Devenish, *A Commentary on the South African Bill of Rights* (Butterworths, Durban, 1999), p. 83. See also M. Reyneke, 'The Right to Dignity and Restorative Justice in Schools' [2011] PER 35, available at: <www.saflii.org/cgi-bin/disp.pl?file=za/journals/PER/2011/35.html&query= harmful traditional practices> accessed 23 April 2015.

> future, to invest in our democracy respect for the intrinsic worth of all human beings. Human dignity therefore informs constitutional adjudication and interpretation at a range of levels. It is a value that informs the interpretation of many, possibly all, other rights. This Court has already acknowledged the importance of the constitutional value of dignity in interpreting rights such as the right to equality, the right not to be punished in a cruel, inhuman or degrading way, and the right to life. Human dignity is also a constitutional value that is of central significance in the limitations analysis. Section 10, however, makes it plain that dignity is not only a *value* fundamental to our Constitution, it is a justiciable and enforceable *right* that must be respected and protected.[22]

The South African Constitution focused on human dignity and provides for it on a number of bases. For example, article 10 of the Bill of Rights, which is part of the 1996 constitution of South Africa, speaks about human dignity as a right: 'Everyone has inherent dignity and the right to have their dignity respected and protected.' The Bill of Rights under the 2005 National Interim Constitution of the Republic of Sudan also explicitly considers inherent human dignity. Article 28 speaks about the right to life and human dignity: 'Every human being has the inherent right to life, dignity and the integrity of his/her person, which shall be protected by law; no one shall be arbitrarily deprived of his/her life.' The term 'dignity' appears in other places in the constitution as well, for example in article 45 on the rights of people with disabilities. Article 32 explicitly speaks about the rights of women and children. Paragraph 3 of this article speaks about the protection of human dignity: 'The State shall combat harmful customs and traditions which undermine the dignity and the status of women.' The article could possibly be interpreted in order to cover a number of harmful practices. The Interim Constitution of the Republic of Sudan was adopted as a part of a peace agreement that was a major step towards ending the civil war in Sudan; therefore, the civil war history is in the background of this constitution.

These worldwide references to the human dignity principle illustrate a consensus on its importance and its strong relevance to every aspect of human life, including children's lives. Unfortunately, this importance is not always reflected in the daily practice of many countries. In this context, article 6(2) is expected to ensure that the practice and the theory support each other.

In fact, both the international documents and the domestic legislation have historical reflections. For instance, the human dignity principle in the Universal Declaration on Human Rights speaks about the equality of all human beings as regards their dignity because it was adopted after the atrocities of the Second World War, including the notion of supremacy of a particular race. Nevertheless,

22 *De Reuck v. Director of Public Prosecutions (Witwatersrand Local Division) and Others* (15 October 2003) (CCT5/03) [2003] ZACC 19 [62] (Constitutional Court of South Africa), para. 62.

there can be certain differences in relation to the meaning and the context of the principle of human dignity in international documents compared to some domestic legislation. Devenish, for instance, refers to the difference between the concept of human dignity in the international documents and the concept of human dignity in the common law in South Africa:

> In the international legal instruments, although the term 'dignity' is not defined, it tends to be used in a broader and less technical manner than in our common law. This is manifestly clear from the African Charter of Rights which speaks of 'dignity inherent in a human being'. The Universal Declaration of Human Rights refers to all human beings as 'born free and equal in dignity and rights'. In contrast, in Roman-Dutch law the term '*dignitas*' relates to the inviolability of an individual's personality or self-esteem. Cachalia et al observes that 'our courts have occasionally, and erroneously, linked dignity with status, honour reputation or what amounts to esteem in other eyes.'[23]

The difference in the meanings and contexts represents the elasticity of the human dignity concept. Whilst considering this factor, the ensuing discussion in this chapter will be limited to understanding the relationship between the human dignity principle and the right of the child to survival and development under article 6(2) of the Convention on the Rights of the Child.

5. DIGNITY AND THE CONVENTION ON THE RIGHTS OF THE CHILD

5.1. GENERAL FEATURES OF DIGNITY

The drafting and later the adoption of the United Nations Convention on the Rights of the Child should, in itself, be considered a milestone in the process of recognition of the human dignity of the child. Initially, the Convention represented a breakthrough in the way childhood is viewed. The Convention is a clear and straightforward recognition that children are human beings and the outcome of this fact is manifest in them having human dignity and human rights. The adoption of a special convention on the rights of the child would, it was hoped, lead to an expansion on the protection of children and their dignity:

> The Convention on the Rights of the Child worked a change in the old paradigms in respect of children, and an opportunity to devise new forms of intervention. The

23 G.E. Devenish, *A Commentary on the South African Bill of Rights* (Butterworths, Durban, 1999), p. 82.

> child, hitherto conceived of as a passive subject of protection by the State, came to be seen as an active subject endowed with rights...[24]

The adoption of the Convention on the Rights of the Child conveys recognition of and respect for children's dignity as a category and as individuals.

> As already noted, the Convention on the Rights of the Child works a substantial change in the manner of addressing children. This transformation is known as replacing the 'irregular situation doctrine' by the 'comprehensive protection doctrine,' in other words, moving from a conception of 'minors' as the object of protection and repression to considering children and youths as full subjects at law. This conceptual change requires a change in the legislation of all countries party to the treaty, as well as public policy initiatives aimed at achieving effective recognition of children as having this new status as subjects at law.[25]

The adoption of a special convention on the child and his or her rights represents the recognition that children as individuals and as a category are different from adults. They have different requirements and different rights that suit their childhood. The preamble of the Convention explicitly refers to the special needs of childhood: 'Recalling that, in the Universal Declaration of Human Rights, the United Nations has proclaimed that Childhood is entitled to special care and assistance.'[26]

On the other hand, this difference, which is an essential requirement of their childhood, does not convey that their rights and their requirements are less important or less developed than those of adults. In fact, no kind of difference, whether in race, age, origin, intellectual capacity, religion or abilities, etc., should ever be considered when it comes to human dignity. This is the reason for human dignity being absolute and universal.

However, for children, the mere recognition of their difference from adults demonstrates recognition of, and respect for, their dignity. Children's rights and requirements are in fact equal to those of adults. The respect for the human dignity of the child is a respect for his or her childhood and unique vulnerability. In General Comment No. 7 of the Committee on the Rights of the Child, titled 'A positive agenda for early childhood', the Committee encourages States Parties to show respect and construct a positive agenda for rights in early childhood:

> A shift away from traditional beliefs that regard early childhood mainly as a period for the socialization of the immature human being towards mature adult status is

---

24 Second Report on the Situation of Human Rights in Peru (2 June 2000) Organization of American States Doc. OEA/Ser.L/V/II.106 Doc. 59 rev., Chapter VIII, para. 6.

25 Third Report on the Situation of Human Rights in Paraguay (9 March 2001) Organization of American States Doc. OEA/Ser.L/V/II.110 Doc. 52. Debates about the extent of parental rights and the attainment of majority are also of relevance in this regard (footnote omitted).

26 Paragraph 4 of the preamble of the Convention on the Rights of the Child, UN Doc. A/RES/44/25 (20 November 1989), Annex.

> required. The Convention requires that children, including the very youngest children, be respected as persons in their own right. Young children should be recognized as active members of families, communities and societies, with their own concerns, interests and points of view. For the exercise of their rights, young children have particular requirements for physical nurturance, emotional care and sensitive guidance, as well as for time and space for social play, exploration and learning. These requirements can best be planned for within a framework of laws, policies and programmes for early childhood, including a plan for implementation and independent monitoring, for example through the appointment of a children's rights commissioner, and through assessments of the impact of laws and policies on children...[27]

According to the Committee on the Rights of the Child it is important to recall that the Convention has introduced a holistic approach to the rights of the child, all rights being interrelated and inherent to the dignity of the child.[28]

In the context of the CRC, human dignity can be considered as an aim as well. For example, training of various professional groups on children's rights 'such as teachers, judges, social workers and police officials. Such programmes should emphasize the promotion and protection of the fundamental rights of the child and the child's sense of dignity',[29] i.e. emphasis on the promotion and protection of the child's dignity being the aim of training programs for professional groups.

The Convention on the Rights of the Child should be viewed as an extension to the other international human rights documents that are also meant for the child and the protection of his or her rights. This implies that the human dignity of the child is equal to that of the adult. However, for the sake of the best interests of the child and the guarantee of his or her survival and development, children's rights and requirements need special attention and awareness than those of adults.

5.2. HUMAN DIGNITY UNDER THE CONVENTION

The term 'dignity' is expressly mentioned eight times in the Convention on the Rights of the Child, but in different contexts. This does not mean that the existence of the human dignity principle cannot be extracted from other parts of the Convention. In fact, some major aspects of the CRC manifest the Convention's recognition of the child's dignity. For instance, the right of the

---

27 Committee on the Rights of the Child, 'General Comment No. 7 on Implementing Child Rights in Early Childhood', UN Doc. CRC/C/GC/7/Rev.1 (20 September 2006), para. 5.

28 Committee on the Rights of the Child, UN Doc. CRC/C/19/Rev.10 (11 March 2002).

29 Committee on the Rights of the Child, 'Concluding Observations on Philippines's Initial Report', UN Doc. CRC/C/15/Add.29 (15 February 1995), para. 22.

child to express his or her views freely in 'all matters affecting the child', and giving his or her thoughts due weight, emphasises and recognises the human dignity of the child. Respect for the child's 'worth and inherent human dignity as valued members of society' is an aspect of the child's participation rights.[30] The participation principle under article 12 of the CRC highlights the role of the child as an active participant in the promotion, protection and monitoring of his or her rights; it applies equally to all measures adopted by States to implement the Convention. The child also needs to have access to all the information concerned. It is not enough that the child expresses his or her opinion; it has to be taken into account:

> But appearing to 'listen' to children is relatively unchallenging; giving due weight to their views requires real change. Listening to children should not be seen as an end in itself, but rather as a means by which States make their interactions with children and their actions on behalf of children ever more sensitive to the implementation of children's rights.[31]

5.3. HUMAN DIGNITY AND THE PARTICIPATION PRINCIPLE

In the context of article 12, the human dignity of the child is an aim that is to be achieved through the participation of the child and a criterion for the quality of the right's implementation, although the aim factor might be more prominent. Taking the example of children below the age of eight or, as they are usually categorised, 'early childhood', granting this category their right to participation will definitely reflect a high level of realisation of their human dignity. This category of children needs to be protected by article 12(1) of the CRC under the umbrella of 'given due weight in accordance with the age and maturity of the child', as the Committee's words describe in relation to the abilities of these children:

> Young children are acutely sensitive to their surroundings and very rapidly acquire understanding of the people, places and routines in their lives, along with awareness of their own unique identity. They make choices and communicate their feelings, ideas and wishes in numerous ways, long before they are able to communicate through the conventions of spoken or written language.[32]

---

30 P. Alderson et al., 'The Participation Rights of Premature Babies' (2005) 13 *The International Journal of Children's Rights* 31–50.

31 Committee on the Rights of the Child, 'General Comment No. 5 on the General measures of implementation for the Convention on the Rights of the Child (arts. 4, 42 and 44, para. 6)', UN Doc. CRC/GC/2003/5 (27 November 2005), para. 12.

32 Committee on the Rights of the Child, 'General Comment No. 7 on Implementing Child Rights in Early Childhood', UN Doc. CRC/C/GC/7/Rev.1 (20 September 2006), para. 14.

The realisation of the right of the child to participate will also reach its peak when the environment and beliefs of the child are considered. The survival and development of the child as a criterion and a quality-control factor can have a big role to play in this regard.

The participation rights of the child also raise the issue of the ability of the child to enter into financial agreements that are in his or her best interests. They also raise the issue of whether the child has a right to property. In many legal systems, children have a right to property. Violations of this right that deny access to property might lead, in cases of poverty, to humiliation, which is the opposite of dignity.

5.4. HUMAN DIGNITY AND THE EVOLVING CAPACITY PRINCIPLE

The other principle of the CRC that manifests the human dignity of the child is the principle of the evolving capacity of the child, which is guaranteed by article 5 of the Convention:

> States Parties shall respect the responsibilities, rights and duties of parents or, where applicable, the members of the extended family or community as provided for by local custom, legal guardians or other persons legally responsible for the child, to provide, in a manner consistent with the evolving capacities of the child, appropriate direction and guidance in the exercise by the child of the rights recognized in the present Convention.

The following statement by Van Bueren explains the interactive relationship between the evolving capacity principle, the child's right to liberty and the child's dignity. This highlights the effects of the principle of the human dignity of the child in relation to article 37(c) of the CRC:

> [C]hildren who are deprived of liberty are entitled throughout their period of deprivation of liberty to be treated 'with humanity and respect for the inherent dignity of the human person, and in a manner which takes into account the needs of persons of their age.'
>
> …
>
> Article 37(c), inter alia, provides,
>
>> in particular, every child deprived of liberty shall be separated from adults unless it is considered in the child's best interest not to do so and shall have the right to maintain contact with his or her family through correspondence and visits, save in exceptional circumstances.[33]

33 G. Van Bueren, *The International Law on the Rights of the Child* (Martinus Nijhoff Publishers, The Hague, 1998), p. 219.

She argues that the CRC adds a new element to the measures that already exist in article 10(1) of the ICCPR. This article is about the right to be treated with humanity and respect for human dignity of, which, according to the Human Rights Committee, is 'a basic standard of universal application which cannot depend entirely on material resources':[34]

> The Convention on the Rights of the Child adds a new element. For the children of States Parties deprived of their liberty, account has to be taken to the needs of their age. This is another application of the concept of the evolving capacities of the child.
>
> The Convention expressly highlights two aspects of respect for the child's humanity and dignity: the separation of child detainees from adult detainees, unless it is not in the best interest of the child, and the right of the child to maintain contact with his or her family. It achieves this by linking all three concepts, dignity, family contacts, and separation in the same article.[35]

5.5. HUMAN DIGNITY AND THE BEST INTEREST PRINCIPLE

Another example of a CRC principle that manifests the human dignity of the child is the best interest principle, which is included in article 3(1): 'In all actions concerning children, whether undertaken by public or private social welfare institutions, courts of law, administrative authorities or legislative bodies, the best interests of the child shall be a primary consideration.' The best interest principle is subjective, i.e. the best interest of one child might be different from that of another one. However, it is of great significance, that the dignity of both children remains the same and should be preserved as such. It is this transformative nature of the best interest principle that guarantees the human dignity of the child and manifests the recognition by the CRC of the quality of the human dignity principle.

5.6. OTHER ASPECTS OF HUMAN DIGNITY WITHIN THE CRC

The notable presence of the human dignity principle in the CRC signifies that it is a major cornerstone in the structure of the Convention. The following words

---

34 Human Rights Committee, 'General Comment No. 9 on humane treatment of persons deprived of liberty (Art. 10)' (30 July 1982), para. 1. Please note that this general comment was replaced by 'General Comment 21', UN Doc. CCPR/C/21/Add.1 (10 April 1992).

35 G. Van Bueren, *The International Law on the Rights of the Child* (Martinus Nijhoff Publishers, The Hague, 1998), p. 219.

of the Committee on the Rights of the Child, which consider human dignity to be the core value of the Convention, confirm this fact:

> Article 29, paragraph 1, of the Convention on the Rights of the Child is of far-reaching importance. The aims of education that it sets out, which have been agreed to by all States parties, promote, support and protect *the core value of the Convention: the human dignity innate in every child...*[36]

Cynthia Cohen has argued that article 16 on the right of the child to privacy – which states that '[n]o child shall be subjected to arbitrary or unlawful interference with his or her privacy, family, home or correspondence, nor to unlawful attacks on his or her honour and reputation', and that '[t]he child has the right to the protection of the law against such interference or attacks' – is put in absolute form, which positively and unquestionably supports his individual dignity.[37]

Overall, the human dignity standard should guide, for instance, all the domestic legislations, policies and administrative measures that the State Party will take in order to fulfil its obligation towards ensuring the survival and development of the child. None of the measures adopted by any State Party in this regard should violate the human dignity of the child. For instance, regarding the legislative recognition of the human dignity principle, when a domestic court requires the opinion of the child in cases of divorce, this is out of respect for the child's dignity. The child will be influenced by this decision; therefore, listening to him or her represents a respect for his or her human dignity.

6. THE HUMAN-DIGNITY PRINCIPLE AND ARTICLE 6(2) OF THE CRC: THE AIM AND THE CRITERION[38]

Arguably, in the context of the right of the child to survival and development, the concept of human dignity is a two-sided coin. It is a criterion and an aim.

---

36 Committee on the Rights of the Child, 'General Comment No. 1 on the Aims of Education', UN Doc. CRC/GC/2001/1 (17 April 2001), para. 1 (emphasis added).

37 C. Cohen, 'A Guide to Linguistic Interpretation of the Convention on the Rights of the Child Articles 1, 4, 41 and 45', in C. Cohen and H.A. Davidson (eds.), *Children's Rights in America: U.N. Convention on the Rights of the Child Compared with United States Law* (American Bar Association Center for Children in the Law and Defense for Children International, Washington D.C., 1990), p. 36.

38 Depending on the context, there are a number of classifications for the human dignity principle. For instance, it can be a right or a mere principle. It can also be regulatory or hermeneutical as in J.M. Cardoso Da Costa, 'The Principle of Human Dignity in European Case Law. The principle of respect for human dignity', Montpellier, 2–6 July 1998, *Science and Techniques of Democracy*, No. 26 (Council of Europe Publishing, 1999), p. 50, p. 53.

6.1. HUMAN DIGNITY AND THE RIGHT OF THE CHILD TO SURVIVAL AND DEVELOPMENT: THE CRITERION

Firstly, it is a criterion, i.e., a gauge of quality, insofar as the human dignity factor determines whether the measure and conditions created by the State Party will ensure to the maximum extent possible the 'dignified survival and development' of the child. In other words, the matter to observe will be whether the State Party is fulfilling its responsibility to implement and realise the right of the child to survival and development in a way that is compatible with the human dignity of the child. According to article 4 of the CRC the State Party is obliged to protect the rights of the child and cannot rely on any excuses including financial ones. Based on that if a child is, for example, severely sick and his or her parents are poor and cannot afford the expenses of his or her treatment and the State has no 'remedy for his or her treatment', this is a violation of the right of the child to survive and develop with dignity, as the State did not protect and provide the dignified criteria for such a remedy.

However, one can argue against this on the basis that dignity is not expressly mentioned in article 6(2). Moreover, dignity lacks clear definition internationally. But one can argue as well that the strong and instinctive link between human rights in general and human dignity does not need to be visibly written in international documents. In fact the link is clearly instinctive to the extent that, as previously mentioned, human dignity has managed to bring together all states with regards to the Universal Declaration on Human Right. As previously mentioned, according to the Committee on the Rights of the Child, dignity is the core value of the Convention. Moreover, the link with the concept of dignity represents the spirit of the effective realisation of all human rights and not only the right of the child to survival and development. Many children in developing countries die because of a lack of treatment as a result of preventable causes of poverty. The everyday suffering that the child witnesses, and the accompanied humiliation in desperately seeking the implementation of his or her rights violate his or her dignity. This qualifies the human dignity principle to represent the quality-control criterion.[39] The African Commission on Human and People's Rights emphasised the use of human dignity as a criterion for the quality of human rights implementation in one of its rulings.[40] The same could be argued with regard to the interrelationship between article 6(2) and human dignity. Respect for dignity emphasises the quality of survival and develoment and makes it more effective. The African Commission on Human and People's

---

39 African Commission on Human and Peoples' Rights, 'Thirteenth Annual Activity Report of the African Commission on Human and People's Rights, 1999–2000', p. 114.

40 The Commission is composed of eleven members serving at their independent capacity. It has its headquarters in Banjul, The Gambia. For further information see the African Commission on Human and People's Rights OAU – OUA, Information Sheet No. 1, Establishment, Organisation of African Unity.

Rights is charged with ensuring the promotion and protection of Human and People's Rights throughout the African continent. It is stated that its primary goal is restoring dignity to the humiliated African peoples. Initially, the client was hiding from the authorities in fear of his life; the commission ruled that living with fear is a violation of one's dignity:

> The Commission notes that the complainant's client (victim) is still alive but in hiding for fear of his life. It would be a narrow interpretation to this right to think that it can only be violated when one is deprived of it. It cannot be said that the right to respect for one's life and the dignity of his person, which this article guarantees, would be protected in a state of constant fear and/or threats, as experienced by Mr. Kazeem Aminu. The Commission therefore finds the above acts of the security agents of the Respondent State in violation of Article 4 of the Charter.[41]

6.1.1. *Human Dignity Criterion: Right to Survival and Development and Right to Life*

This criterion of quality will also reflect on article 6(1) on the right of the child to life, because article 6(2) on survival and development provides a quality factor to the right to life. Initially, during the drafting of article 6(2), there was a discussion about the relationship between the concept of survival and the right to life. 'In summing up the debate, the Chairman-Rapporteur stated that the right to life had been omitted from the draft convention, and that the proposal made in working paper 13 was intended to remedy that shortcoming.' Working Paper 13 includes the original proposal from India for the inclusion of article 6(2). The Chairman-Rapporteur continues:

> The right to life, already enshrined in the International Covenants on Human Rights, should be included in the draft convention and listed as a priority before other rights of the child. The approach to the right to life in the Covenants was rather negative,

41 African Commission on Human and Peoples' Rights, 'Thirteenth Annual Activity Report of the African Commission on Human and People's Rights, 1999–2000', p. 114, OAU Doc. AHG/222 (XXXVI). See also *John D. Ouko v. Kenya*, African Commission on Human and Peoples' Rights Communication 232/1999, para. 23 where the Commission stated that the conditions of the complainant in prison violated his human dignity: 'The Commission finds the above condition, to which the Complainant was subjected, in contravention of the Respondent State Party's obligation to guarantee to the Complainant the right to the respect of his dignity and freedom from inhuman and degrading treatment under article 5 of the Charter', in African Commission on Human and Peoples' Rights, 'Fourteenth Annual Activity Report of the African Commission on Human and People's Rights, 2000–2001', OAU Doc. AHG/229(XXXVII), p. 75. In *Kalenga v. Zambia*, UN Doc. CCPR/C/48/D/326/1988, Annex, para. 6.5, the UN Human Rights Committee stated that where the complainant was denied access to food and medical assistance during his detention, the detention did not respect the inherent dignity of the human being.

while that of the convention should be positive and should take into account economic, social, and cultural conditions.[42]

Following this discussion, a small drafting group worked out the compromise text of the present article 6(2). It was stated that 'the text had been drafted in order to cover the following main concerns: (a) the inherent right to life of the child...'[43] This means that the context of human dignity under article 6(2) will affect article 6(1) on the right to life, i.e., human dignity as a criterion for quality will have its direct and indirect implications for the right to life. The Supreme Court of India referred to the relationship between survival rights – such as the provision of adequate medical facilities to the people, which serves to secure and guarantee the welfare of the people, and the right to life – in one of its cases. The case represented an interpretation of the right to life when considering whether the denial of emergency medical treatment at a government-run hospital violated an individual's right to life.[44] Similarly, it is possible to argue, in this context, that for many different reasons, many children in developing countries are denied access to medical services. The effects of the right to survive and develop in dignity on the right of the child to life are very significant. In least developed countries, for instance, the annual number of deaths of children of under five was as high as 85 per 1,000 live births in 2012, while in CEE/CIS it was 19 per 1,000 live birth.[45] Many of these children died for simple reasons, such as lack of oral rehydration, which reflects a clear violation of the right of the child to live, survive and develop with dignity.

The Supreme Court of India has a rich amount of literature concerning the right to life and human dignity. The right to health of a worker is a fundamental right. Therefore, the right to life enshrined in article 21 of the Indian Constitution means something more than the mere survival of animal existence. The right to live with human dignity with minimum sustenance and shelter, and

42 UN Doc. E/CN.4/1988/28, para. 21, available in Office of the United Nations High Commissioner for Human Rights, *Legislative History of the Convention on the Rights of the Child*, Volume I (United Nations, New York, 2007), pp. 365–366.

43 *Ibid.*, para. 23, p. 366.

44 *Paschim Banga Khet Mazdoor Samity v. State of West Bengal* 1996 SCC (4) 37 (Supreme Court of India). There are also some other cases where the relationship between the quality of the right to life and some economic and social rights has been raised in a number of cases before the Supreme Court of India, e.g. *Shantistar Builders v. Narayan Khimalal Totame*, Civil Appeal No. 2598/1989 (1990) 1 SCC 520. The court stated that shelter for a human being has to be different from that of the animal. For the human being it has to be suitable accommodation which would allow him to grow and develop in every aspect (physical, mental and intellectual). The court stated the Constitution aimes at ensuring the fuller development of every child. This, according to the court, would be possible only if the court lives in a proper home. Another example is the *State of Himachal Pradesh v. Umed Ram Sharma* (1986) 1 SCR 251, which discussed the quality of the right to life under article 21 of the Constitution and the State budget with regard to the construction of a road.

45 UNICEF, 'The State of the World's Children 2014 in Numbers: Every child counts' (UNICEF, 2014), p. 35.

all those rights and aspects of life which would go towards making a human's life complete and worth living, would form part of the right to life. Enjoyment of life and its social, cultural and intellectual attainment, without which life cannot be meaningful, would embrace the protection and preservation of life guaranteed by article 21 of the Constitution. The right to health and social justice was stated to be a fundamental right for workers.[46] The court considered social justice to be the Constitution's 'weapon to ensure life to be meaningful and liveable with human dignity'. The right to economic justice is also a fundamental right.[47] In one case, it was held that the right to social and economic justice is a fundamental right.[48]

6.2. HUMAN DIGNITY AND THE RIGHT OF THE CHILD TO SURVIVAL AND DEVELOPMENT: THE AIM

Secondly, under article 6(2) of the CRC, human dignity is also an aim, i.e., an end in itself. In other words, the standard of measures and conditions that are adopted by the State Party and that are conducive to the survival and development of the child should lead to the protection and realisation of the human dignity of the child. This understanding is probably derived from the fact that human dignity is actually a foundation and the end for rights. The following argument by Goldewijk supports this: 'Indeed, whereas human dignity is the core and the foundation of human rights, it is through the operationalization of rights that dignity is protected … In processes of the implementation of human rights this interaction between dignity and rights is being realised'.[49] In this context, human dignity is both a source of rights and the aim of rights. Human dignity is also an aim in the sense that its recognition will lead to having freedom, justice and peace in the world, as stated in the preamble of the Universal Declaration of Human Rights and the preamble of the Convention on the Rights of the Child: 'Considering that, in accordance with the principles proclaimed in the Charter of the United Nations, recognition of the inherent dignity and of the equal and inalienable rights of all members of the human family is the foundation of freedom, justice

---

46 *Consumer Education and Research Centre v. Union of India* (1995) SCC (3) 42 (Supreme Court of India) 1995 AIR 922, 1995 SCC (3) 42. See also *Life Insurance Corporation v. Consumer Education and Research Centre* (1995) 5 SCC 482.

47 *Suresh Kumar & Ors., Dalmia Cement Bharat Ltd. & Anr. etc. v. Union of India & Ors. etc.* 25 April 1996 (Supreme Court of India).

48 *C.E.S.C. Ltd. & Ors. v. S.C. Bose & Ors.* 1992 AIR 573, 1991 SCR Suppl. (2) 267 (Supreme Court of India).

49 B.K. Goldewijk, 'From Seattle to Porto Alegre: Emergence of a new focus on dignity and the implementation of economic, social and cultural rights', in B.K. Goldewijk, A.C. Baspineiro and P.C. Carbonari (eds.), *Dignity and Human Rights: The implementation of economic, social, and cultural rights* (Intersentia, Antwerp, 2002), p. 6.

and peace in the world...'[50] There are a number of cases that reflect this aspect of the human dignity principle.[51]

The Convention on the Rights of the Child provides for human dignity as an aim in itself and as a status that should always be protected and realised. It also provides for human dignity as a basic requirement or a criterion for the implementation of the right to survival and development.[52] Arguably, both forms of human dignity are absolute rights that need to be realised. However, some argue that human dignity represents an ethical basis, separate from the juridical and political ones required for the notion of the universality, indivisibility and independence of human rights.[53]

The mere existence of human rights norms does not grant the child his or her dignity; but the realisation of human rights does protect the dignity of the child. The realisation of human rights is a tool towards the protection of the child's dignity. For instance, the qualitative realisation of the economic and social rights of the child aims at protecting the human dignity of the child. The spirit of the Convention implies such an understanding. Inherent human dignity as a criterion for quality and as an aim will lead to the preservation of the child's humanity.

The human dignity principle is absolute to the extent that there is no justification for infringing this right and its realisation cannot be halted.[54] This explains the importance of viewing human dignity from different aspects in order to protect the principle. However, the chance always remains for any expansions to be added to the meaning of the Committee's words when it expressed that the State Party should create the measures and conditions necessary for the survival and development of the child to the maximum extent possible and in a manner compatible with the human dignity of the child.

---

50 Convention on the Rights of the Child, UN Doc. A/RES/44/25 Annex (20 November 1989), preambular para. 1.

51 See for example, for human dignity being the foundation for justice, the UN Human Rights Committee's views in *Kelly v. Jamaica*, UN. Doc. CCPR/C/41/D/253/1987 where it held that respect of the inherent dignity of the human being requires the provision of adequate food, medical care and basic sanitation facilities whilst in detention.

52 P.C. Carbonari, 'Human Dignity as a Basic Concept of Ethics and Human Rights', in B.K. Goldewijk, A.C. Baspineiro and P.C. Carbonari (eds.), *Dignity and Human Rights: The implementation of economic, social, and cultural rights* (Intersentia, Antwerp, 2002), p. 39.

53 *Ibid.*

54 J.A. Frowein, 'Human Dignity in International Law', in D. Kretzmer and E. Klein (eds.), *The Concept of Human Dignity in Human Rights Discourse* (Kluwer Law International, The Hague, 2002), pp. 123–124.

7. HUMAN DIGNITY AND ARTICLE 6(2) IN ITS CAPACITY AS A GENERAL PRINCIPLE

The complexity of article 6(2) as being the right of the child to everything on the one hand and a general principle of the CRC on the other hand enriches the following discussion.

As a general principle of the Convention on the Rights of the Child, the spirit of article 6(2) should be conveyed and reflected within the implementation of all the other articles of the Convention. This represents a form of indirect implementation of article 6(2). It is similar to the concept of the holistic approach to the implementation of the Convention which the Committee on the Rights of the Child adopts. This aspect of article 6(2) does not mean, however, that the articles of the Convention should depend on each other for their implementation. This is discussed in more detail in Chapter 5.

Similar to other articles of the CRC, article 6(2) should be implemented in a manner that is compatible with the human dignity of the child, which is a core value of the CRC. This means that the implementation of the remaining articles of the substantive part of the Convention should reflect the survival and development of the child in a manner that is compatible with his or her human dignity. Accordingly, it is important in a discussion on the relationship between the human dignity principle and the right of the child to survival and development to analyse this relationship in the context of article 6(2) as a general principle of the Convention.

7.1. CHILD'S DIGNITY, GENERAL PRINCIPLE OF SURVIVAL AND DEVELOPMENT AND CRC PROVISIONS THAT MAKE EXPLICIT REFERENCE TO 'DIGNITY'

The wording of some articles of the Convention clearly express that the implementation should be compatible with the human dignity of the child. For instance, article 28(2) on the right to education states that: 'States Parties shall take all appropriate measures to ensure that school discipline is administered in a manner consistent with the child's human dignity'. In this context, human dignity is a criterion for quality, because it 'monitors' the administration of the school discipline. It is basically a matter of a 'how' question more than a 'why' one. Nevertheless, one may also argue that the 'why' factor is also implicit, because the administration of school discipline in a humiliating manner will result in a violation of the child's dignity.

The Committee has explained the relationship between article 28 and the development of the child, which is protected by article 6(2), as a relevant right, in its General Comment No. 7 on early childhood education. Note the existence of human dignity as the (why) factor in the background of this relationship between the right to development and the right to education. Compulsory education that realises the development of the child provides for the recognition of the child's dignity:

> The Convention recognizes the right of the child to education, and primary education should be made compulsory and available free to all (art. 28). The Committee recognizes with appreciation that some States parties are planning to make one year of preschool education available and free of cost for all children. The Committee interprets the right to education during early childhood as beginning at birth and closely linked to young children's right to maximum development (art. 6.2)...[55]

The same can be said about the link between the aims of education and development, which is elaborated upon in article 29(1) (although article 29 does not expressly refer to dignity): 'States parties agree that the education of the child shall be directed to: (a) the development of the child's personality, talents and mental and physical abilities to their fullest potential...' In General Comment No. 1 of the Committee on the Rights of the Child on the aims of education, there is an explanation that the goal is to 'empower the child by developing his or her skills, learning and other capacities, human dignity, self-esteem and self-confidence.'[56] In addition, it must be achieved in ways that are child-centred, child-friendly and reflect the rights and inherent dignity of the child.[57]

Articles 28 and 29 also cover the relationship between human dignity and self-esteem, especially in relation to disabled children:

> It is crucial that the education of a child with disability includes the strengthening of positive self-awareness, making sure that the child feels he or she is respected by others as a human being without any limitation of dignity. The child must be able to observe that others respect him or her and recognize his or her human rights and freedoms. Inclusion of the child with disability in the groups of children of the classroom can show the child that he or she has recognized identity and belongs to the community of learners, peers, and citizens.[58]

Another example is article 23(1) on the rights of the disabled child: 'States Parties recognize that a mentally or physically disabled child should enjoy a full and decent life, in conditions which ensure dignity, promote self-reliance and facilitate the child's active participation in the community.' In these cases, where the individual article refers to human dignity, the realisation of article 6(2)

---

55 Committee on the Rights of the Child, 'General Comment No. 7 on Implementing Child Rights in Early Childhood', UN Doc. CRC/C/GC/7/Rev.1 (20 September 2006), para. 28.

56 Committee on the Rights of the Child, 'General Comment No. 1 on the Aims of Education', UN Doc. CRC/GC/2001/1 (17 April 2001), para. 2.

57 *Ibid.*

58 Committee on the Rights of the Child, 'General Comment No. 9 on the rights of children with disabilities', UN Doc. CRC/C/GC/9 (27 February 2007), para. 64.

as a general principle through it will strengthen the realisation of the entire principle of the human dignity of the child. Article 23(1) is an empowering right of the disabled child. It aims at empowering vulnerable members of society who, because of their disability, might be targeted in a disadvantageous way that will increase their suffering. The relationship with article 6(2) will provide an empowering environment for their development with dignity. In the day of general discussions on children with disabilities, the words of thanks to all the participants – which were delivered in the name of the Committee on the Rights of the Child by Mrs Karp, former Vice-Chairperson of the Committee – emphasised the importance of the human dignity principle. She said:

> Inclusion was the goal, but it was as well a means to improve society. The aim was to have a society which accommodated a wide spectrum of individual abilities, and not a society which simply expected all to conform to one hypothetical, and often unachieved, standard of 'normally'. The key issue was respect for the human dignity of children with disabilities. Inclusion of children with disabilities into society was part of a process of social change to make a society in which human dignity was a living value.[59]

7.2. CHILD'S DIGNITY, GENERAL PRINCIPLE OF SURVIVAL AND DEVELOPMENT AND CRC PROVISIONS THAT DO NOT MAKE EXPLICIT REFERENCE TO 'DIGNITY'

7.2.1. Child's Dignity, General Principle of Survival and Development, Exploitation of Children

However, when there is no explicit reference made to human dignity, this does not mean that the link with article 6(2) will not strengthen the realisation of the human dignity of the child. To illustrate, violations of the dignified survival and development of the child are evident, for example, in cases of exploitation under article 36 CRC, whether it is economic exploitation, sexual exploitation or any other form of exploitation. Exploitation interferes with the child's respect, which leads to humiliation. Humiliation in its turn interferes with the child's dignity. The following words of the Committee support this argument:

> [I]n the case of all ... forms of exploitation (art. 36), the Committee urges States parties to incorporate the particular situation of young children into all legislation, policies and interventions to promote physical and psychological recovery and social reintegration within an environment that promotes dignity and self-respect (art. 39).[60]

---

59 Committee on the Rights of the Child, 'Children with Disabilities', UN Doc. CRC/C/66, Annex V (6 October 1997), para. 337.

60 Committee on the Rights of the Child, 'General Comment No. 7 on Implementing Child Rights in Early Childhood', UN Doc. CRC/C/GC/7/Rev.1 (20 September 2006), para. 37. It is worth mentioning that article 39 makes explicit reference to dignity.

The repercussions of child labour on the child's health are evident. Article 32(1) of the CRC refers to this: 'States Parties recognize the right of the child to be protected from economic exploitation and from performing any work that is likely to be hazardous or to interfere with the child's education, or to be harmful to the health or physical, mental, spiritual, moral or social development.' In the International Commission of Jurists v. Portugal, the European Committee for Social Rights found that Portugal's failure to enforce its child labour legislation constituted a breach of its obligations under the European Social Charter.[61] In its ruling, the Committee pointed out the risks of child labour and its repercussions on the child's development: 'This provision prohibits child labour under the age of fifteen, with certain exceptions. It aims to ensure the protection of children and adolescents against the risks associated in performing work which may have negative repercussions on their health, their moral welfare, their development and their education.'[62]

Economic exploitation in the form of child labour represents a continuous violation of the child's dignity because it negatively interferes with the child's development. In addition, child labour usually takes place in working conditions that are humiliating to the child's dignified development. Working without having days off or without being paid represents a form of violation of the child's dignity. Human dignity under article 32 of the CRC is both a 'why' and a 'how' question.

Sexual exploitation also has serious repercussions for children's development and raises obvious concerns in relation to the dignity of the child. In De Reuck v. Director of Public Prosecutions, Witwatersrand Local Division and Others, Langa DCJ discussed the negative effects of sexual exploitation of children on the child's physical development and, importantly, his or her dignity:

> Similarly, article 1 of the Universal Declaration of Human Rights stresses the importance of human dignity. It states: 'All human beings are born free and equal in dignity and rights.' Children merit special protection by the state and must be protected by legislation which guards and enforces their rights and liberties. This is recognised in section 28 of our Constitution. Children's dignity rights are of special importance. The degradation of children through child pornography is a serious harm which impairs their dignity and contributes to a culture which devalues their worth. Society has recognised that childhood is a special stage in life which is to be both treasured and guarded. The state must ensure that the lives of children are not disrupted by adults who objectify and sexualise them through the production and

---

61 The European Committee of Social Rights (ECSR) is responsible for judging whether States Parties are in conformity in law and in practice with the provisions of the European Social Charter. It is composed of 15 independent, impartial experts, elected by the Committee of Ministers. It adopts conclusions in respect of national reports, and makes decisions in respect of collective complaints.

62 Complaint No. 1/1998 *The International Commission of Jurists v. Portugal*, European Committee of Social Rights, para. 26.

> possession of child pornography. There is obvious physical harm suffered by the victims of sexual abuse and by those children forced to yield to the demands of the paedophile and pornographer, but there is also harm to the dignity and perception of all children when a society allows sexualised images of children to be available. The chief purpose of the statutory prohibitions against child pornography is to protect the dignity, humanity and integrity of children.[63]

Exploitation has negative results because there is no respect for the child's dignity. Human dignity equals respect. Respect for the human dignity of the child should lead to the harmonious development of the child.

> If we take the Convention as the framework for our approach, we will recognize the existence of a material interest in activities such as child labour, child pornography or the use of children for criminal activities, as in the case of drug trafficking. On the other hand, we are confronted with a situation of exploitation essentially when the human dignity of the child or the harmonious development of the child's personality is not respected – situations such as the sale of children, child bondage or child prostitution.[64]

7.2.2. Child's Dignity, General Principle of Survival and Development and Harmful Traditional Practices

The repercussions of some harmful traditional practices on various domains of the child's development are also evident. Article 24(3) CRC deals with this issue: 'States Parties shall take all effective and appropriate measures with a view to abolishing traditional practices prejudicial to the health of children.' Female genital mutilation (FGM) is probably the most widely discussed topic under the expression 'harmful traditional practice'. But the term is flexible enough to include other practices as well. Breast ironing is an example of a traditional practice that negatively interferes with the female child's physical and psychological development and violates her dignity:

> A number of reasons are given for the persistence of traditional practices detrimental to the health and status of women, including the fact that, in the past, neither the Governments concerned nor the international community challenged the sinister implications of such practices, which violate the rights to health, life, dignity and personal integrity.[65]

---

63 *De Reuck v. Director of Public Prosecutions (Witwatersrand Local Division) and Others* (CCT5/03) [2003] ZACC 19 [63] (Constitutional Court of South Africa), para. 63 (footnotes omitted).

64 Statement by Mrs Maria Santos Pais, available in UN Doc. CRC/C/20 (25 October 1993), Annex V, Opening Statements of the Day of General Discussion on the Economic Exploitation of Children, p. 51.

65 UN Office of the High Commissioner for Human Rights, Fact Sheet No. 23, 'Harmful Traditional Practices Affecting the Health of Women and Children' (August 1995). See

Often the practice is forced on the female child in order to protect her from rape. This conveys that there is a good intention behind it, but the fact that the practice is non-consensual is significant. This has its repercussions for the girl child's dignity, the freedom over her body and interferes with her right to decide and her will. Does this convey that the human dignity will be preserved if the girl child agrees to the act of breast ironing? In this context human dignity as a gauge will have a role to play in determining if breast ironing interferes with child's dignified survival and development, especially as it interferes with the girl child's health.

The mental dignity of the child is related to his or her developing mind. Respect for the child's dignity and mental abilities and development is realised through many rights, for example the right to nutritious food. Any violation of this right infringes his or her dignity. Despite this, some traditional practices, such as nutritional taboos that have a basis in gender discrimination, prevent the female child from having a nutritious diet:

> Poor health can be improved by a more balanced diet. The choice of food consumed is determined by a number of factors, including availability of natural resources, economics, religious beliefs, social status and traditional taboos. Because these factors place limits in one way or another on the intake of food, communities and individuals are deprived of essential nutriments and, as a result, physical and mental development is impaired.[66]

Another example of a traditional practice that interferes with the right to survival and development with dignity is the virginity test. This practice is carried out for good reasons, e.g., to check that the girl is free from HIV/AIDS and to stop teenage pregnancies. However, the circumstances under which it is done represent a violation of article 6(2) of the CRC. In fact, sometimes the test is actually the reason that diseases are contracted, because the conditions are unhygienic. Moreover, it affects her self-esteem. The Committee refers to the 'traditional practice of virginity testing which threatens the health, affects the self-esteem, and violates the privacy of girls.'[67] The test could be worrying

---

also Committee on the Elimination of All Forms of Discrimination against Women and Committee on the Rights of the Child, 'Joint General Recommendation/General Comment No. 31 of the Committee on the Elimination of Discrimination against Women and No. 18 of the Committee on the Rights of the Child on harmful practices', UN. Doc. CEDAW/C/CG/31-CRC/C/GC/18 (14 November 2014).

66 UN Office of the High Commissioner for Human Rights, Fact Sheet No. 23, 'Harmful Traditional Practices Affecting the Health of Women and Children' (August 1995). See also Committee on the Elimination of All Forms of Discrimination against Women and Committee on the Rights of the Child, 'Joint General Recommendation/General Comment No. 31 of the Committee on the Elimination of Discrimination against Women and No. 18 of the Committee on the Rights of the Child on harmful practices', UN. Doc. CEDAW/C/CG/31-CRC/C/GC/18 (14 November 2014).

67 Committee on the Rights of the Child, 'Concluding Observations on South Africa's Initial Report', UN Doc. CRC/C/15/Add.122 (23 February 2000), para. 33.

because it violates the right of the child to privacy. Later the girls who are found to be virgins will be distinguished by a mark that is different from those who are not. All of this represents a clear violation of the right to survive and develop with dignity in addition to the violation under article 16(1) of the CRC: 'No child shall be subjected to arbitrary or unlawful interference with his or her privacy, family, home or correspondence, nor to unlawful attacks on his or her honour and reputation.' In relation to the good intention behind the practice of breast ironing and virginity tests, it is important to emphasise the role of the State with regard to awareness raising. The aim should be to convince the partners involved about other safe and human dignity oriented forms of protection for the girl child. More details on this obligation are discussed in Chapter 5.

Some also argue against ear-piercing. For example, in some cases it is non-consensual. It could be argued that the imposition of ear-piercing conveys that the child has been forced to do it. Others also argue against it from the view that it involves mutilation of the body or that there are occasional health risks. The right of the child to survive and develop in dignity and for dignity will definitely have a role to play. One aspect of the debate is the consent of the child.

According to the Committee on the Rights of the Child and the Committee on the Elimination of all Forms of Discrimination against Women, dignity is a criterion for determining harmful practices: 'For the purposes of the present general recommendation/general comment, practices should meet the following criteria to be regarded as harmful: a. They constitute a denial of the dignity and/or integrity of the individual and a violation of human rights and fundamental freedoms enshrined in the two Conventions...'[68]

The repercussions of some harmful traditional practices are evident, but it is always good to remain optimistic about their gradual disappearance through awareness-raising campaigns and positive social changes. The case of the *Shulukh* is a good illustration. *Shulukh* are facial marks that leave permanent scars on the face. The practice is done to both boys and girls, thus it has no gender-discrimination basis. In a tribal society the *Shulukh* are probably a form of identification. Each tribe has a specific form of *Shulukh* that will make it easy to identify someone's tribe. However, leaving permanent scars on a person's face in order to identify him or her is indeed a violation of his or her dignity.[69]

---

68 Committee on the Elimination of All Forms of Discrimination against Women and Committee on the Rights of the Child, 'Joint General Recommendation/General Comment No. 31 of the Committee on the Elimination of Discrimination against Women and No. 18 of the Committee on the Rights of the Child on Harmful Practices', UN. Doc. CEDAW/C/CG/31-CRC/C/GC/18 (4 November 2014), para. 16(a).

69 Basically, the *shulukh* شلوخ were performed in a tribal society where the feeling of honour, because one belongs to a particular tribe, was at a very high level. Thus, having a particular form of *shulukh* because one belongs to a certain tribe was a reason for feeling honoured, e.g. the form of *shulukh* for the *Gaaliyya* جعليه tribe in Sudan was ┬. In this environment it was very common for someone to show off his or her sense of honour and worth by saying 'I am a Gaaly (belonging to the *Jaaliyya* Tribe) and I have the ┬ sign for my *shulukh*' '┬ جعلي مشلخ'.

The physical appearance of the human child is a feature of the child's inherent dignity and needs to be protected.

Issues of sustainable development are also relevant to all aspects of the child's development and the child's dignity (this is discussed in more detail later in Chapter 6). The protection of Planet Earth, for instance, will lead to enhancing and protecting the child's dignity and development, because a child needs a clean environment for his or her survival and development, which should protect his or her dignity.

In relation to the child's mental development, laws that ban underage drinking, for instance, are important. This is because underage drinking interferes with the mental development of the child and obstructs the realisation of his or her full potential, i.e., the full realisation of his or her human dignity.

However, despite the existence of a strong link between the human dignity of the child and the above-mentioned cases of child's rights, there are two cases that always attract scholars' attention as regards their influence on the child's dignity: corporal punishment and juvenile justice. These cases can both have some repercussions for the child's right to survive and develop with dignity.

8. CASE STUDY ON HUMAN DIGNITY OF THE CHILD AND CORPORAL PUNISHMENT

8.1. INTRODUCTION

The human dignity principle is vital for all the rights that are included in the CRC. However, there are some cases where the principle, as mentioned, received scholary attention. Examples include corporal punishment, juvenile justice and deprivation of liberty. This is probably the case as these three issues deal with a straightforward aspect of human dignity, i.e., human dignity as opposed to humiliation. Reference to corporal punishment is inevitable for a discussion of the relationship between human dignity and article 6(2) as a general principle. In many cases a number of the child developmental domains, such as the child's physical, mental, spiritual, etc. development, are seriously affected by corporal punishment. A simple and clear example is the repercussions of the feeling of humiliation for the child's psychological development. The ensuing discussion is on the right of the child to survival and development in relation to human dignity, corporal punishment and parental rights.

Ironically, the *shulukh*, which is a harmful traditional practice, was considered a source of the feelings of respect and dignity. Fortunately the practice of *shulukh* has dramatically declined, at least in the northern parts of Sudan, as a result of societal changes.

8.2. PARENTAL RIGHTS AND CORPORAL PUNISHMENT

Certainly, children, by virtue of their childhood, need someone to take care of them. In many cases this care is provided by parents, guardians or another person. This makes the contents of the Convention on the Rights of the Child unique, because it has to organise this horizontal-level relationship. In other words, the State as the obligation holder has to organise this relationship.

The authority of the parent needs to be organised in order to guarantee respect for the human dignity of both, the child and his or her parents. This brings the State into the middle, because, under traditional international human rights law, it is responsible for the protection and realisation of the rights of the child as an 'individual' who is separate from both of his or her parents. On the other hand, however, the issue of corporal punishment raises some concerns about diminishing parental rights. Some see and argue that the prohibition of corporal punishment will lead to loss of parental authority. However, this concern has been handled by article 5 of the CRC:

> States Parties shall respect the responsibilities, rights and duties of parents or, where applicable, the members of the extended family or community as provided for by local custom, legal guardians or other persons legally responsible for the child, to provide, in a manner consistent with the evolving capacities of the child, appropriate direction and guidance in the exercise by the child of the rights recognized in the present Convention...

The discussion of parental rights brings the discussion on the interrelationship between human dignity and article 6(2) to a horizontal level. However, the question remains as to whether the issue of parental responsibility should be considered in this way. After all, the parent–child relationship is a prerequisite of childhood, which means that it is inevitable. It is actually a fact of life that children need someone to take care of them. Parents, however, should treat the child with great respect and consideration for his or her human dignity which will lead to the child's full development:

> The Committee notes the growing body of theory and research which confirms that young children are best understood as social actors whose survival, well-being and development are dependent on and built around close relationships. These relationships are normally with a small number of key people, most often parents, members of the extended family and peers, as well as caregivers and other early childhood professionals.[70]

70 Committee on the Rights of the Child, 'General Comment No. 7 on Implementing Child Rights in Early Childhood', UN Doc. CRC/C/GC/7/Rev.1 (20 September 2006), para. 8.

As previously mentioned, this horizontal aspect, however, highlights the issue of State Party responsibility. In South Africa, for instance, the State can interfere in cases of parental neglect, whereas in the United States the Supreme Court ruled in Deshaney v. Winnebago County Department Social Services that the State has no responsibility.[71]

Furthermore, in the context of parental rights, some might argue against children's rights. As mentioned earlier, their argument is that it limits parental rights, thus, creating a situation where there is a 'conflict of dignities', i.e., the dignity of the child against the dignity of the parents. Do standards established by the CRC, such as the Committee's 'total prohibition of corporal punishment' interfere with the rights of parents?[72] Is the parent's dignity jeopardised if his or her authority is limited? On the other hand, is the child's dignity affected by the practice of parental rights?

Dignity of parents is separate from that of children and vice versa. The mere fact that children have rights is a manifestation of their dignity. It is very important to emphasise that it is not to be understood as being against their parent's dignity. It is not meant to be a scenario for any conflict of dignities between the two sides.

This raises the issue of behaving in a dignified way or behaviour, for both, the parent and the child. Delpérée speaks about what he calls a relational right. For him, human dignity has a dual meaning of 'autonomous right' and 'relational right'. 'Autonomous right' means that the public authorities must help to ensure that it is given appropriate substance. He outlines 'relational right', in a part of his argument that matches the discussion about parental rights and corporal punishment, by saying: 'It serves to draw the outlines of other rights and helps to justify them. At the same time it sets limits on interference by public authorities or private individuals'.[73] Parental rights are not there in order to give the parent absolute and non-questionable power over the child. Parental rights should serve the right of the child to development on the basis of her or his interests on the one hand and the interests of the parent on the other hand. The Convention on the Rights of the Child is already an applied law. This means that article 5 guarantees that parental rights are valid and in force, and this is expected to give parents some assurance. As for any argument on 'conflict of dignities', this, however, does not mean that, under the Convention, human dignity of the child conflicts with that of their parents. The CRC does not promote such assumed 'conflict of dignities'.

---

71 *Deshaney v. Winnebago Cty. DSS*, 489 U.S. 189 (1989) (United States Supreme Court); see also G.E. Devenish, *A Commentary on the South African Bill of Rights* (Butterworths, Durban, 1999), pp. 386–387.

72 Corporal punishment in the context of the child's survival and development and human dignity is discussed later in detail.

73 F. Delpérée, 'The Right to Human Dignity in Belgian Constitutional Law. Concluding Report: The principle of respect for human dignity', Montpellier, 2–6 July 1998, *Science and Techniques of Democracy*, No. 26 (Council of Europe Publishing, 1999), pp. 57–67, p. 60.

8.3. VIEWS OF HUMAN RIGHTS BODIES

A number of regional human rights bodies have adopted the view that the State has the authority to interfere in cases of violations in horizontal relationships. For instance, the Inter-American Court of Human Rights has stated in one of its advisory opinions that the State is under the obligation to protect children in cases of individuals who violate the child's right.[74] However, from a practicability perspective the protection of the child can prove to be somewhat complicated and this requires the parties involved to keep away from abstracts. In this context the subjective and contextual aspect of the survival and development of the child is essential. One might argue against the subjective and case-by-case approach on the basis that they would lower the standards established by the Committee. But this is not how it should be viewed. The case-by-case approach allows for efficiency and effectiveness. The main aim of the CRC is to have a realisation of children's rights. Case-by-case studies allow for such realisation. On the contrary generalised and abstract approaches do not.

8.3.1. View of the Committee on the Rights of the Child on Corporal Punishment

Generally speaking, corporal punishment has a direct link with the child's development. The Committee on the Rights of the Child has been very specific about both corporal punishment and other degrading forms of treatment. It gives a lengthy definition that does not differentiates between violence and humiliation and identifies some acts that amount to corporal punishment and other degrading forms of treatment:

> The Committee defines 'corporal' or 'physical' punishment as any punishment in which physical force is used and intended to cause some degree of pain or discomfort, however light. Most involves hitting ('smacking', 'slapping', 'spanking') children, with the hand or with an implement – a whip, stick, belt, shoe, wooden spoon, etc. But it can also involve, for example, kicking, shaking or throwing children, scratching, pinching, biting, pulling hair or boxing ears, forcing children to stay in uncomfortable positions, burning, scalding or forced ingestion (for example, washing children's mouths out with soap or forcing them to swallow hot spices). In the view of the Committee, corporal punishment is invariably degrading. In addition, there are other non-physical forms of punishment that are also cruel and degrading and thus incompatible with the Convention. These include, for example, punishment which belittles, humiliates, denigrates, scapegoats, threatens, scares or ridicules the child.[75]

---

74 *Juridical Condition and Human Rights of the Child*, Advisory Opinion OC-17/2002, Inter-American Court of Human Rights (28 August 2002), paras. 87 and 91.

75 Committee on the Rights of the Child, 'General Comment No. 8 on the right of the child to protection from corporal punishment and other cruel or degrading forms of punishment (arts. 19; 28, para. 2; and 37, inter alia)', UN Doc. CRC/C/GC/8 (2 March 2007), para. 11.

In addition, the Committee keeps adding more forms of acts to this list in the course of its work as a monitoring body to the Convention, for instance, when it stated, under the heading of ill treatment and violence:

> The Committee is concerned that corporal punishment is widely practiced in the State party, including within the family, schools and other institutions; that children have been the victims of violence by, among others, the police; and that acts of torture, rape and other cruel, inhuman or degrading treatment have been committed against children in the context of the armed conflict.[76]

The Committee is very clear about its understanding of the Convention's total prohibition of corporal punishment. It makes reference to it, where it is relevant, in almost all of its concluding observations on the State Party reports. For instance in its concluding observations on the initial report of Grenada:

> The Committee expresses grave concern that corporal punishment is still widely practised in the State party and that domestic legislation does not prohibit its use. In this regard, the Committee recommends that the State party take all appropriate measures, including of a legislative nature, to prohibit corporal punishment within the family, schools, the juvenile justice and alternative care systems and generally within the society. It further suggests that awareness raising campaigns be conducted to ensure that alternative forms of discipline are administered in a manner consistent with the child's human dignity and in conformity with the Convention, especially article 28.2.[77]

Another example can be found in its concluding observations on the Initial report of Guyana:

> The Committee expresses its concern at the fact that corporal punishment is still widely practised in the family, in schools and in institutions, and that domestic legislation does not prohibit its use.
> ... The Committee recommends that the State party:
> a) Expressly prohibit corporal punishment by law in the family, schools and other institutions;
> b) Conduct awareness-raising campaigns to ensure that alternative forms of discipline are administrated in a manner consistent with the child's human dignity and in conformity with the Convention, especially article 28 (2);
> c) Seek international technical assistance from, among others, UNICEF in this regard.[78]

---

76 Committee on the Rights of the Child, 'Concluding Observations on Sudan's Second Periodic Report', UN Doc. CRC/C/15/Add.190 (9 October 2002), para. 35.

77 Committee on the Rights of the Child, 'Concluding Observations on Grenada's Initial Report', UN Doc. CRC/C/15/Add.121 (28 February 2000), para. 21.

78 Committee on the Rights of the Child, 'Concluding Observations on Guyana's Initial Report', UN Doc. CRC/C/15/Add.224 (26 February 2004), paras. 31–32.

The Committee promotes the adoption of non-violent forms of discipline and child-rearing. It also calls corporal punishment 'the use of force for the purpose of correction', as in the concluding observations on Belize's second periodic report:

> The Committee ... urges the State party:
> a) To critically review its current legislation with a view to abolishing the use of force for the purpose of correction and to introduce new legislation prohibiting all forms of corporal punishment of children in the family and within all institutions, including schools and the alternative care system...[79]

The Committee called for the adoption of disciplinary forms that are consistent with the human dignity of the child and are in conformity with article 28(2).[80] In some recommendations the Committee promoted for positive, participatory and non-violent forms of discipline, as in its concluding observations on the initial report of Antigua and Barbuda.[81]

It also argued against the argument that moderate or reasonable corporal punishment is in the best interests of the child as follows:

> When the Committee on the Rights of the Child has raised eliminating corporal punishment with certain States during the examination of their reports, governmental representatives have sometimes suggested that some level of 'reasonable' or 'moderate' corporal punishment can be justified as in the 'best interests' of the child. The Committee has identified, as an important general principle, the Convention's requirement that the best interests of the child should be a primary consideration in all actions concerning children (art. 3, para. 1). The Convention also asserts, in article 18, that the best interests of the child will be parents' basic concern. But interpretation of a child's best interests must be consistent with the whole Convention, including the obligation to protect children from all forms of violence and the requirement to give due weight to the child's views; it cannot be used to justify practices, including corporal punishment and other forms of cruel or degrading punishment, which conflict with the child's human dignity and right to physical integrity.[82]

---

79 Committee on the Rights of the Child, 'Concluding Observations on Belize's Second Periodic Report', UN Doc. CRC/C/15/Add.252 (31 March 2005), para. 41.

80 Committee on the Rights of the Child, 'Concluding Observations on the Bahamas Initial Report', UN Doc. CRC/C/15/Add.253 (31 March 2005), para. 36.

81 Committee on the Rights of the Child, 'Concluding Observations on Antigua and Barbuda's Initial Report', UN Doc. CRC/C/15/Add.247 (3 November 2004), para. 36(d). See also Committee on the Rights of the Child, 'Concluding Observations on the Combined Second and Third Periodic Report of Cambodia', UN Doc. CRC/C/KHM/CO/2-3 (3 August 2011), para. 41(d).

82 Committee on the Rights of the Chid, 'General Comment No. 8 on the right of the child to protection from corporal punishment and other cruel or degrading forms of punishment (arts. 19; 28, para. 2; and 37, inter alia)', UN Doc. CRC/C/GC/8 (2 March 2007), para. 26.

8.4. FINAL REMARKS

According to the Convention on the Rights of the Child, children should be disciplined on the bases of its general principles. In this respect, the child's right to survival and development, and the child's right to participate and express his or her views, are of great importance. Violent, degrading and humiliating punishment should not be accepted. In this context, the child should be disciplined in a manner that will realise the contextual facts of the right of the child to dignified survival and development, where a subjective standard should be implemented. Some might possibly argue against this 'subjective', case-by-case assessment of government's performances on the bases that it could question the standards established by the Committee. This could potentially be counter-balanced by emphasising the dignity aspect in applying standards to individual situations. Narrow interpretation does not reflect the spirit of the Convention. The Convention sets international standards; therefore narrow interpretations limit them.

9. CASE STUDY: HUMAN DIGNITY AND JUVENILE JUSTICE

9.1. INTRODUCTION

In nineteenth-century Great Britain, a child as young as eight years old could be convicted of theft and be sent to Australia to serve his prison sentence. Young criminals were set to work on the crank, where, if they fainted, a bucket of cold water would be thrown over them. These severe forms of punishment might not exist in our present world, but what is already there still needs to be improved. In some cases, children are subject to extrajudicial executions, disappearances, humiliation and torture.

The significance of the juvenile justice system is that it focuses on handling children who are in conflict with the law. Ironically, this is the term that the Committee uses, but it includes concepts such as the presumption of innocence. This concept means that the child is not yet an offender, i.e., not in conflict with the law. The system is comprehensive and aims at the protection of the child concerned. In addition to being a system for dealing with children in a manner which is appropriate to their age, juvenile justice is also about the general, dignified well-being of the children concerned.[83] The system does not aim at punishing the child, but about his or her rehabilitation and the reintegration into the society. The system also respects the participation rights of the child.

---

[83] G. Van Bueren, *The International Law on the Rights of the Child* (Martinus Nijhoff Publishers, The Hague, 1998), p. 172.

While the protection of the child is important debates about his or her criminal responsibility are of relevance in this context.

9.2. GENERAL OBSERVATIONS ON THE INTERCONNECTEDNESS OF CHILD'S DIGNITY AND JUVENILE JUSTICE

The human dignity of the child is a basic principle for the juvenile justice system. When the child's dignity is protected and preserved this will support his or her overall well-being, which includes his or her survival and development:

> Another facet of promoting the child's sense of well being is that, in all cases where children are 'alleged as, accused of, or recognised as having infringed the penal law' they should, according to the Convention on the Rights of the Child, be treated in a manner consistent with the promotion of their sense of dignity and worth, and which reinforces their respect for human rights.[84]

In its General Comment No. 10, the Committee on the Rights of the Child points out a direct link between the juvenile justice system and the survival and development of the child under article 6(2):

> This inherent right of every child should guide and inspire States Parties in the development of effective national policies and programmes for the prevention of juvenile delinquency, because it goes without saying that delinquency has a (very) negative impact on the child's development. Furthermore, this basic right should result in a policy of responding to juvenile delinquency in ways that support the child's development ... The use of deprivation of liberty has (very) negative consequences for the child's harmonious development and seriously hampers his/her reintegration in society. In this regard, article 37(b) CRC explicitly provides that deprivation of liberty, including arrest, detention and imprisonment, should be used only as a measure of last resort and for the shortest appropriate period of time, so that the child's right to development is fully respected and ensured...[85]

This statement by the Committee conveys references to the two facets of human dignity, namely the criterion for quality and the aim. Juvenile delinquency has very negative results for the child's development. Reaching the full potential of the child will result in the realisation of her or his human dignity and vice versa. In addition, the Committee's statement refers to the deprivation of liberty, which interferes with the child's development. This is actually a clear example of how human dignity is a criterion for quality.

84 *Ibid.*

85 Committee on the Rights of the Chid, 'General Comment No. 10 on Children's rights in juvenile justice', UN Doc. CRC/C/GC/10 (25 April 2007), para. 11.

The juvenile justice system has a special focus on the child's dignity. In particular, the treatment to be accorded to the children concerned as a reflection of the realisation of their dignity:

> Treatment that is consistent with the child's sense of dignity and worth. This principle reflects the fundamental human right enshrined in article 1 UDHR that all human beings are born free and equal in dignity and rights. This inherent right to dignity and worth, to which the preamble of the CRC makes explicit reference, has to be respected and protected throughout the entire process of dealing with the child...[86]

Article 37(c) of the CRC refers to the treatment of children who are deprived of their liberty as follows:

> Every child deprived of liberty shall be treated with humanity and respect for the inherent dignity of the human person, and in a manner which takes into account the needs of persons of his or her age. In particular, every child deprived of liberty shall be separated from adults unless it is considered in the child's best interest not to do so and shall have the right to maintain contact with his or her family through correspondence and visits, save in exceptional circumstances...

9.3. JUVENILE JUSTICE UNDER INTERNATIONAL HUMAN RIGHTS LAW

Juvenile justice was guaranteed by article 14(4) of the ICCPR long before its adoption in the CRC. Article 14(4) reads: 'In the case of juvenile persons, the procedure shall be such as will take account of their age and the desirability of promoting their rehabilitation.' Other relevant documents are the Beijing Rules and the Riyadh Guidelines.[87] The basic idea behind juvenile justice is the provision of rehabilitation rather than punishment as such. In all cases of juvenile justice, however, the human dignity principle should be preserved.

> Adequate protection should also be afforded to children in conflict with the law. ... [I]t is suggested that general principles underlying the Convention such as consideration of the best interest and dignity of the child and its role into society, be taken into account. Deprivation of liberty should always be envisaged as the very last resort, and particular attention should be paid to rehabilitation measures, psychological recovery and social reintegration. Furthermore, deprivation of

---

86 *Ibid.*, para. 13.

87 See United Nations General Assembly, 'United Nations Guidelines for the Prevention of Juvenile Delinquency (The Riyadh Guidelines)', UN Doc. A/RES/45/112 (14 December 1990); and United Nations General Assembly, 'United Nations Standard Minimum Rules for the Administration of Juvenile Justice ("The Beijing Rules")', General Assembly Resolution 40/33 (29 November 1985).

liberty in social care institutions should be regularly monitored by a judge or an independent body.[88]

9.4. CHILD'S DIGNITY AND TRAINING OF PERSONNEL OF LAW ENFORCEMENT AGENCIES

Law enforcement agencies are to be trained on children's rights and juvenile justice, as violations occur in all phases of the juvenile justice process. Importantly, indeed, is the provision of effective supervision over the law enforcement agencies work as regards their implementation of the right to juvenile justice. This should ensure respect for the dignity of the child:

> *Respect for the dignity of the child requires that all forms of violence in the treatment of children in conflict with the law must be prohibited and prevented.* Reports received by the Committee show that violence occurs in all phases of the juvenile justice process, from the first contact with the police, during pre-trial detention and during the stay in treatment and other facilities for children sentenced to deprivation of liberty.[89]

It is important to emphasise the interrelationship between the child's dignity and the work of the law involvement agencies. As a criterion for quality, the human dignity principle requires that the personnel involved in juvenile justice should be well informed, trained and highly familiar with the child's development. In particular, they should be trained on 'adolescent's physical, psychological, mental and social development, and about the special needs of the most vulnerable children, such as children with disabilities, displaced children, street children, refugee and asylum-seeking children, and children belonging to racial, ethnic, religious, linguistic or other minorities'.[90] Unfortunately, in some cases, police brutality happens in a discriminatory manner, for example targeting only refugee children, street children and those who are in conflict with the law. In its concluding report concerning Tanzania, the Committee expressed its concern that these acts would negatively affect the child's human dignity: 'The Committee is concerned about the incidence of police brutality, particularly against children living and/or working on the streets, refugee children and those in conflict with the law. Concern is also expressed at the inadequate enforcement of existing legislation to ensure that all children are

---

88 Committee on the Rights of the Chid, 'Concluding Observations on Egypt's Initial Report', UN Doc. CRC/C/15/Add.5 (18 February 1993), para. 14.

89 Committee on the Rights of the Chid, 'General Comment No. 10 on Children's rights in juvenile justice', UN Doc. CRC/C/GC/10 (25 April 2007), para. 13.

90 *Ibid.*, para. 40.

treated with respect for their physical and mental integrity and their inherent dignity.'[91]

Considerations of the child's social and cultural backgrounds are also relevant. For instance, in some cultures, theft is acceptable within the child's tribal cultural background. This emphasises the importance of the subjective and case-by-case handling of the problem. The training of the law enforcement personnel on juvenile justice allows for the dignified and effective handling of such matters. Furthermore, States Parties are expected to take special measures to ensure that children are protected against the occurrence of cases of extrajudicial executions, disappearances and torture. These are human rights violations contrary to the human dignity of the child. Those accused should be tried and, when found guilty, punished. Furthermore, States Parties are expected to ensure that children benefit from recovery and reintegration programmes in an environment which fosters the dignity and the self-confidence of the child.[92]

9.5. DEPRIVATION OF LIBERTY AND THE CHILD'S DIGNITY

Deprivation of liberty may seriously interfere with the child's dignity. It may occur for different reasons as it is not limited to cases of juvenile justice only. It includes, among other cases, deprivation of liberty in mental health institutions, detention camps (for immigrants) and correctional institutions.[93] In some cases, the State deprives children of their liberty in order to protect them. The Committee has called on States Parties to refrain from such practice as it interferes with the right of the child to survival and development.[94] In the United Kingdom, for example, the Independent Asylum Commission pointed out that it is not only the concept of detention that is against human dignity but

---

91 Committee on the Rights of the Child, 'Concluding Observations on United Republic of Tanzania's Initial Report', UN Doc. CRC/C/15/Add.156 (9 July 2001), para. 36.

92 Committee on the Rights of the Chid, 'Concluding Observations on Peru's Initial Report', UN Doc. CRC/C/15/Add.8 (18 October 1993), para. 16.

93 See *A. v Australia,* UN Doc. CCPR/C/59/D/560/1993. See also Committee on the Rights of the Child, 'Concluding Observations on Austria's Initial Report', UN Doc. CRC/C/15/Add.98 (7 May 1999), para. 27. See also Committee on the Rights of the Child, 'Concluding Observations on Canada's Initial Report', UN Doc. CRC/C/15/Add.37 (20 July 1995), para. 24. Also 'Deserving Dignity – the Independent Asylum Commission's Third Report of Conclusions and Recommendations: How we treat people seeking sanctuary', (July 2008), United Kingdom, pp. 27–28. Also 'General Comment No. 21', UN Doc. CCPR/C/21/Add.1 (10 April 1992), para. 2 which replaces General Comment No. 9 concerning humane treatment of persons deprived of liberty (article 10).

94 Committee on the Rights of the Child, 'Concluding Observations on the Combined Fourth and Fifth Periodic Reports of Jordan', UN Doc. CRC/C/JOR/CO/4-5 (8 July 2014), paras. 21–22.

also the conditions of detention such as lack of healthcare, length of detentions and the mixture with convicted criminals in some cases. The Commission recommended that there should be no detention for children. The Commission referred to some issues with detention in its report, for example, where the child is detained with his family. It also recommended that the best interests of the child be paramount and that the UK should revoke its reservation to article 22 of the Convention on the Rights of the Child in the case of unaccompanied children. The Commission also recommends that detention of children should end.[95]

The principle of human dignity in this situation is absolute:

> Treating all persons deprived of their liberty with humanity and with respect for their dignity is a fundamental and universally applicable rule. Consequently, the application of this rule, as a minimum, cannot be dependent on the material resources available in the State party. This rule must be applied without distinction of any kind, such as race, colour, sex, language, religion, political or other opinion, national or social origin, property, birth or other status.[96]

According to this statement by the Human Rights Committee, the nature of the human dignity principle is strengthened by the fact that it is not influenced by budgetary or material resources. In this regard it is similar to the essence and nature of article 6(2) because it is a general principle of the Convention.[97]

Other forms of discipline that violate the human dignity of the child who is deprived of her or his liberty include 'placement in a dark cell, closed or solitary confinement, or any other punishment that may compromise the physical or mental health or well-being of the child concerned'.[98]

---

95 Independent Asylum Commission, Third Report of Conclusions and Recommendations: How we treat people seeking sanctuary (July 2008), pp. 2, 27–28 and 41.

96 Human Rights Committee, 'General Comment No. 21', UN Doc. CCPR/C/21/Add.1 (10 April 1992), para. 2, which replaces General Comment No. 9 concerning humane treatment of persons deprived of liberty (article 10), para. 4.

97 Committee on the Rights of the Chid, 'Concluding Observations on Bolivia's Initial Report', UN Doc. CRC/C/15/Add.1 (18 February 1993), para. 14; and Committee on the Rights of the Child, 'Concluding Observations on Indonesia's' Initial Report', UN Doc. CRC/C/15/Add.7 (18 October 1993), para. 13.

98 Committee on the Rights of the Chid, 'General Comment No. 10 on Children's rights in juvenile justice', UN Doc. CRC/C/GC/10 (25 April 2007), para. 89.

10. THE RELATIONSHIP BETWEEN HUMAN DIGNITY AND ARTICLE 6(2) IN ITS CAPACITY AS AN ECONOMIC, SOCIAL AND CULTURAL RIGHT OF THE CHILD (BASIC HEALTH AND WELFARE RIGHT)

It is important, in this context, to re-emphasise that article 6(2) is a comprehensive right of the child that basically means the right of the child to everything. However, the ensuing discussion is about the interdependence between the right of the child to survival and development, in its capacity as an economic and social right, and the child's dignity.

Economic, social and cultural rights are for everyone to enjoy, no matter whether they are poor or rich. Differences between human beings are irrelevant as far as the entitlement to human rights is concerned. Children are also equal in their dignity; therefore, they are equal in having their rights as well. But in some cases of poverty and deprivation, poor children need to be specifically targeted so as to guarantee effective protection. In this respect, human dignity is expected to play an important role. For instance, migrant children, whether alone or accompanied by someone, in many cases, are a large group of vulnerable children. They suffer from violations of their dignity in order to survive; economic, social and cultural rights of migrant children are frequently targeted.

> The challenge now is to create a situation in which migration can take place in conditions of dignity and become an informed choice rather than a survival strategy. A good starting point would be for States to acknowledge that the Convention on the Protection of Migrant Workers stems directly from those principles expressed in the Universal Declaration of Human Rights and the Convention on the Rights of the Child, and should therefore be given a wider and much needed ratification. This could be a first step towards a future that really belongs to children.[99]

Goldewijk argues in favour of the protection of children. For her, poor people are those who, first of all, have rights, and their dignity needs to be protected. She considers that economic, social and cultural rights offer precisely this protection by law of human dignity, of people's basic human needs and of their fundamental freedoms. She also argues that this implies that these rights have a transformative character. They present a legal framework for processes of social, political and cultural change. In this regard, human rights need to be seen as legal resources and as political instruments for transformation.[100] Sometimes,

---

99 F. Musiani, 'Migrant Children's Rights: Working to Fill the Gap' (2006) 43(4) *UN Chronicle* 33.

100 B.K. Goldewijk, 'From Seattle to Porto Alegre: Emergence of a new focus on dignity and the implementation of economic, social and cultural rights', in B.K. Goldewijk, A.C. Baspineiro

the realisation of economic, social and cultural rights may take a while. This time factor should not negatively affect the human dignity of the child.

Article 27(3) provides the right of the child to an adequate standard of living: 'States Parties, in accordance with national conditions and within their means, shall take appropriate measures to assist parents and others responsible for the child to implement this right and shall in case of need provide material assistance and support programmes, particularly with regard to nutrition, clothing and housing.' This right has a strong link with the human dignity of the child and article 6(2) because violations of this right will affect his or her right to survive and develop with dignity. The following words of the Committee on Economic, Social and Cultural Rights, with regard to the right to housing, restate this fact:

> In the Committee's view, the right to housing should not be interpreted in a narrow or restrictive sense which equates it with, for example, the shelter provided by merely having a roof over one's head or views shelter exclusively as a commodity. Rather it should be seen as the right to live somewhere in security, peace and dignity. This is appropriate for at least two reasons. In the first place, the right to housing is integrally linked to other human rights and to the fundamental principles upon which the Covenant is premised. This 'the inherent dignity of the human person' from which the rights in the Covenant are said to derive requires that the term 'housing' be interpreted so as to take account of a variety of other considerations, most importantly that the right to housing should be ensured to all persons irrespective of income or access to economic resources. Secondly, the reference in article 11 (1) must be read as referring not just to housing but to adequate housing. As both the Commission on Human Settlements and the Global Strategy for Shelter to the Year 2000 have stated: 'Adequate shelter means ... adequate privacy, adequate space, adequate security, adequate lighting and ventilation, adequate basic infrastructure and adequate location with regard to work and basic facilities – all at a reasonable cost'.[101]

In Defence for Children International v. The Netherlands, which was a complaint to the European Committee on Social Rights, several references to the relationship between human dignity and the right of children and young people to housing were made. In this case, Defence for Children International has argued out that the violation of this right is a violation of children's dignity and development. It has asked the Committee to hold the Netherlands responsible for violations against the rights of children to housing, which violates their dignity and affects their development: 'By not being able to secure a safe shelter children not lawfully present in the Netherlands are denied their human dignity and the right to develop themselves fully, both physically and

---

and P.C. Carbonari (eds.), *Dignity and Human Rights: The implementation of economic, social, and cultural rights* (Intersentia, Antwerp, 2002), p. 8.

101 Available in 'Compilation of the General Comments and General Recommendations Adopted by Human Rights Treaty Bodies', UN Doc. HRI/GEN/1/Rev.7 (12 May 2004), p. 20.

mentally.'[102] However, the Committee acknowledged 'that States have the right under international law to control the entry, residence and expulsion of aliens from their territories'.[103]

In favour of the arguments of the government of Netherlands, the Committee acknowledged:

> As far as Article 31§1 of the Revised Charter is concerned, the Committee acknowledges that the denial of adequate housing, which includes a legal guarantee of security of tenancy, to children unlawfully present on its territory, does not automatically entail a denial of the basic care needed to avoid persons living in intolerable conditions. Moreover, to require that a Party provide such lasting housing would run counter the State's aliens policy objective of encouraging persons unlawfully on its territory to return to their country of origin.
>
> ... Accordingly the Committee concludes that children unlawfully present on the territory of a State Party do not come within the personal scope of Article 31§1, which thus does not apply in the instant case.[104]

10.1. THE PROVISION OF HEALTH AND OTHER WELL-BEING SERVICES SHOULD REFLECT THE HUMAN DIGNITY OF THE CHILD BOTH AS A CRITERION FOR QUALITY AND AS AN AIM

Violations of economic and social rights reflect negatively on the child's dignity. For instance, a child wearing ragged cloth will certainly look servile and this will interfere with his or her dignified appearance. Carrying children around and begging in order to bring sympathy is obviously a violation of the child's dignity.

Poverty and disease are facts of life, and thus it might not be easy to get rid of them forever, as some might think.[105] However, it is important to get rid of poverty and diseases which are unnecessary and are the result of preventable causes because they are the ones that interfere with the human dignity of the child. It is also important to get rid of the undignified interventions into the economic and social rights of the child, such as the right to safe water, the right

---

102 European Committee of Social Rights, *Defence for Children International (DCI) v. The Netherlands* (Complaint No. 47/2008) ECSR Case Document No. 1, 12 February 2008.

103 European Committee of Social Rights, *Defence for Children International (DCI) v. The Netherlands* (Complaint No. 47/2008) ECSR Case Document No. 1, decision on the merits, para. 41, available at: <https://www.coe.int/t/dghl/monitoring/socialcharter/complaints/CC47Merits_en.pdf> accessed 24 April 2015.

104 European Committee of Social Rights, *Defence for Children International (DCI) v. The Netherlands* (Complaint No. 47/2008) ECSR Case Document No. 1, decision on the merits, para. 44, available at: <https://www.coe.int/t/dghl/monitoring/socialcharter/complaints/CC47Merits_en.pdf> accessed 24 April 2015.

105 For human dignity and freedom from poverty see G.E. Devenish, *A Commentary on the South African Bill of Rights* (Durban, Butterworths, 1999), p. 83.

to food and the right to health, which are highly relevant to the right of the child to survival and development. The Constitutional Court of South Africa, for instance, discussed this essential relationship between dignity and access to health and the responsibility of the State in a case involving children's rights to minimum shelter. The Court held that the realisation of socio-economic rights, including access to housing, health-care, sufficient food and water, and social security, is necessary to ensure the human dignity, freedom and equality of all individuals. The failure of the government to make any provision at all for the housing needs of the poorest was a violation of the South African constitution.[106]

Economic, social and cultural rights aim at transforming and improving the standards and quality of people's lives, i.e. children's lives, in a real sense, not only as an end in themselves, but as a means to preserving the dignity of the person (children). Hence, the very core of economic, social and cultural rights is human dignity and equality.[107]

In the same regard, it is important, however, in this context to realise the quality control aspects of the right of the child to survival and development:

> The mere provision of a house, water, education etc, is not enough in terms of the realisation of economic, social and cultural rights. The methodologies used, the resources made available for delivery, education, the standard and quality of the service, the sustainability of the service, the timeousness of the intervention, the development of basic infrastructure, the involvement of the recipients, the creation of accessible mechanisms etc have to be met, for us to agree that the right has been realised. In other words, the human being as a holistic individual is the central focus and not the act of delivering a service or product.[108]

Social grants for children are economic rights. They are also relevant to the child's dignity as in the South African case of Khosa and Others v. Minister of Social Development and Others.[109] The applicants had permanent residence in South Africa. They challenged legislative provisions, which limited entitlement to social grants for the aged to South African citizens and prevented children of non-South African citizens, in the same position as the applicants, from claiming any of the childcare grants available to South African children (regardless of the citizenship status of the children themselves).

---

106 *Government of the Republic of South Africa and Others v. Grootboom*, 2001 [1] SA 46 [CC], 2000 [11] BCLR 1169 [CC] (Constitutional Court of South Africa).

107 V. Govender, 'Economic, Social and Cultural Rights in South Africa: Entitlement, Not Mere Policy Options', in B.K. Goldewijk, A.C. Baspineiro and P.C. Carbonari (eds.), *Dignity and Human Rights: The implementation of economic, social, and cultural rights* (Intersentia, Antwerp, 2002), p. 89.

108 *Ibid.*, p. 90.

109 *Khosa and Others v. Minister of Social Development and Others, Mahlaule and Another v. Minister of Social Development* (CCT 13/03, CCT 12/03) [2004] ZACC 11; 2004 (6) SA 505 (CC); 2004 (6) BCLR 569 (CC) (4 March 2004) (Constitutional Court of South Africa).

The Court held that the Constitution gave 'everyone' the right to have access to social security – not only citizens – and that 'everyone' would include those residing in the country legally. Justice Mokgoro emphasised the interdependence and interconnectedness of rights and observed that the right to equality was implicit in the Section 27 entitlement of everyone to have access to social security. She held that when other constitutional rights are implicated by a socio-economic right, compliance with those other implicated rights will be important in evaluating whether the measures taken by the state in fulfilling the socio-economic rights are reasonable within the meaning of Section 27(2). The Court stated that, due to their position as people who have become part of South African society and have made their homes in South Africa, the exclusion of permanent residents from the legislative scheme amounted to unfair discrimination in violation of Section 9(3). The court applied the reasonableness standard as in Section 27(2). It found the scheme's exclusion of permanent residents to be unreasonable. It stated out the importance of providing access to social assistance for all who live permanently in South Africa. It also pointed out the impact upon life and dignity that a denial of such access would have, far outweighed the financial and immigration considerations on which the State relied.[110] In addition, in a case before the European Committee on Social Rights about medical assistance and human dignity in relation to children, the Committee found that there was a violation in relation to children but not adults.[111]

The literature of the Committee on the Rights of the Child also refers to human dignity and the right to health. In its concluding observations on Kyrgyzstan's second periodic report, the Committee referred to the inhumane treatment of children in psychiatric hospitals. This implies a link between human dignity and the right to health because the word 'inhumane' often refers to undignified situations.[112] This association between article 6(2) and the economic and social rights of the child should lead to the realisation of the human dignity of the child.

Delpérée's argument on human dignity as a relational right is clear when he speaks about article 23 of the Belgian Constitution.[113] He clearly states that the

---

110 *Khosa and Others v. Minister of Social Development and Others, Mahlaule and Another v. Minister of Social Development* (CCT 13/03, CCT 12/03) [2004] ZACC 11; 2004 (6) SA 505 (CC); 2004 (6) BCLR 569 (CC) (4 March 2004) (Constitutional Court of South Africa).

111 European Committe on Social Rights, *International Federation of Human Rights Leagues (FIDH) v. France* (Complaint No. 13/2003), available at: <www.escr-net.org/docs/i/400976> accessed 14 April 2015.

112 Committee on the Rights of the Child, 'Concluding Observations on Kyrgyzstan's Second Periodic Report', UN Doc. CRC/C/15/Add.244 (3 November 2004) paras. 49–50.

113 Everyone has the right to lead a life in keeping with human dignity. To this end, the laws, federate laws and rules referred to in article 134 guarantee economic, social and cultural rights, taking into account corresponding obligations, and determine the conditions for exercising them. These rights include among others:

1. The right to employment and to the free choice of an occupation within the context of a general employment policy, aimed among others at ensuring a level of employment

Constitution makes the right to human dignity the objective to be achieved via the attainment of economic, social and cultural rights. This in fact is, indeed, very similar to the argument in this chapter about the use of the concept of human dignity as an aim that is to be achieved through the implementation of article 6(2).

10.2. SIGNIFICANCE OF THE 'DIGNITY' FOUNDATIONS OF THE CHILD'S ECONOMIC, SOCIAL AND CULTURAL RIGHTS

What does it mean to have social and economic rights based on human dignity? In other words, what will the criterion aspect of human dignity lead to? Delpérée gives the Belgian example of the right to a minimum electricity supply (Brussels ordinance of July 1991). The main aim of this ordinance was to make it illegal for an electricity company to cut off the electricity supply to households that are unable to pay their bills.[114] The same question could be put in a different way. What does it mean to base the right of the child to survival and development on human dignity? In this context, consider the following example. It is about the right of children, in some States, who are suffering government-programmed electricity cuts in their homes because the government claims that it cannot afford to have a continuous electricity supply. Sometimes, children who have exams the next day have only street lights to go and study under. Such electricity cuts and the general examinations schedule could be timed so that there is coordination between the two governmental bodies that are responsible for these particular issues.[115] This would guarantee some respect for the human dignity of the child who is studying for his or her exams.

In South Africa, the High Court had to deal with the same aspects of human dignity, i.e., as a criterion and as an aim – in the Mazibuk case.[116] Significantly, Judge Tsoka stated that water is life but sanitation is dignity. Arguably, in

---

that is as stable and high as possible, the right to fair terms of employment and to fair remuneration, as well as the right to information, consultation and collective negotiation;

2. The right to social security, to health care and to social, medical and legal aid;
3. The right to decent accommodation;
4. The right to the protection of a healthy environment;
5. The right to cultural and social fulfilment.

114 F. Delpérée, 'The Right to Human Dignity in Belgian Constitutional Law. The principle of respect for human dignity', Montpellier, 2–6 July 1998, *Science and Techniques of Democracy*, No. 26 (Council of Europe Publishing, 1999), pp. 57–67, p. 63.

115 The electricity company usually promises that the electricity cuts are going to be programmed and based on a particular schedule, but unfortunately the company does not keep to its promise and starts to make a totally unpredictable supply of the electricity. The unprogrammed cuts cause lots of suffering as electricity is a major factor in the daily life of children.

116 *S v. Mazibuko* (A1246/2006) [2008] ZAGPHC 106 (18 April 2008) (High Court of South Africa).

paragraph 160 he conveyed both aspects of human dignity under article 6(2) of the CRC, thereby denying the applicants the right to water is to refuse them the right to live a dignified human existence.[117] In this statement the court used the principle of human dignity as a quality-of-life measurement. The same also applies when the court stated that: 'The denial would perpetuate the decades-long poverty, deprivation, want and undignified existence of the recent past.'[118] The other aspect of human dignity, i.e., as an aim to be achieved, was conveyed in the judge's words that the denial of the right to water will deny the applicants the right to live a South African dream, that is: 'To live in a democratic, open, caring, responsive and equal society that affirms the values of human dignity, equality, and freedom.'[119] In this case, all the residents of the city of Johannesburg were provided with six kilolitres of free water per month per household/account holder. The residents of Phiri were exempted from this and their six-kilolitre supply was to be dispensed by a prepayment meter system. Once the six kilolitres were consumed, the water supply was automatically cut off. The affected account holder had to purchase water credits in order to be entitled to the water supply until he or she became entitled to the next month's free water supply. Phiri is a residential area with large numbers of poor, uneducated and unemployed South Africans who suffer from high rates of HIV/AIDS infection. The court discussed the importance of water for the lives of HIV sufferers and their carers. It also referred to article 24 of the Convention on the Rights of the Child.[120]

10.3. INTERACTION BETWEEN THE RIGHT TO SURVIVAL AND DEVELOPMENT (ARTICLE 6(2)), RIGHT TO LIFE (ARTICLE 6(1)) AND THE CHILD'S DIGNITY

Article 6(2) is a basic right that reflects the qualified implementation of the right of the child to life. Arguably, the quality of the right of the child to life, as guaranteed by article 6(1) of the Convention – 'States Parties recognize that every child has the inherent right to life' – is guided by article 6(2) on the survival and development of the child. Moreover, article 6(2) has a strong association with the human dignity of the child which manifests as a quality control for article 6(1).

The right to life is a vital right. There are varied forms of the right to life. The Supreme Court in India, for example, held that the right to live with human dignity derives from the directive principles of State policy. Accordingly, opportunities and facilities should be provided to children to develop in a healthy manner and in conditions of freedom and dignity. The Court stated that adequate

117 *Ibid.*
118 *Ibid.*
119 *Ibid.*
120 *Ibid.*

facilities, just and humane conditions of work, etc. are the minimum requirements which must exist in order to enable a person to live with human dignity. It adds that the State has to take every action to ensure that 'no State, neither the Central Government nor any State Government, has the right to take any action which will deprive a person of the enjoyment of these basic essentials'.[121] This case highlights the strong level of responsibility of the State Party. In another case, the court also held that the right to life includes the right to enjoyment of pollution-free water and air for the full enjoyment of life.[122] The Inter-American Court of Human Rights gave a comprehensive definition of the right to life as the right to access conditions of living that guarantee a dignified life. Significantly, the Court based its interpretation on the Convention on the Rights of the Child.[123]

11. CONCLUSION

The chapter discussed the significant and unbreakable link between the right of the child to survival and development and human dignity. In this context, it argued against criticisms that might not view such a strong link. In particular, criticisms based on the understanding that article 6(2) does not explicitly refer to dignity. It also argued against criticisms that the reasoning for the strong emphasis of dignity and the added value for clarifying the already broad concepts of survival and development do not appear entirely clear. This argument continues that this is even special when (given the already complex nature of article 6(2)), it appears not really convincing why a kind of 'inherent', but also parallel, concept of dignity, which, admittedly, remains 'wide and vague' should help in interpretation of these already very broad concepts of 'survival' and 'development'. In this respect, the chapter argued for the child's dignity aspect of article 6(2) on the basis that dignity represents the aim and the quality factor for the implementation of the right of the child to survival and development. This means that the child's human dignity actually surrounds all aspects of the right of the child to survival and development, including its importance and comprehensiveness as the right of the child to everything. Moreover, as stated by the Committee on the Rights of the Child, dignity is the core value of the Convention.

Since the adoption of the Universal Declaration on Human Rights in 1948, the relationship between human rights and human dignity has become inseparable. In this respect, the child's dignity has become a component of all children' rights. As pointed out by the Committee on the Rights of the Child,

121 *Bandhua Mukti Morcha v. Union of India* 1984 SCR (2) 67 (Supreme Court of India).

122 *Subhash Kumar v.State of Bihar* AIR 1991 420 (Supreme Court of India).

123 *Villagrán Morales et al. (The "Street Children" Case)* Inter-American Court of Human Rights Series C No. 63 [1999] IACHR 17 (19 November 1999), paras. 191–196, available at: <www.corteidh.or.cr/docs/casos/articulos/seriec_63_ing.pdf> accessed 14 April 2015.

human dignity is the core value of the Convention. The multi-identity nature of the right of the child to survival and development and the fact that it is the right of the child to 'everything' make this connection inevitable.

This kind of link finds a basis in article 22 of the Universal Declaration of Human Rights as well:

> Everyone, as a member of society, has the right to social security and is entitled to realization, through national effort and international co-operation and in accordance with the organization and resources of each State, of the economic, social and cultural rights indispensable for his dignity and the free development of his personality.[124]

Article II of the initial Polish proposal for a convention on the rights of the child reads: 'The child shall enjoy special protection, and shall be given opportunities and facilities, by law and by other means, to enable him to develop physically, mentally, morally, spiritually and socially in a healthy and normal manner and in conditions of freedom and dignity.' This previous declaration addressed the issue of the rights of the child and included concepts similar to those of article 6(2). As would often be seen within the legislative process of international law, the principles or concepts of a particular article would be based on an already existing article or principle from a previous international declaration.[125]

As for the strong relationship between the survival and development and human dignity, the complexity of article 6(2) is an asset. This is because it enriches the interaction between the two. The human dignity principle is linked to article 6(2) in two unique forms. The first one makes the human dignity of the child an aim that needs to be achieved through the implementation of article 6(2). The second form makes the human dignity of the child a criterion for the proper implementation of article 6(2). These two forms are manifest in the wide range of recommendations for implementation and links that article 6(2) enjoys within the Convention on the Rights of the Child.

This kind of link between the human dignity principle and article 6(2) strengthens both the principle and the article. This strength is conveyed in the basic understanding of both concepts and in their implementations.

---

124 Universal Declaration of Human Rights (adopted 10 December 1948) UNGA Res 217 A (III) (UDHR), article 22.

125 C. Cohen, 'The Developing Jurisprudence of the Rights of the Child' (1993–1994) 6 *St. Thomas Law Review* 1, 1–96.

CHAPTER 5

WHO IS RESPONSIBLE?

The Obligation of the State Party to Create Measures and Conditions Necessary for the Survival and Development of the Child

'I am afraid that God might ask me about a stumbled mule in Iraq.'

Caliphate Omar Ibn Alkhattab,
Seventh century

1. INTRODUCTION

The adoption of the Convention on the Rights of the Child (CRC) has been a major step towards the recognition of children as legal rights holders. For the CRC, children are not only to be protected as subjects – they are also rights holders. Normally, in a 'traditional' human-rights context there are two main parties, namely the rights holders and the duty bearers. The Convention made it a reality that children are the rights holders *vis-à-vis* the State under whose jurisdiction they fall.

The main aim of this chapter is to discuss the responsibility of the State, as the duty bearer, for the implementation and realisation of the rights of children to survival and development as guaranteed by article 6(2) of the CRC. To achieve this, the chapter focuses on two main points. The first one is that the survival and development of the child is not simply a right that is included in the CRC, it is actually an aim of the entire Convention. It is also a general principle of the CRC and a tool to measure the State Party's implementation of the Convention. As a general principle, it is similar to the best interests of the child, the non-discrimination principle and the participation principle. States Parties that implement the Convention in a way that interferes with the survival and development of the child are in violation of the CRC.

The second main point that the chapter discusses is related to the 'formulation' of the right of the child to survival and development itself. Based on an understanding that the survival and development is simply about the right of the child to everything, the chapter discusses the concept of the State Party obligation, under article 6(2), and the degree of this duty.[1] This formulation of article 6(2) conveys that the survival and development of the child includes different 'kinds' of rights. In turn, different kinds of rights involve different kinds of State obligations.

Initially, by becoming a Party to the Convention on the Rights of the Child, the State Party has to consider the rights of the child in every aspect of the relationship between the State and the individuals (children) under its jurisdiction. In article 6(2), this aspect of the State Party obligation is even more pronounced, as it was initially put in the CRC in order to bring focus to the obligations of the State Party and the measures they ought to create.[2]

However, it is very important to point out that while the chapter identifies and discusses State Party obligations, it does not claim that it will include an exhaustive list of them. This is because, under article 6(2), there are a wide range of State duties that include, for example, political, social, economic and moral commitments. As the Constitutional Court of South Africa indicated: 'It is necessary to recognise that a wide range of possible measures could be adopted by the State to meet its obligations.'[3] Another reason for the impossibility of having an exhaustive list is that State Party obligations should always be reviewed, reassessed and renewed; therefore, the list will never be an exhaustive or final one. This is especially true considering that there are 194 States Parties to the CRC. Certainly, this huge number of States has its opinions on the nature and contents of the measures and conditions that are to be adopted.[4]

The chapter includes a discussion on the concept of 'ensuring to the maximum extent possible' as it is the standard under article 6(2). The chapter then looks at some examples of the possible measures and conditions that the State Party needs to adopt and create in order to ensure the survival and

---

1 Words of Benyam Dawit Mezmur, the Vice-Chairperson of the Committee on the Rights of the Child, in a Lecture at the Children's Rights Summer School, Nottingham, United Kingdom, June 2013.

2 UN Doc. E/CN.4/1988/28, para. 23, available in Office of the United Nations High Commissioner for Human Rights, *Legislative History of the Convention on the Rights of the Child*, Volume I (United Nations, New York, 2007), p. 366.

3 *Government of the Republic of South Africa and Others v Grootboom and Others Case* (CCT11/00) [2000] ZACC 19 [41] (Constitutional Court of South Africa).

4 Information available at: <https://treaties.un.org/Pages/ViewDetails.aspx?src=TREATY&mtdsg_no=IV11&chapter=4&lang=en> accessed 14 September 2014. However, according to the United Nations (UN News Centre) Somalia ratified the CRC on 20 January 2015. This brings the number of State Parties to 195. See <www.un.org/apps/news/story.asp?NewsID=49845#.VNivTWb6hMS> accessed 23 April 2015. However, according the United Nations Office of the High Commissioner for Human Rights, Somalia did not ratify the Convention on the Rights of the Child. See <http://tbinternet.ohchr.org/_layouts/TreatyBodyExternal/Treaty.aspx?CountryID=161&Lang=EN> accessed 23 April 2015. See also <https://treaties.un.org/Pages/ViewDetails.aspx?src=TREATY&mtdsg_no=IV-11&chapter=4&lang=en> accessed 23 April 2015.

development of the child. It also discusses the general obligations under article 4 of the CRC, with specific reference to their context under article 6(2). Overall, the chapter aims at analysing the elaborate and complicated nature of State Party obligations under article 6(2).

2. IMPORTANCE OF IMPOSING OBLIGATIONS ON THE STATE PARTY

2.1. THE SIGNIFICANT ROLE OF THE STATE

Over the years, human life has developed so as to create the present international community, in which the State is a major actor. The following words of Cassese describe this significant development and the importance of belonging to a particular state:

> [T]he various communities in Europe and elsewhere gradually consolidated and 'hardened' into States. It may suffice now to stress that this powerful drive has been a constant and salient feature of the world community, so much so that most individuals now belong to one State or another: the world population of about six billion human beings is currently divided up amongst nearly two hundred States ... Today it could be maintained with greater truthfulness that without the protection of the State human beings are likely to endure more suffering and hardship than what is likely to be their lot in the normal course of events...[5]

Cassese's comment leads to the following question: what is it, exactly, that the State needs to undertake in order to prove that without the protection of the State, children are likely to endure more suffering and hardship? This question could be put in a different way: what is the unique thing that the State could provide to its children in order to ensure their right to survival and development? Why is it that under 'traditional' international human rights law the survival and development of the child is basically the responsibility of the State?

The present international community, armed with contemporary international law, obliges each individual State to care for the human rights of its citizens, individuals and those under its jurisdiction. As stated by the Inter-American Court of Human Rights in the Serrano Cruz Sisters case:

> The Court recalls that the purpose of international human rights law is to provide the individual with the means to protect internationally recognized human rights before the State (its bodies, agents and all those who act in its name), and that it is a basic principle of the law of the international responsibility of the State, embodied in international human rights law, that all States are internationally responsible

5 A. Cassese, *International Law* (Oxford University Press, Oxford, 2001), p. 4.

for any and every act or omission of any of their powers or bodies that violates internationally enshrined rights.[6]

The simple and straightforward understanding of the obligations of the State in international human rights law lies in the philosophy that the individual child can effectively enjoy all of his or her rights, through his or her State. This dictates that if A, who is a national of country B, travels to country C for his or her holidays, he or she has no right to enjoy the health services that country C provides for free for its nationals or those who reside legally in the country. This kind of perspective reflects the importance that all States should fulfil their duties regarding the implementation of the human rights of the children under their jurisdiction. Obviously, there are some exemptions, such as in cases of accidents and emergencies, and rights of refugee children under article 22 of the CRC. There are also other political and economic regional and international bodies that allow for the nationals of other States to enjoy the human rights implementations in another State, e.g., the European Union, which allows for some voting rights, within the Union.[7] Also important in this context is the rights of aliens and the concept of extra-territorial human rights obligations of the State (ETOs).[8] It is worth mentioning in this context that ETOs are gaining significance with regard to holding States accountable for human rights violations, particularly, in the area of economic, social and cultural rights.[9]

2.2. STATE OBLIGATIONS AND THE INTERNATIONAL HUMAN RIGHTS SYSTEM

State responsibility and accountability is a major aspect of all the United Nations conventions on human rights. Under the CRC the responsibilities of the State towards the children under its jurisdiction are stated in article 2(1):

---

6 *Serrano Cruz Sisters v. El Salvador*, Inter-American Court of Human Rights Series C No. 120 [2005] IACHR 1 (1 March 2005), para. 54.

7 For more information see: <http://ec.europa.eu/justice/citizen/voting-rights/index_en.htm> accessed 23 April 2015.

8 For further reading see S. Skogly, *Beyond National Borders: States' Human Rights Obligations in International Cooperation* (Intersentia, Antwerp, 2006). See also F. Coomans and R. Künnemann (eds.), *Cases and Concepts on Extraterritorial Obligations in the Area of Economic, Social and Cultural Rights* (Intersentia, Cambridge, 2012). As for the position of aliens in the State Party in relation to civil and political rights see United Nations Human Rights Committee, 'General Comment No. 15 on the position of aliens under the Covenant', Twenty-seventh session, 11 April 1986, available in 'Compilation of the General Comments and General Recommendations Adopted by Human Rights Treaty Bodies', UN Doc. HRI/GEN/1/Rev.7 (12 May 2004), p. 140.

9 See, for example, Maastricht Principles on Extraterritorial Obligations of States in the Area of Economic, Social and Cultural Rights (28 September 2011), available at: <www.maastrichtuniversity.nl/web/Institutes/MaastrichtCentreForHumanRights/MaastrichtETOPrinciples.htm> accessed 23 April 2015.

> States Parties shall respect and ensure the rights set forth in the present Convention to each child within their jurisdiction without discrimination of any kind, irrespective of the child's or his or her parent's or legal guardian's race, colour, sex, language, religion, political or other opinion, national, ethnic or social origin, property, disability, birth or other status.

A discussion on the detailed nature and features of State jurisdiction is beyond the scope of this chapter. Suffice to say, however, that there are debates about the extra-territorial obligations of the State Party. For example, in her argument for the extra-territorial obligations of the State, Skogly identifies State jurisdiction as a principle that should not be seen as 'primarily limiting the responsibility of the State.'[10] She argues that the importance of jurisdiction in a human rights context is for the protection of the individual. 'Each individual person should be under the jurisdiction of some state in order to receive human rights protection. This is to be recognised as a person before the law to receive protection from the law.'[11] Extra-territorial legislation is of relevance in the context of article 6(2) because it simply means that the State has the legal 'permission' to exercise its jurisdiction beyond its geographical boundaries. For example, this has been adopted in cases of sexual abuse of minors which no one argues about its negative impact on the survival and development of the child. The extraterritorial obligations of the State have allowed the State to prosecute its citizens when they returned home.[12]

Skogly, however, argues that in the last fifty years, and with the development of international criminal law, the fact that it is only States that have human rights obligations under international human rights law has been questioned because the individual can be held responsible for crimes against humanity, war crimes and genocide. She also refers to the human rights obligations of other international law subjects, such as the UN.[13] The question remains valid as regards the strength of this basic concept of international human rights law, i.e., that the State is the only responsibility holder. Article 29(1) of the Universal Declaration of Human Rights, for example states:

> Everyone has duties to the community in which alone the free and full development of his personality is possible.

Nevertheless, it is important to restate that in the context of article 6(2) of the CRC, the State Party's responsibility for the survival and development of the

10 S. Skogly, *Beyond National Borders: States' Human Rights Obligations in International Cooperation* (Intersentia, Antwerp, 2006), p. 45.

11 *Ibid.* (footnotes omitted).

12 K. Arts, 'General Introduction: A Child Rights-Based Approach to International Criminal Accountability', in K. Arts and V. Popovski (eds.), *International Criminal Accountability and the Rights of Children* (Hague Academic Coalition, The Hague, 2006), p. 9.

13 S. Skogly, *Beyond National Borders: States' Human Rights Obligations in International Cooperation* (Intersentia, Antwerp, 2006) pp. 62–63.

child is essential and has specific relevance. As previously mentioned, this is because the small drafting group on the article clarified that it was initially put in the Convention in order to focus on the obligation of the State Party to create measures and conditions that are necessary for the survival and development of the child. 'The representative of India stated that the text had been drafted in order to cover the following main concerns: … the focus on obligations for States parties to promote measures and conditions for the survival and development of the child.'[14] The emphasis on State Party obligation by the Indian delegate indicates a deeper and more specific level of obligation by the State Party. This is inferred from the fact that all human rights conventions focus on State obligation; therefore, the explicit reference to State Party obligations could mean something more.

3. WAYS OF IDENTIFYING THE OBLIGATIONS OF THE STATE PARTY UNDER ARTICLE 6(2)

The Convention on the Rights of the Child brings with it its own design for the protection of the child and the way he or she is to be viewed. For instance, the child, according to the CRC, is entitled to the kind of protection that respects his or her dignity. The following detailed argument of the Centre for Justice and International Law in its Advisory Opinion to the Inter-American Court of Human Rights clarifies this:

> The main normative reaction to the system of the 'irregular situation' was the adoption of the Convention on the Rights of the Child in 1989, which involved a change of paradigm to recognize minors as subjects of rights and to establish the principle of the 'best interests of the child' as a 'form for resolution of conflicts among rights, and/or as a guide to evaluate laws, practices and policies pertaining to children,' as well as principles such as respect for the opinion of the child, the principle of survival and development, and the principle of nondiscrimination. The Convention on the Rights of the Child also legally codified the 'doctrine of comprehensive protection,' which delimited the role of the Judge to that of solving juridical conflicts, strengthened procedural guarantees, and determined obligations of the State to establish 'comprehensive policies that respect the rights and guarantees protected' by the aforementioned Convention.[15]

---

14 UN Doc. E/CN.4/1988/28, para. 23, available in Office of the United Nations High Commissioner for Human Rights, *Legislative History of the Convention on the Rights of the Child*, Volume I (United Nations, New York, 2007), p. 366.

15 *Juridical Condition and Human Rights of the Child*, Advisory Opinion OC-17/2002, Inter-American Court of Human Rights (28 August 2002) (Oral Comments by the Centre for Justice and International Law).

However, while it is beyond the discussion, it is worth mentioning in this context that debates on the attainment of majority are also of relevance as regards this doctrine. Debates about child soldiers, the criminal responsibility of the child and his or her civil liability are of relevance to this doctrine of comprehensive protection.

Before proceeding with the identification of State Party obligations, it is important to re-emphasise that article 6(2) of the CRC includes two rights, namely the right to survival and the right to development. In this context, the State Party is obliged to ensure the implementation, realisation and actualisation of both rights. It is not enough for the State Party, for instance, to claim that the realisation of the right of the child to breastfeeding will result in the child's development, therefore the State is satisfied that it has fulfilled its obligations under article 6(2). Breastfeeding is a major part of the right to survival, as will be discussed later in Chapter 6 and it should lead to a child's successful development, but this does not mean that the State Party has fulfilled all of its obligations towards the right of the child to development.

Arguably, within the CRC, there are two sources for identifying the obligations of the State. The first one, which is general in its nature, is article 4. This important article already specifies some State obligations with regard to all the rights in the Convention. It reads:

> States Parties shall undertake all appropriate legislative, administrative, and other measures for the implementation of the rights recognized in the present Convention. With regard to economic, social and cultural rights, States Parties shall undertake such measures to the maximum extent of their available resources and, where needed, within the framework of international co-operation.

The second source is specific in nature and can be found within each individual article of the substantive part of the Convention. This kind of source specifies the requirements that are necessary for the implementation and realisation of the article concerned. These requirements and obligations can vary in their nature and their strength.

Before going into the level and nature of State Party obligations in more detail, it is worth looking at the method that the Committee identified for the implementation of the entire Convention, i.e., the method of the 'holistic approach'. In addition to this, the following paragraphs also look at other methods of implementation.

4. VARIOUS METHODS FOR IMPLEMENTING ARTICLE 6(2)

4.1. THE 'HOLISTIC APPROACH' TO THE IMPLEMENTATION OF THE CONVENTION

This has been discussed in detail in Chapter 2; therefore, the discussion here is somewhat brief. The Committee has identified the 'holistic approach' as vital for the implementation of the entire CRC. In its concluding observations to Cuba's initial report the Committee stated that it:

> encourages the State party to pursue the efforts required to ensure a holistic approach to the implementation of the Convention, which reaffirms that the rights of the child are indivisible, interdependent and interrelated and that the rights of the child should be addressed in an integrated manner.[16]

The 'holistic approach' for the implementation of the entire convention finds support in the fact that the CRC includes different 'types of rights'. The following statement by the Committee in its General Comment No. 7 highlights some various forms of State Party obligations with regards to article 6 by focusing on the holistic approach:

> Article 6 refers to the child's inherent right to life and States parties' obligation to ensure, to the maximum extent possible, the survival and development of the child. The Committee reminds States parties (and others concerned) that the right to survival and development can only be implemented in a holistic manner, through the enforcement of all the other provisions of the Convention, including rights to health, adequate nutrition, social security, an adequate standard of living, a healthy and safe environment, education and play ... as well as through respect for the responsibilities of parents and the provision of assistance and quality services ... From an early age, children should themselves be included in activities promoting good nutrition and a healthy and disease-preventing lifestyle.[17]

4.2. INTERDEPENDENCE OF DIFFERENT KINDS OF RIGHTS AS A METHOD FOR IMPLEMENTING ARTICLE 6(2)

The interdependence of rights is also another method of implementation. As it has been categorised by the Committee, one aspect of article 6(2) is that it is

---

16 Committee on the Rights of the Child, 'Concluding Observations on Cuba's Initial Report', UN Doc. CRC/C/15/Add.72 (18 June 1997), para. 34.

17 Committee on the Rights of the Child, 'General Comment No. 7 on Implementing Child Rights in Early Childhood', UN Doc. CRC/C/GC/7/Rev.1 (20 September 2006), para. 10.

a basic health and welfare right of the child, i.e., an economic and social right. In 1989, the Human Rights Committee issued a general comment regarding article 24 of the International Covenant on Civil and Political Rights, which is concerned with the rights of the child and reads:

> 1. Every child shall have, without any discrimination as to race, colour, sex, language, religion, national or social origin, property or birth, the rights to such measures as are required by his status as a minor, on the part of his family, society and the State.
> 2. Every child shall be registered immediately after birth and shall have a name.
> 3. Every child has the right to acquire a nationality.

Paragraph 3 of this general comment stated that the full enjoyment of civil and political rights requires the adoption of measures for economic, social and cultural rights. In this comment the Human Rights Committee stated that the implementation of the civil and political rights that are included in the Covenant requires, in addition to civil and political measures, economic, social and cultural ones:

> In most cases, however, the measures to be adopted are not specified in the Covenant and it is for each State to determine them in the light of the protection needs of children in its territory and within its jurisdiction. The Committee notes in this regard that such measures, although intended primarily to ensure that children fully enjoy the other rights enunciated in the Covenant, may also be economic, social and cultural. For example, every possible economic and social measure should be taken to reduce infant mortality and to eradicate malnutrition among children and to prevent them from being subjected to acts of violence and cruel and inhuman treatment or from being exploited by means of forced labour or prostitution, or by their use in the illicit trafficking of narcotic drugs, or by any other means. In the cultural field, every possible measure should be taken to foster the development of their personality and to provide them with a level of education that will enable them to enjoy the rights recognized in the Covenant...[18]

This is a two-sided coin. Similarly, one can argue that the implementation of economic, social and cultural rights requires the existence of civil and political measures, as stated in article 5 of the Vienna Declaration and Programme of Action:

> All human rights are universal, indivisible and interdependent and interrelated. The international community must treat human rights globally in a fair and equal manner, on the same footing, and with the same emphasis. While the significance of national and regional particularities and various historical, cultural and religious

---

18 Available in 'Compilation of the General Comments and General Recommendations Adopted by Human Rights Treaty Bodies', UN Doc. HRI/GEN/1/Rev.7 (12 May 2004), pp. 144–145.

backgrounds must be borne in mind, it is the duty of States, regardless of their political, economic and cultural systems, to promote and protect all human rights and fundamental freedoms.[19]

4.3. THE GENERAL PRINCIPLE CAPACITY AND INTERPRETATIVE CAPACITY OF ARTICLE 6(2)

Arguably, the prestigious position of article 6(2) as a general principle of the Convention provides for a third method of implementation. In this sense, the spirit of article 6(2) should be reflected in the implementation of the individual articles of the substantive part of the CRC.[20] However, it is possible, also, to ask the following question: what is the implication of or the value added of article 6(2) as an interpreter into other rights? This interaction between article 6(2) as an interpreting general principle and other individual rights of the child should make the implementation of the entire Convention more effective and coherent. Moreover, it will add value to the meaning and implementation of article 6(2) as it will broaden its perspectives and areas of its implementation. It will also give more volume and emphasis to the quality interpretation of article 6(2) and strengthens its dynamic implementation. In practice this could mean that birth registration, for instance, according to article 7, should be implemented on the basis of the right of the child to survival and development. If the implementation infringes article 6(2) it is contrary to the CRC. In some countries where there is a collapse in the system due to corruption in public institutions, or in countries where there is a large nomadic population, or in cases of failing States, birth registration could be negatively affected. In cases of chaos due to natural disasters such as earthquakes and tsunamis, for example, birth registrations could be affected as well. In such kinds of situations, the State Party should guarantee the survival and development of the child to the maximum extent possible by using it as an interpretative tool for the implementation of all kinds of rights.

Hence, it is possible to argue that the implementation through the aforementioned methods stands as one of the enhancement factors. However, because the concepts of survival and development have a wide scope, there are other aspects to article 6(2) that need consideration as well. For example, the right of the child not to be subjected to arbitrary or unlawful interference with his or her privacy, family, or correspondence, and in addition not to be subjected to unlawful attacks on his or her honour and reputation, is an aspect of the right of the child to survive and develop in exactly the same way as the right of the child to health and education. In addition, rights of the child cannot be implemented

---

19 Vienna Declaration and Programme of Action, UN Doc. A/CONF. 157/24 (12 July 1993), article 5.

20 This applies to all four general principles of the Convention.

without reference to article 6(2); for example, the right of the child to education should be implemented by taking into consideration the survival and development of the child and through means that guarantee the child's survival and development. This kind of understanding makes it possible to argue that, within the CRC, article 6(2) plays different roles as an aim, a general principle, a quality-control factor and an article that holds within it different kinds of rights. Thus any method of implementation should take this into consideration. This important value of article 6(2), however, as pointed out in Chapter 3, has not reached a consensus among scholars.

5. THE STANDARDS OF 'TO THE MAXIMUM EXTENT POSSIBLE' AND 'TO THE MAXIMUM EXTENT OF THEIR AVAILABLE RESOURCES'

5.1. THE STANDARD OF 'TO THE MAXIMUM EXTENT POSSIBLE'

The standard of 'to the maximum extent possible' represents the level to which the State Party needs to exert its efforts with regards to its implementation of some rights in the Convention including article 6(2). In other words, the phrase 'to the maximum extent possible' is a measuring tool. A major aspect of the obligation of the State Party in article 6(2) is the fact that the State Party is obliged to ensure the implementation of the right of the child to survive and develop and not to ensure that the child will actually survive and develop. It is not possible for any Party to guarantee this. The phrase 'to the maximum extent possible' appears in the body of article 6(2) and in many of the recommendations of the Committee on the Rights of the Child that are concerned with the right of the child to survive and develop. For instance, States Parties are requested to

> describe specific measures taken to guarantee the child's right to life and to create an environment conducive to ensuring to the maximum extent possible the survival and development of the child, including physical, mental, spiritual, moral, psychological and social development, in a manner compatible with human dignity, and to prepare the child for an individual life in a free society.[21]

Although the wording of this standard appears to be limiting and loosening the level of State Party obligations, the standard of 'to the maximum extent possible'

---

21 Committee on the Rights of the Child, 'General guidelines for periodic reports' (Basic Reference Document), UN Doc. CRC/C/58 (20 November 1996), para. 40.

in fact recognises that the State cannot afford to do more than it has already done. This represents a realistic approach to the implementation of the right concerned.

In relation to economic, social and cultural rights, article 4 of the CRC speaks about the standard of 'to the maximum extent possible of their available resources'. The Committee on the Rights of the Child have asked States Parties to live up to that position as it is not convinced that any government fully lives up to that ambition today.

> A key article in the Convention – article 4 – states that Governments should implement the economic, social and cultural rights of the child 'to the maximum extent of their available resources'. We are not convinced that any Government which has reported to us has managed to show that it has lived up to that obligation.[22]

5.2. THE STANDARD OF 'TO THE MAXIMUM EXTENT OF THEIR AVAILABLE RESOURCES'

The question arising here is whether this standard is similar to that of 'to the maximum extent possible'? In its advisory opinion on the Juridical Condition and Human Rights of the Child, the Inter-American Court of Human Rights explained the concept of 'to the maximum extent of their available resources' as follows:

> Full exercise of economic, social, and cultural rights of children has been associated with the possibilities of the State that is under the obligation (Article 4 of the Convention on the Rights of the Child), which must make its best effort, in a constant and deliberate manner, to ensure access of children to those rights, and their enjoyment of such rights, avoiding regressions and unjustifiable delays, and allocating as many available resources as possible to this compliance.[23]

The Limburg Principles, which were adopted by a group of experts for the interpretation of State obligations under the International Covenant on Economic, Social and Cultural Rights, also explain the following aspects of 'to the maximum extent of its available resources' standard.

> States parties are obligated, regardless of the level of economic development, to ensure respect for minimum subsistence rights for all.

---

22 Committee on the Rights of the Child, 'Day of General Discussion on Economic Exploitation of Children', UN Doc. CRC/C/20 (25 October 1993) Annex V, p. 53.

23 *Juridical Condition and Human Rights of the Child*, Advisory Opinion OC-17/2002, Inter-American Court of Human Rights (28 August 2002), para. 81. Citing the Inter-American Court is useful in the understanding of the Convention on the Rights of the Child. The Court has stated that on the basis of article 64 of the American Convention on Human Rights it has the power to interpret any international treaty applicable in the American states.

> ... 'Its available resources' refers to both the resources within a State and those available from the international community through international co-operation and assistance.
>
> ... In determining whether adequate measures have been taken for the realization of the rights recognized in the Covenant attention shall be paid to equitable and effective use of and access to the available resources.
>
> ... In the use of the available resources due priority shall be given to the realization of rights recognized in the Covenant, mindful of the need to assure to everyone the satisfaction of subsistence requirements as well as the provision of essential services.[24]

5.3. COMPARISON OF THE STANDARD OF 'TO THE MAXIMUM EXTENT POSSIBLE' AND THE STANDARD OF 'TO THE MAXIMUM EXTENT OF THEIR AVAILABLE RESOURCES'

As regards the difference between the standard of 'to the maximum extent possible' and that of 'to the maximum extent of their available resources', it is possible to argue that the standard of 'to the maximum extent of its available resources' has, generally speaking, been used in relation to economic, social and cultural rights only, in particular to economic and other resources? In this respect, it could be argued that the standard of 'to the maximum extent possible' always has a wider context. In a number of its concluding observations on States Parties' reports, the Committee on the Rights of the Child links the standard of 'to the maximum extent of its available resources' to financial and other resources for fighting poverty. For example, the following statement by the Committee on the Rights of the Child, in its concluding observations on the initial report of Canada, considers financial resources:

> The Committee encourages the Government of Canada to ensure the full implementation of article 4 of the Convention in the light of the general principles of the Convention ... Available resources should be allocated to their maximum extent to ensure the implementation of economic, social and cultural rights. The Committee also emphasizes the need to take immediate steps to tackle the problem of child poverty and make every feasible effort to ensure that all families, particularly single parent families, have adequate resources and facilities.[25]

---

24 Limburg Principles on the Implementation of the International Covenant on Economic, Social and Cultural Rights, Maastricht, 2–6 June 1986, paras. 25–28; available in UN Doc. E/CN.4/1987/17 (8 January 1987).

25 Committee on the Rights of the Child, 'Concluding Observations on Canada's Initial Report', UN Doc. CRC/C/15/Add.37 (20 June 1995), para. 21.

Another example is in the Committee's concluding observations on the Initial Report of Poland:

> The Committee encourages the Government of Poland to pay particular attention to the full implementation of article 4 of the Convention and to ensure a judicious distribution of the resources at the central, regional and local levels. Budget allocations for the implementation of economic, social and cultural rights should be ensured to the *maximum extent of available resources* and in the light of the best interests of the child.[26]

Or:

> With respect to the implementation of article 4 of the Convention, the Committee recommends that particular attention be paid to the need to ensure budget allocations, to *the maximum extent of available resources*, to implement economic, social and cultural rights in the light of the principles of non-discrimination and the best interest of the child...[27]

Or:

> The Committee remains concerned at the small proportion of the budget devoted to the social sectors, particularly primary health care and primary education, in contradiction to the provisions of article 4 of the Convention which emphasize that economic, social and cultural rights should be implemented *to the maximum extent of available resources*. The Committee further notes that international agencies have questioned the present level of resources allocated in the State party to the social sector.[28]

This is how, in general terms, the Committee views the phrase 'to the maximum extent of their available resources' in broader context.[29]

Arguably, in this context, the standard of 'to the maximum extent possible' is broader and more comprehensive. It is not limited to economic or to any other resources. It is linked to the efforts and exertions of the State Party in every

---

26 Committee on the Rights of the Child, 'Concluding Observations on Poland's Initial Report', UN Doc. CRC/C/15/Add.31 (15 January 1995), para. 24 (emphasis added).

27 Committee on the Rights of the Child, 'Concluding Observations on Senegal's Initial Report', UN Doc. CRC/C/15/Add.44 (27 November 1995), para. 23 (emphasis added).

28 Committee on the Rights of the Child, 'Concluding Observations on Indonesia's Initial Report', UN Doc. CRC/C/15/Add.25 (24 October 1994), para. 12 (emphasis added).

29 The standard does not mean that the State should be exempted from its obligations because of financial difficulties. There are several reasons for this. The first is that article 6(2) is a general principle of the CRC which gives the article immunity against being subject to financial difficulties; see Committee on the Rights of the Child, 'Concluding Observations on Indonesia's Initial Report', UN Doc. CRC/C/15/Add.7 (18 October 1993), para. 13. Secondly, article 4 of the CRC states that, in cases of financial difficulties, States should ask for international cooperation. Thirdly, the concept of interdependence of rights means that the implementation of other articles of the CRC is in itself part of the implementation of article 6(2).

aspect of its implementation of any relevant right. It could even be argued that the standard of 'to the maximum extent of its available resources' is part of the standard of 'to the maximum extent possible'. For example, the State has to prove that it has done the maximum planning required for the implementation of the right of the child to survival and development. It means that the State Party needs to provide the maximum quality of care, the maximum effort possible, and the maximum knowledge possible, etc. For instance, the State should start working immediately on the eradication of poverty, which indicates that the State has applied the 'to the maximum extent possible' standard. The immediate start conveys that the State Party applied the standard of 'to the maximum extent possible'. This indication could be considered an important step for claiming that the State Party has implemented its obligation in ensuring the implementation of the right of the child to survival and development.

As a quality-measuring standard, however, both the standard of 'to the maximum extent of their available resources' and the standard of 'to the maximum extent possible' work on subjective bases. The method of analysing whether the State Party has applied the standard is left to each individual case. To illustrate, if when considering the financial abilities of a particular State, the State spent a small amount of money when it was expected that it could have spent more, then in this case the State did not fully implement the 'to the maximum extent possible' nor 'to the maximum extent of its available resources' standards.

In other cases, the criterion for claiming that the State Party applied the standard of 'to the maximum extent possible' could mean that the State is expected to ask for international cooperation.[30]

Another example is that, in order to prove that the State Party has applied the 'to the maximum extent possible' standard, the State needs to prove transparency and to demonstrate that it is fighting corruption, especially corruption in public institutions. The Committee has taken a similar path as it interpreted the phrase 'to the maximum extent of their available resources', which, as mentioned before, is arguably part of 'to the maximum extent possible, to include issues of transparency and corruption, as shown by its concluding observations on the initial report of Angola:

> The Committee recommends that the State party continue and strengthen its efforts to increase budgetary allocations for the realization of children's rights … to the 'maximum extent … of available resources'… In this regard the Committee recommends that the State party increase budgetary allocations for the social sector and make sure that revenues from oil and other sources is handled in a transparent manner in order to prevent embezzlement and corruption. The State

30 Committee on the Rights of the Child, 'Concluding Observations on Denmark's Initial Report', UN Doc. CRC/C/15/Add.33 (15 February 1995), para. 19.

party is encouraged, in this regard, to ratify the United Nations Convention against Corruption which is signed in December 2003.[31]

The standard of 'to the maximum extent of their available resources' is also useful in cases of structural adjustment policies:

> [S]tructural adjustment policies have created difficulties in the full application of the rights guaranteed by the Convention and have had a specific impact on the situation of children, in particular children in low-income categories and in rural areas. The Committee, however, takes this opportunity to recall that, under article 4 … States parties are called upon to implement the Convention to the maximum extent of their available resources.[32]

In relation to the timeframe for implementation, both standards are of an immediate nature; this is to block out any unjustified claims from the State Party with regards to lack of implementation. In this context, the obligation of conduct and obligation of result is also another context under which the comparison between the two standards could be made.

5.4. COMPARISON OF THE STANDARD OF 'TO THE MAXIMUM EXTENT POSSIBLE' AND THE STANDARD OF 'TO THE MAXIMUM OF THEIR AVAILABLE RESOURCES' IN THE CONTEXT OF SPECIFIC OBLIGATIONS OF THE STATE

Article 2(1) of the International Covenant on Economic and Social Rights states that:

> Each State Party to the present Covenant undertakes to take steps, individually and through international assistance and co-operation, especially economic and technical, to the maximum of its available resources, with a view to achieving progressively the full realization of the rights recognized in the present Covenant by all appropriate means, including particularly the adoption of legislative measures.

The Committee on Economic, Social and Cultural Rights has also, significantly, clarified this in the following statement:

---

31 Committee on the Rights of the Child, 'Concluding Observations on Angola's Initial Report', UN Doc. CRC/C/15/Add.246 (3 November 2004), para. 14. See also Committee on the Rights of the Child, 'Concluding Observations on the Combined Third and Fourth Periodic Reports of India', UN Doc. CRC/C/IND/CO/8–4 (7 July 2014), paras. 17–18.

32 Committee on the Rights of the Child, 'Concluding Observations on Egypt's Initial Report', UN Doc. CRC/C/15/Add.5 (18 February 1993), para. 5.

> On the basis of the extensive experience gained by the Committee, as well as by the body that preceded it, over a period of more than a decade of examining State parties' reports the Committee is of the view that *a minimum core obligation to ensure the satisfaction of, at the very least, minimum essential levels of each of the rights is incumbent upon every State party. Thus, for example, a State party in which any significant number of individuals is deprived of essential foodstuffs, of essential primary health care, of basic shelter and housing, or of the most basic forms of education is, prima facie, failing to discharge its obligations under the Covenant.* If the Covenant were not to be read to establish such a minimum core obligation, it would be largely deprived of its raison d'être ... In order for a State party to be able to attribute its failure to meet at least its minimum core obligations to a lack of available resources it must demonstrate that every effort has been made to use all resources that are at its disposition in an effort to satisfy, as a matter of priority, those minimum obligations.[33]

The Committee on Economic, Social and Cultural Right has also importantly made the following comment:

> The other is the undertaking in article 2 (1) 'to take steps', which in itself, is not qualified or limited by other considerations. The full meaning of the phrase can also be gauged by noting some of the different language versions. In English the undertaking is 'to take steps', in French it is 'to act' ('s'engage à agir') and in Spanish it is 'to adopt measures' ('a adoptar medidas'). Thus while the full realization of the relevant rights may be achieved progressively, steps towards that goal must be taken within a reasonably short time after the Covenant's entry into force for the States concerned. Such steps should be deliberate, concrete and targeted as clearly as possible towards meeting the obligations recognized in the Covenant.[34]

The Committee on Economic, Social and Cultural Rights also refers to the difference between the implementation of economic, social and cultural rights

33 UN Committee on Economic, Social and Cultural Rights, 'General Comment No. 3 on the Nature of States Parties Obligations (Art. 2, para. 1)', 1990, para, 10. Available in 'Compilation of the General Comments and General Recommendations Adopted by Human Rights Treaty Bodies', UN Doc. HRI/GEN/1/Rev.7 (12 May 2004), p. 17 (emphasis added). See also the Limburg Principles on the Implementation of the International Covenant on Economic, Social and Cultural Rights, Maastricht, 2–6 June 1986, para. 28. Available in: UN Doc. E/CN.4/1987/17 (8 January 1987); and the Maastricht Guidelines on Violations of Economic, Social and Cultural Rights, Maastricht from 22–26 January 1997, para. 9. Available in: 'Substantive Issues Arising in the Implementation of the International Covenant on Economic, Social and Cultural Rights (Day of General Discussion)', UN Doc. E/C.12/2000/13 (2 October 2000). See also *Government of the Republic of South Africa and Others v. Grootboom and Others* 2001 (1) SA 46 (CC); 2000 (11) BCLR 1169 (CC) (Constitutional Court of South Africa).

34 Committee on Economic, Social and Cultural Rights, 'General Comment No. 3 on the Nature of States Parties Obligations (Art. 2, para. 1)', 1990, para, 2. Available in 'Compilation of the General Comments and General Recommendations Adopted by Human Rights Treaty Bodies', UN Doc. HRI/GEN/1/Rev.7 (12 May 2004), p. 15.

and the implementation of civil and political rights. The Committee made the following statement to what it identifies as the obligation of result:

> The principal obligation of result reflected in article 2 (1) is to take steps 'with a view to achieving progressively the full realization of the rights recognized' in the Covenant. The term 'progressive realization' is often used to describe the intent of this phrase. The concept of progressive realization constitutes a recognition of the fact that full realization of all economic, social and cultural rights will generally not be able to be achieved in a short period of time. In this sense the obligation differs significantly from that contained in article 2 of the International Covenant on Civil and Political Rights which embodies an immediate obligation to respect and ensure all of the relevant rights. Nevertheless, the fact that realization over time, or in other words progressively, is foreseen under the Covenant should not be misinterpreted as depriving the obligation of all meaningful content. It is on the one hand a necessary flexibility device, reflecting the realities of the real world and the difficulties involved for any country in ensuring full realization of economic, social and cultural rights. On the other hand, the phrase must be read in the light of the overall objective, indeed the *raison d'être*, of the Covenant which is to establish clear obligations for States parties in respect of the full realization of the rights in question. It thus imposes an obligation to move as expeditiously and effectively as possible towards that goal. Moreover, any deliberately retrogressive measures in that regard would require the most careful consideration and would need to be fully justified by reference to the totality of the rights provided for in the Covenant and in the context of the full use of the maximum available resources.[35]

From the way the Committee on Economic, Social and Cultural Rights has linked the standard of 'to the maximum available resources' to the progressive realisation of economic and social rights, it is possible to argue that in the context of article 6(2) the same applies, only to one aspect of article 6(2): in other words, the aspect of the economic, social and cultural rights of the child. Survival and development of the child is not only about the child's economic, social and cultural rights. It is actually about the right of the child to everything. Thus, the standard of 'to the maximum extent possible' that is mentioned in article 6(2) is not only about the progressive realisation or an obligation to take steps with regard to this kind of rights. The civil and political aspects of article 6(2), such as the right of the child to name and birth registration, which are important for the survival and development of the child, are of an immediate nature. The same applies to the right to development aspect of article 6(2).

Indeed, as a right relating to the survival and development of the child to the maximum extent possible, article 6(2) holds the power to be implemented both

---

35 Committee on Economic, Social and Cultural Rights, 'General Comment No. 3 on the Nature of States Parties Obligations (Art. 2, para. 1)', 1990, para. 9. Available in 'Compilation of the General Comments and General Recommendations Adopted by Human Rights Treaty Bodies', UN Doc. HRI/GEN/1/Rev.7 (12 May 2004), p. 17.

immediately and through progressive realisation. In fact, article 6(2) enhances the immediate implementation of the other rights of the child as well. As Van Bueren argues, the right to survival is a dynamic concept, the codification of which 'represents an acknowledgement that individual rights, such as the right to health, cannot be protected in isolation.'[36]

6. THE OBLIGATION TO 'ENSURE' TO THE MAXIMUM EXTENT POSSIBLE THE SURVIVAL AND DEVELOPMENT OF THE CHILD AND OTHER OBLIGATIONS OF THE STATE

6.1. THE OBLIGATION TO ENSURE

Under article 6(2) the State is, essentially, obliged to 'ensure' the creation of a situation and the adoption of measures that allow for the implementation and realisation of the right of the child to survival and development. Paragraph 6 of the Maastricht Guidelines, which were adopted on the occasion of the 10th anniversary of the Limburg Principles, mentions that: 'Like civil and political rights, economic, social and cultural rights impose three different types of obligations on States: the obligations to respect, protect and fulfil.'[37] These obligations are also known as the 'tripartite typology'. As Nowak argues, in the context of the indivisibility and interdependence of all human rights the State is obliged to respect, protect and fulfil all human rights.[38]

Article 6(2) sets the obligation of the State Party to 'ensure' the survival and development of the child. In this regard, the question that arises is: what is the relationship between the obligation of the State Party to 'ensure' and the obligation to respect, protect and fulfil? Nowak, for instance, suggests that the obligation to ensure is about the protection and the fulfilment of the right. He presents a diagram in which he explains that the right to positive State action, i.e., the obligation to fulfil and the right to be protected – or in other words the obligation to protect from the acts of third parties – are both parts of the obligation to 'ensure'. He adds that, with privatisation – outsourcing the health-care, educational system, refugee care, security and prison administration and leaving them for the free market to

36 G. Van Bueren, *The International Law on the Rights of the Child* (Martinus Nijhoff Publishers, The Hague, 1998), p. 293.

37 Maastricht Guidelines on Violations of Economic, Social and Cultural Rights, Maastricht from 22–26 January 1997, para. 6. Available on: United Nations Committee on Economic, Social and Cultural Rights, 'Substantive Issues Arising in the Implementation of the International Covenant on Economic, Social and Cultural Rights (Day of General Discussion)', UN Doc. E/C.12/2000/13 (2 October 2000).

38 See M. Nowak, *Introduction to the International Human Rights Regime* (Martinus Nijhoff Publishers, Leiden, 2003), p. 48.

take over – opportunities for direct State intervention and consequently the State's obligation to respect such rights has diminished. He then suggests that, in this context, relevant obligations to protect and fulfil increase.[39] Reflecting Nowak's arguments into article 6(2) as a general principle of the Convention it is probably not possible to argue that the obligation of the State Party to respect the right of the child to survival and development has diminished. The fact that the right of the child to survival and development is an aim of the Convention should result in a stronger level of State responsibility.[40] This suggests that with survival and development as an aim and a general principle, the obligation to respect, did not diminish. The same applies to article 6(2) as an aim and a quality-control factor.

Basically, the term 'ensure' conveys that the State has taken into consideration all the issues that would guarantee the survival and development of the child. The obligation to ensure is about blocking any remote possibility that will interfere with the right of the child to survival and development. As UNICEF commented during the drafting of the Convention, 'the obligation to "ensure" implies an affirmative obligation on the part of the State to take *whatever measures* are necessary to enable individuals to enjoy and exercise the relevant rights.'[41] The obligation to ensure is about 'guaranteeing' the survival and development of the child. The Inter-American Court of Human Rights, for example, also referred to the 'guarantee' aspect of the obligation to ensure under article 6(2) of the CRC in its famous judgment in the Street Children case. The Court indirectly explained the way article 6(2), among others, throws light on the behaviour that the State should have observed towards street children:

> These provisions allow us to define the scope of the 'measures of protection' referred to in Article 19 of the American Convention, from different angles. Among them, we should emphasize those that refer to non-discrimination, special assistance for children deprived of their family environment, the *guarantee* of survival and development of the child, the right to an adequate standard of living ... It is clear to the Court that the acts perpetrated against the victims in this case, in which State agents were involved, violate these provisions.[42]

The guarantee aspect widens the spectrum of the obligation to ensure. The obligation to respect requires States to refrain from interfering directly or indirectly with the enjoyment of the rights of the child. The obligation to protect requires States to take measures that prevent third parties from

39 *Ibid.*, p. 49.

40 See the above discussion on the value added of having article 6(2) as a general principle.

41 See UN Doc. E/CN.4/1989/WG.1/CRP.1, pp. 15–17, available in: Office of the United Nations High Commissioner for Human Rights, *Legislative History of the Convention on the Rights of the Child*, Volume 1 (United Nations, New York, 2007), p. 330 (emphasis added).

42 *Villagrán Morales et al. (The "Street Children" Case)* Inter-American Court of Human Rights Series C No. 63 [1999] IACHR 17 (19 November 1999), para. 196 (emphasis added), available at: <www.corteidh.or.cr/docs/casos/articulos/seriec_63_ing.pdf> accessed 14 April 2014.

interfering with article 6(2). Finally, the obligation to fulfil requires States to adopt appropriate legislative, administrative, budgetary, judicial, promotional and other measures towards the full realisation of the rights.[43] The obligation to fulfil contains aspects such as to facilitate, to provide and to promote. By focusing on the aim of the obligation to 'ensure', i.e., to guarantee, it is possible to argue that this obligation has a wider context as it includes obligations of the State Party to respect, to protect and to fulfil. Thus, the term 'ensure' in the context of article 6(2) embraces all the obligations of respect, protect and fulfil.

Arguably, all State Party obligations enjoy a degree of strength, but as Cantwell argues the obligation to ensure is among the stronger ones:

> In my view, it is more realistic and justifiable to look on the provisions of the CRC not as a list of children's rights per se, but as a compilation of State responsibilities towards children from which 'rights' of greater or lesser force automatically devolve. Thus, those articles – the majority – that affirm that the 'State Party undertakes' to act in a given way, to 'ensure' given measures, or to abstain from such and such an act, are far stronger in their implications than those under which the State simply agrees to 'recognise' a specified right of the child.[44]

6.2. THE OBLIGATION TO ENSURE IN THE CONTEXT OF THE OBLIGATIONS OF CONDUCT AND OBLIGATION OF RESULT

As discussed earlier, another categorisation of the State Party obligations under human rights treaties is the obligations of conduct and obligations of result. Paragraph 7 of the Maastricht Guidelines states that:

> The obligations to respect, protect and fulfil each contain elements of obligation of conduct and obligation of result. The obligation of conduct requires action reasonably calculated to realize the enjoyment of a particular right. In the case of the right to health, for example, the obligation of conduct could involve the adoption and implementation of a plan of action to reduce maternal mortality. The obligation of result requires States to achieve specific targets to satisfy a detailed substantive standard. With respect to the right to health, for example, the obligation of result requires the reduction of maternal mortality to levels agreed at the 1994 Cairo International Conference on Population and Development and the 1995 Beijing Fourth World Conference on Women.

---

43 Committee on Economic, Social and Cultural Rights, 'General Comment No. 14 on the Right to the Highest Attainable Standards of Health', UN Doc. E/C.12/2000/4 (11 August 2000), para. 33.

44 N. Cantwell, 'Veni, Vidi... et Vici? A review of the history and impact of the CRC', in A. Weyts (ed.), *Understanding Children's Rights* (Ghent University, Ghent, 2004), p. 296.

Arguably, due to the status of article 6(2) within the Convention on the Rights of the Child as an aim of the entire CRC and a right in itself, the obligations of conduct and the obligations of result are varied. For instance, in countries where there is an internal armed conflict, a typical obligation of conduct would be the decision to enter into peace negotiations.[45] In this case, the obligation of result would be the prevalence of a peaceful environment that allows for the implementation of the right of the child to development, family, name, education, etc. In its turn, the obligation of the State in relation to the child's name, for example, will then be implemented on the bases of the obligation of conduct and obligation of result.

6.3. THE OBLIGATION TO ENSURE IN THE CONTEXT OF THE 'OBLIGATION APPROACH' AND THE 'ENJOYMENT APPROACH'

Another categorisation that could help in the understanding of the nature of the obligation to 'ensure' the survival and development is related to the 'obligation approach' and the 'enjoyment approach':

> It is quite conceivable in a particular social system that, for example, not all people have enough to eat due to natural resources constraints, yet all duty-bound persons have met their obligations to provide the maximum possible amount of food fairly to all. In this case, by the enjoyment approach to assessment the right to food has not been realized, yet by the obligation approach all duties have been met.[46]

The logical question to ask in this case would be: is the obligation to ensure an 'obligation approach' or an 'enjoyment approach'? Skogly argues that '[e]ven if the codification of human rights into international law has provided individuals with a legitimate legal claim to their fulfilment, their immediate and full enjoyment may not always be possible.'[47] She argues that economic, social and cultural rights, according to article 4 of the CRC, are to some extent considered dependent upon economic resources.

> Thus, non-implementation of rights or restrictions on their enjoyment will not always imply that there have been breaches or violations on the part of the obligation holder. Therefore, an assessment of the compliance with human rights obligations cannot

45 See, for example, the effects of political unrest on the child's survival and development in: Committee on the Rights of the Child, 'Concluding Observations on the Consolidated Second and Third Periodic Report of Bahrain', UN Doc. CRC/C/BHR/CO/2–3 (3 August 2011), paras. 34–35.

46 Available in S. Skogly, *Beyond National Borders: States' Human Rights Obligations in International Cooperation* (Intersentia, Antwerp, 2006), p. 36.

47 *Ibid.*

> necessarily be carried out with a view to non-enjoyment only, but will have to take into consideration the context in which the human rights are being implemented as well.[48]

This kind of argument is related to the part of article 6(2) that deals with the economic, social and cultural rights aspect of the survival and development of the child. But the survival and development of the child is about all kinds of rights. Thus the obligation to ensure the survival and development of the child is both an 'obligation approach' and an 'enjoyment approach'. The right of the child to a name, which gives the child an identity that supports the child's enjoyment of his right to health services or education, is both an obligation right and an enjoyment right on the part of the State. As argued in Chapter 3, it is always good to remember that the survival and development of the child is more than an economic and social right of the child.[49] Under the CRC, the survival and development of the child is a comprehensive right, an aim of the entire Convention, a general principle of the entire Convention and a quality measurement of the entire Convention. Accordingly, it is expected that it enjoys the prestigious status of being approached by means of an 'obligation approach' or an 'enjoyment approach'.[50]

7. SPECIFIC FEATURES OF THE OBLIGATION TO 'ENSURE'

Another question that could shed some light on the nature of the obligation to ensure is whether it conveys that the State Party should immediately implement its obligations or whether the implementation could be of a progressive nature. This is also relevant to the broad spectrum of article 6(2) as a right that incorporates various kinds of rights. The progressive realisation of rights, as mentioned above, was noted by the Committee on Economic, Social and Cultural Rights in its General Comment No. 3, 'is ... a necessary flexibility device, reflecting the realities of the real world and the difficulties involved for any country in ensuring full realization of economic, social, and cultural rights.'[51] Again, this works well for

48 *Ibid.*, pp. 36–37.

49 See for example K. Arts, 'General Introduction: A Child Rights-Based Approach to International Criminal Accountability', in K. Arts and V. Popovski (eds.), *International Criminal Accountability and the Rights of Children* (Hague Academic Coalition, The Hague, 2006), pp. 10–11.

50 For the terms 'obligation approach' and 'enjoyment approach' see S. Skogly, *Beyond National Borders: States' Human Rights Obligations in International Cooperation* (Intersentia, Antwerp, 2006), p. 36. Skogly discusses the extra-territorial obligations of the State. Her discussion opens the door as to whether the jurisdiction under the CRC is limited to geographical jurisdiction or not.

51 Committee on Economic, Social and Cultural Rights, 'General Comment No. 3 on the Nature of States Parties Obligations (Art. 2, para. 1)', 1990, para. 9. Available in: 'Compilation of

the aspect of article 6(2) that is related to the economic, social and cultural rights of the child. The nature of the obligation to ensure as an obligation to guarantee, i.e., having the State Party close all loopholes, makes it relevant to speak about the minimum core obligation of the State, as mentioned above, in General Comment No. 3 of the Committee on Economic, Social and Cultural Rights.

The State Party is obliged to start immediately with the legislative and administrative measures for the implementation of article 6(2). Even the obligation of the State Party with regard to seeking and accepting international cooperation has an immediate aspect. In this regard, the level of responsibility of the least developed countries and the responsibility of the developed States is the same. For instance, in the case of the responsibility of the developing countries to seek international cooperation, it has to do it in order to prove that it has 'ensured' the survival and development of the child 'to the maximum extent possible'. The immediate nature of the obligation to ensure should be emphasised in cases of emergencies as well. This should minimise the number of children who suffer in cases of emergencies or other exceptional cases such as armed conflicts or natural disasters. For instance, the State Party is under an obligation to ensure the right to education in cases of man-made disasters and natural ones.[52] Moreover, in cases of wars in which there is *de facto* control by a group that is fighting the State, the State Party is still accountable for children's rights.[53] This accountability, for example, might be represented by the State not to bomb schools.

The immediate aspect of the obligation to 'ensure' is significantly manifested in relation to the rights of children who are vulnerable and at risk, such as street children. The following statement by the Inter-American Court of Human Rights clarifies the serious way in which the States violate the right of street children to survival and development. Decisions by this Court affect the conduct of a large number of States who are party to both the CRC and the American Convention on Human Rights; therefore, citing it could prove useful in this matter under consideration:

> In the light of Article 19 of the American Convention, the Court wishes to record the particular gravity of the fact that a State Party to this Convention can be charged with having applied or tolerated a systematic practice of violence against at-risk children in its territory. When States violate the rights of at-risk children, such as 'street children', in this way, it makes them victims of a double aggression. First, such States do not prevent them from living in misery, thus depriving them of the minimum conditions for a dignified life and preventing them from the 'full and harmonious development

the General Comments and General Recommendations Adopted by Human Rights Treaty Bodies', UN Doc. HRI/GEN/1/Rev.7 (12 May 2004), p. 17.

52 Committee on the Rights of the Child, 'Day of General Discussion on the Right of the Child to Education in Emergency Situations', 49th session (3 October 2008), para. 23 (Unedited Version).

53 Committee on the Rights of the Child, 'Concluding Observations on Sudan's Second Periodic Report', UN Doc. CRC/C/15/Add.190 (9 October 2002), para. 6.

> of their personality' ..., even though every child has the right to harbor a project of life that should be tended and encouraged by the public authorities so that it may develop this project for its personal benefit and that of the society to which it belongs. Second, they violate their physical, mental and moral integrity and even their lives.[54]

In the case of street children, the State is obliged to immediately start fulfilling its obligation with regard to the rights of these children, for example by the provision of shelter, and by working to find the children's families. In the same case, however, the State Party is under an obligation to fulfil its duties in progressively realising the right of street children to education.

However, the various and complex classification of article 6(2) influences the nature of the requirements for the obligation to ensure. For example, the requirements of the obligation to 'ensure' the survival and development of the child could be guided by its position as an aim, a general principle, and a gauge of the implementation of the CRC. The State Party is expected to abide by the requirements of each individual article of the Convention. In some cases, the State Party's responsibility could diminish and become restricted only to providing assistance. In such cases, the State Party's responsibility is all about assisting the parents in carrying out their responsibilities towards their children. According to article 27 of the CRC, for instance, the State should help the parents with their responsibilities if they fail to fulfil them. The State should also help the parents in fulfilling their parental duties as in article 5 of the CRC. Article 18 of the CRC places the obligation on the State Party to provide assistance, which includes quality child-care. The role of the State and the role of the parents are complementary and both roles make the other effective. Parents are responsible for offering care, direction and guidance, because this is the nature of parenthood. The State needs to respect the parental role and to:

> take all necessary steps to ensure that parents are able to take primary responsibility for their children; to support parents in fulfilling their responsibilities, including by reducing harmful deprivations, disruptions and distortions in children's care; and to take action where young children's well-being may be at risk. States parties' overall goals should include reducing the number of young children abandoned or orphaned, as well as minimizing the numbers requiring institutional or other forms of long-term care, except where this is judged to be in a young child's best interests...[55]

There is also a contextual aspect to the contents of the obligation to ensure. For example, in cases of street children, the State Party needs to ensure the provision of adequate nutrition, clothing, housing, health-care, educational opportunities,

---

54 *Villagrán Morales et al. ("Street Children" Case)*, Inter-American Court of Human Rights Series C No. 63 [1999] IACHR 17 (19 November 1999) para. 191, available in: <www.corteidh.or.cr/docs/casos/articulos/seriec_63_ing.pdf> accessed 14 April 2015..

55 Committee on the Rights of the Child, 'General Comment No. 7 on Implementing Child Rights in Early Childhood', UN Doc. CRC/C/GC/7/Rev.1 (20 September 2006), para. 18.

including vocational and life-skills, and training of children in order to support their full development.[56] In other cases, the obligation to 'ensure' could mean the provision of sufficient basic requirements, as in the South African case of Mazibuko, where the judge stated that, in order for the State to ensure access to water to economically and other disadvantaged groups, the obligation to ensure meant the provision of basic requirements: 'Specifically, in the context of the State's obligations to ensure access to water to economically and other disadvantaged groups, the right to water must relate to a sufficient amount of water to meet basic requirements.'[57]

One last point in relation to the features of the obligation to ensure is that it is comprehensive and expands to other areas that are of relevance to the implementation of the right under consideration. For example, Kent argues that the obligation to ensure good nutrition does not only come from nutrition programmes, and the obligation to ensure good health does only not come from health-care services.

> The advocates of comprehensive public health care recognize that health is influenced not only by health services but by a multitude of environmental, social and economic factors. These factors include income, education, housing, food production, sanitation, and motivations among others. The management of health needs to include not only the management of health services but also the management of agriculture, schooling, irrigation and markets for produce ... [H]ealth is not merely a disease problem but a development problem ... It is not enough to keep responsibility for health in the health ministry alone ... Health services may help, but they are not the source of good health. Immunization and oral rehydration programs may increase child survival rates, but they do not address the social situation and the government policy-making...[58]

In Velásquez Rodriguez v. Honduras, the Inter-American Court of Human Rights explained the comprehensiveness of the obligation to 'ensure':

> The second obligation of the States Parties is to 'ensure' the free and full exercise of the rights recognized by the Convention to every person subject to its jurisdiction. This obligation implies the duty of the States Parties to organize the governmental apparatus and, in general, all the structures through which public power is exercised, so that they are capable of juridically ensuring the free and full enjoyment of human rights. As a consequence of this obligation, the States must prevent, investigate and punish any violation of the rights recognized by the Convention and, moreover, if possible, attempt to restore the right violated and provide compensation as warranted for damages resulting from the violation.[59]

---

56 Committee on the Rights of the Child, 'Concluding Observations on Angola's Initial Report', UN Doc. CRC/C/15/Add.246 (3 November 2004), para. 69(c).

57 *S v. Mazibuko* (A1246/2006) [2008] ZAGPHC 106 (18 April 2008) (High Court of South Africa).

58 G. Kent, *The Politics of Children's Survival* (Praeger Publishers, New York, 1991) p. 55.

59 *Velásquez Rodriguez v. Honduras*, Inter-American Court of Human Rights Series C No. 4 Judgment of (29 July 1988), para. 166.

8. THE RESPONSIBILITY OF THE STATE TO CREATE SUITABLE VARIOUS MEASURES AND CONDITIONS FOR THE SURVIVAL AND DEVELOPMENT OF THE CHILD

As mentioned earlier, during the drafting of article 6(2), '[t]he representative of India stated that the text had been drafted in order to cover the following main concerns: ... (b) the focus on obligations for States parties to promote measures and conditions for the survival and development of the child.'[60] This part of the chapter focuses on the possible measures and conditions that the State Party needs to create. The argument will be made on the basis that the obligation to 'ensure' includes within it the obligations to respect, protect and fulfil. Thus, there are varied conditions that the State is obliged to identify, promote and create. It is not possible to list all the circumstances that the State should create, but, suffice to say, the State must establish conditions that do not negatively interfere with the enjoyment of the right of the child to survival and development. In this sense, survival and development is both a quality-measuring tool and an end in itself.

Accordingly, the formation of suitable conditions could include any kinds of situations, such as the ones mentioned in article 3 of the Declaration on Social Progress and Development.[61] Therefore, in order to make a framework, it would probably be wiser to say that the State Party needs to care for and consider any issue that could lead to the full implementation of article 6(2), e.g., fighting and eliminating poverty, hunger and famine, droughts, wars, discrimination, exploitation, inequalities, unfairness, colonialism, etc. After all, the scope of article 6(2) is extensive, because it is about the right of the child to everything, which means survival and development in every condition and situation of the child's life. The survival and development of the child cannot be divided into different parts, i.e., to survive and develop in a particular situation and not to

---

60 UN Doc. E/CN.4/1988/28, para. 23, available in Office of the United Nations High Commissioner for Human Rights, *Legislative History of the Convention on the Rights of the Child*, Volume I (United Nations, New York, 2007), p. 366.

61 United Nations General Assembly, 'Declaration on Social Progress and Development', UN Doc. A/RES/24/2542 (11 December 1969), article 3: 'The following are considered primary conditions of social progress and development:
(a) National independence based on the right of peoples to self-determination;
(b) The principle of non-interference in the internal affairs of States;
(c) Respect for the sovereignty and territorial integrity of States;
(d) Permanent sovereignty of each nation over its natural wealth and resources;
(e) The right and responsibility of each State and, as they are concerned, each nation and people to determine freely its own objectives of social development, to set its own priorities and to decide in conformity with the principles of the Charter of the United Nations the means and methods of their achievement without any external interference;
(f) Peaceful coexistence, peace, friendly relations and cooperation among States irrespective of differences in their social, economic or political systems.'

survive and develop in another one. In addition, the fulfilment of the right to survival and development is both a short- and a long-term matter. This makes the obligation to ensure to the maximum extent possible the survival and development of the child an ongoing one.

In addition, with almost all countries around the world being parties to the CRC, the circumstances that must be created are varied and complex. The Arab Human Development Report, for instance, speaks about a number of conditions that are, for empirical purposes, expected to suit the nature of the Arab world and lead to the enhancement of the well-being of the individual and the human development of the overall population of the Arab world:

> [F]ive distinct types of instrumental freedom have been identified as being of special importance for policy purposes on the grounds that they contribute directly to the general capability of a person to live more freely and that they complement one another. The five types are:
>
> - political freedoms, which relate to the opportunities that people have to determine who should govern and on what principles, and also include the possibility to scrutinize and criticize authorities and to have freedom of political expression and an uncensored press...[62]

Some might argue against political freedom for children on the ground that children may benefit from the existence of political freedoms for their survival and development, but generally speaking they do not participate in political decisions such as voting in public elections. However, in a few countries children do have a right to vote. Austria and Brazil are some examples of countries where children are allowed to vote at the age of 16. Children at the age of 16 have also participated in important national referenda such as the Scottish independence referendum which took place in September 2014.[63] However, in general, in a political freedom environment, where there are free and honest elections, parents are the ones who mostly vote for the candidates who promise policies that support the rights of their children to health services and an education that support the building up of the child's character. Nevertheless, Kent argues that children do not benefit from such political freedom, because some governments neglect children's interests, as children do not vote, but not those of the elderly, who do.[64] The Arab Human Development Report continues with the five distinct types of instrumental freedoms as follows:

> - economic facilities, which can be understood as the ways in which economies function to generate income opportunities and promote the distribution of wealth;

62 United Nations Development Programme (UNDP), *Arab Human Development Report 2002: Creating Opportunities for Future Generations* (UNDP, New York, 2002), p. 19.

63 Available at: <https://www.scotreferendum.com/questions/who-can-vote-in-the-referendum/> accessed 23 April 2015.

64 G. Kent, *The Politics of Children's Survival* (Praeger Publishers, New York, 1991), p. 116.

- social opportunities, which refer to the arrangements that society makes for education and health care, both of which influence the individual's substantive freedom to live better, as well as to transparency guarantees and protective security;
- transparency guarantees, which safeguard social interactions between individuals and which are undertaken on the basis of some presumption of what they are being offered and what they expect to get;
- protective security, which deals with the provision of the relevant social safety nets for vulnerable groups in society.[65]

There are some standard measures and conditions for the implementation of the right of the child to survival and development. Nevertheless, the individuality of every State in the creation of conditions needs to be considered in order to efficiently ensure the survival and development of the child. The Arab Human Development Report argues for the individuality of the State; indeed, the quality-measuring aspect of the obligation to ensure indicates the need for the identification and recognition of some local values that should prove supportive for the survival and development of the child. The identification of such factors makes the guarantee aspect of the obligation to ensure more efficient. For example, the Arab Human Development Report states that in some instances the problem is related to the existence of a commitment and not the existence of resources. This, in fact, is the case in many countries where there is no lack of resources but there is lack of commitment, which could be due to public corruption or any other reason. While it is beyond the scope of the discussion in this chapter, it is worth mentioning the series of revolutions that spread accros the Arab world (famously known as the Arab Spring). The revolutions manifested the change needed. In this context, the identification of the kind of commitment needed should be governed by the metric of survival and development:

> A solid, unequivocal political commitment – based on ethical, social, political and moral imperatives as well as the region's religious and cultural traditions – to well-articulated human development objectives, including poverty reduction, is the critical ingredient for securing a brighter future for all the people of the Arab region.[66]

The Vienna Declaration obliges States Parties to seek international cooperation in order to create the suitable conditions and measures for the enjoyment of human rights:

> Increased efforts should be made to assist countries which so request to create the conditions whereby each individual can enjoy universal human rights and fundamental freedoms. Governments, the United Nations system as well as other

65 United Nations Development Programme (UNDP), *Arab Human Development Report 2002: Creating Opportunities for Future Generations* (UNDP, New York, 2002), p. 19.

66 United Nations Development Programme (UNDP), *Arab Human Development Report 2002: Creating Opportunities for Future Generations* (UNDP, New York, 2002), p. 12.

> multilateral organizations are urged to increase considerably the resources allocated to programmes aiming at the establishment and strengthening of national legislation, national institutions and related infrastructures which uphold the rule of law and democracy, electoral assistance, human rights awareness through training, teaching and education, popular participation and civil society.[67]

An example of a situation or condition that the State Party needs to create is security. There are different kinds of securities that could be created, such as crime prevention, which obliges the State Party to fight poverty, because, in some cases, it is a reason for crime. The State also needs to adopt deterrence measures, because the law should have the power to deter and this will lead to the safety of the community. However, while it is beyond the discussion in this chapter, some may argue against the deterrent character of law as most evidence indicates that this is not the case. State party obligations extend to fighting international crime, such as international trafficking of children. In some countries, children, for example those in institutional care, go missing. The child should be safe for his or her physical, mental and psychological development. The State is obliged to assess risks to the child's safety, whether in the home or outside. Significant numbers of children are unsafe even inside their own homes for many reasons, for example because of a mother's boyfriend.[68] The obligations of States Parties also include the creation of conditions of peace. The State will remain the primary party responsible for the survival and development of the child in situations of war and lack of security; it is the responsibility of the State to establish and maintain situations of peace in order to ensure the survival and development of the child. The wording of paragraph 20(8) of the World Declaration on the Survival, Protection and Development of Children clearly refers to this. It reads:

> We will work carefully to protect children from the scourge of war and to take measures to prevent further armed conflicts, in order to give children everywhere a peaceful and secure future. We will promote the values of peace, understanding and dialogue in the education of children. The essential needs of children and families must be protected even in times of war and in violence-ridden areas. We ask that periods of tranquillity and special relief corridors be observed for the benefit of children, where war and violence are still taking place.[69]

This includes the obligation to create, promote, and maintain peace at both international and national levels. In some regions a number of rights are

---

67 Vienna Declaration and Programme of Action, UN Doc. A/CONF.157/24 (12 July 1993), para. 34.

68 B. Morrison-Rodriguez, 'Twenty-Six Steps to article 27: The Example of African American Children in South Carolina', in A.B. Andrews and N.H. Kaufman (eds.), *Implementing the U.N. Convention on the Rights of the Child: A Standard of Living Adequate for Development* (Praeger Publishers, Westport, 1999), p. 202.

69 United Nations World Summit for Children, 'World Declaration on the Survival, Protection and Development of Children' (30 September 1990) New York, para. 20(8).

negatively affected by years of domestic civil war. As a consequence of conflict, millions of people, including children, are internally displaced. Many children are separated from their parents; schools, health services and the infrastructure of many communities are destroyed or severely damaged; and children suffer serious physical, psychological and other trauma that could affect their development.[70] The responsibility of the State extends to the aftermath of the war; particular reference here should be made to landmines. Landmines are a threatening factor to the child's life, survival and development, as they cause many deaths and injuries.[71] Overall, it is possible to identify three categories of children who are affected by internal wars: children in the warzone, children who fled the warzone and the rest of the children under the jurisdiction of the State. The State is under various obligations to each category. The obligation to secure the development of the child should be extended within each individual State Party to the CRC all over the world. This was mentioned by the General Assembly in 1985 in its document 'Question of a Convention on the Rights of the Child'. In this document, the General Assembly stated on the fortieth anniversary of the United Nations: 'that children's rights require special protection and call for continuous improvement of the situation of children all over the world, as well as their development and education in conditions of peace and security'.[72] In this context, it is worth noting that the General Assembly referred to peace and security as they were at the heart of establishing the United Nations.[73] The General Assembly continually confirms the importance of international peace and security for the protection of human rights in general and children's rights in particular. In its 1986 publication 'State of the World's Children', UNICEF gave an example of the way peace and security represent a vital condition for the survival and development of children. This took place during the civil war in El Salvador, the government and rebels observed a three-day ceasefire which led to the immunisation of 400,000 children.[74] The UN also successfully negotiated a week-long ceasefire in Afghanistan to allow nearly 35,000 health workers and volunteers to reach 5.7 million children under five in a countrywide polio vaccination campaign.[75]

---

70 Committee on the Rights of the Child, 'Concluding Observations on Angola's Initial Report', UN Doc. CRC/C/15/Add.246 (3 November 2004), para. 4. Also see *Serrano Cruz Sisters v. El Salvador*, Inter-American Court of Human Rights Series C No. 120 [2005] IACHR 1 (1 March 2005), para. 48(7).

71 Committee on the Rights of the Child, 'Concluding Observations on Angola's Initial Report', UN Doc. CRC/C/15/Add.246 (3 November 2004), para. 62.

72 United Nations General Assembly, 'Question of a Convention on the Rights of the Child', UN Doc. A/RES/40/113 (13 December 1985), preambular para. 3.

73 See article 1(1) of the United Nations Charter.

74 UN Chronicle, Volume: 23 August 1986, pp. 97 ff. See also UNICEF, 'The State of the World's Children 1987' (Oxford University Press, Oxford, 1987), p. 52.

75 UNICEF, Press Release, *UN Successfully Negotiates Ceasefire in Afghanistan for Polio Immunization*, available at: <www.unicef.org/newsline/01pr33.htm> accessed 23 April 2015.

In addition, in some of its concluding observations on State Party reports, the Committee on the Rights of the Child noted that the climate of fear, insecurity and impunity resulting from armed conflicts and the states of emergency that were declared have had seriously negative physical and psychological effects on the sound development of children in the State Party concerned.[76]

Arguably, the conditions created are not limited to political or security-related ones alone. Environmental conditions, for instance, are as important as the other kinds of conditions. This is discussed in detail in Chapter 6.

The responsibility of the State in relation to the creation of conditions extends to cover issues of democracy and other forms of ruling that involve the will of the people, such as *Shura*, transparency, accountable governance, and administration in all sectors of society, because they are indispensable foundations for the realisation of social development, which, in addition to other aspects of development, is part of the right of the child to development.[77] In many countries around the world, the level of corruption is a major obstacle to the creation of conditions that support the right of the child to development.[78]

9. TYPES OF OBLIGATIONS IN RELATION TO PARTICULAR RIGHTS

It is important to re-emphasise that the right of the child to survival and development under article 6(2) is actually about the right of the child to everything. However, the ensuing discussion is about the nature of the State Party obligations under article 6(2) with specific reference to the right to education. Generally speaking, the obligation of the State should be about the integration of the right to survival and development into every aspect of governmental responsibilities and duties, in other words into the system of the State, which is a party to the CRC. Any identification of State Party obligations should bear in mind that children's survival and development must be considered as a guiding right, aim, criterion and principle to create and implement provisions pertaining to all aspects of children's lives, including children's rights. When a State Party

76 Committee on the Rights of the Child, 'Concluding Observations on Nepal's Second Periodic Report', UN Doc. CRC/C/15/Add.261 (21 September 2005), para. 10.

77 'Report adopted by the World Summit for Social Development in Copenhagen', UN Doc. A/CONF.166/9 (19 April 1995), Annex, para. 4. The Committee on the Rights of the Child stated in its General Comment No. 5 on the General Measures of Implementation for the Convention on the Rights of the Child (arts. 4, 42 and 44, para. 6): 'The Committee expects States to interpret "development" in its broadest sense as a holistic concept, embracing the child's physical, mental, spiritual, moral, psychological and social development.' UN Doc. CRC/GC/2003/5 (27 November 2003), para. 12.

78 See for instance, Committee on the Rights of the Child, 'Concluding Observations: Syrian Arab Republic', UN Doc. No. CRC/C/SYR/CO/3-4 (9 February 2012), paras. 20–21(e).

ratifies the Convention, this articulates children's rights and could serve as a benchmark for governmental implementation of child-focused programmes.[79]

The economic and social rights aspect of article 6(2) has a special relationship with some other articles of the CRC. As pointed out in previous chapter, this link was highlighted by the Committee on the Rights of the Child on a number of events.[80]

One right that has a special relationship with article 6(2) is the right to education. Education is important for the realisation of economic and social development.[81] The State Party is obliged to allocate enough funds for education, under the theme of the child's survival and development as a right, aim and quality-control measure. States Parties have to make education, especially primary education, affordable, i.e. free, for every child. They have to provide school equipment and teachers. Schools need to provide healthy, safe and child-friendly classes for children. In some countries lack of governmental planning and spending on education, due to corruption, has resulted in a school environment that could be described as hazardous, unhygienic and harmful to the child's health and development.[82]

It could be argued here that there is great inequality of education in both developed and developing countries, but in many developing countries there are very extreme examples of violations of the right to education. In some developing countries the educational system has collapsed, and there is a lack of well-equipped schools in terms of seating for the children and buildings, as children sometimes have to sit in schools with no roofs, in a very hot climate. Many children who go to schools in poor neighbourhoods, where there is no water supply at home, work on selling water. When they go to school, these extremely poor children sit on the containers that they use to sell water, or on boxes, which they use to work as shoe cleaners. In addition, in these countries, primary education is not free because of State policies.[83] States Parties should provide enough budgetary resources to build safe, healthy and child-friendly schools and to appoint qualified teachers. The State is also obliged to fight corruption. The State Party also needs to focus on the nature, content, and quality of the curriculum taught. The curriculum should effectively coincide with the right of the child to survival and development and raise the children's awareness on children's rights.

79 R.G. Thornton, 'Children in Poverty and Their Access to Health Care' (1999/2000) 3 *Quinnipiac Health L.J.* 111, 126.

80 UN Doc. CRC/C/58/Rev.1. (Basic Reference Document) (29 November 2005), paras. 30–31.

81 Committee on the Rights of the Child, 'Concluding Observations on China's Initial Report', UN Doc. CRC/C/15/Add.56 (7 June 1996), para. 6.

82 See Amal Friends of Children Society, 'The Status of Implementation of the Child Rights Convention in the Sudan', An alternative report prepared by national NGOs (June 2002), para. 7(3).

83 Author's personal observations and experiences.

10. SPECIFIC OBLIGATIONS UNDER ARTICLE 4 OF THE CRC

Article 4 of the CRC reads:

> States Parties shall undertake all appropriate legislative, administrative, and other measures for the implementation of the rights recognized in the present Convention. With regard to economic, social and cultural rights, States Parties shall undertake such measures to the maximum extent of their available resources and, where needed, within the framework of international cooperation.

Article 4 is a cornerstone in terms of understanding and identification of the obligations of the State as regards the survival and development of the child. It clearly states two kinds of obligations: specific obligations, i.e., legislative and administrative obligations; and non-specific obligations, which are referred to by the statement 'other measures'. This second kind of obligation opens the door for unlimited and renewable forms of obligation that the State Party will be obliged to fulfil. The standard for identification of the latter forms of State Party obligation under article 4 has a subjective factor. This will give one State Party the chance to adopt certain obligations that suit it, while another State Party might not choose the same approach. As for article 6(2), it does not mention the specific obligations, referring only to the level of obligation 'to ensure to the maximum extent possible', whereas article 4 states both.

10.1. OBLIGATIONS OF THE STATE PARTY IN RELATION TO LEGISLATION

This is probably the most obvious form of State Party obligations. The Convention is a binding international treaty, and under international human rights law the State Party needs to ensure that its legislation is compatible with article 6(2) of the CRC on the right of the child to survival and development. States are obliged to implement their treaty obligations in good faith,[84] including by means of incorporating the rights and duties concerned into their national legal order.[85] State legislation should guarantee the right of the child to survive and develop by changing any law that will negatively interfere with this right. This is a key aspect of the obligation to 'ensure', which implies that the State needs to prevent every foreseeable matter from interfering with the right. Some governments argue against the immediate obligation of the State to bring its laws

84 Vienna Convention on the Law of Treaties, U.N.T.S. 1155 (1969) 331, Article 26.

85 See also, for example, Article 2(2) of the International Covenant on Civil and Political Rights, 999 U.N.T.S. 171 (1969).

into conformity with the CRC. In Minister of State for Immigration and Ethnic Affairs v. Ah Hin Teoh, which was a case that involved the best interests of the child and referred to the CRC, Judge McHugh stated in paragraph 37:

> The people of Australia may note the commitments of Australia in international law, but, by ratifying the Convention, the Executive government does not give undertakings to its citizens or residents. The undertakings in the Convention are given to the other parties to the Convention. How, when or where those undertakings will be given force in Australia is a matter for the federal Parliament...[86]

In response to the judgment, the Australian government issued a statement: 'Therefore, we indicate on behalf of the Government that the act of entering into a treaty does not give rise to legitimate expectations in administrative law which could form the basis for challenging any administrative decision made from today.'[87]

The State Party is expected to use the Convention as a kind of guideline for its interpretation of domestic laws, i.e., interpretation in conformity with the treaty.[88] It needs to meticulously and carefully review its existing legislation. It has to be comprehensive. It also has to be continuous, rather than one-off.[89] The review should also not lead to a setback in terms of the level of protection of the right to survival and development that already exists. According to article 41 of the CRC reference to already existing provisions also includes domestic legislations and standards. It is also important in this context to highlight that some domestic legislation may provide higher standards for the survival and development of the child than the CRC. In this case, according to article 41 of the CRC States are obliged to implement the national legislation as it is more conducive for the child's right to survival and development: 'Nothing in the present Convention shall affect any provisions which are more conducive to the realization of the rights of the child and which may be contained in: (a) The law of a State party; or (b) International law in force for that State.

An important document in relation to legislative implementation is the State constitution, which is expected to guarantee the right of the child to survival

86 *Minister of State for Immigration and Ethnic Affairs v. Ah Hin Teoh* (1995) 183 CLR 273 (High Court of Australia). See also P. Alston and R. Goodman, *International Human Rights* (Oxford University Press, Oxford, 2013), p. 1067.

87 Available in H.J. Steiner and P. Alston, *International Human Rights in Context: Law, Politics, Morals*, 2nd edition (Oxford University Press, Oxford, 2000), pp. 1016–1021.

88 A. Vandaele and P. Wouter, 'International Human Rights Treaties and their Relation with National Law: Monism, Dualism and the Self-executing Character of Human Rights', in A. Weyts (ed.), *Understanding Children's Rights: Collected papers presented at the seventh International Interdisciplinary Course on Children's Rights* (Ghent University (Belgium), November–December 2004), p. 278.

89 Committee on the Rights of the Child, 'General Comment No. 5 on the General measures of implementation of the Convention on the Rights of the Child (arts. 4, 42 and 44, para. 6)', UN Doc. CRC/GC/2003/5 (27 November 2003), para. 18.

and development. In South Africa, for instance, the responsibility of the State is recognised in the constitution, which imposes a basic responsibility on the State for some socio-economic rights of children.[90] But sometimes the constitution is only inspirational and sometimes it is more than that. Incorporation of the Convention into the constitution is important in both cases, but it is given more emphasis in the latter case.[91] In order to have constitutionalism, the constitution should guarantee the right to survival and development through, for example, genuine elections and a multi-party system and independent judiciary.[92] This is in conformity with article 6(2) as an aim. One important question, however, is whether the CRC requires States Parties to include children's rights in their constitutions? The Convention does not make explicit reference to the constitutional inclusion of the rights: 'The Convention, like other human rights instruments, does not require States to have a constitution. But where there is a constitution, its provisions must be consistent with the Convention, or, in the terms of article 41, must be more conducive to the realization of the rights of the child.'[93]

Tobin has identified three broad categories of methods with regards to the inclusion, treatment and status of children within States' national constitutions:

> the 'invisible child' constitution in which children are neither seen nor heard and are accorded no special treatment or recognition ... the 'special protection' constitution in which children are given special recognition within the text because of their vulnerability and need for care and special protection, and ... the 'children's rights' constitution in which the special recognition of children is addressed in terms of children's rights rather than the welfare approach that characterises their treatment under 'special protection' constitutions.[94]

---

90 G.E. Devenish, *A Commentary on the South African Bill of Rights* (Butterworths, Durban, 1999), pp. 384–386. Worth noting is that the word 'basic', which qualifies the duty of the State and the right, is subject to the resources available to the State.

91 H.J. Steiner and P. Alston, *International Human Rights in Context: Law, Politics, Morals,* 2nd edition (Oxford University Press, Oxford, 2000), p. 989. See P. Alston and R. Goodman, *International Human Rights* (Oxford University Press, Oxford, 2013), p. 1051. See also J. Tobin, 'Increasingly Seen and Heard: The Constitutional Recognition of Children's Rights' (2005) 21 *SAJHR* 94 (footnotes omitted); and K. Mahgoub, 'Children's Rights and the Forthcoming Constitutional Bill of Rights of Sudan' (January 2014), pp. 63–74, available at: <www.redress.org/downloads/publications/140127FINAL%20Sudan%20UoK%20Report.pdf> accessed 18 April 2015.

92 H.J. Steiner and P. Alston, *International Human Rights in Context: Law, Politics, Morals,* 2nd edition (Oxford University Press, Oxford, 2000), p. 990.

93 R. Hodgkin and P. Newell, *Implementation Handbook for the Convention on the Rights of the Child* (UNICEF, Geneva, 2007), p. 21.

94 J. Tobin, 'Increasingly Seen and Heard: The Constitutional Recognition of Children's Rights' (2005) 21 *SAJHR* 94 (footnotes omitted).

The Constitutional Court of Sudan in Nagmeldin Gasm Alseed v. Government of Sudan and the relatives of Abd Alraheem Muhammad Ali, for instance, ruled that the CRC is part of the 2005 Interim National Constitution by virtue of its article 27(3).[95]

The legislation, whether permanent or temporary, should be a reasonable one. For example, the South African Constitutional Court referred to this in relation to the South African Bill of Rights: 'As the Bill of Rights indicates, their function in respect of socio-economic rights is directed towards ensuring that legislative and other measures taken by the State are reasonable.'[96] The State Party is obliged to pass new laws that are needed in order to ensure the implementation of the right of the child to survival and development and to cancel any existing laws that will interfere with the article and its spirit. The adoption of legislation includes the kinds of laws that might not focus directly on the right of the child to survival and development, but that will support and activate the actual implementation of the two rights, like the adoption of a Good Governance Act 2001.[97] In its concluding observations on the initial report of Angola, the Committee mentioned a number of things that the State needs to do with regard to legislation:

> The Committee urges the State party to accelerate the process of revising its legislation, including the ongoing process of drafting a new constitution, to bring it into conformity with the Convention. It further recommends that the State party take the necessary measures to ensure the timely publication of laws and rules and regulations and the efficient and effective implementation of laws.[98]

The State Party is also under obligation to ensure that its criminal laws are deterrent in order to guarantee the survival and development of the child. The European Court of Human Rights spoke about this point and referred to articles 19 and 37 of the CRC in the case of A. v. United Kingdom, which was the case of a 9-year-old who had been beaten with a garden cane by his stepfather. 'Children and other vulnerable individuals, in particular, are entitled to State protection, in the form of effective deterrence, against such

---

95 *Nagmeldin Gasm Alseed v. Government of Sudan and the relatives of Abd Alraheem Muhammad Ali*, Journal of the Constitutional Court, Volume 2, 2011, p. 399 (Republic of Sudan, Constitutional Court) (in Arabic). See also REDRESS, *Arrested Development: Sudan's Constitutional Court, Access to Justice and the Effective Protection of Human Rights* (REDRESS, London, August 2012), p. 21, available at: <www.refworld.org/docid/50641ad82.html> accessed 15 April 2015.

96 *Minister of Health and Others v. Treatment Action Campaign and Others (No 2)* (CCT8/02) [2002] ZACC 15; 2002 (5) SA 721; 2002 (10) BCLR 1033 (5 July 2002) [36] (Constitutional Court of South Africa).

97 Committee on the Rights of the Child, 'Concluding Observations on United Republic of Tanzania's Initial Report', UN Doc. CRC/C/15/Add.156 (9 July 2001), para. 3.

98 Committee on the Rights of the Child, 'Concluding Observations on Angola's Initial Report', UN Doc. CRC/C/15/Add.246 (3 November 2004), para. 6.

serious breaches of personal integrity'.[99] The Committee on the Rights of the Child also stated:

> The Committee suggests that firm measures be taken urgently to ensure the right to survival for all children in Colombia, including those from vulnerable groups. Such measures should include a quick response to reports of and complaints from children who are victims of violence, disappearance, assassination or alleged organ trafficking. Thorough and systematic investigation should be carried out and severe penalties applied in cases involving violence against children. The outcome of investigations and cases of convictions should be widely publicized in order to deter future offences.[100]

The State Party should make sure that the legislative remedy for the implementation of the right of the child to survival and development is effective. For instance, sometimes the implementation of the right to life is important for the implementation of article 6(2); therefore, the State has to ensure its realisation effectively. This also applies in cases of children with disabilities, where the State Party is under legal obligation to protect the inherent right to survival and development of the disabled child by focusing on the right of the child to life:

> The inherent right to life, survival and development is a right that warrants particular attention where children with disabilities are concerned. In many countries ... children with disabilities are subject to a variety of practices that completely or partially compromise this right. In addition to being more vulnerable to infanticide, some cultures view a child with any form of disability as a bad omen that may 'tarnish the family pedigree' and, accordingly, a certain designated individual from the community systematically kills children with disabilities. These crimes often go unpunished or perpetrators receive reduced sentences. States parties are urged to undertake all the necessary measures required to put an end to these practices, including setting up appropriate legislation and enforcing laws that ensure appropriate punishment to all those who directly or indirectly violate the right to life, survival and development of children with disabilities.[101]

In order for a legislation to be effective, the State needs to ensure that it is possible to seek remedies in cases where rights have been breached. The State Party needs to ensure that children are well informed and that they have access to advocacy.

> For rights to have meaning, effective remedies must be available to redress violations. This requirement is implicit in the Convention and consistently referred to in the

99 *A. v. United Kingdom* (100/1997/884/1096) (23 September 1998) [1999] 27 EHRR 611 (European Court of Human Rights).

100 Committee on the Rights of the Child, 'Concluding Observations on Colombia's Initial Report', UN Doc. CRC/C/15/Add.15 (7 February 1994), para. 10.

101 Committee on the Rights of the Child, 'General Comment No. 9 on the Rights of Children with Disabilities', UN Doc. CRC/C/GC/9 (27 February 2007), para. 31.

> other six major international human rights treaties. Children's special and dependent status creates real difficulties for them in pursuing remedies for breaches of their rights. So States need to give particular attention to ensuring that there are effective, child-sensitive procedures available to children and their representatives.[102]

The Inter-American Court of Human Rights referred to the effectiveness aspect in the Street Children v. Guatemala case:

> This Court has established that 'Article 25 is closely linked to the general obligation in Article 1.1 of the American Convention, in that it assigns duties of protection to the States Parties through their domestic legislation' ... from which it is clear that the State has the obligation to design and embody in legislation an effective recourse, and also to ensure the due application of the said recourse by its judicial authorities.[103]

Sometimes the problem might not be in the legislation, but in some discretionary measures taken by the party responsible.[104] Justiciability is also an important aspect.[105] In order to have effective implementation of the right of the child to survival and development, the right should be justiciable and a court should have the power to order remedies that will ensure implementation. In other words, courts should bear a duty to ensure the realisation of the rights by issuing far-reaching remedial orders:

> Where a breach of any right has taken place, including a socio-economic right, a court is under a duty to ensure that effective relief is granted. The nature of the right infringed and the nature of the infringement will provide guidance as to the appropriate relief in a particular case ... Where necessary this may include both the issuing of a mandamus and the exercise of supervisory jurisdiction.[106]

This kind of measurement comes under the obligation of the State Party to 'ensure' which requires the State to prove that it has done all that it could afford, i.e., to the maximum extent possible.[107] It could be argued, however,

---

102 Committee on the Rights of the Child, 'General Comment No. 5 on the General measures of implementation of the Convention on the Rights of the Child (arts. 4, 42 and 44, para. 6)', UN Doc. CRC/GC/2003/5 (27 November 2003), para. 24.

103 *Villagrán Morales et al. ("Street Children" Case)*, Inter-American Court of Human Rights Series C No. 63 [1999] IACHR 17 (19 November 1999), para. 237, available at: <www.corteidh.or.cr/docs/casos/articulos/seriec_63_ing.pdf> accessed 14 April 2015.

104 *Eldridge v. British Columbia (Attorney General)* (1997) 3 S.C.R. 624 (Supreme Court of Canada).

105 *Government of the Republic of South Africa and Others v. Grootboom and Others* (2001) (1) SA 46 (CC); (2000) (11) BCLR 1169 (CC) [19–20] (Constitutional Court of South Africa).

106 *Minister of Health and Others v. Treatment Action Campaign and Others (No 2)* (CCT8/02) [2002] ZACC 15; 2002 (5) SA 721; 2002 (10) BCLR 1033 (5 July 2002) [106] Constitutional Court of South Africa).

107 The State, including all its legislative, executive and judiciary organs, is responsible for the implementation of article 6(2). Accordingly, the State has to ensure that its entire system is

that justiciability of rights for children is a bit complicated, because some legal systems do not allow children to appear before the courts. The Third Optional Protocol to the Convention on the Rights of the Child on a Communications Procedure has the potential to ease this problem.[108]

One final word with regard to legislation is about the relationship between the incorporation of the CRC into domestic State legislation, epecially when the State legislation has a religious basis. In this respect, it is important in some cases to bring the dialogue between the Committee on the Rights of the Child and the State concerned to a common ground. In some instances, the framework for this common ground is that the CRC norms, particularly article 6(2), and religious-based legislation are intertwined. It is sometimes the interpretations given by both sides that need to be addressed.

10.2. ADMINISTRATIVE OBLIGATIONS OF THE STATE PARTY UNDER ARTICLE 4 OF THE CRC

10.2.1. Budgetary Allocations

Budgetary allocations have been identified by the Committee on the Rights of the Child as a form of administrative measure for the State to adopt. Financial resources are very important to the implementation of the economic, social and cultural rights aspect of article 6(2), but lack of them should never obstruct the implementation of these rights, according to article 4 of the CRC. Budgetary allocations should be implemented from the perspective of a child's rights-based approach to survival and development:

> With a view to strengthening its implementation of article 4 of the Convention and in the light of articles 2, 3 and 6, the Committee recommends that the State party prioritize budgetary allocations to ensure the implementation of the rights of children to the maximum extent of available resources and where needed, within the framework of international cooperation and using a rights-based approach.[109]

Budgetary allocations are somewhat relevant to all children's rights, but in some cases they become more prominent because the problem in question is directly

---

comprehensive and complementary in a way that does not prejudice some constitutional principle such as the separation of powers.

108 Third Optional Protocol to the Convention on the Rights of the Child on a Communications Procedure is expected to ease up this problem. Resolution adopted by the General Assembly on 19 December 2011. UN Doc. A/RES/66/138 (27 January 2012). On 14 April 2014, the Third Optional Protocol to the Convention on the Rights of the Child (OP3-CRC) entered into force.

109 Committee on the Rights of the Child, 'Concluding Observations on Antigua and Barbuda's Initial Report', UN Doc. CRC/C/15/Add.247 (3 November 2004), para. 19.

linked to poverty, which is sometimes the cause of the problem, or the problem causes it.[110] One example is children with disabilities: 'The question of children with disabilities living in poverty should be addressed by allocating adequate budgetary resources as well as by ensuring that children with disabilities have access to social protection and poverty reduction programmes.'[111] Allocation of budgetary resources needs to be done with a transparent, meticulous, conscious and well-planned attitude; this is because the allocation has a direct effect on the implementation of economic, social and cultural rights aspect of the right of the child to survival and development. The following gives an example of the way the budget should be allocated to children in general and disabled ones in particular:

> States parties shall undertake such measures to the maximum extent of their available resources ... Although the Convention does not make a specific recommendation regarding the most appropriate percentage of the State budget that should be dedicated to services and programmes for children, it does insist that children should be a priority. The implementation of this right has been a concern to the Committee since many States parties not only do not allocate sufficient resources but have also reduced the budget allocated to children over the years. This trend has many serious implications especially for children with disabilities who often rank quite low, or even not at all, on priority lists. ... Furthermore, funding must also be ensured for other programmes aimed at including children with disabilities into mainstream education, inter alia by renovating schools to render them physically accessible to children with disabilities.[112]

The State Party must ensure balanced distribution of resources at the central, local and regional levels. In doing so it will promote and provide for the implementation of the economic, social and cultural rights aspect of article 6(2).[113] Arguably, in many cases, the problem can be relieved by focusing on national prioritisation of budgetary resources, rather than on national poverty.[114] The allocation of budgetary resources should aim at providing financial and other kinds of assistance to the national actors on the rights of the child and to increase budgetary allocations with regard to some children's programmes, within the context of economic growth.[115] The allocation of budgetary resources according to article 4 should be made 'to the maximum

---

110 Similar to article 6(2) the Committee classified the rights of the disabled child as a basic health and welfare right.

111 Committee on the Rights of the Child, 'General Comment No. 9 on The Rights of Children with Disabilities', UN Doc. CRC/C/GC/9 (27 February 2007), para. 3.

112 Committee on the Rights of the Child, 'General Comment No. 9 on The Rights of Children with Disabilities', UN Doc. CRC/C/GC/9 (27 February 2007), para. 20.

113 Committee on the Rights of the Child, 'Concluding Observations on Spain's Initial Report', UN Doc. CRC/C/15/Add.28 (24 October 1994), para. 14.

114 G. Kent, *The Politics of Children's Survival* (Praeger Publishers, New York, 1991), p. 120.

115 Committee on the Rights of the Child, 'Concluding Observations on Grenada's Initial Report', UN Doc. CRC/C/15/Add.121 (28 February 2000), para. 10.

extent of the available resources' and in favour of children and their rights. The standard is subjective. Priorities differ from one State to another. It is true that some social welfare and general well-being rights, such as the right to health and the right to education, are always a priority, but it is also important to prioritise on the basis of the individual needs of the States Parties.[116] According to article 4, budgetary allocations should adopt a rights-based approach to the prioritisation of economic, social and cultural rights. This should strengthen and give more realisation to the spirit of the Convention and its general principles, including the principle of survival and development.[117]

In countries where the level of malnutrition is high, the priority in budgetary allocations would be to financially support some kinds of food in order not to affect the nutritional health of the child. No country in the world was able to reduce malnutrition without financial aid for food.[118]

As pointed out earlier, the State Party is obliged to seek international cooperation and donor States are obliged to provide it.[119] The Committee on Economic, Social and Cultural Rights confirms this on the basis of articles 55 and 56 of the Charter of the United Nations, which establish the principle of international cooperation as an obligation of all States Parties, and in particular of those States that are in a position to assist others in this regard. It is very important for States to have an active programme of international assistance and cooperation if they are in a position to do so.[120] This is a part of the obligation to 'ensure' and it is in conformity with the standard of 'to the maximum extent possible'. Skogly, for instance, observes that: 'to the maximum extent of its available resources' refers to resources within the State and to those from international cooperation.[121] She continues: 'This will imply that states attempting to fulfil their obligations under the Covenant are under a positive obligation to seek international assistance, if domestic resources are not sufficient.'[122] In the context of the obligation to 'ensure' as guaranteed by article 6(2), this means that the State is under positive obligation to seek assistance. States Parties need to cooperate on the implementation of the CRC as stated in paragraph 32 of

116 Committee on the Rights of the Child, 'Concluding Observations on the Bahamas's Initial Report', UN Doc. CRC/C/15/Add.253 (31 March 2005), para. 18.

117 See 'General Comment No. 5 on the general measures of implementation of the Convention on the Rights of the Child (arts. 4, 42 and 44, para. 6)', UN Doc. CRC/GC/2003/5 (27 November 2003), para. 51.

118 UNICEF, *The State of the World's Children* (Oxford University Press, Oxford, 1990), p. 33.

119 For further reading see S. Skogly, *Beyond National Borders: States' Human Rights Obligations in International Cooperation* (Intersentia, Antwerp, 2006).

120 Committee on Economic, Social and Cultural Rights, 'General Comment No. 3 on the Nature of States Parties Obligations (Art. 2, para. 1)', 1990, para. 14. Available in 'Compilation of the General Comments and General Recommendations Adopted by Human Rights Treaty Bodies', UN Doc. HRI/GEN/1/Rev.7 (12 May 2004), p. 18.

121 S. Skogly, *Beyond National Borders: States' Human Rights Obligations in International Cooperation* (Intersentia, Antwerp, 2006), p. 145.

122 *Ibid.*

the Limburg Principles on the interpretation of State obligations under the International Covenant on Economic, Social and Cultural Rights: 'States parties shall take steps by international means to assist and co-operate in the realization of the rights recognized by the Covenant.'[123] International cooperation is not only for financial issues as per article 45(b) of the CRC:

> The Committee shall transmit, as it may consider appropriate, to the specialized agencies, the United Nations Children's Fund and other competent bodies, any reports from States Parties that contain a request, or indicate a need, for technical advice or assistance, along with the Committee's observations and suggestions, if any, on these requests or indications.

Indeed an important category problem that interferes with budgetary allocations is the expenditure on arms. This is a problem in the case of developing countries in particular, which are not all poor. As Kent argues, 'Contrary to common assumptions, poor countries, like poor people, do have money. Poor countries are not uniformly poor; most have a middle class and a wealthy elite'.[124] He argues that the middle class and the poor in most 'poor countries' have no hunger or medical services problems.

> But most countries spend very little on children. Poverty is their explanation. But even very poor countries seem to find money for monuments and armaments. The limited allocation of national resources to serving the interests of children is due more to the ways in which available funds are allocated than to the absolute shortage of funds.[125]

The State Party is under an obligation to consider the economic effects of disarmament. The Committee has provided evidence of cases where the allocation of further resources for the benefit of children came as a consequence of the economic effects of disarmament. This made a positive contribution in favour of children and their rights.[126]

Corruption, particularly public corruption, interferes with budgetary allocations. In many States, corruption in public administration seriously jeopardises the implementation and realisation of the right to survival and development. There are different shapes and forms of corruption, such as the appointment of civil servants on the basis of ideological political affiliation rather than competence, nepotism, and financial corruption. This is the case in

---

123 Limburg Principles on the Implementation of the International Covenant on Economic, Social and Cultural Rights, Maastricht, 2–6 June 1986, para. 32; available in: UN Doc. E/CN.4/1987/17 (8 January 1987).

124 G. Kent, *The Politics of Children's Survival* (Praeger Publishers, New York, 1991), p. 119.

125 *Ibid.*

126 Committee on the Rights of the Child, 'Concluding Observations on Russian Federation's Initial Report', UN Doc. CRC/C/15/Add.4 (18 February 1993), para. 4.

a number of totalitarian regimes. The obligation on the State Party is to ensure to the maximum extent possible the survival and development of the child, which requires that the State adopts effective and well-activated measures, such as transparency and good planning and accountability, to eliminate the menace and bureaucracy. For example, in cases of allocation of budgetary resources: 'that the State party, in accordance with article 4 of the Convention, develops its general budget, including the budget's different missions, in a more systematic manner so that resources and investments for children are more transparent, enabling a better monitoring of spending.'[127] Corruption has widely spread in some countries and reached levels where even the money collected from *Zakat* (an Islamic system whereby alms are collected and distributed on a particularly set basis) has been abused by the State authorities responsible for the collection of *Zakat*. The system, if correctly implemented, will greatly help in the reduction of poverty within the relevant State.[128] In addition, it will limit the claims of some States that lack of financial resources is what is impairing the implementation of the right of the child to survival and development. It is important to note, however, that as a general principle of the CRC, the implementation of article 6(2) should not be dependent upon budgetary allocations.[129]

10.2.2. State Party Policies

Other administrative measures that have been identified include the adoption of appropriate and effective policies. The kind of policy that the State adopts represents a cornerstone for the realisation of article 6(2). If the State Party chooses the wrong policy, this might obstruct and hamper all the other efforts that the State Party has made to ensure the survival and development of the child. Policies are also important because in some countries the financial resources are there, but the policy is not good enough. Some argue, for instance, that in the United States of America there is no public health policy to grant pregnant mothers the required health-care, even though the resources are there; free health-care is given only to elderly people.[130]

---

127 Committee on the Rights of the Child, 'Concluding Observations on Venezuela's Second Periodic Report', UN Doc. CRC/C/VEN/CO/2 (5 October 2007) (Unedited Version), para. 19.

128 Author's personal observations and experiences.

129 Committee on the Rights of the Child, 'Concluding Observations on Bolivia's Initial Report', UN Doc. CRC/C/15/Add.1 (18 February 1993), para. 14, and Committee on the Rights of the Child, 'Concluding Observations on Indonesia's Initial Report', UN Doc. CRC/C/15/Add.7 (18 October 1993), para. 13.

130 See K.A. Johnson and M. McNulty, 'Assuring Adequate Health and Rehabilitative Care for the Child Articles 6, 23, 24 and 25', in C.P. Cohen and H.A. Davidson (eds.), *Children's Rights in America: U.N. Convention on the Rights of the Child Compared with United States Law* (American Bar Association and Defence for Children International, Washington D.C., 1990), pp. 222–223. However, the United States Congress agreed to a new Health Bill March 2010 (The Patient Protection and Affordable Care Act); this might have an effect on this situation.

The effects of some policies are sometimes catastrophic and represent a great violation of the right of the child to survival and development. For instance, Judge Cançado explained the repercussions of the wrong social policies in the advisory opinion of the Inter-American Court of Human Rights on the Juridical Condition and Human Rights of the Child. Despite the fact that he saw some hope with the adoption of the CRC and its general principles, he explained how the deterioration in social policies can affect the right of the child to survival and development:

> The advances, in the present context, at the juridical level ... cannot make us forget the current deterioration of basic social policies everywhere, aggravating the economic-social problems which so much affect children, and which transform the necessity to secure the right to create and develop their project of life an undeniable question of justice ... The recurring, and aggravated, problems, which nowadays affect the children (added to the tragedy of refugee, displaced and stateless children, and of the children involved in armed conflicts), warn that we remain far from their 'integral protection'. Nevertheless, one ought to persevere in the endeavours in favour of the prevalence of the general principle of the 'superior interest of the child' ... and evoked in the present Advisory Opinion ... from which emanates their dignity as human beings.[131]

Like all the other kinds of State Party obligations, the development and later the adoption of policies should be governed by the four general principles of the Convention.[132] This can be seen in the Committee's comments on the UK's initial report:

> With regard to the implementation of article 4 of the Convention, the Committee would like to suggest that the general principles of the Convention ... should guide the determination of policy-making at both the central and local levels of government. This approach is of relevance to decisions taken about the allocation of resources to the social sector at the central and local governmental levels...[133]

As for the content of the policy, Kent, for instance, in relation to the child's survival, argues for policies at the macro level. Factors such as maternal education and poverty are important in determining the level of child mortality. He argues that this should in turn raise new questions, such as:

It is also worth noting that the United States of America has signed the CRC but did not ratify it.

131 *Juridical Condition and Human Rights of the Child*, Advisory Opinion OC-17/2002, Inter-American Court of Human Rights (28 August 2002), para. 60.

132 Committee on the Rights of the Child, 'Concluding Observations on Sudan's Initial Report', UN Doc. CRC/C/15/Add.10 (18 October 1993), para. 21.

133 Committee on the Rights of the Child, 'Concluding Observations on United Kingdom of Great Britain and Northern Ireland's Initial Report', UN Doc. CRC/C/15/Add.34 (15 February 1995), para. 24.

why are so many people in poverty? Why are amenities such as clean water and health-care services in short supply in so many places? He continues his argument by saying that, after all, schools and health services are not natural resources which are available only in fixed and given quantities, but that their availability is largely the result of deliberate decisions that humans make. These are decisions at the macro or societal level, but not the micro or household level.

> It is tempting to respond to problems of malnutrition with new programs for nutrition intervention and food production. But the food situation is shaped far more by the character of the economy and by government policies than by specific nutrition programs and projects. Governments' macroeconomic policies affecting such things as the prices of exports and imports and the level of unemployment have a very strong influence in determining the extent of malnutrition and of child survival. Nutrition interventions – even those which work – may distract attention from more fundamental issues...[134]

The State needs to adopt successful economic policies to balance and stabilise the State budget, health policies, educational policies, and social policies, i.e., comprehensive policies. There should be a National Plan of Action for children which may take into account the Plan of Action which was adopted by 'A World Fit for Children' adopted by the General Assembly special session in May 2002 and or other comprehensive policies on children.[135]

The national comprehensive policies should be uniformly implemented.[136] The State Party is obliged to adopt comprehensive social policies. In this regard the decentralisation of social services is a good technique for the development of the child because it will create easy access to basic social services and education.[137] The decentralisation of social services can prove to be very useful in cases of States that are, for whatever reason, facing difficulties in reaching remote geographical areas within the State. It could also decrease the repercussions of corruption on the survival and development of the child.

In the context of the survival and development of the child as a quality-measuring factor, the State Party needs to adopt the right policy and be willing to change it if the survival and development of the child will be affected. Accordingly, the State has an obligation to constantly review, evaluate and assess

134 G. Kent, *The Politics of Children's Survival* (Praeger Publishers, New York, 1991), p. 55.

135 Committee on the Rights of the Child, 'Concluding Observations on Luxembourg's Second Periodic Report', UN Doc. CRC/C/15/Add.250 (31 March 2005), para. 11.

136 *Minister of Health and Others v Treatment Action Campaign and Others (No 2)* (CCT8/02) [2002] ZACC 15; 2002 (5) SA 721; 2002 (10) BCLR 1033 (5 July 2002) [90] (Constitutional Court of South Africa).

137 Committee on the Rights of the Child, 'Concluding Observations on Lebanon's Initial Report', UN Doc CRC/C/15/Add.54 (7 June 1996), para. 31.

its policies.[138] In the South African case of the Minister of Health, the State policy in relation to the administration of nevirapine (a drug) for the prevention of mother-to-child transmission of HIV/AIDS was questioned. The applicants questioned two issues with regard to the policy: 'The applicants' contentions raise two questions, namely, is the policy of confining the supply of nevirapine reasonable in the circumstances; and does government have a comprehensive policy for the prevention of mother-to-child transmission of HIV.'[139] With regard to the discussion in this chapter, the fact that State policy affected the rights of newborns should, in itself, be reason enough for the State to reconsider its policies.

> In evaluating government's policy, regard must be had to the fact that this case is concerned with newborn babies whose lives might be saved by the administration of nevirapine to mother and child at the time of birth. The safety and efficacy of nevirapine for this purpose have been established and the drug is being provided by government itself to mothers and babies at the pilot sites in every province.[140]

The obligation of ensuring the survival and development of the child to the maximum extent possible means that the State Party could act against an existing State policy in order to guarantee the survival and development of the child. In the South African case of the Minister of Health, the court stated that even if there was some good reason behind the State policy this should not prevent the State from administering the drug. 'However, this is not a reason for not allowing the administration of nevirapine elsewhere in the public health system when there is the capacity to administer it and its use is medically indicated.'[141]

The State policy should be a reasonable one as well. The standard of reasonableness may differ from one case to another. In the same South African case, for instance, the court spoke about evaluation programmes versus accessibility of the drug in order to decide whether the State policy was a reasonable one or not.

> The policy of confining nevirapine to research and training sites fails to address the needs of mothers and their newborn children who do not have access to these sites.
>
> It fails to distinguish between the evaluation of programmes for reducing mother-to-child transmission and the need to provide access to health care services

138 The responsibility of the State to review policies as in the 'Limburg principles': Limburg Principles on the Implementation of the International Covenant on Economic, Social and Cultural Rights, Maastricht, 2–6 June 1986, para. 11, available in: UN Doc. E/CN.4/1987/17 (8 January 1987).

139 *Minister of Health and Others v. Treatment Action Campaign and Others (No 2)* (CCT8/02) [2002] ZACC 15; 2002 (5) SA 721; 2002 (10) BCLR 1033 (5 July 2002) [47] (Constitutional Court of South Africa).

140 *Ibid.*, para. 72.

141 *Ibid.*, para. 64.

> required by those who do not have access to the sites ... In *Grootboom* this Court held that '[t]o be reasonable, measures cannot leave out of account the degree and extent of the denial of the right they endeavour to realise. Those whose needs are the most urgent and whose ability to enjoy all rights therefore is most in peril, must not be ignored by the measures aimed at achieving realisation of the right.' The fact that the research and training sites will provide crucial data on which a comprehensive programme for mother-to-child transmission can be developed and, if financially feasible, implemented is clearly of importance to government and to the country. So too is ongoing research into safety, efficacy and resistance. This does not mean, however, that until the best programme has been formulated and the necessary funds and infrastructure provided for the implementation of that programme, nevirapine must be withheld from mothers and children who do not have access to the research and training sites. Nor can it reasonably be withheld until medical research has been completed. A programme for the realisation of socio-economic rights must 'be balanced and flexible and make appropriate provision for attention to ... crises and to short, medium and long term needs. A programme that excludes a significant segment of society cannot be said to be reasonable.'[142]

Sometimes difficulties appear at the implementation stage of the policy rather than the planning one. It is not enough for the State Party to have reasonable programmes if the implementation is wrong. The obligation of ensuring to the maximum extent possible dictates that the formulation of programmes is only the first step.[143]

But does the judgment in the Minister of Health case make it possible to say that there should be remedies for changing policies that interfere with the survival and development of the child? Should a policy that is made to stamp out child pornography, for instance, be rigid or flexible? In order to complement the obligation of the State Party to ensure the survival and development of the child, the role of article 6(2) as a measuring tool is manifest.

> A factor that needs to be kept in mind is that policy is and should be flexible. It may be changed at any time and the executive is always free to change policies where it considers it appropriate to do so. The only constraint is that policies must be consistent with the Constitution and the law.[144]

In the context of a flexible policy, the standard of 'to the maximum extent possible' means that the State has left the door open for future policies that could prove to be better for the realisation of the right of the child to survival and development. The formulation of policies is also relevant to the issue of

142 *Minister of Health and Others v. Treatment Action Campaign and Others (No 2)* (CCT8/02) [2002] ZACC 15; 2002 (5) SA 721; 2002 (10) BCLR 1033 (5 July 2002) [67–68] (Constitutional Court of South Africa).

143 *Ibid.*, para. 100.

144 *Ibid.*, para. 114.

budgetary constraints. 'The Policy as reformulated must meet the constitutional requirement of providing reasonable measures within available resources for the progressive realisation of the rights of ... newborn children.'[145]

The State Party is also obliged to adopt specific policies, such as policies on juvenile justice or on children affected by HIV/AIDS.[146] In cases of people living with HIV/AIDS, the State needs to develop preventive policies including information, awareness, education, and full assistance programmes.[147]

10.3. OTHER OBLIGATIONS OF THE STATE PARTY UNDER ARTICLE 4 OF THE CRC

10.3.1. Obligation for Data Collection

Article 4 of the CRC on the general measures of implementation also speaks about the adoption of other measures, but does not specify the kinds of measures: 'States Parties shall undertake all appropriate legislative, administrative, and other measures for the implementation of the rights recognized in the present Convention.' According to the *travaux préparatoires*, 'other measures' is open-ended.[148] Moreover, one can easily spot a number of measures that the Committee has identified in order to ensure the implementation and realisation of the articles of the CRC. For instance, in order for the State to effectively implement and realise the right of children to survival and development, it needs to identify the children first. Thus, the State Party is under obligation to systematically collect data and make use of it. The State Party should:

> develop a system of data collection and indicators consistent with the Convention and disaggregated by gender, age, and in different parishes and dependencies. This system should cover all children up to the age of 18 years, with specific emphasis on those who are particularly vulnerable, including children living in poverty, children with disabilities and children from single-parent families. It further encourages the State party to use these indicators and data in the formulation of law, policies and programmes for the effective implementation of the Convention.[149]

---

145 *Ibid.*, para. 122.

146 *Juvenile Re-education Institute v. Paraguay*, Inter-American Court of Human Rights Series C No. 112, judgment of 2 September 2004, para. 73 (i).

147 *Cruz del Valle Bermúdez y otros v. MSAS s/amparo* (15 Mayo 1999) Expediente No. 15.789. Sentencia No. 196. (Tribunal Supremo de Venezuela), available at: <www.escr-net.org/docs/i/406005> accessed 15 April 2015.

148 See UN Doc. E/CN.4/1989/WG.1/CRP.1, pp. 17–20, available in: Office of the United Nations High Commissioner for Human Rights, *Legislative History of the Convention on the Rights of the Child*, Volume 1 (United Nations, New York, 2007), p. 353.

149 Committee on the Rights of the Child, 'Concluding Observations on Nepal's Second Periodic Report', UN Doc. CRC/C/15/Add.261 (21 September 2005), para. 30.

The obligation of ensuring to the maximum extent possible under article 6(2) requires that the State Party ensures the collection of data even in cases of emergencies, such as internal wars, earthquakes and other natural or man-made disasters. Data collection should be systematic and comprehensive, meaning it should include a collection of desegregated quantitative and qualitative data. The data collected should cover all groups of children, including vulnerable and non-vulnerable ones, i.e., data on disabled children, children living in poverty, children in the juvenile justice system, children of single-parent families, sexually abused children, institutionalised children, immigrant children, and disappeared children, etc.,[150] in addition to other vulnerable groups of children. The State Party should classify the data collected on the basis of the type of data collected and the group or kind of children, e.g., urban children and rural children. Data collection could prove very useful in locating children who are victims of crimes, such as disappeared children. The Inter-American Court of Human Rights, for example, ruled that the State Party should use the latest science and technology for this matter:

> Consequently, the Court considers that the State must adopt all necessary measures to create a system of genetic information that allows genetic data that can contribute to determining and clarifying the relationships and identification of the disappeared children and their next of kin to be obtained and conserved ... The State must comply with this reparation within a reasonable time.[151]

Data collection is very useful in many countries where the collapse of the system and corruption led to the State registry being rigged. This could seriously interfere with the right of the child to survival and development by facilitating child trafficking, illegal adoptions and crimes against humanity, such as forced evictions and changes of communities and societies through forced deportations. The data collected is very useful for monitoring and evaluating the progress achieved and for assessment of the impact of policies adopted with respect to children, such as the policies that aim at the prevention of child trafficking. Data collection could help in this regard, by means of a comprehensive study to examine the sexual exploitation of children and by the State Party gathering accurate data on its prevalence.[152] The State Party could use the data collected to design policies and programmes to prevent the commercial sexual exploitation of children, including through the development of a National Plan of Action

---

150 Committee on the Rights of the Child, 'Concluding Observations on Grenada's Initial Report', UN Doc. CRC/C/15/Add.121 (28 February 2000), para. 8. Also Committee on the Rights of the Child, 'Concluding Observations on the Bahamas's Initial Report', UN Doc. CRC/C/15/Add.253 (31 March 2005), paras. 20–21.

151 *Serrano Cruz Sisters v. El Salvador*, Inter-American Court of Human Rights Series C No. 120 [2005] IACHR 1 (1 March 2005), para. 193.

152 Committee on the Rights of the Child, 'Concluding Observations on Antigua and Barbuda's Initial Report', UN Doc. CRC/C/15/Add.247 (3 November 2004), para. 65(b).

on Commercial Sexual Exploitation of Children.[153] The collection of data is critical for the allocation of budgetary resources as well. The State Party needs to disaggregate the relevant budgetary data, so as to make it possible to obtain a clearer picture of the allocation of budgetary resources and to assess them.[154] States Parties should seek international and regional cooperation in the matter, as in the case of Grenada, which participated 'in a regional initiative funded by the Caribbean Development Bank for the collection, collation and publication of data, based on social development indicators, among the member countries of the Organization of Eastern Caribbean States.'[155] However, it is important to emphasise that the State has to utilise the data collected for the purposes of implementing the right of the child to survival and development, especially in cases of some non-democratic regimes, where the data collected is sometimes used for the interests of the regime and not of children, such as recruiting children for the non-democratic regime's own armed groups.

10.3.2. Obligation to Raise Awareness

Another measure that the Committee on the Rights of the Child has identified is the obligation of the State Party to raise awareness. This obligation is significant. It is also a typical aspect of the obligation to 'ensure' because it aims at guaranteeing to the maximum extent possible that both adults and children are aware of the child's survival and development and the factors that interfere with it. Many of the problems that children are facing can be solved if those involved, including public authorities, had a certain degree of awareness about the risks, causes, problems, solutions, etc. Raising awareness would probably be more useful in the long run. The State needs to promote the right of the child to development among parents, religious leaders, judges, state officials, teachers – in other words, almost all categories of society.[156] Children themselves should also be a targeted group.[157]

---

153 Committee on the Rights of the Child, 'Concluding Observations on the Bahamas's Initial Report', UN Doc. CRC/C/15/Add.253 (31 March 2005), para. 58.

154 Committee on the Rights of the Child, 'Concluding Observations on Barbados's Initial Report', UN Doc. CRC/C/15/Add.103 (24 August 1999), para. 11.

155 Committee on the Rights of the Child, 'Concluding Observations on Grenada's Initial Report', UN Doc. CRC/C/15/Add.121 (28 February 2000), para. 8.

156 For instance, with regard to raising awareness that families stop giving preferential treatment to boys when sending their children to school, see General Comment No. 16 on Substantive Issues Arising in the Implementation of the International Covenant on Economic, Social and Cultural Rights: The equal right of men and women to the enjoyment of all economic, social and cultural rights (art. 3 of the International Covenant on Economic, Social and Cultural Rights), UN Doc. E/C.12/2005/4 (11 August 2005), para. 30.

157 Committee on the Rights of the Child, 'Concluding Observations on the Combined Third and Fourth Periodic Reports of China', UN Doc. CRC/C/CHN/CO/3-4 (29 October 2013), paras. 45(c) and 46(c).

As the survival and development of the child is both an aim and a standard, the obligation includes simple matters such as raising awareness about safety issues for parents as regards accidents at home, wearing helmets when riding bikes and scooters, and wearing safety belts in the car, especially as driving in some cities is potentially dangerous.[158] Up to now, for instance, in some countries, safety belts in cars has not been a legal requirement. In some developing countries, the expensive and scarce public transport system can lead groups of people to cram themselves inside a fee-free vehicle, with great carelessness for the safety of the passengers. These kinds of rides are socially and legally acceptable to the extent that the police will never stop the driver for illegally and carelessly loading passengers inside his or her vehicle.[159] In some other developing countries children are, carelessly and dangerously, being seated on the driver's lap while driving.[160] The State Party should fulfil its obligation to raise awareness about the dangers and hazards of such rides. The State is under an obligation to identify methods to reach out to people. In addition, the State Party should make public transport available to all sectors of the society through the allocation of budgetary resources and good planning.

States also fail to fulfil their obligation to raise awareness when, for whatever personal or political interests, government officials are permitted to lobby against international human rights standards especially in the media or public speeches.

10.3.3. Obligation to Identify the Factors that Impede the Implementation of the Convention

Something else that falls under the obligation of the State Party to adopt the appropriate measures is the obligation of the State to identify the factors that impede the implementation of article 6(2). These factors could include debt burden, widespread poverty, racial tensions, political instability, corruption, and difficulty in reaching children. In the latter case, the State is obliged to find the children and ensure to the maximum extent possible that it reaches out for them.[161] The State should also ensure that children have access to the relevant public department or facility. The State Party should also identify the serious economic, social and political challenges that constitute threats.[162]

158 See for example Committee on the Rights of the Child, 'Concluding Observations on the Combined Second and Third Periodic Reports of Cambodia', UN Doc. CRC/C/KHM/CO/2-3 (3 August 2011), paras. 32–33.

159 Author's personal experiences and observations.

160 Author's personal experiences and observations. Also see M. Nowak, 'Article 6. The Right to Life, Survival and Development', in: A. Alen, J. Vande Lanotte, E. Verhellen, F. Ang, E. Berghmans and M. Verheyde (eds.), *A Commentary on the United Nations Convention on the Rights of the Child* (Martinus Nijhoff Publishers, Leiden, 2005), pp. 6–9.

161 Committee on the Rights of the Child, 'Concluding Observations on Guyana's Initial Report', UN Doc. CRC/C/15/Add.224 (26 February 2004), para. 7.

162 Committee on the Rights of the Child, 'Concluding Observations on Kyrgyzstan's Second Periodic Report', UN Doc. CRC/C/15/Add.244 (3 November 2004), para. 6.

Lack of coordination also impedes the implementation of the Convention. In some countries, the almost total collapse of the system creates a state of anarchy, which seriously interferes with the right of the child to survival and development. Initially, the State needs to have a child's rights-oriented system that should survive and effectively work under any circumstances. For instance, in order for the States Parties to effectively implement the right of the child to survival and development, there should be coordination between all State departments. The coordination should happen between central authorities, and regional and local authorities. Coordination is also necessary for the purpose of monitoring in order to avoid any disparities that are likely to develop during and after the implementation of programmes that relate to children.[163] In many cases, obstacles to the implementation of the right of the child to survival and development are not always related to the lack of available resources alone; it is actually a matter of how to spend. The State would have to put careful, meticulous and well-designed plans in place. For instance, in cases of budgetary allocations, and as a practical technique, the State should prioritise and adopt a rights-based perspective, for the resources allocated within the framework of international cooperation. This should strengthen the State Party implementation of article 6(2) of the Convention and bring it more towards effectiveness.[164]

In the context of the obligation to ensure being an obligation to respect, protect and fulfil, the identification of factors that impede the implementation includes the identification of environmental conditions that impede the survival and development of the child. This is argued for in Chapter 6: environmental conditions, in particular climate change extremes, could have serious effects on the survival and development of the child.

10.3.4. Obligation to Conduct Research and Studies

Another measure that has been identified is the responsibility of the State to conduct research and studies. This kind of obligation is of particular help to the State Party and those involved with the realisation of the right of the child to survival and development. For instance, in cases of youth suicide, the State is obliged to make studies in order to understand the possible causes of this serious problem.

In his argument for broader level research Kent, for example, mentions that, in relation to socioeconomic issues such as race or low-income occupations, the State needs to conduct research at a broader level. He considers that individual and household studies absolve the society as a whole from its responsibility for

163 Committee on the Rights of the Child, 'Concluding Observations on Spain's Initial Report', UN Doc. CRC/C/15/Add.28 (24 October 1994), para. 7.

164 Committee on the Rights of the Child, 'Concluding Observations on Nepal's Second Periodic Report', UN Doc. CRC/C/15/Add.261 (21 September 2005), para. 28.

child mortality.[165] He highlights that this kind of connection blames the victim and not the social order in which they live:

> The causes of malnutrition are found primarily among the malnourished, and not in the social order in which they live. Since it is the characteristic of the malnourished and their families which function as the determinants of malnutrition, changes are required only for those suffering nutritional deficiencies and not for the rest of society. There has been no serious examination of the alternative hypothesis that the persistency of widespread malnutrition is largely a reflection of social and political organization, institutional and economic arrangements, and choices of development strategies. Malnutrition is reduced to the status of a technical problem.[166]

10.3.5. Obligation of the State to Monitor the Implementation of the Convention

Part of the obligation to ensure is the protection of the child from non-State actors, i.e., the protection aspect of the 'comprehensive' obligation to ensure. In this context, the State Party is also obliged to monitor the implementation of the Convention.[167] This obligation applies, for example, in cases where public services have been partially or fully privatised.

11. CONCLUSION

This chapter has discussed in detail the varied and complex nature, content, quality and standard of State Party obligations under article 6(2) of the CRC. The comprehensive nature of article 6(2) as being the right of the child to 'everything' and the multi-identities of article 6(2), within the CRC, have enriched the discussion. The comprehensiveness of the CRC itself had also made the discussion somehow complicated. The aim was to cover the elaborate and complex nature of the topic in detail. Obligations of the State Parties under article 6(2) vary. In this respect they include, for example, issues such as raising awareness for healthy eating or the importance of wearing seat belts while driving, to issues such as fighting corruption, having good governance, rule of law and democratic process, and the obligation, in cases of armed conflict, to opt for peace and reject conflict.

---

165 Available in: G. Kent, *The Politics of Children's Survival* (Praeger Publishers, New York, 1991), p. 53.

166 *Ibid.*

167 General Comment No. 16 on Substantive Issues Arising in the Implementation of the International Covenant on Economic, Social and Cultural Rights: The equal right of men and women to the enjoyment of all economic, social and cultural rights (art. 3 of the International Covenant on Economic, Social and Cultural Rights), UN Doc. E/C.12/2005/4 (11 August 2005), para. 20.

Under traditional international human rights law, the State remains the main party that is obliged to promote, implement and realise the right of the child to survival and development. In the context of article 6(2), State responsibility is more emphasised as the article was initially put in the Convention in order to focus on State Party obligations.

The standard of 'to the maximum extent possible' represents a measuring tool for assessing whether the State Party has fulfilled its obligations under article 6(2). It has some substantive aspects, which allows for each case to be viewed separately. This allows for the individuality and uniqueness of each individual State Party to be considered. The obligation to 'ensure' represents the level to which the State Party is obliged to implement article 6(2). The obligation to 'ensure' is a strong one. It embodies the famous three types of State obligations, i.e., the obligations to respect, protect and fulfil. The obligation to 'ensure' includes both immediate and progressive realisation of the right of the child to survival and development. It is also of a comprehensive nature.

The list of State Party obligations in this chapter is not an exhaustive one. Article 4 of the CRC sheds some light on the nature and types of specific and non-specific State Party obligations. There are always constant additions to the list of obligations. The identification and later the implementation of State Party obligations should always be governed by the general principles of the Convention on the Rights of the Child, including article 6(2). It should also be governed by the survival and development of the child as an aim of the CRC and as a quality-control measure.

Finally, it is important to re-emphasise the obligation of the State Party to raise awareness and disseminate the CRC. This is particularly important in cases of totalitarian and dictatorial regimes, which strive to mislead people about international human rights standards. In this context, governments sometimes mobilize significant public resources to vilify and defame international human rights instruments in school curricula, public and weekly religious speeches, and the media. This puts the State in violation of its obligations under article 6(2) and the entire CRC.

CHAPTER 6
CASE STUDIES ON ARTICLE 6(2)

1. INTRODUCTION

This chapter includes two detailed case studies that aim at highlighting the broad spectrum of article 6(2) on the right of the child to survival and development. This furthers the conclusion that the right of the child to survival and development is basically about the right of the child to 'everything'. The case studies also emphasise the complex and evolving nature of State Party obligations under article 6(2). The two topics are discussed in detail. The discussion starts with the first case study, which adresses the interaction of climate change and the right of the child to survival and development. The second case study focuses on the connection between breastfeeding and the right of the child to survival and development.

However, legitimate questions might arise with regard to the bases for choosing the two topics. Why choose climate change and breastfeeding? Are there any very far-reaching considerations? The interaction between human rights and the current issue of climate change is an important and pressing topic. In fact, climate change negatively interacts with the right of the child to survival and development. In this respect, it is important for a 'comprehensive' study on the right of the child to survival and development to cover this current and significant topic. As for the case study on the right of the child to survival and development and breastfeeding, it is important to emphasise that the relationship between the two was emphasised, as discussed in Chapter 1, during the drafting of article 6(2). It is also important to point out that the discussion is not about a subjective right of the baby against his or her mother. In fact it is more about the responsibility and obligations of the State in such a horizontal relationship.

2. FIRST CASE STUDY: CLIMATE CHANGE AND THE RIGHT OF THE CHILD TO SURVIVAL AND DEVELOPMENT

2.1. INDIVIDUALITY AND INDEPENDENCE OF THE RIGHT OF THE CHILD TO SURVIVAL AND DEVELOPMENT

It is important to re-emphasise that the right of the child to survival and development is a right on its own which is separate from other children's rights. It has its own broad formulation and components. It suffices in this regard, however, to state that it includes various kinds of rights, such as economic, social and cultural rights, civil and political rights, and right to development, including its integral aspect, i.e. the right to human development.[1]

In this context a number of pertinent questions, however, arise as to whether it is a collective right to development or individual right? Is it possible, for instance, to argue through article 6(2), that after all '[l]east developed countries (LDCs) … are particularly vulnerable to climate change because of the overwhelming dependence of their economies on natural resources, and their low adaptive capacity?'[2] Who is responsible for the realisation of the right of the child to survive and develop? Is it only the responsibility of the State to which he or she belongs to its jurisdiction? Do other states have an obligation to protect or to provide for the right of the child to survive and develop? In this respect, the case study focuses on the relationship between climate change and the right of the child to survival and development from the perspective that the right of the child to development is an individual right. The case study does not expand into other aspects of the right to development.

2.2. RELEVANT SCIENTIFIC FACTS

There is sufficient scientific evidence to support the claims that our climate is changing. Undoubtedly, changes in the climate have extreme negative impacts which could interfere with the child's right to survival and development, as they interfere with every aspect of children's lives. Significantly, the danger is both a present and a future one.

---

1 For further reading see: M. Nowak, 'Article 6. Right to Life, Survival and Development'; in: A. Alen, J. Vande Lanotte, E. Verhellen, F. Ang, E. Berghmans and A. Verheyde (eds.), *A Commentary on the United Nations Convention on the Rights of the Child* (Martinus Nijhoff Publishers, Leiden, 2005), pp. 6–7.

2 S.A. Zakieldeen, 'Adaptation to Climate Change: A Vulnerability Assessment for Sudan', *Gatekeeper* Series, 142 (2009), p. 11.

Present impacts of the climate change are witnessed in various parts of the world where there is medium confidence that melting snow and changing precipitation cause alteration in hydrological systems and affect the quantity and quality of water resources.[3] Moreover, despite the fact that the worldwide burden of human ill health from climate change is relatively small when compared with the effects of other stressors, 'there has been increased heat-related mortality … in some regions as a result of warming … Local changes in temperature and rainfall have altered the distribution of some water-borne illnesses and disease vectors'.[4] Impacts of extreme heat vary according to people's age, socioeconomic factors and location.[5] This puts children in particular at risk.

Malaria, an environment-related killer, for example, causes an estimated 1 million deaths each year, and around 80 per cent of these are among children under five.[6] As the World Health Organization (WHO) has stated, malaria is one of the major environment-related killers in 'children under five', in Africa.[7]

Although malaria existed long before the issue of 'climate change', it is evidently triggered by a form of change in the climate: 'With increasing temperatures, malaria is returning to places where it was once eradicated. For example, after 50 years of little incidence, malaria is being reported in the highlands of Kenya. This is after subtle increases in temperature.'[8]

Violent conflicts inflicted by climate change also interfere with the right of the child to survival and development. Climate change can indirectly put children at the increased risk of violent conflict. This interferes with their right to peace as part of their right to development.[9]

---

3 Intergovernmental Panel on Climate Change (IPCC), Fifth Assessment Synthesis Report, 'Climate Change 2014 Synthesis Report', pp. 49–51, available at: <http://ipcc.ch/pdf/assessment-report/ar5/syr/AR5_SYR_FINAL_All_Topics.pdf> accessed 16 April 2015.

4 *Ibid.*, p. 51.

5 *Ibid.*, p. 53.

6 UNICEF Innocenti Research Centre, *Climate Change and Children: A Human Security Challenge*, 2008, available at: <www.unicef-irc.org/publications/pdf/climate_change.pdf> (Florence, UNICEF Innocenti Research Centre, November 2008), p. 9 (accessed 16 April 2015). See also K. Arts, 'A Child Rights Perspective on Climate Change', in M.A. Mohamed Salih (ed.), *Climate Change and Sustainable Development: New Challenges for Poverty Reduction* (Edward Elgar, Cheltenham, 2009), pp. 79–93.

7 World Health Organization (WHO), *The Environment and Health for Children and Their Mothers*, Fact sheet no. 284, available at: <www.who.int/ceh/publications/factsheets/fs284/en/> accessed 16 April 2015.

8 UNICEF Innocenti Research Centre, *Climate Change and Children: A Human Security Challenge*, 2008, available at: <www.unicef-irc.org/publications/pdf/climate_change.pdf> (Florence, UNICEF Innocenti Research Centre, November 2008), p. 12 (accessed 16 April 2015).

9 Intergovernmental Panel on Climate Change (IPCC), Fifth Assessment Synthesis Report, 'Climate Change 2014 Synthesis Report', p. 73, available at: <http://ipcc.ch/pdf/assessment-report/ar5/syr/AR5_SYR_FINAL_All_Topics.pdf> accessed 16 April 2015.

Future risks are also projected. For instance children's right to water, food, health, security and livelihoods, which are all major components of the child's right to survival and development, are increasingly at risk. There is *high agreement* that some fractions of the global population that experience some impacts of global warming will continue to increase in the 21st century.[10] Interferences with the right to water will continue to occur as the frequency of droughts will likely increase by the end of the 21st century.[11] In some parts of the world there is *high agreement* that the quality of raw water will reduce, which poses risks to drinking water quality.[12]

There is also *high confidence* that future climate change will interfere with the child's right to food, which is part of the right to development. This includes all aspects of food security as they are potentially affected by climate change.[13] Also at stake is the child's right to health as there is *very high confidence* that future climate changes will interfere with the right to health which is part of the right of the child to development.[14]

Future impacts on health also project greater likelihood of 'increased risks from foodborne and waterborne diseases ... Risks of undernutrition in poor regions will increase'.[15] UNICEF has also stated that: 'Vector-borne diseases, including malaria, dengue fever, yellow fever and schistosomiasis, are likely to increase as their vectors are affected by the changing climate.'[16] The rate of reduction of poverty, which is essential for the realisation of the right of the child to survival and development, is also expected to slow down.[17] Moreover, climate change puts children more at risk of displacement, which can expose them to many risks such as statelessness, resulting in further negative impacts on their right to survival and development.[18] Projected deficiencies in essential infrastructure and services can also amplify risks.[19]

All of the aforementioned projected future risks put the rights of future generations at risk too. In the OPOSA case, the plaintiff children claimed that they represent their generation as well as the generations yet to come. 'The

10 Intergovernmental Panel on Climate Change (IPCC), Fifth Assessment Synthesis Report, 'Climate Change 2014 Synthesis Report', p. 67, available at: <http://ipcc.ch/pdf/assessment-report/ar5/syr/AR5_SYR_FINAL_All_Topics.pdf> accessed 16 April 2015.

11 *Ibid.*, p. 69.

12 *Ibid.*

13 *Ibid.*

14 *Ibid.*

15 *Ibid.*

16 UNICEF Innocenti Research Centre, *Climate Change and Children: A Human Security Challenge*, 2008, available at: <www.unicef-irc.org/publications/pdf/climate_change.pdf> (Florence, UNICEF Innocenti Research Centre, November 2008), p. 12 (accessed 23 April 2015).

17 Intergovernmental Panel on Climate Change (IPCC), Fifth Assessment Synthesis Report, 'Climate Change 2014 Synthesis Report', p. 73, available at: <http://ipcc.ch/pdf/assessment-report/ar5/syr/AR5_SYR_FINAL_All_Topics.pdf> accessed 16 April 2015.

18 *Ibid.*

19 *Ibid.*

Supreme Court of the Philippines held that the principle of intergenerational responsibility was legally recognizable, and that the assertion of the children in *OPOSA* was a legitimate expression of their interest in protecting the rights of future generations. The Court granted that the plaintiffs had the legal capacity to sue on behalf of succeeding generations 'based on the concept of intergenerational responsibility insofar as the right to a balanced and healthful ecology is concerned'.[20] Rights of future generations are discussed later in this chapter.

2.3. CAUSES OF CLIMATE CHANGE

The main focus is on the human influence and responsibility with regard to the change in the climate. It is now an established scientific fact that human activities affect the climate:

> The evidence for human influence on the climate system has grown ... Human influence has been detected in warming of the atmosphere and the ocean, in changes in the global water cycle, in reductions in snow and ice, and in global mean sea-level rise; and it is *extremely likely* to have been the dominant cause of the observed warming since the mid-20th century.[21]

Humans are responsible for this historic anthropogenic greenhouse gas emissions which have increased since the pre-industrial era and are driven largely by economic and population growth.[22] The main question in this respect is whether this has an effect on establishing a child's right to survival and development approach to climate change?

2.4. CLIMATE CHANGE EXTREMES, VULNERABILITY AND EXPOSURE

In order to have an appreciable understanding of the consequences of climate change extremes, a relevant question needs to be asked: why do human beings (children) get seriously impacted by climate change extremes? The rationale behind the following discussion is to identify two 'preventable' factors that allow climate change extremes to negatively impact the right of the child to survival and development, namely vulnerability and exposure.

---

20 *Oposa et al. v. Fulgencio S. Factoran, Jr. et al* (G.R. No. 101083), (1993), Supreme Court of the Philippines, available at: <www.escr-net.org/docs/i/401226> accessed 16 April 2015.

21 Intergovernmental Panel on Climate Change (IPCC), Fifth Assessment Synthesis Report, 'Climate Change 2014 Synthesis Report', p. 47, available at: <http://ipcc.ch/pdf/assessment-report/ar5/syr/AR5_SYR_FINAL_All_Topics.pdf> accessed 16 April 2015.

22 *Ibid.*, p. 44.

Climate change affects everyone but vulnerability makes it worse. Vulnerability is basically the susceptibility to harm.[23] Vulnerability may also be defined as 'the potential to be adversely affected by an event or a change and the ability to cope with or recover from its impacts. ... Physical vulnerability refers to exposure to stress and crises resulting from physical hazards, while social vulnerability refers to the inability of individuals and communities to respond to physical impacts.'[24]

Many human systems are significantly vulnerable and exposed to climate related extremes such as draughts, floods and wildfires. Children need to be prepared for such extremes. In other words States have to prepare children against climate change extremes. This is important as '[f]or countries at all levels of development, these impacts are consistent with a significant lack of preparedness for current climate variability in some sectors'.[25] Vulnerability is determined by a number of factors, such as age, gender and social status.[26] This puts girls in particular at risk. The State is obliged to empower vulnerable children and eliminate the factors that cause vulnerability. Exposure, however, is people and assets at risk.[27] States are expected to significantly reduce the amount of exposure.

2.5. ADAPTATION

As States are obliged to limit vulnerability and exposure to the impacts of climate change extremes, the inevitable question is about the nature of the possible actions for the State to undertake, i.e., 'adaptation options'. The Fifth Assessment Report of the Intergovernmental Panel on Climate Change (IPCC) has defined adaptation and its aims as the 'process of adjustment to actual or expected climate and its effects. In human systems, adaptation seeks to moderate harm or exploit beneficial opportunities. In natural systems, human intervention

---

23 I.R. Noble et al., 'Adaptation needs and options', in C.B. Field (eds.), *Climate Change 2014: Impacts, Adaptation, and Vulnerability. Part A: Global and Sectoral Aspects. Contribution of Working Group II to the Fifth Assessment Report of the Intergovernmental Panel on Climate Change* (Cambridge University Press, Cambridge, 2014), pp. 833–868, 841.

24 S.A. Zakieldeen, 'Adaptation to Climate Change: A Vulnerability Assessment for Sudan', *Gatekeeper* Series, 142 (2009), p. 4.

25 Intergovernmental Panel on Climate Change (IPCC), Fifth Assessment Synthesis Report, 'Climate Change 2014 Synthesis Report', p. 53, available at: <http://ipcc.ch/pdf/assessment-report/ar5/syr/AR5_SYR_FINAL_All_Topics.pdf> accessed 16 April 2015.

26 I.R. Noble et al., 'Adaptation needs and options', in C.B. Field (eds.), *Climate Change 2014: Impacts, Adaptation, and Vulnerability. Part A: Global and Sectoral Aspects. Contribution of Working Group II to the Fifth Assessment Report of the Intergovernmental Panel on Climate Change* (Cambridge University Press, Cambridge, 2014), pp. 833–868, 841.

27 Intergovernmental Panel on Climate Change (IPCC), Fifth Assessment Synthesis Report, 'Climate Change 2014 Synthesis Report', p. 54, available at: <http://ipcc.ch/pdf/assessment-report/ar5/syr/AR5_SYR_FINAL_All_Topics.pdf> accessed 16 April 2015.

may facilitate adjustment to expected climate and its effects)'.[28] Zakieldeen also defines adaptation as 'the adjustment in natural or human systems in response to actual or expected climatic change or their effects, to reduce harm or exploit beneficial opportunities.'[29] What follows is a brief review of the possible adaptation options to be adopted by the State in relation to the right of the child to survival and development.

Children are among the most vulnerable to the extremes of climate change.[30] Accordingly, they should receive special consideration when effective institutional adaptation options are selected.[31] It is probably better for governments to start by adopting policies that integrate adaptations in order to reduce vulnerability and exposure.[32] The government's role is essential in developing 'national adaptation strategies and plans. This includes National Adaptation Programmes of Action (NAPAs) by least developed countries, the National Adaptation Plan (NAP) process, and strategic frameworks for national adaptation in OECD countries.'[33] All these measures should have a focus on children's rights including the right of the child to survival and development. This should also reflect some aspects of effective governance which is expected to guarantee efficient operation of institutional adaptations within the state.[34]

Other institutional adaptations include the legislation of relevant laws and regulations such as 'Land zoning laws ... building standards ... water regulations ... laws to support disaster risk reduction ... defining property rights ... marine protected areas ... fishing quotas ...'[35] Adaptations are also required with respect to judicial decisions. Significantly, it may be suggested one judicial adaptation measure could be found, for instance in the principle

---

28 I.R. Noble et al., 'Adaptation needs and options', in C.B. Field (eds.), *Climate Change 2014: Impacts, Adaptation, and Vulnerability. Part A: Global and Sectoral Aspects. Contribution of Working Group II to the Fifth Assessment Report of the Intergovernmental Panel on Climate Change* (Cambridge University Press, Cambridge, 2014), pp. 833–868, 838.

29 S.A. Zakieldeen, 'Adaptation to Climate Change: A Vulnerability Assessment for Sudan', *Gatekeeper* Series, 142 (2009), p. 4.

30 W.N. Adger et al., 'Human security', in C.B. Field (eds.), *Climate Change 2014: Impacts, Adaptation, and Vulnerability. Part A: Global and Sectoral Aspects. Contribution of Working Group II to the Fifth Assessment Report of the Intergovernmental Panel on Climate Change* (Cambridge University Press, Cambridge, 2014), pp. 755–791, 761.

31 I.R. Noble et al., 'Adaptation needs and options', in C.B. Field (eds.), *Climate Change 2014: Impacts, Adaptation, and Vulnerability. Part A: Global and Sectoral Aspects. Contribution of Working Group II to the Fifth Assessment Report of the Intergovernmental Panel on Climate Change* (Cambridge University Press, Cambridge, 2014), pp. 833–868, 850.

32 Intergovernmental Panel on Climate Change (IPCC), Fifth Assessment Synthesis Report, 'Climate Change 2014 Synthesis Report', p. 107, available at: <http://ipcc.ch/pdf/assessment-report/ar5/syr/AR5_SYR_FINAL_All_Topics.pdf> accessed 16 April 2015.

33 *Ibid.*

34 I.R. Noble et al., 'Adaptation needs and options', in C.B. Field (eds.), *Climate Change 2014: Impacts, Adaptation, and Vulnerability. Part A: Global and Sectoral Aspects. Contribution of Working Group II to the Fifth Assessment Report of the Intergovernmental Panel on Climate Change* (Cambridge University Press, Cambridge, 2014), pp. 833–868, 849.

35 *Ibid.*, p. 845.

of the suspension of the *hadd* (Islamic Sharia ruling) for theft during years of famine. For instance, the High Court in Sudan made an important decision in 1989 when it decided in Government of Sudan v. Shaiboo Saeed Muhammad to suspend the *hadd* for theft. Judge Zain Alabideen based his decision on the reasoning that the president of the Transitional Military Council had announced to the whole world, back in 1985, and after the uprising, that Sudan was suffering from famine. On this basis, he decided that the courts are entitled to take judicial notice, of this announcement, without having to provide evidence; and, therefore, suspended the *hadd* for theft.[36] Constitutional guarantees to the right to a clear environment are also a form of adaptation. For instance, section 24 of the South African Bill of Rights has been given, by some authors a positive role in connection to climate change. 'It is predicted that plaintiffs will rely on … statutory obligations for bringing actions for property damage such as coastal properties affected by rising sea levels as a result of climate change.'[37] It is, however, also possible to argue that constitutional guarantees are not that strong as some constitutions allow in cases of emergency for the derogative suspension of human rights.[38]

Adaptation itself is a social learning process.[39] It requires a participatory approach to guarantee its effectiveness. Participation, in turn, is an important aspect of the right of the child to development. Effective participation, however, requires well-informed citizens. It is important, in this context, to educate citizens (including children), and raise their level of awareness and readiness:

> The complexity of climate adaptation means that adaptation options are heavily influenced by forms of learning and knowledge sharing … Many scholars have noted that education is a key indicator for how people select adaptation options … while a lack of education is a constraint that contributes to vulnerability… For example, in a study of how farmers in the Nile Basin of Ethiopia select adaptation options, the researchers found a positive relationship between the education level of the household head and the adoption of improved technologies and adaptation to climate change…[40]

36 *Sudan Law Journal & Reports* (SLJR), 1989, *Government of Sudan v. Shaiboo Saeed Muhammad* (in Arabic), author's translation.

37 J. Glazewski and D. Collier, 'South Africa', in R. Lord et al. (eds.), *Climate Change Liability: Transnational Law and Practice* (Cambridge University Press, Cambridge, 2011), pp. 328–329.

38 S. Humphreys (ed.), *Human Rights and Climate Change* (Cambridge University Press, Cambridge, 2010), p. 6.

39 I.R. Noble et al., 'Adaptation needs and options', in C.B. Field (eds.), *Climate Change 2014: Impacts, Adaptation, and Vulnerability. Part A: Global and Sectoral Aspects. Contribution of Working Group II to the Fifth Assessment Report of the Intergovernmental Panel on Climate Change* (Cambridge University Press, Cambridge, 2014), pp. 833–868, 842.

40 *Ibid.*, p. 847. See also see Convention on Access to Information, Public Participation in Decision-Making and Access to Justice in Environmental Matters (with annexes). Aarhus, Denmark, 25 June 1998, United Nations, *Treaty Series*, vol. 2161, p. 447. More information is available at: <http://ec.europa.eu/environment/aarhus/> accessed 23 April 2015.

It should be for the benefit of the child's survival and development, and in the child's best interest if climate change knowledge and information is introduced into the school curricula.[41] However, in Dimmock v. Secretary of State for Education and Skills the claimant argued that the distribution of a film on global warming to school children by the Secretary of State is a promotion of partisan political views. The court ruled that: 'The mere distribution by the Secretary of State to schools to facilitate their showing of a film regarding global warming, and accompanied by guidance, was not per se, or irremediably, a promotion of partisan political views so as to be contrary to ss406 and 407.'[42]

Adaptation options are also important in the health sector. Public health services are vital in handling the current and projected future increases in climate change related disease instances.[43] States are required to ensure availability, provision and access:

> For example, in countries where malaria is endemic, frequent adaptation options for addressing possible outbreaks include increasing use of mosquito nets, insecticides sprays, and controlling mosquito breeding by reclaiming land and filling drains ... Governments at all levels are often also responsible for maintaining adequate access to services that are projected to be further stressed due to climate change ... Frequently cited options in this domain include, among others, clearing drainage systems to prevent floods, diversifying water supply services to account for changing water supplies...[44]

It is considered to be an aspect of good governance and good management of the available resources if adaptation options start by strengthening the existing delivery systems:

> The most effective vulnerability reduction measures for health in the near-term are programs that implement and improve basic public health measures such as provision of clean water and sanitation, secure essential health care including vaccination and child health services...[45]

Adaptation options also require States to opt for peace against war. As discussed in Chapter 5, the right of the child to survival and development as an aim is also

---

41 S.A. Zakieldeen, 'Adaptation to Climate Change: A Vulnerability Assessment for Sudan', *Gatekeeper* Series, 142 (2009), p. 17.

42 [2007] All ER (D) 117 (Oct).

43 I.R. Noble et al., 'Adaptation needs and options', in C.B. Field (eds.), *Climate Change 2014: Impacts, Adaptation, and Vulnerability. Part A: Global and Sectoral Aspects. Contribution of Working Group II to the Fifth Assessment Report of the Intergovernmental Panel on Climate Change* (Cambridge University Press, Cambridge, 2014), pp. 833–868, 847.

44 *Ibid.*

45 Intergovernmental Panel on Climate Change (IPCC), Fifth Assessment Synthesis Report, 'Climate Change 2014 Synthesis Report', p. 97, available at: <http://ipcc.ch/pdf/assessment-report/ar5/syr/AR5_SYR_FINAL_All_Topics.pdf> accessed 16 April 2015.

about the right to peace. As previously mentioned, climate change impacts are sometimes reported to be linked to conflict. For instance, some argue that the effects of climate change were among the significant causes of the mass killings that occurred in Darfur in 2003;[46] however, some studies argue against this.

2.6. FORMULATION OF A CHILD'S RIGHTS (RIGHT TO SURVIVAL AND DEVELOPMENT) APPROACH TO CLIMATE CHANGE

The following paragraphs attempt to define the possible children's rights (right to survival and development) perspective of the topic, obviously with a particular emphasis on article 6(2) as being the right of the child to 'everything'. This is not a straight forward topic, as one scholar has once commented: 'perhaps the biggest challenge is to identify what a human rights approach to climate change might look like in practice.'[47]

Basically, the discussion draws two levels of presumed State responsibility. The first one is responsibility at the international level and the second one is responsibility at the national level. Within the responsibility at the international level, it is possible to argue that this has two components. First is the difficult question of whether it is possible to place responsibility on the developed States who are mainly causing the climate change, to stop what they are doing? The second component of the responsibility at the international level is the responsibility of the developed States to cooperate with the affected developing States in adapting to impacts of climate change. As for the responsibility at the national or domestic level of States, it is basically centred on the obligation to adapt to the extreme impacts of climate change. The main challenge, at this level of responsibility, is whether it is possible to establish a human rights approach to any of the above-mentioned adaptation options or any others.

Human rights and climate change is indeed a challenging topic. Some might view the whole thing as a utopia. Climate change could be considered as the debate of the powerful against the weak. Some even argue that the two do not meet at all.[48]

---

46 W.N. Adger et al., 'Human security', in C.B. Field (eds.), *Climate Change 2014: Impacts, Adaptation, and Vulnerability. Part A: Global and Sectoral Aspects. Contribution of Working Group II to the Fifth Assessment Report of the Intergovernmental Panel on Climate Change* (Cambridge University Press, Cambridge, 2014), pp. 755–791, 773. Their argument is that five detailed studies dispute the identification of the Darfur conflict as being primarily caused by climate change. They found that the violence in Darfur has multiple causes.

47 P. Alston and R. Goodman, *International Human Rights* (Oxford University Press, Oxford, 2013), p. 1542. See also S. Humphreys, *Human Rights and Climate Change* (Cambridge University Press, Cambridge, 2010), p. 45.

48 See P. Alston and R. Goodman, *International Human Rights* (Oxford University Press, Oxford, 2013), p. 1535.

In fact, some even consider that the United Nations Framework Convention on Climate Change (UNFCCC), which was signed in 1992 in the United Nations Conference on Environment and Development, was more about equity and not at all about human rights law.[49] Importantly, indeed, some authors of the Fifth Assessment Report of the Intergovernmental Panel on Climate Change (IPCC) argue against a human rights context to climate change on the grounds that:

> Research on climate change risks to human rights examines legal issues in policy, litigation, and compensation ... Many legal commentators argue that claims to human rights may ultimately not offer greater explanation of the harm to individuals or realize political traction in climate policy ... Several cases have tested these rights, especially of women, children, indigenous peoples, and other minorities...[50]

However, there is almost an agreement among scholars that the subject of human rights and climate change needs more study and analysis. Some others argue that there could be some kind of disconnection between the two disciplines as there are not too many studies about the topic and not because there is a real disconnection between the two disciplines.[51]

Nevertheless, a more forward argument recognises some kind of a link between the two disciplines despite arguing that it is not strong enough. This kind of link is based on the understanding that human rights talk in the climate change debate is not centred about human rights law, policy or jurisprudence. It is more centred on the philosophical aspects of human rights. In other words, it is more about the ethical aspects of human rights or, as Stephen Humphreys describes them, they are of 'schematic fashion'.[52]

Karin Arts, for instance, argues that the CRC allows only for an indirect construction of a child's rights approach to climate change:

> [I]n doctrine supporting the progressive development of international law ... there is broad backing for the idea that an adequate environment is an essential precondition for the protection of human rights ... the human rights aspects of climate change are mainly construed indirectly. Climate change in itself is not a (potential) human rights violation, but the fact that climate change makes it impossible to realize the rights to life, health ... turns it into a factor that contributes to the creation of a

49 S. Humphreys (ed.), *Human Rights and Climate Change* (Cambridge University Press, Cambridge, 2010), p. 48.

50 W.N. Adger et al., 'Human security', in C.B. Field (eds.), *Climate Change 2014: Impacts, Adaptation, and Vulnerability. Part A: Global and Sectoral Aspects. Contribution of Working Group II to the Fifth Assessment Report of the Intergovernmental Panel on Climate Change* (Cambridge University Press, Cambridge, 2014), pp. 755–791, 759.

51 S. Humphreys (ed.), *Human Rights and Climate Change* (Cambridge University Press, Cambridge, 2010), p. 3.

52 *Ibid.*, p. 12.

> disabling environment for human rights ... the human rights to survival ... imply 'a right to the conditions that make these goals achievable'.[53]

In defence of a link between climate change and human rights, some argue that the relationship between the two could find some common ground in the kind of the sophisticated debate that evolved after the end of the Cold War. The main line of argument in this context is that notions such as participation, good governance and accountability 'inevitably' have human rights dimensions.[54]

In the author's opinion, the link between children's right and climate change could also be viewed as common sense. There is an obvious link between the right of the child to survival and development, and, climate change as it interferes with the implementation, realisation and fulfilment of the right. However, it is important to stress that the nature of any children's rights approach to this topic still needs to be defined. Is it merely an ethical and philosophical one? Is it a social one? Is it a matter of justice? Is it one of logic? Or is it a legal and obligatory one? And if it is a legal one, is it about legal principles or about legal responsibilities and accountabilities?

Some of those who advocate for the children's rights approach to climate change argue from the perspective of children's vulnerability and the fact that they have the least contribution in the actions that prompted the global climate change and have the weakest influence on climate policies. For instance, Navi Pillay, the former United Nations High Commissioner for Human Rights, argues that: 'Under international human rights law, States are legally bound to address such vulnerability in accordance with human rights principles of equality and non-discrimination.'[55] With relevance to article 6(2) it also is possible to add the principle of survival and development.

Earlier in 2006 Mary Robinson, the former, United Nations High Commissioner for Human Rights, viewed human rights and climate change from the perspective of equality between the rich and the poor and that it is the human rights framework and not a charity one anymore. This takes the discussion into the broader international level, of developed and developing countries. The following two points are of importance in this regard, i.e., the human rights obligations for developed countries and the nature of these obligations. Moreover, what are the human rights obligations of developing countries?

---

53 K. Arts, 'A Child Rights Perspective on Climate Change', in M.A. Mohamed Salih (ed.), *Climate Change and Sustainable Development: New Challenges for Poverty Reduction* (Edward Elgar, Cheltenham, 2009), pp. 79–93, p. 87 (footnotes omitted).

54 P. Alston and R. Goodman, *International Human Rights* (Oxford University Press, Oxford, 2013), pp. 1516–1517.

55 United Nations General Assembly, UN Human Rights Council, 'Annual Report of the United Nations High Commissioner for Human Rights and Reports of the Office of the High Commissioner and the Secretary-General Report of the Office of the United Nations High Commissioner for Human Rights on the Relationship Between Climate Change and Human Rights', UN Doc. A/HRC/10/61 (15 January 2009), para. 42.

Firstly human rights obligations of developed countries relate to the following: is there a human right to stop the change to the climate? In other words, is there a human right to mitigation? In the context of this case study, mitigation will be discussed from the perspective of developed countries, as some developing countries are also contributing to the change in the climate. Is it possible to formulate, through article 6(2), a child's rights approach to limiting the change to the climate? Is it possible to oblige relevant States to reduce greenhouse gas emissions? Another relevant question is whether, according to article 6(2), there is a child's right to international cooperation.

Secondly, human rights obligations of developing countries relate to the effects of climate change on the enjoyment of rights at the national level. In other words, is there a human right to adaptation options? Again, it is important to point out that developed countries are also required to adopt adaptation measures.

2.7. POSSIBLE CHILD'S RIGHTS APPROACH TOWARDS DEVELOPED STATES

With regard to the question of whether we can make a child rights claim against rich countries to stop the change to the climate and to compensate poor countries for climate change. 'These claims may be based either upon the specific attribution of responsibility to the countries of the North for the carbon emissions which are responsible for global warming ...'[56] Is it logical enough to argue that the parties who caused the problem should pay for their wrongdoings? Also relevant is the question whether an individual child in country X have a human right against country Y to stop its activities that cause climate change? Does article 6(2) on the right of the child to survival and development provide for such a claim?

Significantly, the Report of the Office of the High Commissioner for Human Rights argued against such a possibility of attributing human rights accountability for climate change to developed States:

> Qualifying the effects of climate change as human rights violations poses a series of difficulties. First, it is virtually impossible to disentangle the complex causal relationships linking historical greenhouse gas emissions of a particular country with a specific climate-related effect ... [and] adverse effects of global warming are often projections about future impacts whereas human-rights violations are normally established after the harm has occurred ... [therefore] it is doubtful that an individual would be able to hold a particular State responsible for harm caused by climate change.[57]

56 P. Alston and R. Goodman, *International Human Rights* (Oxford University Press, Oxford, 2013), p. 1537.

57 United Nations General Assembly, UN Human Rights Council, 'Annual Report of The United Nations High Commissioner for Human Rights and Reports of the Office of the High

Speaking about the right to health and climate change Stephen Humphreys also identifies four justice claims that have been raised from the outset in the context of climate change. Some of them are relevant to the possible responsibility of the 'wrongdoers'. As for a human rights approach to mitigation, he observes that requesting the States who are causing the harm that is affecting a larger group to stop and compensate is more an act of tort than of human rights. He speaks about the familiar contours of corrective justice to stop the perpetrators and questions the human rights approach by asking if it is human rights then what kind of mechanisms could be adopted to stop the perpetrators.[58] Humphreys opens the discussion to some procedural claims. He poses the following question: 'who should pay how much of the cost of dealing with it? How should the burden of solving the problem be distributed? … It is in the context of … the "polluter pays principle"'.[59] Humphreys continues that there is no obvious wrong doing and that many carbon-intensive economies have risen and that many livelihoods depend on them 'a legitimate entitlement has been generated among carbon users that cannot be rescinded arbitrarily in favour of a larger policy goal … a persuasive argument might even be made that compensation should be due to the *polluters* if they are to give up their acquired entitlement to the global carbon dump … This might be regarded … as a formal justice … it warns against the elimination of private rights in the public interest except under the strictest necessity, and against retroactive penalisation of actions that were legal at the time they were taken'.[60]

The Committee on Economic, Social and Cultural Rights identifies the obligation to '[r]efrain from interfering with the enjoyment of human rights in other countries' as an extraterritorial obligation of states to promote and protect economic, social and cultural rights.[61] Nevertheless, in climate change debate, this will be difficult to implement so as to hold developed States accountable for a human rights violation towards developing countries. This difficulty can be attributed to many practical reasons. Probably, there is almost an agreement that rather than focusing on blaming any particular State, the focus should be on international cooperation. Nevertheless, the United Nations High Commissioner for Human Rights argues that: 'Human rights standards and principles,

Commissioner and the Secretary-General Report of the Office of the United Nations High Commissioner for Human Rights on the Relationship Between Climate Change and Human Rights', UN Doc. A/HRC/10/61 (15 January 2009) para. 70.

58 S. Humphreys (ed.), *Human Rights and Climate Change* (Cambridge University Press, Cambridge, 2010), p. 40.

59 *Ibid.*, p. 41. See also *ibid.*, p. 42.

60 *Ibid.*, p. 42.

61 United Nations General Assembly, UN Human Rights Council, 'Annual Report of the United Nations High Commissioner for Human Rights and Reports of the Office of the High Commissioner and the Secretary-General Report of the Office of the United Nations High Commissioner for Human Rights on the Relationship Between Climate Change and Human Rights', UN Doc. A/HRC/10/61 (15 January 2009), para. 86.

underpinned by universally recognized moral values, can usefully inform debates on equity and fair distribution of mitigation and adaptation burdens.'[62]

2.8. INTERNATIONAL COOPERATION AND CLIMATE CHANGE

The other relevant point with regard to the responsibility at the international level is about the responsibility of rich developed countries towards poor developing ones. In other words, from a child's rights perspective, does article 6(2) allow for a human right to international cooperation in order to solve climate change effects?

As for international cooperation, the foundation for the human rights claim against rich countries is 'that the wealthy must assist those who are at risk of large-scale rights deprivation and are effectively unable to help themselves.'[63] Humphreys, for instance, speaks about global solidarity in solving the global problem that affects everyone 'global problem requiring global solution'.[64] But are there any moral or legal foundations for such a claim?[65] To be more precise, is there any legal obligation under article 6(2) on the right of the child to survival and development for such a claim?

The CRC, in particular, explicitly refers in article 4 to international cooperation with regards to economic, social and cultural rights. Moreover, international cooperation is one of the basics of the UN Charter. Other international documents such as the ICESCR and the Declaration on the Right to Development also state the importance of international cooperation. But the right to survival and development is comprehensive, and it is not only about economic, social and cultural rights. So what are the 'other' bases for a claim on an obligation for international cooperation within article 6(2)?

Basically, the Office of the United Nations High Commissioner for Human Rights argues that international cooperation is the only effective method to address climate change.[66] It also contends that 'the obligation to take steps to the maximum of available resources to implement economic, social and cultural

---

62 United Nations General Assembly, UN Human Rights Council, 'Annual Report of the United Nations High Commissioner for Human Rights and Reports of the Office of the High Commissioner and the Secretary-General Report of the Office of the United Nations High Commissioner for Human Rights on the Relationship Between Climate Change and Human Rights', UN Doc. A/HRC/10/61 (15 January 2009), para. 88.

63 P. Alston and R. Goodman, *International Human Rights* (Oxford University Press, Oxford, 2013), p. 1537.

64 S. Humphreys (ed.), *Human Rights and Climate Change* (Cambridge University Press, Cambridge, 2010), p. 41.

65 P. Alston and R. Goodman, *International Human Rights* (Oxford University Press, Oxford, 2013), pp. 1537–1538.

66 United Nations General Assembly, UN Human Rights Council, 'Annual Report of the United Nations High Commissioner for Human Rights and Reports of the Office of the High Commissioner and the Secretary-General Report of the Office of the United Nations High

rights includes an obligation of States, where necessary, to seek international cooperation.'[67] Some also draw the link between article 2(1) in the ICESCR and UNFCCC, which has a nearly universal participation, with regard to seeking international cooperation in article 4(7).[68] However, in this respect, and as discussed in more details in Chapter 5, article 6(2) puts a wider standard than that of 'the maximum extent of available resources'. In fact article 6(2) adopts the standard of 'to the maximum extent possible' which has a wider spectrum. This should allow a valid claim for international cooperation on the survival and development of the child.

According to the Office of the High Commissioner for Human Rights report:

> Human rights standards and principles are consistent with and further emphasize 'the principle of common but differentiated responsibilities' contained in the United Nations Framework Convention on Climate Change. According to this principle, developed country Parties ... commit to assisting developing country Parties ... in meeting the costs of adaptation to the adverse effects of climate change and to take full account of the specific needs of least developed countries in funding and transfer of technology. The human rights framework complements the Convention by underlining that 'the human person is the central subject of development', and that international cooperation is not merely a matter of the obligations of a State towards other States, but also of the obligations towards individuals.[69]

Human development is clearly at the heart of article 6(2). It is possible to argue that international cooperation to achieve human development in the context of climate change is the same as international cooperation to achieve the child's development under article 6(2). Several concepts of development may assist in establishing a child's right approach to climate change through article 6(2), for instance the concept of development as a 'process of expanding the real freedoms that people enjoy',[70] also as a principle for the realisation of human rights, particularly the right of the child to development. In this regard, article 6(2) as an aim of the CRC is manifest.

Commissioner for Human Rights on the Relationship Between Climate Change and Human Rights', UN Doc. A/HRC/10/61 (15 January 2009), paras. 84–85.

67 *Ibid.*, para. 85.

68 See S. Humphreys (ed.), *Human Rights and Climate Change* (Cambridge University Press, Cambridge, 2010), p. 50. See also Intergovernmental Panel on Climate Change (IPCC), Fifth Assessment Synthesis Report, 'Climate Change 2014 Synthesis Report', p. 102, available at: <http://ipcc.ch/pdf/assessment-report/ar5/syr/AR5_SYR_FINAL_All_Topics.pdf> accessed 16 April 2015.

69 United Nations General Assembly, UN Human Rights Council, 'Annual Report of the United Nations High Commissioner for Human Rights and Reports of the Office of the High Commissioner and the Secretary-General Report of the Office of the United Nations High Commissioner for Human Rights on the Relationship Between Climate Change and Human Rights', UN Doc. A/HRC/10/61 (15 January 2009), para. 87.

70 P. Alston and R. Goodman, *International Human Rights* (Oxford University Press, Oxford, 2013), p. 1517.

2.9. HUMAN RIGHTS APPROACHES TO ADAPTATION OPTIONS

As for the responsibility at the national level, it is possible to argue that unlike human rights approaches at the international level, this is a more straightforward case. In terms of the obligation of the State to identify, select and adopt any adaptation option, the obligation to ensure according to article 6(2) is vital. It provides for present adaptation options through the obligation to protect and provide. It also provides for future adaptation options through the obligation to predict, provide, prepare and fulfil.

This conveys the broad spectrum of obligations that fall on the shoulder of the state at the national level.[71] Article 6(2), for example, provides a chance for a right to conditions of adequate environment, which is essential for the survival and development of the child. The State Party should create conditions that protect man-made and natural environments and bio-diversity in order to implement the right of the child to survival and development.[72]

2.9.1. Specific Adaptation Options for the Survival and Development of the Child

Adaptation options have to be more child's-rights-oriented. As pointed out earlier, extreme impacts of climate change impose on States to adopt a number of adaptation options. It is important to emphasise that the standard for selecting the adaptation options depends on the individuality of each case. The State is obliged to improve children's adaptive capacity. This is not an easy task, especially for least developed countries where people's adaptive capacity is already weakened by factors such as endemic poverty, institutional weakness and conflict which makes them more vulnerable to predicted climate change.[73]

2.10. SOME DIFFICULTIES IN THE PATH OF THE HUMAN RIGHTS APPROACH

2.10.1. Litigation and Climate Change

Litigation for climate change still needs to be studied and it is probably difficult to establish. Some might argue, in this context, that '[w]hile States are legally

71 See for instance E.D. Gibbons, 'Climate Change, Children's Rights, and the Pursuit of Intergenerational Climate Justice' (2014) 16(1) *Health and Human Rights Journal* 26, available at: <www.hhrjournal.org/wp-content/uploads/sites/13/2014/06/Gibbons1.pdf> accessed 17 April 2015.

72 See for instance *Virender Gaur & Ors. v. State of Haryana & Ors.* (1995) 2 SCC 577 (Supreme Court of India).

73 S.A. Zakieldeen, 'Adaptation to Climate Change: A Vulnerability Assessment for Sudan', *Gatekeeper* Series, 142 (November 2009), p. 3.

obliged to ensure the widest possible enjoyment of economic, social, and cultural rights of children under their jurisdiction, and to ensure adequate safeguards to protect children from harm caused by climate change, legal enforcement of rights violations seen as stemming from climate change may be problematic.'[74] Gibbons, for example, suggests that: 'Nevertheless, legal scholars are exploring climate change litigation as one avenue for forcing action on public utilities, fossil fuel companies, car manufacturers, and other private sector actors who have power to limit the greenhouse gas emissions at the source of much of climate change's impact.'[75]

The availability of human rights bases for litigation may facilitate the human rights approach to climate change. The South African case of Trustees, Biowatch Trust v. The Registrar: Genetic Resources, for instance, confirmed the constitutional right of citizens to information. This constitutional right provides an opportunity to help the plaintiff in climate change litigation to get relevant information. The right to obtain information and the right of the holder of the information to be protected is considered by some as affording a plaintiff in a climate change litigation the opportunity to obtain the documents that may support him/her in the climate change claim.[76]

2.10.2. The Concept of 'Climate Migrants'

Another difficulty in the path of the human rights approach is the concept of 'climate migrants'. Some argue that climate change might have an impact on migration, but it is still very difficult to legally classify any one as a 'climate migrant' because of some scientific and legal problems.[77] Others argue that the concept does not exist: 'McAdam calls the concept "erroneous as a matter of law and conceptually inaccurate"'.[78] In 2014 a case about climate migrant was brought before New Zealand authorities. A man from Kiribati, a 'sinking island State',[79] argued for refugee status for himself, wife and three children on the basis of climate change. He argued that rising sea levels will make it too dangerous for him and his wife and children to return to Kiribati. He also

---

74 E.D. Gibbons, 'Climate Change, Children's Rights, and the Pursuit of Intergenerational Climate Justice' (2014) 16(1) *Health and Human Rights Journal* 26, available at: <www.hhrjournal.org/wp-content/uploads/sites/13/2014/06/Gibbons1.pdf> accessed 17 April 2015.

75 *Ibid.*

76 J. Glazewski, and D. Collier, 'South Africa', in R. Lord et al. (eds.), *Climate Change Liability: Transnational Law and Practice* (Cambridge University Press, Cambridge, 2011), p. 325.

77 W.N. Adger et al., 'Human security', in C.B. Field (eds.), *Climate Change 2014: Impacts, Adaptation, and Vulnerability. Part A: Global and Sectoral Aspects. Contribution of Working Group II to the Fifth Assessment Report of the Intergovernmental Panel on Climate Change* (Cambridge University Press, Cambridge, 2014), pp. 755–791, 768–771.

78 *Ibid.*, p. 771.

79 J. McAdam, 'Disappearing States, Statelessness and the Boundaries of International Law', in J. McAdam (ed.), *Climate Change and Displacement: Multidisciplinary Perspectives* (Hart Publishing, Oxford, 2012), p. 107.

argued against a number of issues, one of which is that many Kiribati people face the same danger and this should not be a reason for dismissing the claim.[80] It is worth mentioning that back in 2006 the Committee on the Rights of the Child had acknowledged that the extreme vulnerability to natural disasters is one of the challenges faced by the State of Kiribati which led to its classification as a least developed country.[81]

However, while 'climate migrants' might be considered one of the difficulties faced by human rights approaches to climate change, Hugo speaks about one aspect of migration and development that might prove to be beneficial for the right of the child to survival and development. Hugo argues that 'there is an increasing body of work which suggests that migration can have beneficial impacts, both in origin and destination countries, within the right policy context. In fact, there has been what amounts to a paradigm shift in thinking on the migration-development relationship.'[82] This should have an indirect positive effect on the right of the child to survival and development.

2.10.3. The Rights of Future Generations

As pointed out earlier, extreme climate change impacts on future generations are now an established fact. Generally speaking, there are positive opinions about the rights of future generations. For instance, the United Nations Millennium Declaration makes explicit reference to future generations:

> We must spare no effort to free all of humanity, and above all our children and grandchildren, from the threat of living on a planet irredeemably spoilt by human activities, and whose resources would no longer be sufficient for their needs.
>
> … We reaffirm our support for the principles of sustainable development, including those set out in Agenda 21, agreed upon at the United Nations Conference on Environment and Development.[83]

The United Nations Framework Convention on Climate Change also argues for the concepts of 'intergenerational equity and justice' and 'the precautionary principle', which are well-established principles in international environmental

80 The Guardian, 'Climate change refugee fights to stay in New Zealand', *The Guardian* (1 October 2013), available at: <www.theguardian.com/environment/2013/oct/01/climate-change-refugee-new-zealand> accessed 23 April 2015.

81 Committee on the Right of the Child, 'Concluding Observations: Kiribati', UN Doc. CRC/C/KIR/CO/1 (29 September 2006), section C.

82 G. Hugo, 'Climate Change-Induced Mobility and the Existing Migration Regime in Asia and the Pacific', in J. McAdam (ed.), *Climate Change and Displacement: Multidisciplinary Perspectives*, (Hart Publishing, Oxford, 2012), p. 29.

83 UN General Assembly, 'United Nations Millennium Declaration', UN Doc. A/RES/55/2 (18 September 2000), paras. 21–22.

law.[84] They are important principles in the debate on climate change, but not well developed in human rights law.[85] Moreover, human rights approaches to the rights of future generations have been referred to in the Report of the High Commissioner for Human Rights. The precautionary principle reflected in article 3 of the United Nations Framework Convention on Climate Change states that lack of full scientific certainty should not be used as a reason for postponing precautionary measures to anticipate, prevent or minimise the causes of climate change and mitigate its adverse effects. As discussed above, human rights litigation is not well-suited to promote precautionary measures based on risk assessments, unless such risks pose an imminent threat to the human rights of specific individuals. Yet, by 'drawing attention to the broader human rights implications of climate change risks, the human rights perspective, in line with the precautionary principle, emphasizes the need to avoid unnecessary delay in taking action to contain the threat of global warming.'[86] Gibbons, for instance argues for the right of future generations, that although the General Comments of the Committee on the Rights of the Child are 'advisory and not enforceable, it is noteworthy that the CRC Committee – in its GC15 on the child's right to health – calls on states to put children's health concerns at the centre of their climate change adaptation and mitigation strategies. As these concerns are long-term by definition, they will protect unborn children far into the future.'[87]

2.11. CONCLUSION

The case study focused on the co-relationship of the right of the child to survival and development and climate change. From the side of the right of the child to survival and development, the study focused on the understanding that it is a comprehensive right which covers a very broad spectrum of issues. Moreover, the multi-identities of the article were kept in consideration. From the side of climate change, the focus of the discussion was on the fact that climate change is mainly caused by humans; as Rajendra Kumar Pachauri the former chair of the Intergovernmental Panel on Climate Change confirmed, '[h]umans are the dominant cause of warming since the mid twentieth

84 United Nations General Assembly, UN Human Rights Council, 'Annual Report of the United Nations High Commissioner for Human Rights and Reports of the Office of the High Commissioner and the Secretary-General Report of the Office of the United Nations High Commissioner for Human Rights on the Relationship Between Climate Change and Human Rights', UN Doc. A/HRC/10/61 (15 January 2009), para. 89.

85 *Ibid.*, paras. 89–90.

86 *Ibid.*, para. 91.

87 E.D. Gibbons, 'Climate Change, Children's Rights, and the Pursuit of Intergenerational Climate Justice' (2014) 16(1) *Health and Human Rights Journal* 28, available at: <www.hhrjournal.org/wp-content/uploads/sites/13/2014/06/Gibbons1.pdf> accessed 17 April 2015.

century'.[88] The discussion also focused on scientific facts and possible adaptation and mitigation options.

The case study focused on the right of the child to survival and development approach to climate change:

> The Convention on the Rights of the Child, which enjoys near universal ratification, obliges States to take action to ensure the realization of all rights in the Convention for all children in their jurisdiction, including measures to safeguard children's right to life, survival and development through, inter alia, addressing problems of environmental pollution and degradation. Importantly, children must be recognized as active participants and stewards of natural resources in the promotion and protection of a safe and healthy environment.[89]

3. SECOND CASE STUDY: BREASTFEEDING AND THE RIGHT OF THE CHILD TO SURVIVAL AND DEVELOPMENT

3.1. INTRODUCTION

The close link between the right of the chid to survival and development, and, breastfeeding was established during the drafting of the article (this was discussed in detail in Chapter 1). Venezuela kept up its opposition to the inclusion of the word 'survival' until the last minute. Then the representative of the World Health Organization (WHO) stated reservations with regard to the replacement of the word 'survival'. He also made a very significant explanation, in reference to a proposal submitted by Venezuela, in which the word 'survival' was replaced by the word 'growth':

> The observer for the World Health Organization expressed reservation with regard to the replacement of the word 'survival' and explained that the term 'survival' had a special meaning within the United Nations context, especially for his organization and UNICEF. 'Survival' included growth monitoring, oral rehydration and disease control, breast feeding, immunization, child spacing, food and female literacy; the

88 Based on this scientific fact, the inevitable question is: since humans are the dominant cause of climate change, it is possible to establish a human rights-based approach to climate change?

89 United Nations General Assembly, UN Human Rights Council, 'Annual Report of the United Nations High Commissioner for Human Rights and Reports of the Office of the High Commissioner and the Secretary-General Report of the Office of the United Nations High Commissioner for Human Rights on the Relationship Between Climate Change and Human Rights', UN Doc. A/HRC/10/61 (15 January 2009), para. 50.

term 'growth' represented only a part of the concept of 'survival' and the change would be a step backwards from standards already accepted.[90]

This statement by the observer for the WHO emphasised the importance of the particular meaning of the words that were to be used as components of the term 'survival'. This clarification by the WHO was an example of the great determination to maintain the terminologies as they were and demonstrated recognition of the fact that any attempt to change them might result in adverse change to the standards already recognised. It is noticeable that most of the meanings of the word 'survival' which the WHO representative referred to are centred on the issue of early childhood development.

The following discussion on the right of the child to breastfeeding also demonstrates that article 6(2) is comprehensive and that it is simply about the right of the child to everything. The discussion in this case study attempts to identify some State Party obligations in reference to the right of the child to breastfeeding, as it represents an aspect of the right of the child to survival.

3.2. FORMULATION OF A RIGHTS-BASED APPROACH TO BREASTFEEDING

How can one formulate a child's rights-based approach to breastfeeding? Is it a right of the child against his or her mother? What are the consequences of having a rights-based approach to something (breastfeeding)? Saudamini Siegrist defines the rights-based approach to something as follows:

> This approach seeks to realise children's rights within the broader cultural, social, economic and political context and to address the root causes of violations. Instead of focusing on specific problems and symptoms within a limited context, the human rights-based approach builds holistic, long-term solutions, laying the foundation for a fair, stable and just society.[91]

Siegrist was referring to the involvement of children in post-conflict justice processes, but the definition of the human rights-based approach that she gives could also be valid with reference to a child's rights-based approach to breastfeeding. For instance, the realisation of children's rights within the broader cultural context opens the door for a number of speculations. For example,

---

90 UN Doc. E/CN/1989/48 (2 March 1989), para. 88, available in Office of the United Nations High Commissioner for Human Rights, *Legislative History of the Convention on the Rights of the Child*, Volume I (United Nations, New York, 2007), p. 367.

91 S. Siegrist, 'Child Participation in International Criminal Accountability Mechanisms: The case of the Sierra Leone Truth and Reconciliation Commission', in K. Arts and V. Popovski (eds.), *International Criminal Accountability and the Rights of the Children* (Hague Academic Coalition, The Hague, 2006), p. 55 (emphasis added).

the cultural aspect of breastfeeding is related to the way a particular society approaches and expects a mother to feed her baby after birth. In some societies, breastfeeding is seen as the norm, while in others it is the exception.

These kinds of cultural differences are an important aspect to consider when referring to the individuality of each State in terms of identifying the obligations of the State Party in relation to breastfeeding. In countries where the level of breastfeeding is low because of ignorance about its recognised benefits, then the obligation of the State Party to raise awareness about breastfeeding is probably an important one. In other cases, where the low level of breastfeeding mothers is not related to lack of commitment by mothers or knowledge, but is due to lack of legislation that is friendly to the needs of breastfeeding mothers, legislative reforms would be more important.

In some cases, legislative reforms could also be made in addition to raising awareness to correct cultural attitudes towards breastfeeding mothers. In the UK, for instance, in 2007 ministers considered new laws to give women a right to breastfeed their babies in public and to take statutory breaks at work to breastfeed their infants. 'The move follows research showing that only a minority of new mothers breastfeed their babies for the full six months recommended by the World Health Organisation.'[92] The laws proposed were to make it an offence for anyone to stop a woman from breastfeeding in public. It followed complaints from mothers that they had been accused of indecency and been barred from breastfeeding when they had attempted to do so in public.[93]

Another point that could arise in the cultural context of the right of the child to breastfeeding is whether the right of the child to breastfeeding could be overshadowed by the 'right of the mother not to breastfeed'. It might be unusual in the real world to find a mother who would make such a challenging argument for not breastfeeding her baby by saying that she was not going to breastfeed because it was her right.[94] This could be attributed to the understanding that, with widespread knowledge about the benefits of breastfeeding, mothers are becoming afraid of being accused of not being good mothers. Thus, even if a mother held such ideas, she might not voice them. However, for the sake of argument, this scenario could cause difficulties as regards the fulfillment of the obligation of the State Party to protect the child versus the obligation of the State Party to respect the right of the individual (mother).

---

92 S.-K. Templeton, 'Women may get right to breastfeed in public', *Sunday Times* (13 May 2007).

93 *Ibid.*

94 According to other international documents, breastfeeding is also about the mother. Examples of these are the Convention on the Elimination of All Forms of Discrimination Against Women, which speaks about lactation rights in article 12; World Health Organization; the International Code of Marketing of Breast-milk Substitutes, adopted by the World Health Assembly in 1981; and the Maternity Protection Convention, revised by the International Labour Organization in 2000, which speaks about a right to breastfeeding in article 10, 'C183 Maternity Protection Convention, 2000'.

The CRC expresses only one reference to the term 'breastfeeding', in article 24(e): 'To ensure that all segments of society, in particular parents and children, are informed, have access to education and are supported in the use of basic knowledge of child health and nutrition, the advantages of breastfeeding, hygiene and environmental sanitation and the prevention of accidents…'

Together, both article 24(e) and article 6(2) work towards strengthening the right of the child to breastfeeding. The right of the child to breastfeeding was put in article 24(e) in an awareness-raising context; therefore, the setting under article 6(2) provides a more comprehensive form of State Party obligations. Article 6(2) is an independent right of the child, an aim of the Convention, a quality measure of the Convention and a general principle of the CRC. This helps to establish the importance of article 6(2) as a separate and independent article of its own: one that, in particular, is independent from the right to health. The State Party has specific obligations in relation to the right of the child to survival, which includes the right to breastfeeding. It is the responsibility of the State and the parents have a great role to play in its implementation. This kind of understanding could answer any worries about the weakness of the CRC in protecting the right of the child to breastfeeding. Kedrowski states:

> However, there are other provisions in the CRC that could be construed to undermine a child's right to be breastfed. First, several provisions recognise the role of the parents, and the parents' rights to make decisions regarding the care of their children. Similarly, the State is required to respect the 'responsibilities, rights and duties of parents' and to ensure that children are not separated unnecessarily from their children, except in cases of abuse or neglect, or when such separation is otherwise in the 'best interests of the child.' Parents could conceivably decide, based on all of the evidence available and against the advice of medical professionals and breastfeeding advocates, that breastfeeding is not the best option for them or is not in their child's best interests. In this case, a child's right to breastfeed, if the CRC is interpreted to include such a right, would be in conflict with, and would probably be subject to, the parents' autonomy in the area of child-rearing.[95]

Kedrowski also argues that another way that the CRC may undermine a child's right to breastfeed is in Article 2, which states that 'States Parties shall take all appropriate measures to ensure that the child is protected against all forms of discrimination or punishment on the basis of the status, activities, expressed opinions or beliefs of the children's parents, legal guardians, or family members.' 'This provision against "punishment" would imply that breastfeeding children should not be placed in prison with their mothers in order to continue the breastfeeding relationship. Thus the child's implied right to be breastfed could

95 K.M. Kedrowski, 'Breastfeeding Policies and Practices in an International Human Rights Context', prepared for presentation at the Oxford Roundtable Women in the Modern World: The Struggle for Equality, March 2008.

come into conflict with the child's expressed right to be free from punishment based on her/his parents' incarcerated status.'[96] The role that article 6(2) plays as a general principle, and the fact that the right of the child to breastfeeding should be sensed and reflected within the interpretation of the Convention, also responds to the same worries about the possibility of undermining the breastfeeding right by the provision and wording of article 2. However, article 6(2) as a quality-control factor and an aim interferes in order to weigh things for the sake of the child's interests.

The UK legislative reforms mentioned above are a good example of the way in which legislation could be changed to guarantee the right of the child to breastfeeding. However, from a child's rights point of view, the legislation that was proposed was not enough, because it only covers children up to the age of one year old: 'It would mean that women breastfeeding infants of up to a year could no longer be told to leave cafes, shops and other places – still a relatively frequent occurrence according to campaigners.'[97] Breastfeeding campaigners argued that the protection should be extended. They cited the World Health Organization advice recommending breastfeeding for two years or more.[98] In fact, the State Party should pass legislation that gives all children the right to be breastfed, including the children of working mothers. Another legislative example that obliges the State to guarantee the right of the child to breastfeeding is article 7(1) of the 2010 Sudanese Child Act. According to this article, the child has a right to breastfeed for a period of two years. The State is also obliged to give the mother maternity leave according to article 7(2).

The comprehensiveness of the obligation to ensure is also a good remedy for the right of the child to breastfeeding. For instance, with respect to State policies, the State Party needs to have a national plan of action specifically designed for breastfeeding. The State also needs to ratify and fully implement regional and international documents that regulate the marketing of breast-milk supplements, such as the International Code of Marketing of Breast-Milk Substitutes, which was passed by the World Health Organization in 1981.[99] The State should also make efforts to regulate advertisements for bottle-feeding.[100] Moreover, States are expected to refrain from making financial subsidies to formula milk. Budgetary

96 *Ibid.*

97 L. Ward, 'Equality laws enshrine mothers' right to breastfeed in public', *The Guardian* (13 June 2007).

98 *Ibid.*

99 See Committee on the Rights of the Child, 'Concluding Observations on the Combined Second and Third Periodic Report of Turkey', UN Doc. CRC/C/TUR/CO/2-3 (20 July 2012), para. 53. For further discussion about the Code see K.M. Kedrowski, 'Breastfeeding Policies and Practices in an International Human Rights Context', prepared for presentation at the Oxford Roundtable Women in the Modern World: The Struggle for Equality, March 2008.

100 See also M. Brady, 'Breastfeeding is a human right. What does that mean?' (11 December, 2012), available at: <http://info.babymilkaction.org/news/campaignblog111212> accessed 23 April 2015.

allocations for establishing baby friendly hospitals are also an obligation of the State.[101] The State is also obliged to acquire relevant information with regards to the rate of exclusive breastfeeding of infants when they are six months of age.[102] The State Party should work hard for the eradication of severe poverty and famine. The State also needs to work for the prevalence of peace, because wars and conflict disrupt stability of family life, which might compromise the right to breastfeeding.

3.3. INTERACTION BETWEEN THE RESPONSIBILITY OF THE STATE AND THE RESPONSIBILITY OF THE PARENTS

Some aspects of the responsibility for the child's survival are shared between the State Party and the parent. This in fact is a unique aspect of children's rights. Childhood requires that the child has someone to take care of him or her. Article 5 of the CRC confirms the rights and duties of the parents:

> States Parties shall respect the responsibilities, rights and duties of parents or, where applicable, the members of the extended family or community as provided for by local custom, legal guardians or other persons legally responsible for the child, to provide, in a manner consistent with the evolving capacities of the child, appropriate direction and guidance in the exercise by the child of the rights recognized in the present Convention…

The fact that there are some obligations placed on the State Party should not relieve the parents or individuals of their responsibilities. The right to breastfeeding lays obligation on both the State and the parent. The State, however, should work hard on the realisation of the rights of all children, especially those who are born to young or unmarried parents. In particular, the State needs to ensure the awareness-raising aspect within society. It is not always the law that is to be blamed. There are also some social problems involved, such as problems related to children born to unmarried parents, as the Committee commented in its concluding observations on the initial report of Barbados about the family environment and alternative care. In this instance, the Committee was concerned about the challenges faced by children as a result of changes in social and family structures, which have led to high numbers of single-parent households and reduced support from extended families; States were asked to review their social-security structures in order to ensure that both parents contribute to the maintenance of the child. States need to provide public assistance to assist

101 Committee on the Rights of the Child, 'Concluding Observations: Hungary', UN Doc. CRC/C/HUN/CO/3-5 (14 October 2014), paras. 50–51.

102 *Ibid.*, paras. 50–51.

children in these circumstances, and tackle the difficulties involved in ensuring respect for the provisions of article 18(1) and (2). States should also continue to give attention to the risks of single parenthood and early parenthood. Moreover, they should promote higher levels of involvement of fathers in the upbringing and development of the child, and to the need to provide necessary support to children in these cases.[103] This approach by the Committee supports the argument that lack of awareness and knowledge plays an important role in the problems of children who are born to unmarried parents, particularly their right to survival.

Budgetary allocations are also relevant in helping breastfeeding mothers. In addition, States are expected to ensure the protection of parents and children from separation.[104] Thus, the State could help in the case of children who have parents that are or have been incarcerated.

The State Party needs to provide and make available a number of programmes and services related to breastfeeding. Thus, it needs to make available adequate data in the area of the mothers' health and adolescents' health, including accidents, violence, suicide, mental health, abortion, HIV/AIDS and STDs. This applies particularly in cases of teenage pregnancies and the situation of teenage mothers, especially in relation to the late attendance, of some of them, at antenatal clinics, as well as their generally poor breastfeeding practices.[105] Children born as a result of rape are also a category that needs special attention. The State should design focused data collection for the benefit of breastfeeding.[106] As previously mentioned, the State also needs to provide data on breastfeeding practices.[107] States Parties need to find ways to encourage and facilitate breastfeeding by establishing child-care places at work, especially governmental work and departments.[108]

Teenage mothers are most likely to lack the knowledge and capabilities to care for their babies and themselves. This is one of the reasons why most of the cases of infant and maternal mortality relate to teenage mothers.[109] To solve this problem, the State Party needs to increase its efforts in promoting adolescent health policies and counselling services. But this is not the only available solution. The State Party also needs to seek international cooperation, including technical assistance in helping teenagers in cases of childhood illnesses by

103 Committee on the Rights of the Child, 'Concluding Observations on Barbados's Initial Report', UN Doc. CRC/C/15/Add.103 (24 August 1999), para. 20.

104 Committee on the Rights of the Child, 'Concluding Observations on Antigua and Barbuda's Initial Report', UN Doc. CRC/C/15/Add.247 (3 November 2004), paras. 39–40.

105 Committee on the Rights of the Child, 'Concluding Observations on Grenada's Initial Report', UN Doc. CRC/C/15/Add.121 (28 February 2000), para. 22.

106 Committee on the Rights of the Child, 'Concluding Observations on Barbados's Initial Report', UN Doc. CRC/C/15/Add.103 (24 August 1999), para. 26.

107 *Ibid.*

108 *Ibid.*

109 Committee on the Rights of the Child, 'Concluding Observations on Grenada's Initial Report', UN Doc. CRC/C/15/Add.121 (28 February 2000), para. 22.

seeking assistance from international bodies such as UNICEF and the WHO. The State Party needs to allocate adequate human and financial resources, to make efforts to increase the number of social workers and psychologists, and to develop youth-friendly care, counselling and rehabilitation facilities for adolescents. The policies that the State Party issues in this regard should be comprehensive policies and programmes to reduce the incidence of infant and maternal mortality and promote proper breastfeeding and weaning practices among teenage mothers.

3.4. CONCLUSION

This case study provided an analysis to the right of the child to breastfeeding as an aspect of the right of the child to survival and development. It was important to emphasise that the approach was not that of right of the child to breastfeeding against his or her mother. In fact the discussion was founded on two important points that were raised during the drafting of article 6(2). Both points were discussed in detail in Chapter 1.

The first one was that within the United Nation the right to survival had a specific meaning so as to include breastfeeding. This does not suggest that the right to survival is only restricted to that specific meaning. In fact, over the years, other aspects of the right to survival had emerged.

The second important point that was raised during the drafting of the article is that the representative of India pointed out that the reason for drafting the text in this way was to focus on the obligations of States Parties to create measures and conditions for the survival of the child. Against this background, the case study analysed a number of State Party obligations with regard to the right of the child to breastfeeding as an aspect of the right of the child to survival and development. This discussion also emphasised the multi-identities of article 6(2) as a right, aim, quality-control factor and a general principle of the CRC.

CONCLUSION

1. INTRODUCTION

The adoption of the Convention on the Right of the Child (CRC) by the United Nations General Assembly has been widely celebrated in many forms. The speedy ratification of the Convention and entry into force represents a celebration of the Convention. This has been followed by the emergence of writings about the then 'new' Convention. The wide spread of positive academic writings on children's rights is also a manifestation of celebration. Initially, most of these writings were mostly identificatory in nature, focusing on introducing a general overview of the then 'new' convention and the idea of 'children's rights'. Some of them also focused on analysing and discussing the lengthy drafting process of the CRC. Over the years children's rights literature has evolved so as to become more specific about particular articles and standards of the Convention. Against this background, however, article 6(2) on the rights of the child to survival and development has remained among the articles that did not receive much attention within these specific children's rights academic studies. One can name only Manfred Nowak's commentary on article 6 of the CRC.[1] Moreover, the implementation of article 6(2) has emerged, for some reason, as somewhat 'limited'. This 'narrow' understanding influenced the effective implementation of the article,

The aim of this book is to provide an in-depth understanding and interpretation of article 6(2) of the CRC. The chapters of the book are all designed to collectively clarify the various perspectives on article 6(2) and the comprehensive nature of the right of the child to survival and development. However, each chapter on its own has added to the richness of the right to survival and development.

This very detailed analysis ranged from the right of the child to vaccination, the right to oral rehydration, the right to be protected from potentially dangerous motor vehicle driving, the right to education, the right to a reasonable State policy on children, the right of children to vote, the right not to be subjected to corporal punishment, the right to a democratic rule or *Shura*-based rule, and the right to survival and development and climate change. The comprehensive

---

1 M. Nowak, 'Article 6. Right to Life, Survival and Development'; in: A. Alen, J. Vande Lanotte, E. Verhellen, F. Ang, E. Berghmans and A. Verheyde (eds.), *A Commentary on the United Nations Convention on the Rights of the Child*, (Martinus Nijhoff Publishers, Leiden, 2005).

understanding that this book offers on the right of the child to survival and development intends to bring this right into its proper, well-deserved position within any discussion on children's rights.

2. HISTORICAL BACKGROUND

The drafting of the Convention on the Rights of the Child was lengthy. It took the drafters ten years, from 1979–1989, to agree on the text of the CRC. However, the proposal for article 6(2) came only in 1988, i.e., the year before the adoption of the CRC by the General Assembly. Discussions during the drafting of the article were mainly about 'terminologies'. The words 'survival' and the non-specification of an aspect of 'development' were a bit controversial. The controversy was represented in the attempts to change the word 'survival' and add a specific aspect of development to the word 'development'. As for the term 'survival', the representative of the World Health Organisation (WHO) emphasised the importance of the specific meaning that has been given to the term 'survival' within the UN. Against this background the representative of Venezuela emphasised that the issue in the future is going to be about domestic interpretations.

In an attempt to have a clearer insight into the drafting history of article 6(2), a chance for an interview with Nigel Cantwell, who participated in the drafting of the CRC, was not to be missed. When asked about the drafting of article 6(2) he clarified that despite being formally proposed by India, it was actually the United Nations Children's Fund (UNICEF) who actually pushed for the inclusion of this article. This led to further research which revealed that UNICEF was having its own 'Child Survival and Development Revolution'. UNICEF's revolution guided all of its actions and policies at the time. From this an 'unofficial drafting history' of article 6(2) started to emerge. However, this 'unofficial history' is not available in the official *travaux préparatoires* of the CRC. Further research into the 'unofficial history' also looked into any possible relevance of the 1986 Declaration on the Right to Development. Human development aspects of the right to development proved to be of relevance. The aim of Chapter 1 was to identify and discuss any possible factors that affected the drafting and later the interpretation of article 6(2).

3. THE INDEPENDENT ARTICLE 6(2)

After the adoption of the CRC in 1989, article 6(2) entered a new era. It was time for interpretation. Interpretation, as such, can happen by various parties. However, for the purposes of the research in this book one party that definitely had an important role to play with regards to the implementation of article 6(2) was the Committee on the Rights of the Child. In this respect, the Committee definitely interacted with all States Parties at a time of their implementation of article 6(2). For that, Chapter 2 focused mainly on studying and analysing the Committee's literature on article 6(2). A brief description of the Committee's interpretation is that it identifies it as a basic health and welfare right and as a general principle of the Convention. It is possible to argue that this was a reflection of UNICEF's survival and development revolution, which impacted on the understanding of article 6(2) during the first few years following the adoption of the CRC.

The Committee, however, has adopted a holistic approach to the implementation of the entire Convention. This means that articles within the substantive part of the Convention should not be separately implemented. The reflection of this approach to article 6(2) was that despite article 6(2) being classified as a basic health and welfare right, it may also cover other kinds of children's rights. To make it clearer, the Committee's interpretation widens the scope of article 6(2) on the basis of the holistic approach to the rights included in the Convention. In this respect, the important argument that this book introduced was that article 6(2) on the right of the child to survival and development independently, and without relying on the holistic approach, provides for such a comprehensive and widely based understanding.

It is also important, however, to mention that the Committee's literature on the matter is evolving. Twenty-five years after the adoption of the CRC, some members of the Committee are now speaking about the right of the child to survival and development as the right of the child to everything. After all, the overall aim of Chapter 2 was to argue that despite the importance of the holistic approach to all the articles of the CRC, article 6(2) on the survival and development of the child is an independent article that holds the power for comprehensiveness and independence from within.

4. MULTI-IDENTITIES

The multi-identities aspect of article 6(2) is derived from its comprehensiveness. The discussion about the Committee's recommendations on article 6(2) continued in Chapter 3. The identity of the right of the child to survival and development as a general principle has been disputed by some scholars. Some view it as an aim only, and others view it as a qualifying right. Chapter 3, in fact, argued for them all. In particular, article 6(2) is a general principle, an aim, a qualifying factor of the Convention and a right in itself. In addition, the way article 6(2) stands within the Convention and the way it is textually designed gives a chance for the article to be comprehensively identified and realised.

5. INTERACTION WITH THE CONCEPT OF HUMAN DIGNITY

Human dignity is the core value of the Convention on the Rights of the Child.[2] The adoption of the Convention on the Rights of the Child, in general and in terms of article 6(2) in particular, is significant for the child's human dignity.[3] However, some might argue that the concept of human dignity is vague; therefore, it is unconvincing to attempt to understand the already wide concepts of survival and development on the basis of dignity. In response to this, Chapter 4 argued for human dignity as being inseparable from article 6(2). It is in the background of article 6(2). The various categorisations of article 6(2) gave a great chance for the interrelationship between the human dignity of the child and his or her survival and development to come to the surface.

6. SPECIAL REFERENCE TO 'OBLIGATIONS OF THE STATE' WITHIN ARTICLE 6(2)

Traditionally, under the international human rights system, State responsibility and obligations are of great importance. Under article 6(2) State responsibility is even more important. This was clarified by the representative of India after the drafting of article 6(2). The aim was to focus on the obligations of States Parties to create measures and conditions for the survival and development of the child. In this context Chapter 5 analysed the special relationship between the right of the child to survival and development and the focus on State Party obligations. State Party interpretation and implementation of the article should reflect the soul of article 6(2) as a general principle, a right, an aim, and a qualifying factor of the Convention. The concept of 'to the maximum extent possible' represents a measuring tool for considering that the State Party has fulfilled its obligations under article 6(2). It is a subjective standard; therefore, each case should be viewed separately. The obligation to 'ensure' represents the level to which the State Party is obliged to implement article 6(2). The obligation to 'ensure' embodies the three types of State obligations, i.e., the obligations to respect,

[2] Committee on the Rights of the Child, 'General Comment No. 1 on the Aims of Education', UN Doc. CRC/GC/2001/1 (17 April 2001), para. 1.

[3] See M. Freeman, 'Taking Children's Rights More Seriously', in P. Alston et al. (ed.), *Children's Rights and the Law* (Oxford University Press, Oxford, 1992), p. 54.

protect and fulfil. The chapter discussed a variety of State Party obligations. The comprehensiveness of article 6(2) enriched the discussion.

7. SUGGESTED FUTURE RESEARCH

The discussion throughout this book has been an attempt to identify, discuss and analyse the comprehensiveness, wide spectrum, and far-reaching perspectives of the right of the child to survival and development. As mentioned before, each chapter in its own, or collectively, adds to the richness of the right of the child to survival and development.

In order to continue with the same theme, further research could, for instance, look into the interaction of the right of the child to survival and development and public corruption. Or it could study the interaction between the two parts of article 6, i.e., article 6(1) on the right to life and article 6(2) on the right to survival and development. Or it could look into the right of specific group of children to survival and development. More studies could also focus on the developing theories of extra-territorial State obligations with respect to the right of the child to survival and development. This is of significance in the context of article 6(2) being specifically adopted in order to focus on State Party obligations for the promotion of measures and conditions.

Moreover, suggested future studies may focus on the interaction of the right of the child to survival and development and the concept of 'free society'. This is in response to the Committee on the Rights of the Child following comment on the existence of a special relationship between the two when calling on States Parties to implement article 6(2) in such a way as to prepare the child to live in a free society:

> Please describe specific measures taken to guarantee the child's right to life and to create an environment conducive to ensuring to the maximum extent possible the survival and development of the child, including physical, mental, spiritual, moral, psychological and social development, in a manner compatible with human dignity, and to prepare the child for an individual life in a free society.[4]

In this context, the relationship between the survival and development of the child and the concept of a 'free society' needs to be discussed in detail. For example, what is 'a free society' within article 6(2)? Why is it important for the survival and development of the child? In addition, the dynamic interpretation of the Convention on the Rights of the Child may reveal new areas for discussion.

4 'General Guidelines for Periodic Reports' (Basic Reference Document), UN Doc. CRC/C/58 (20 November 1996), para. 40.

BIBLIOGRAPHY

BOOKS

Adger W.N. et al., 'Human Security', in C.B. Field et al. (eds.), *Climate Change 2014: Impacts, Adaptation, and Vulnerability. Part A: Global and Sectoral Aspects. Contribution of Working Group II to the Fifth Assessment Report of the Intergovernmental Panel on Climate Change* (Cambridge: Cambridge University Press, 2014), 755–791.

Alston P. and R. Goodman, *International Human Rights* (Oxford: Oxford University Press, 2013).

Andrews A.B. and N.H. Kaufman (eds.), *Implementing the U.N. Convention on the Rights of the Child: A Standard of Living Adequate for Development* (Westport: Praeger Publishers, 1999).

Ansbach T., 'Peoples and Individuals as Subjects of the Right to Development', in S.R. Chowdhury, E.M.G. Denters, and P.J.I.M. De Waart (eds), *The Right to Development in International Law* (Calcutta: Law Research Institute, 1992).

Arts K., 'A Child Rights Perspective on Climate Change', in M.A. Mohamed Salih (ed.), *Climate Change and Sustainable Development: New Challenges for Poverty Reduction* (Cheltenham: Edward Elgar, 2009).

Arts K. and V. Popovski (eds.), *International Criminal Accountability and the Rights of Children* (The Hague: Hague Academic Press, 2006).

Barrett D. and P.E. Veerman, *A Commentary on the United Nations Convention on the Rights of the Child: Article 33, Protection from Narcotic Drugs and Psychotropic Substances* (Leiden: Martinus Nijhoff Publishers, 2012).

Black M., *Children First: The Story of UNICEF, Past and Present* (Oxford: Oxford University Press, 1996).

Cantwell N., 'The Origins, Development and Significance of the United Nations Convention on the Rights of the Child', in S. Detrick (ed.), *The United Nations Convention on the Rights of the Child: A Guide to the Travaux Préparatoires* (Dordrecht: Martinus Nijhoff Publishers, 1992).

Cassese A., *International Law* (Oxford: Oxford University Press, 2001).

Cardoso Da Costa J.M., 'The Principle of Human Dignity in European Case Law: The principle of respect for human dignity', *Science and Techniques of Democracy*, No. 26 (Council of Europe Publishing, 1999).

Cohen C., 'Drafting of the United Nations Convention on the Rights of the Child: Challenges and Achievements', in E. Verhellen (ed.) *Understanding Children's Rights* (Ghent Papers on Children's Rights, Ghent: Children's Rights Centre, University of Ghent, 1996).

Cohen C., 'A Guide to Linguistic Interpretation of the Convention on the Rights of the Child Articles 1, 4, 41 and 45', in C. Cohen and H.A. Davidson (eds.), *Children's Rights in America: U.N. Convention on the Rights of the Child Compared with United States Law* (Washington D.C.: American Bar Association Center for Children in the Law and Defense for Children International, 1990).

Coomans F. and R. Künnemann (eds.), *Cases and Concepts on Extraterritorial Obligations in the Area of Economic, Social and Cultural Rights* (Cambridge: Intersentia, 2012).

Cornell C. et al. (eds.), *The Dignity Jurisprudence of the Constitutional Court of South Africa: Cases and Materials* (New York: Fordham University Press, 2013).

Delpérée F., 'The Right to Human Dignity in Belgian Constitutional Law. Concluding Report: The principle of respect for human dignity', *Science and Techniques of Democracy,* No. 26 (Council of Europe Publishing, 1999).

Detrick S., *A Commentary on the United Nations Convention on the Rights of the Child* (The Hague: Martinus Nijhoff, 1999).

Doek J.E., 'The CRC General Principles', in J. Connors et al. (eds), *The Convention on the Rights of the Child Reaches Majority* (Switzerland: Institut international des droits de l'enfant (IDE), 2007).

Devenish G.E., A *Commentary on the South African Bill of Rights* (Durban: Butterworths, 1999).

Frowein J.A., 'Human Dignity in International Law', in D. Kretzmer and E. Klein (eds.), *The Concept of Human Dignity in Human Rights Discourse* (The Hague: Kluwer Law International, 2002).

Freeman M., 'Taking Children's Rights More Seriously', in P. Alston et al. (ed.) *Children's Rights and the Law* (Oxford: Oxford University Press, 1992).

Glazewski J. and D. Collier, 'South Africa', in R. Lord et al. (eds.) *Climate Change Liability: Transnational Law and Practice* (Cambridge: Cambridge University Press, 2011).

Goldewijk B.K., A.C. Baspineiro and P.C. Carbonari (eds.), *Dignity and Human Rights: The implementation of economic, social, and cultural rights* (Antwerp, Intersentia, 2002).

Hammarberg T., 'The Rights of the Child in Developing Countries: International Norms and Procedures for Real Change?', in P. Baehr, H. Hey, J. Smith and T. Swinehart (eds.), *Human Rights in Developing Countries*, Yearbook (Deventer: Kluwer Law and Taxation Publishers, 1994).

Harris D.J., *Cases and Materials on International Law,* 4th edition (London: Sweet and Maxwell, 1991).

Harris D.J., *Cases and Materials on International Law,* 7th edition (London: Sweet and Maxwell, 2010).

Hodgkin R. and P. Newell, *Implementation Handbook for the Convention on the Rights of the Child* (Geneva: UNICEF, 2007).

Homby A.S., *Oxford Advanced Learner's Dictionary of Current English,* 5th edition (Oxford: Oxford University Press, 1995).

Humphreys S. (ed.), *Human Rights and Climate Change* (Cambridge: Cambridge University Press, 2010).

Johnson K.A. and M. McNulty, 'Assuring Adequate Health and Rehabilitative Care for the Child Articles 6, 23, 24 and 25', in C. Cohen and H.A. Davidson (eds),

Children's Rights in America: U.N. Convention on the Rights of the Child Compared with United States Law (Washington D.C.: American Bar Association and Defence for Children International, 1990).

Kent G., *The Politics of Children's Survival* (New York: Praeger Publishers, 1991).

LeBlanc L., *The Convention on the Rights of the Child: United Nations Lawmaking on Human Rights* (Lincoln: University of Nebraska Press, 1995).

Lopatka A., 'The Rights of the Child Are Universal: The Perspective of the UN Convention on the Rights of the Child', in M. Freeman and P. Veerman (eds.), *The Ideologies of Children's Rights* (Dordrecht: Martinus Nijhoff Publishers, 1992).

McAdam J., (ed.), *Climate Change and Displacement: Multidisciplinary Perspectives*, (Oxford: Hart Publishing, 2012).

Noble, I.R. et al., 'Adaptation needs and options', in C.B. Field et al. (eds.), *Climate Change 2014: Impacts, Adaptation, and Vulnerability. Part A: Global and Sectoral Aspects. Contribution of Working Group II to the Fifth Assessment Report of the Intergovernmental Panel on Climate Change* (Cambridge: Cambridge University Press, 2014).

Nowak M., *Introduction to the International Human Rights Regime* (Leiden: Martinus Nijhoff Publishers, 2003).

Nowak M., 'Article 6. Right to Life, Survival and Development'; in: A. Alen, J. Vande Lanotte, E. Verhellen, F. Ang, E. Berghmans and A. Verheyde (eds.), *A Commentary on the United Nations Convention on the Rights of the Child* (Leiden: Martinus Nijhoff Publishers, 2005).

Office of the High Commissioner for Human Rights, *Legislative History of the Convention on the Rights of the Child*, Volume I (New York: United Nations, 2007).

Office of the United Nations High Commissioner for Human Rights, *Legislative History of the Convention on the Rights of the Child*, Volume II (New York: United Nations, 2007).

Rousseau, D. 'Concluding Report. The principle of respect for human dignity', *Science and Techniques of Democracy*, No. 26 (Council of Europe Publishing, 1999).

الدين محمد عبد الحكيم الصافي, حق الانسان في التنمية الاقتصادية و حمايته دوليا (الطبعة الاولى), منشورات صفاء العربي الحقوقية, بيروت 2005.

Schabas W., *The Abolition of the Death Penalty in International Law*, 3rd edition (Cambridge: Cambridge University Press, 2002).

Skogly S., *Beyond National Borders: States' Human Rights Obligations in International Cooperation* (Antwerp: Intersentia, 2006).

Steiner H.J. and P. Alston, *International Human Rights in Context: Law, Politics, Morals*, 2nd edition (Oxford: Oxford University Press, 2000).

UNICEF Innocenti Research Centre, *Climate Change and Children: A Human Security Challenge* (Florence, UNICEF Innocenti Research Centre, November 2008), available at: www.unicef-irc.org/publications/pdf/climate_change.pdf (accessed 16 April 2015).

UNICEF, 'The State of the World's Children 1996: Fifty years for children' (New York: UNICEF, 1996).

UNICEF, 'The State of the World's Children 1987' (Oxford University Press, Oxford, 1987).

UNICEF, 'The State of the World's Children 1989' (Oxford University Press, Oxford, 1989).

UNICEF, 'The State of the World's Children 1990' (Oxford: Oxford University Press, 1990).

UNICEF, 'The State of the World's Children 1996' (Oxford University Press, Oxford, 1996).

UNICEF, 'The State of the World's Children 2007: The Double Dividend of Gender Equality' (UNICEF, New York, 2006).

UNICEF, 'The State of the World's Children 2010: Celebrating 20 Years of the Convention on the Rights of the Child' (UNICEF, November 2009).

UNICEF, 'The State of the World's Children 2014 in Numbers' (UNICEF, January 2014).

United Nations Development Programme (UNDP), *Arab Human Development Report 2002: Creating Opportunities for Future Generations* (New York: UNDP, 2000).

United Nations Development Programme (UNDP), *Human Development Report Sustaining Human Progress: Reducing Vulnerabilities and Building Resilience* (New York: UNDP, 2014).

Van Bueren G., *The International Law on the Rights of the Child* (The Hague: Martinus Nijhoff Publishers, 1998).

Van Bueren G., 'International Children's Rights – A Stop-go History', in E. Verhellen (ed.) *Understanding Children's Rights* (Ghent Papers on Children's Rights, Ghent: Children's Rights Centre, University of Ghent, 1996).

Verhellen E. (ed.), *Monitoring Children's Rights* (The Hague: Martinus Nijhoff Publishers, 1996).

Verhellen E., *Convention on the Rights of the Child: Background, motivation, strategies, main themes* (Leuven: E. Verhellen and Garant Publishers, 2000).

Walter, C., 'Human Dignity in German Constitutional Law. The principle of respect for human dignity', *Science and Techniques of Democracy*, No. 26 (Strasbourg: Council of Europe Publishing, 1999).

Weyts A. (ed.), *Understanding Children's Rights: Collected papers presented at the seventh International Interdisciplinary Course on Children's Rights* (Ghent: Ghent University, 2004).

JOURNALS AND NEWSPAPERS

Alderson P. et al., 'The Participation Rights of Premature Babies', *The International Journal of Children's Rights* 13 (2005), pp. 31–50.

Alston, P., 'The legal framework of the Convention on the Rights of the Child', *United Nations Bulletin of Human Rights: The Rights of the Child* 91/2 (1992), pp. 1–15.

Brady M., 'Breastfeeding is a human right. What does that mean?' (11 December 2012), available at: http://info.babymilkaction.org/news/campaignblog111212 (accessed 18 November 2014).

Cohen C., 'United Nations Convention on the Rights of the Child: Introductory Note', *International Legal Materials* 28 (1989), p. 1448.

Cohen C., 'The Developing Jurisprudence of the Rights of the Child', *St. Thomas L. Rev.* 6(1) (1993).

Cohen C. and S. Kilbourne, 'Jurisprudence of the Committee on the Rights of the Child: A Guide for Research and Analysis', *Michigan Journal of International Law* 19 (1998), p. 633.

De Chazournes L.B. and L. Condorelli, 'Common Article 1 of the Geneva Conventions revisited: Protecting collective interests', *International Review of the Red Cross* 837 (03–2000).

European Union, 'Charter of Fundamental Rights of the European Union', *Official Journal of the European Communities* (2000/C 364/01), December 2000.

Gibbons E.D., 'Climate Change, Children's Rights, and the Pursuit of Intergenerational Climate Justice', *Health and Human Rights Journal* 16(1)1 (June 2014), available at: www.hhrjournal.org/wp-content/uploads/sites/13/2014/06/Gibbons1.pdf (accessed 17 April 2015).

Himes J.R., 'Children's Rights: Moralists, Lawyers and the Right to Development', *The International Journal of Children's Rights* 1(1) (1993), pp. 81–97.

Hodgson D., 'The Child's Right to Life, Survival and Development', *The International Journal of Children's Rights* 2 (1994), pp. 369–394.

Ksentini F.Z., 'The Convention on the Rights of the Child: norms for protection and an instrument of co-operation for the survival, development and well-being of the child', *United Nations Bulletin of Human Rights: The Rights of the Child* 91/2 (1992), pp. 43–55.

Lopatka A., 'Importance of the Convention on the Rights of the Child', *United Nations Bulletin of Human Rights* 91/2 (1992), pp. 56–65.

Maglione M.A. et al., 'Safety of Vaccines Used for Routine Immunization of US Children: A Systemic Review', *Paediatrics* 134 (2014), pp. 325–375.

Mahgoub K., 'Article 33 of the Convention on the Rights of the Child: The Journey from Drafting History to the Concluding Observations of the Committee on the Rights of the Child', *Human Rights and Drugs* 2(1) (2012), pp. 45–63.

Musiani F., 'Migrant Children's Rights: Working to Fill the Gap', *UN Chronicle* 43(4) (2006), p. 33.

Newman-Williams M., 'How Things Changed', *UN Chronicle* 36(2) (1999), p. 38.

Rabkin J., 'What We Can Learn about Human Dignity from International Law', *Harvard Journal of Law & Public Policy* 27 (2003), p. 145.

Sengupta A., 'On the Theory and Practice of the Right to Development', *Human Rights Quarterly* 24(4) (2002), pp. 837–889.

Templeton S.K., 'Women may get right to breastfeed in public', *The Sunday Times* (13 May 2007).

The Guardian, 'Climate change refugee fights to stay in New Zealand', *The Guardian* (1 October 2013).

Thornton R.G., 'Children in Poverty and Their Access to Health Care' *Quinnipiac Health L.J.* 3 (1999/2000), pp. 111–132.

Tobin J., 'Increasingly Seen and Heard: The Constitutional Recognition of Children's Rights', *South African Journal on Human Rights* 21 (2005), pp. 86–126.

Thornton R.G., 'Children in Poverty and Their Access to Health Care', *Quinnipiac Health L.J.* 3 (1999/2000), p. 111.

Ward L., 'Equality laws enshrine mothers' right to breastfeed in public', *The Guardian* (13 June 2007).

Weissbrodt D., J.C. Hansen and N.H. Nesbitt, 'The Role of the Committee on the Rights of the Child in Interpreting and Developing International Humanitarian Law', *Harvard Human Rights Journal* 24 (2011), pp. 115–153.
Zakieldeen S.A., 'Adaptation to Climate Change: A Vulnerability Assessment for Sudan', *Gatekeeper Series* 142 (2009).

OFFICIAL DOCUMENTS

LEAGUE OF NATIONS

Declaration of the Rights of the Child, League of Nations Official Journal, Spec. Supp. No. 21 (26 September 1924).
Records of the Fifth Assembly, League of Nations Official Journal, Spec. Supp. No. 23.

UN CHARTER AND HUMAN RIGHTS CONVENTIONS AND DECLARATIONS

Charter of the United Nations, signed on 26 June 1945, in San Francisco, 59 Stat. 1031, T.S. 993, 3 Bevans 1153.
Universal Declaration of Human Rights, adopted 10 December 1948, UNGA Res 217 A (III) (UDHR).
Declaration of the Rights of the Child, UN Doc. A/RES/1386 (XIV) (20 November 1959).
Convention on the Elimination of All Forms of Discrimination against Women, United Nations, *Treaty Series*, vol. 1249, p. 13.
International Covenant on Civil and Political Rights, United Nations, *Treaty Series*, vol. 999, p. 171.
International Covenant on Economic, Social and Cultural Rights, United Nations, *Treaty Series*, vol. 993, p. 3.
Declaration on the Right to Development', UN Doc. A/RES/41/128 (4 December 1986).
Convention on the Rights of the Child, United Nations, *Treaty Series*, vol. 1577, p. 3.

UNITED NATIONS COMMISSION ON HUMAN RIGHTS

UN Doc. E/CN.4/1284 (18 January 1978).
UN Doc. E/CN.4/L.1366 (7 February 1978).
Question of a convention on the rights of the child, Resolution 20 (XXXIV) (8 March 1978).
UN Doc. E/CN.4/1324 (27 December 1978).
UN Doc. E/CN.4/1983/62 (25 March 1983).
UN Doc. E/CN.4/1983/WG.1/WP.27.
UN Doc. E/CN.4/1984/71 (23 February 1984).
UN Doc. E/CN.4/1984.WG.1/WP.3.

UN Doc. E/CN.4/1985/WG.1/WP.1.
UN Doc. E/CN.4/1986/39, annex IV.
UN Doc. E/CN.4/1988/28.
UN Doc. E/CN.4/1988/WG.1/WP.2.
UN Doc. E/CN.4/1989/WG.1 /CRP.1.
UN Doc. E/CN.4/1989/WG.1/WP.2.
UN Doc. E/CN.4/1989/WG.1/WP.10.
UN Doc. E/CN.4/1989/WG.1/WP.18.
UN Doc. E/CN.4/1989/48.
UN Document Fact Sheet No. 23, 'Harmful Traditional Practices Affecting the Health of Women and Children' (August 1995).

UNITED NATIONS GENERAL ASSEMBLY

'Health as an integral part of development', UN Doc. A/RES/34/58 (29 November 1979).
UN Doc. A/4249 and Corr.2.
'Declaration on Social Progress and Development', UN Doc. A/RES/24/2542 (11 December 1969).
'International Year of the Child', UN Doc. A/RES/31/169 (21 December 1976).
'Question of a Convention on the Rights of the Child', UN Doc. A/RES/40/113 (13 December 1985).
Vienna Declaration and Programme of Action, A/CONF.157/24 (25 June 1993).
'Agenda for Development', UN Doc. A/RES/51/240 (15 October 1997).
UN Doc. A/RES/53/155 (25 February 1999).
'The UN Declaration on the Right and Responsibility of Individuals, Groups and Organs of Society to Promote and Protect Universally Recognized Human Rights and Fundamental Freedoms', UN Doc. A/RES/53/144 (8 March 1999).
'Optional Protocol to the Convention on the Rights of the Child on a Communications Procedure', UN Doc. A/RES/66/138, Annex (27 January 2012).

COMMITTEE ON THE RIGHTS OF THE CHILD

GENRAL COMMENTS

General Comment No. 1 on the Aims of Education, UN Doc. CRC/GC/2001/1 (17 April 2001).
General Comment No. 3 on HIV/AIDS and the Rights of the Child, UN Doc. CRC/GC/2003/3 (17 March 2003).
General Comment No. 4 on Adolescent Health and Development in the Context of the Convention on the Rights of the Child, UN Doc. CRC/GC/2003/4 (1 July 2003).
General Comment No. 5 on the General Measures of Implementation for the Convention on the Rights of the Child (arts. 4, 42 and 44, para. 6), UN Doc. CRC/GC/2003/5 (27 November 2003).

General Comment No. 6 on the Treatment of Unaccompanied and Separated Children Outside their Country of Origin, UN Doc. CRC/GC/2005/6 (1 September 2005).
General Comment No. 7 on Implementing Child Rights in Early Childhood, UN Doc. CRC/C/GC/7/Rev.1 (20 September 2006).
General Comment No. 8 on the Right of the Child to Protection from Corporal Punishment and Other Cruel or Degrading Forms of Punishment (arts. 19; 28, para. 2; and 37, inter alia), UN Doc. CRC/C/GC/8 (2 March 2007).
General Comment No. 9 on the Rights of Children with Disabilities, UN Doc. CRC/C/GC/9 (27 February 2007).
General Comment No. 10 on Children's Rights in Juvenile Justice, UN Doc. CRC/C/GC/10 (25 April 2007).
General Comment No. 13 on the Right of the Child to Freedom from All Forms of Violence, UN Doc. CRC/GC/13 (18 April 2011).
General Comment No. 15 on the Right of the Child to the Enjoyment of the Highest Attainable Standard of Health (Art. 24), UN Doc. CRC/C/GC/15 (17 April 2013).
General Comment No. 16 (2013) on State Obligations Regarding the Impact of the Business Sector on Children's Rights, UN Doc. CRC/C/GC/16 (17 April 2013).
General Comment No. 17 (2013) on the Right of the Child to Rest, Leisure, Play, Recreational Activities, Cultural Life and the Arts (art. 31), UN. Doc. CRC/C/GC/17 (17 April 2013).
Committee on the Elimination of All forms of Discrimination against Women and Committee on the Rights of the Child, Joint General Recommendation/General Comment No. 31 of the Committee on the Elimination of Discrimination against Women and No. 18 of the Committee on the Rights of the Child on Harmful Practices, UN Doc. CEDAW/C/CG/31-CRC/C/GC/18 (14 November 2014).

CONCLUDING OBSERVATIONS

Concluding Observations on Egypt's Initial Report, UN Doc. CRC/C/15/Add.5 (18 February 1993).
Concluding Observations on Russian Federation's Initial Report, UN Doc. CRC/C/15/Add.4 (18 February 1993).
Concluding Observations on Bolivia's Initial Report, UN Doc. CRC/C/15/Add.1 (1993) (18 February 1993).
Concluding Observations on Indonesia's Initial Report, UN Doc. CRC/C/15/Add.7 (1993) (18 October 1993).
Concluding Observations on Costa Rica's Initial Report, UN Doc. CRC/C/15/Add.11 (18 October 1993).
Concluding Observations on Peru's Initial Report, UN Doc. CRC/C/15/Add.8 (18 October 1993).
Concluding Observations on Sudan's Initial Report, UN Doc. CRC/C/15/Add.10 (18 October 1993).
Concluding Observations on Romania's Initial Report, UN Doc. CRC/C/15/Add.16 (7 February 1994).

Concluding Observations on Belarus's Initial Report, UN Doc. CRC/C/15/Add.17 (7 February 1994).
Concluding Observations on Colombia's Initial Report, UN Doc. CRC/C/15/Add.15 (7 February 1994).
Concluding Observations on France's Initial Report, UN Doc. CRC/C/15/Add.20 (25 April 1994).
Concluding Observations on Pakistan's Initial Report, UN Doc. CRC/C/15/Add.18 (25 April 1994).
Concluding Observations on Honduras's Initial Report, UN Doc. CRC/C/15/Add.24 (24 October 1994).
Concluding Observations on Indonesia's Initial Report, UN Doc. CRC/C/15/Add.25 (24 October 1994).
Concluding Observations on Spain's Initial Report, UN Doc. CRC/C/15/Add.28 (24 October 1994).
Concluding Observations on Poland's Initial Report, UN Doc. CRC/C/15/Add.31 (15 January 1995).
Concluding Observations on Denmark's Initial Report, UN Doc. CRC/C/15/Add.33 (15 February 1995).
Concluding Observations on Philippines's Initial Report, UN Doc. CRC/C/15/Add.29 (15 February 1995).
Concluding Observations on United Kingdom of Great Britain and Northern Ireland's Initial Report, UN Doc. CRC/C/15/Add.34 (15 February 1995).
Concluding Observations on Canada's Initial Report, UN Doc. CRC/C/15/Add.37 (20 June 1995).
Concluding Observations on Italy's Initial Report, UN Doc. CRC/C/15/Add.41 (27 November 1995).
Concluding Observations on Senegal's Initial Report, UN Doc. CRC/C/15/Add.44 (27 November 1995).
Concluding Observations on Ukraine's Initial Report, UN Doc. CRC/C/15/Add.42 (27 November 1995).
Concluding Observations on Croatia's Initial Report, UN Doc. CRC/C/15/Add.52 (13 February 1996).
Concluding Observations on Finland's Initial Report, UN Doc. CRC/C/15/Add.53 (13 February 1996).
Concluding Observations on the Republic of Korea's Initial Report, UN Doc. CRC/C/15/Add.51 (13 February 1996).
Concluding Observations on Croatia's Initial Report, UN Doc. CRC/C/15/Add.52 (13 February 1996).
Concluding Observations on Iceland's Initial Report, UN Doc. CRC/C/15/Add.50 (13 February 1996).
Concluding Observations on Mongolia's Initial Report, UN Doc. CRC/C/15/Add.48 (13 February 1996).
Concluding Observations on Yemen's Initial Report, UN Doc. CRC/C/15/Add.47 (13 February 1996).
Concluding Observations on Nepal's Initial Report, UN Doc. CRC/C/15/Add.57 (7 June 1996).

Concluding Observations on Lebanon's Initial Report, UN Doc. CRC/C/15/Add.54 (7 June 1996).
Concluding Observations on China's Initial Report, UN Doc. CRC/C/15/Add.56 (7 June 1996).
Concluding Observations on Guatemala's Initial Report, UN Doc. CRC/C/15/Add.58 (7 June 1996).
Concluding Observations on Nigeria's Initial Report, UN Doc. CRC/C/15/Add.61 (30 October 1996).
Concluding Observations: United Kingdom of Great Britain and Northern Ireland: Dependent Territories Hong Kong Initial Report, UN Doc. CRC/C/15/Add.63 (30 October 1996).
Concluding Observations on Uruguay's Initial Report, UN Doc. CRC/C/15/Add.62 (30 October 1996).
Concluding Observations on Myanmar's Initial Report, UN Doc. CRC/C/15/Add.69 (24 January 1997).
Concluding Observations on Syrian Arab Republic's Initial Report, UN Doc. CRC/C/15/Add.70 (24 January 1997).
Concluding Observations on Bulgaria's Initial Report, UN Doc. CRC/C/15/Add.66 (24 January 1997).
Concluding Observations on Bangladesh's Initial Report, UN Doc. CRC/C/15/Add.74 (1997) (18 June 1997).
Concluding Observations on Cuba's Initial Report, UN Doc. CRC/C/15/Add.72 (18 June 1997).
Concluding Observations on Ghana's Initial Report, UN Doc. CRC/C/15/Add.73 (18 June 1997).
Concluding Observations on Trinidad and Tobago's Initial Report, UN Doc. CRC/C/15/Add.82 (10 October 1997).
Concluding Observations on Austria's Initial Report, UN Doc. CRC/C/15/Add.98 (7 May 1999).
Concluding Observations on Barbados's Initial Report, UN Doc. CRC/C/15/Add.103 (24 August 1999).
Concluding Observations on South Africa's Initial Report, UN Doc. CRC/C/15/Add.122 (23 February 2000).
Concluding Observations on Grenada's Initial Report, UN Doc. CRC/C/15/Add.121 (28 February 2000).
Concluding Observations: Australia, UN Doc. A/55/40(SUPP) (24 July 2000).
Concluding Observations: Palau's Initial Report, UN Doc. CRC/C/15/Add.149 (21 February 2001).
Concluding Observations on United Republic of Tanzania's Initial Report, UN Doc. CRC/C/15/Add.156 (9 July 2001).
Concluding Observations on Sudan's Second Periodic Report, UN Doc. CRC/C/15/Add.190 (9 October 2002).
Concluding Observations on Jamaica's Second Periodic Report', UN Doc. CRC/C/15/Add.210 (4 July 2003).
Concluding Observations on Antigua and Barbuda's Initial Report, UN Doc. CRC/C/15/Add.247 (3 November 2004).

Concluding Observations on Angola's Initial Report, UN Doc. CRC/C/15/Add.246 (3 November 2004).
Concluding Observations on Guyana's Initial Report, UN Doc. CRC/C/15/Add.224 (26 February 2004).
Concluding Observations on Kyrgyzstan's Second Periodic Report, UN Doc. CRC/C/15/Add.244 (3 November 2004).
Concluding Observations on the Bahamas's Initial Report, UN Doc. CRC/C/15/Add.253 (31 March 2005).
Concluding Observation on Albania's Initial Report, UN Doc. CRC/C/15/Add.249 (31 March 2005).
Concluding Observations on Luxembourg's Second Periodic Report, UN Doc. CRC/C/15/Add.250 (31 March 2005).
Concluding Observations on Belize's Second Periodic Report, UN Doc. CRC/C/15/Add.252 (31 March 2005).
Concluding Observations on Nepal's Second Periodic Report, UN Doc. CRC/C/15/Add.261 (21 September 2005).
Concluding Observations: Uganda (Unedited Version), UN Doc. CRC/C/15/Add.270 (30 September 2005).
Concluding Observations: Denmark, UN Doc. CRC/C/DNK/CO/3 (23 November 2005).
Concluding Observations: China (including Hong Kong and Macau Special Administrative Regions), UN Doc. CRC/C/CHN/CO/2 (24 November 2005).
Concluding Observations: Kiribati, UN Doc. CRC/C/KIR/CO/1 (29 September 2006).
Concluding Observations on Venezuela's Second Periodic Report (Unedited Version), UN Doc. CRC/C/VEN/CO/2 (5 October 2007).
Concluding Observations: Romania's Third and Fourth Periodic Reports, UN Doc. CRC/C/ROM/CO/4 (30 June 2009).
Concluding Observations on the Consolidated Third and Fourth Periodic Reports of Egypt, UN. Doc.CRC/C/EGY/CO/3-4 (15 July 2011).
Concluding Observations on the Consolidated Second and Third Periodic Reports of Bahrain, UN Doc. CRC/C/BHR/CO/2-3 (3 August 2011).
Concluding Observations on the Combined Second and Third Periodic Reports of Cambodia, UN Doc. CRC/C/KHM/CO/2-3 (3 August 2011).
Concluding Observations on the Combined Third and Fourth Periodic Reports of the Syrian Arab Republic, UN Doc. CRC/C/SYR/CO/3-4 (9 February 2012).
Committee on the Rights of the Child, Concluding Observations on the Combined Second and Third Periodic Report of Turkey, UN Doc. CRC/C/TUR/CO/2-3 (20 July 2012).
Concluding Observations on the Combined Third and Fourth Periodic Reports of China, UN Doc. CRC/C/CHN/CO/3-4 (29 October 2013).
Concluding Observations on the Second Periodic Report of the Holy See, UN Doc. CRC/C/VAT/CO/2 (25 February 2014).
Concluding Observations on the Combined Third and Fourth Periodic Reports of India, UN Doc. CRC/C/IND/CO/3-4 (7 July 2014).
Concluding Observations on the Combined Fourth and Fifth Periodic Reports of Jordan, UN Doc. CRC/C/JOR/CO/4-5 (8 July 2014).

Concluding Observations on the Combined Third, Fourth and Fifth Periodic Reports of Hungary, UN Doc. CRC/C/HUN/CO/3-5 (14 October 2014).

OTHER DOCUMENTS

General guidelines regarding the form and content of initial reports to be submitted by States parties under article 44, paragraph 1 (a), of the Convention, UN Doc. (CRC/C/5) (30 October 1991).
Committee on the Rights of the Child, Report on the fourth session, UN Doc. CRC/C/20 (25 October 1993).
Overview of the Reporting Procedures, UN Doc. CRC/C/33 (24 October 1994).
Children with Disabilities, UN Doc. CRC/C/66 (6 October 1997), Annex V.
Summary record of the 464th meeting: Japan, UN Doc. CRC/C/SR.464 (2 June 1998).
General Guidelines regarding the form and contents of periodic reports to be submitted by States Parties under article 44, paragraph 1 (b), of the Convention, UN Doc. CRC/C/58 (20 November 1996) (Basic Reference).
Consideration of Reports Submitted by States Parties Under Article 44 of the Convention, Second periodic reports of States Parties due in 1999 Addendum Belgium, UN Doc. CRC/C/83/Add.2 (25 October 2000).
UN Doc. CRC/C/19/Rev.10 (11 March 2002).
Day of Discussion: Implementing Child Rights in Early Childhood (17 September 2004) – Palais Wilson.
General guidelines regarding the form and content of periodic reports, UN Doc. CRC/C/58/Rev.1 (29 November 2005).
Day of General Discussion on the Right of the Child to Education in Emergency Situations, 49th session (3 October 2008) (Unedited Version).
Treaty-specific guidelines regarding the form and content of periodic reports to be submitted by States parties under article 44, paragraph 1 (b), of the Convention on the Rights of the Child, UN Doc. CRC/58/Rev.2 (23 November 2010).
Compilation of General Comments and General Recommendations Adopted by Human Rights Treaty Bodies, UN Doc. HRI/GEN/1/Rev.7 (May 2004).

HUMAN RIGHTS COMMITTEE

ICCPR General Comment No. 9 on Humane Treatment of Persons Deprived of Liberty (Art. 10) (30 July 1982).
ICCPR General Comment No. 15 (Twenty-seventh session, 1986): The Position of Aliens under the Covenant, A/41/40 (1986) 117.
Mónaco v. Argentina, UN Doc. CCPR/C/53/D/400 (1990).
General Comment No. 21, UN Doc. CCPR/C/21/Add.1 (10 April 1992).
A v. Australia (1993) UN Doc. CCPR/C/59/D/560/1993.
Kalenga v. Zambia, UN Doc. CCPR/C/48/D/326/1988 (2 August 1993), Annex.

General Comment No. 25 on the right to participate in public affairs, voting rights and the right of equal access to public service (Art. 25), UN Doc. CCPR/C/ 21/Rev. 1/ Add.7 (12 July 1996).
The Rights of the Child Fact Sheet No. 10 (Rev.1).
ICCPR General Comment No. 31 [80]: Nature of the General Legal Obligation Imposed on States Parties to the Covenant, UN Doc. CCPR/C/21/Rev.1/Add.13 (26 May 2004).

COMMITTEE ON ECONOMIC, SOCIAL AND CULTURAL RIGHTS

Substantive Issues Arising in the Implementation of the International Covenant on Economic, Social and Cultural Rights (Day of General Discussion), UN Doc. E/C.12/2000/13 (2 October 2000).
General Comment No. 14 on the Right to the Highest Attainable Standards of Health, UN Doc. E/C.12/2000/4 (11 August 2000).
General Comment No. 16: Substantive Issues Arising In The Implementation of the International Covenant on Economic, Social and Cultural Rights: The equal right of men and women to the enjoyment of all economic, social and cultural rights (art. 3 of the International Covenant on Economic, Social and Cultural Rights), UN Doc. E/C.12/2005/4 (11 August 2005).
United Nations Economic and Social Council Official Records, 1978, Supplement No. 4 (E/1978/34), chap. XXVI, sect. A.

ORGANIZATION OF AFRICAN UNITY

Organization of African Unity, 'The African Charter on the Rights and Welfare of the Child', (11 July 1990), OAU Doc. CAB/LEG/24.9/49 (1990), article 31.
African Commission on Human and Peoples' Rights, 'Thirteenth Annual Activity Report of the African Commission on Human and People's Rights, 1999–2000', p. 114, OAU Doc AHG/222 (XXXVI).
African Commission on Human and Peoples' Rights, 'Fourteenth Annual Activity Report of the African Commission on Human and People's Rights, 2000–2001', OAU Doc. AHG/229 (XXXVII).
John D. Ouko v. Kenya, African Commission on Human and Peoples' Rights Communication 232/1999.

INDIAN CASES

Bandhua Mukti Morcha v. Union of India 1984 SCR (2) 67 (Supreme Court of India).
State of Himachal Pradesh v. Umed Ram Sharma (1986) 1 SCR 251.

Shantistar Builders v Narayan Khimalal Totame, Civil Appeal No. 2598/1989, (1990) 1 SCC 520.
Subhash Kumar v. State of Bihar AIR 1991 420 (Supreme Court of India).
C.E.S.C. Ltd. & Ors. v. S.C. Bose & Ors. 1992 AIR 573, 1991 SCR Suppl. (2) 67 (Supreme Court of India).
Virender Gaur & Ors. v. State of Haryana & Ors. (1995) 2 SCC 577 (Supreme Court of India).
Consumer Education and Research Centre v. Union of India (1995) SCC (3) 42 (Supreme Court of India).
Life Insurance Corporation v. Consumer Education and Research Centre (1995) SCC (3) 42 (Supreme Court of India).
Suresh Kuma & Ors., Dalmia Cement Bharat Ltd. & Anr. etc. v. Union of India & Ors. etc. 25 April 1996 (Supreme Court of India).
Paschim Banga Khet Mazdoor Samity v State of West Bengal 1996 SCC (4) 37 (Supreme Court of India).

ORGANIZATION OF INTER-AMERICAN STATES

Velásquez Rodriguez v. Honduras, Inter-American Court of Human Rights Series C No. 4, judgment of 29 July 1988.
Villagrán Morales et al. ("Street Children" Case), Inter-American Court of Human Rights Series C No. 63 [1999] IACHR 17 (19 November 1999).
Second Report on the Situation of Human Rights in Peru (2 June 2000) Organization of American States Doc. OEA/Ser.L/V/II.106 Doc. 59 rev., Chapter VIII.
Third Report on the Situation of Human Rights in Paraguay (9 March 2001) Organization of American States Doc. OEA/Ser.L/V/II.110 Document52.
Juridical Condition and Human Rights of the Child, Advisory Opinion OC-17/2002, Inter-American Court of Human Rights (28 August 2002).
Juvenile Re-education Institute v. Paraguay, Inter-American Court of Human Rights Series C No. 112, judgment of 2 September 2004.
Serrano Cruz Sisters v. El Salvador, Inter-American Court of Human Rights Series C No. 120 [2005] IACHR 1 (1 March 2005).

SOUTH AFRICAN CASES

Christian Education South Africa v. Minister of Education (18 August 2000) (CCT4/00) [2000] ZACC 11 (Constitutional Court of South Africa), (2000).
Government of the Republic of South Africa and Others v. Grootboom and Others (CCT11/00) [2000] ZACC 19; 2001 (1) SA 46; 2000 (11) BCLR 1169 (4 October 2000) (CC) (Constitutional Court of South Africa).
Minister of Health and Others v. Treatment Action Campaign and Others (No 2) (CCT8/02) [2002] ZACC 15; 2002 (5) SA 721; 2002 (10) BCLR 1033 (5 July 2002) (Constitutional Court of South Africa).

Khosa and Others v. Minister of Social Development and Others, Mahlaule and Another v. Minister of Social Development (CCT13/03, CCT12/03) [2004] ZACC 11; 2004 (6) SA 505 (CC); 2004 (6) BCLR 569 (CC) (4 March 2004) (Constitutional Court of South Africa).
De Reuck v. Director of Public Prosecutions (Witwatersrand Local Division) and Others (CCT5/03) [2003] ZACC 19 [62] (Constitutional Court of South Africa) (15 October 2003).
S v. Mazibuko (A1246/2006) [2008] ZAGPHC 106 (18 April 2006) (High Court of South Africa).

OTHER CASES

Aegean Sea Continental Shelf (Greece v. Turkey) (Judgment) [1978] ICJ Rep.
European Court of Human Rights, *Marckx v. Belgium*, 13 June 1979, Series A no. 31.
Kelly v. Jamaica, UN. Doc. CCPR/C/41/D/253/1987.
Government of Sudan v. Shaiboo Saeed Muhammad, Sudan Law Journal & Reports (SLJR), 1989 (in Arabic).
European Court of Human Rights, *Soering v. United Kingdom* (Series A, vol. 161, 11 E.H.R.R.) (1989) 439.
Deshaney v. Winnebago City. DSS, 489 U. S. 189 (1989) (United States Supreme Court).
Oposa et al. v. Fulgencio S. Factoran, Jr. et al (G.R. No. 101083), (1993), Supreme Court of the Philippines, available at: www.escr-net.org/docs/i/401226 (accessed 16 April 2015).
High Court of Australia, *Minister of State for Immigration and Ethnic Affairs v. Ah Hin Teoh* (1995) 183 CLR 273.
Supreme Court of Canada, *Eldridge v. British Columbia (Attorney General)* (1997) 3 S.C.R. 624.
European Committee on Social Rights, *The International Commission of Jurists v. Portugal,* Complaint No. 1/1998.
European Court of Human Rights, *A. v. United Kingdom* [1999] 27 EHRR 611.
Cruz del Valle Bermúdez y otros v. MSAS s/amparo (15 May 1999) Expediente No. 15.789. Sentencia No. 196 (Tribunal Supremo de Venezuela).
Manuel Wackenheim v. France, UN Doc. CCPR/C/75/D/854/1999 (2002).
European Committee on Social Rights, *International Federation of Human Rights Leagues (FIDH) v. France,* Complaint No. 13/2003 ECSR.
European Court of Human Rights, *Paeffgen GMBH v. Germany* (App nos. 25379/04, 21688/05, 21722/05 and 21770/05) (18 September 2007).
Dimmock v. Secretary of State for Education and Skills [2007] All ER (D) 117 (Oct).
European Committee on Social Rights, *Defence for Children International (DCI) v. The Netherlands* (Complaint No. 47/2008) ECSR Case Document No. 1, (12 February 2008).
Constitutional Court of Sudan, *Nagmeldin Gasm Alseed v. Government of Sudan and the relatives of Abd Alraheem Muhammad Ali*, Journal of the Constitutional Court, Volume 2, 2011, p. 399 (in Arabic).

OTHER DOCUMENTS

UNICEF's mission statement', available at: www.unicef.org/about/who/index_mission.html (accessed 24 April 2015).

Constitution of the World Health Organization, (1946) 14 UNTS 185.

C183 – Maternity Protection Convention, 2000 (No. 183), (Convention concerning the revision of the Maternity Protection Convention (Revised), 1952) (Entry into force: 7 February 2002).

Vienna Convention on the Law of Treaties, U.N.T.S. 1155 (1969) 331.

World Health Organization, the International Code of Marketing of Breast-milk Substitutes, adopted by the World Health Assembly in 1981 World Health Assembly, Rresolution WHA34.22 in 1981, Annex.

United Nations, UN Chronicle, Volume: 23 August 1986.

Innocenti Declaration on the Protection, Promotion and Support of Breastfeeding (1 August 1990), Florence, Italy. www.unicef.org/nutrition/files/Innocenti_plus15_BreastfeedingReport.pdf (accessed 13 December 2014).

World Declaration and Plan of Action on the Survival, Protection and Development of Children (30 September 1990).

United Nations Framework Convention on Climate Change (1992).

James P. Grant, Statement of UNICEF at the International Conference on Population and Development, Cairo (6 September 1994), available at: www.un.org/popin/icpd/conference/una/940907130633.html (accessed 13 December 2014).

Report of the World Summit for Social Development (Copenhagen, 6–12 March 1995) UN Doc. A/CONF.166/9 (19 April 1995).

Statement delivered by Hoda Badran, the Chairperson of the Committee on the Rights of the Child at the International Conference on Population and Development (ICPD) in Cairo, Egypt (7 September 1994).

United Nations Economic Commission for Europe (UNECE) Convention on Access to Information, Public Participation in Decision-Making and Access to Justice in Environmental Matters, available at: http://ec.europa.eu/environment/aarhus/ (accessed 3 October 2014).

Amal Friends of Children Society, 'The Status of Implementation of the Child Rights Convention in the Sudan', an alternative report prepared by national NGOs (June 2002).

Limburg Principles on the Implementation of the International Covenant on Economic, Social and Cultural Rights, Maastricht, 2–6 June 1986. Available in: UN Doc. E/CN.4/1987/17 (8 January 1987).

Maastricht Guidelines on Violations of Economic, Social and Cultural Rights, Maastricht, 22–26 January 1997, para. 6. Available in: United Nations Committee on Economic, Social and Cultural Rigths, 'Substantive Issues Arising in the Implementation of the International Covenant on Economic, Social and Cultural Rights (Day of General Discussion)', UN Doc. E/C.12/2000/13 (2 October 2000).

World Health Organization (WHO), *The Environment and Health for Children and Their Mothers*, Fact sheet no. 284. Available at: www.who.int/ceh/publications/factsheets/fs284/en (accessed 16 April 2015).

United Nations Secretary-General Kofi Annan, 'Statement to the General Assembly', New York, 21 March 2005.

'Deserving Dignity – the Independent Asylum Commission's Third Report of Conclusions and Recommendations: How we treat people seeking sanctuary' (July 2008), United Kingdom.

UNICEF Innocenti Research Centre. 2008. *Climate Change and Children: A Human Security Challenge,* available at: www.unicef-irc.org/publications/pdf/climate_change.pdf (Florence, UNICEF Innocenti Research Centre, November 2008) (accessed 20 November 2014).

Kedrowski K.M., 'Breastfeeding Policies and Practices in an International Human Rights Context', prepared for presentation at the Oxford Roundtable Women in the Modern World: The Struggle for Equality, March 2008, available at: http://faculty.winthrop.edu/kedrowskik/international%20human%20rights%20paper.htm (accessed 20 November 2014).

UN High Commissioner for Human Rights Report of the Office of the United Nations High Commissioner for Human Rights on the relationship between climate change and human rights. (UN Human Rights Council, A/HRC/10/61, 15 January 2009).

Food and Agriculture Organization of the United Nations, 'The State of Food Insecurity in the World: Addressing food insecurity in protracted crises' (Rome 2010).

Reyneke M., 'The Right to Dignity and Restorative Justice in Schools' [2011] PER 35, available at: www.saflii.org/cgi-bin/disp.pl?file=za/journals/PER/2011/35.html&-query= harmful traditional practices (accessed 23 November 2014).

Brady M., 'Breastfeeding is a human right. What does that mean?' (11 December 2012), available at: http://info.babymilkaction.org/news/campaignblog111212 (accessed 18 November 2014).

REDRESS, *Arrested Development: Sudan's Constitutional Court, Access to Justice and the Effective Protection of Human Rights* (REDRESS, London, August 2012), available at: www.refworld.org/docid/50641ad82.html (accessed 15 April 2015).

Mahgoub K., 'Children's Rights and the Forthcoming Constitutional Bill of Rights of Sudan' (January 2014), pp. 63–74, available at: www.redress.org/downloads/publications/140127FINAL%20Sudan%20UoK%20Report.pdf (accessed 18 April 2015).

UNICEF, Press Release, *UN Successfully Negotiates Ceasefire in Afghanistan for Polio Immunization,* available at: www.unicef.org/newsline/01pr33.htm (accessed 24 September 2014).

Intergovernmental Panel on Climate Change (IPCC), Fifth Assessment Synthesis Report 'Climate Change 2014 Synthesis Report', available at: http://ipcc.ch/pdf/assessment-report/ar5/syr/AR5_SYR_FINAL_All_Topics.pdf (accessed 16 April 2015).

Michel L., 'The Ideal Gift', in *UNICEF, 20 Years, The Convention on the Rights of the Child,* available at: www.unicef.org/rightsite/364_587.htm (accessed 13 April 2015).

The United Nations Economic Commission for Europe (UNECE) Convention on Access to Information, Public Participation in Decision-Making and Access to Justice in Environmental Matters, available at: http://ec.europa.eu/environment/aarhus/ (accessed 3 October 2014).

www.ingramcontent.com/pod-product-compliance
Ingram Content Group UK Ltd.
Pitfield, Milton Keynes, MK11 3LW, UK
UKHW051921100926
8556IPUK00021B/1294

9 781780 682334